Politics and Process at the United Nations

Politics and Process at the United Nations

The Global Dance

Courtney B. Smith

LYNNE
RIENNER
PUBLISHERS

BOULDER
LONDON

Published in the United States of America in 2006 by
Lynne Rienner Publishers, Inc.
1800 30th Street, Boulder, Colorado 80301
www.rienner.com

and in the United Kingdom by
Lynne Rienner Publishers, Inc.
3 Henrietta Street, Covent Garden, London WC2E 8LU

Library of Congress Cataloging-in-Publication Data
Smith, Courtney B., 1971–
    Politics and process at the United Nations : the global dance / Courtney B. Smith.
      p. cm.
    Includes bibliographical references and index.
    ISBN 978-1-58826-323-0 (hardcover : alk. paper)
    ISBN 978-1-58826-348-3 (pbk. : alk. paper)
    1. United Nations.   I. Title.
    JZ4984.5.S65   2005
    341.23—dc22

                                        2005011004

British Cataloguing in Publication Data
A Cataloguing in Publication record for this book
is available from the British Library.

Printed and bound in the United States of America

    The paper used in this publication meets the requirements
∞ of the American National Standard for Permanence of
    Paper for Printed Library Materials Z39.48-1992.

5 4 3 2

Contents

Acknowledgments

WRITING A BOOK REQUIRES BOTH PASSION AND PERSISTENCE, AND I HAVE been fortunate to benefit from a wide range of individuals who have helped me develop these qualities. My passion for the United Nations and its political processes stems from several sources: the more than one hundred nationalities represented in my high school near Washington, D.C.; the study abroad experiences I had in high school and college; the intellectual environment created by my mentor, Professor Chadwick F. Alger, in graduate school; and the indispensable mission of the United Nations itself, so eloquently stated in the Preamble to its Charter.

Over the past decade, many individuals have helped me translate this passion into the pages that follow. First, I owe a debt of gratitude to my students at Seton Hall University and Ohio State University, who, through their questions and comments, pushed me to share with a larger audience my ideas and stories regarding the UN's political processes. I am also grateful to numerous colleagues in the International Studies Association and the Academic Council on the United Nations System who provided feedback regarding the tradeoffs in content and approach that I faced. Much of their insight came through panel discussions, but some spent literally hours talking with me in hallways, over meals, and while traveling.

This book would not have been possible without the insights of another essential set of individuals: the more than fifty UN delegates and staff members who graciously took the time to meet with me and were more than generous in answering my many questions regarding their daily experiences. Their assistance was invaluable, although none of them bears any responsibility for the conclusions I reached.

During the preparation of the manuscript, I benefited from the supportive environment provided by the dean of the John C. Whitehead School of Diplomacy and International Relations, Ambassador Clay Constantinou, and my colleagues on the faculty there. Many of them have been through this process themselves, and they were more than willing to help me along. In addition, I was assisted in my research by three graduate students at Seton Hall—Nancy Tanella, Whitney Rubison, and Jacob Dryden. Likewise, I am extremely thankful for the support and guidance provided by the staff of Lynne Rienner Publishers, especially Lynne herself. Her reputation for nurturing young authors and for publishing excellent material on the United Nations is well earned, and I am pleased that I was able to work with her team. In particular, Sally Glover, Lisa Tulchin, and Lesli Athanasoulis were patient and responsive editors, and the two anonymous reviewers selected by the press provided helpful feedback that was both detailed and encouraging.

Finally, a word of thanks to my family for understanding more than anyone else the long hours that persistence requires. None of this work would have been possible without the love and encouragement of my wife, Sharyn. She pushed me when required and supported me always. The same is true for my children, Peyton and Kiley. They taught me, among other things, that there really is no better cure for writer's block than a rousing game of monster hide-and-seek. While my family did not do the research or write this book, their contribution is found on every page. Plus they made it all worthwhile.

Politics and
Process at the
United Nations

1

Introduction to
the Global Dance

IN MARCH 2003 AN INTENSE PERIOD OF DIPLOMATIC ACTIVITY AT THE
United Nations collapsed when the United States failed to secure
Security Council authorization for its military action against Iraq. The
tension and hostility that characterized these difficult negotiations
resulted in a divided and paralyzed Council. However, just two months
later Council unity was restored when the United States was able to
lobby the other member states to endorse a US-authored plan for
rebuilding Iraq. This series of events raises important questions: Why
was the most powerful UN member, the United States, unable to obtain
Council support on an issue in which the Bush administration clearly
felt the vital interests of the country were at stake? Conversely, why
was the United States able to achieve a postwar resolution very favorable to its interests in the face of what had been such a hostile environment at the United Nations? Finally, why were both permanent and
elected members of the Council unwilling to compromise in March but
prepared to do so in May?

Complicated questions about the political processes of the United
Nations are not limited to peace and security issues. Economic interdependence, technological change, faster travel, and other aspects of globalization have resulted in increased activity in all areas of global policymaking in the early twenty-first century. On issues as diverse as global
warming, terrorism, drug trafficking, infectious diseases, weapons of
mass destruction, and political oppression, the international community
has come together in search of coordinated responses to address these
complex and challenging problems more effectively. As the world's
only universal membership and general purpose international organization, the United Nations has become the primary vehicle for pursuing
these efforts.

1

As can be expected, the results of these efforts have been mixed. In some cases the countries involved have agreed to and followed through on concrete steps to overcome the problems; in other cases dramatic policy statements were drafted, only to be neglected once the spotlight of attention was removed; and in still other cases the participants were unable to come to any meaningful agreement at all. This variation in outcomes can be found across the different political bodies of the United Nations system and in the series of global conferences that have been held under UN auspices since the early 1990s.

Understanding how and why this variation occurs requires a deeper examination of how the United Nations makes its decisions. More precisely, it involves considering how an organization that is composed of 191 sovereign member states, influenced by numerous nongovernmental organizations, lobbied by multinational corporations, and serviced by an international secretariat works to reconcile these potentially diverse interests in search of effective international solutions to pressing global problems. This is a challenging enterprise, and it represents the focus of this book.

■ The Nature of Parliamentary Diplomacy: An Analogy

Diplomatic interaction in international organizations like the United Nations is complex and multifaceted. Due to the wide range of participants involved and the numerous issues potentially on the table, a number of interrelated processes often unfold simultaneously. One of these processes reflects the need for participants in international decision-making to pursue the interests of the actor they represent. This is most pressing for representatives of member states, and here the mechanisms of multilateral diplomacy have a number of important similarities to traditional bilateral diplomacy. Representing the interests of your state (or for that matter any other actor in international organizations) certainly involves trying to persuade other participants of the merits of your position when there are areas of disagreement. However, it also involves listening to their arguments, gathering information about the roots of their positions, and laying the groundwork for future interaction (Muldoon, 1999, pp. 2–3). Beyond these various tasks, diplomatic representation can also require some internal coordination within the actors involved (Jacobson, 1979, pp. 120–122). Member states, nongovernmental organizations, multinational corporations, and even members of the Secretariat face diverse constituencies whose preferences must be reconciled, or at least considered, when it comes time to advocate for certain policies in a diplomatic negotiation. Since international organizations often require participants to adopt positions on a broader range of issues than is typical in bilateral diplomacy, these problems of representation and coordination are made all the more challenging.

Despite some similarities to bilateral diplomacy, the political processes found in international organizations are significantly more complex because the decisionmaking involved is both multilateral and parliamentary. The fact that decisionmaking is multilateral, with anywhere from a handful to several hundred actors involved, quite simply results in a much larger range of interests that must be reconciled. This, in turn, means there are at least three differences in the skills required of diplomats in multilateral versus bilateral settings (Muldoon, 1999, p. 3; Hamilton and Langhorne, 1995, pp. 199–209). First, skills such as adaptability, flexibility, and the ability to multitask are helpful in bilateral settings, but they are essential in multilateral settings. Second, since multilateral diplomacy often includes a more public and open component and involves more frequent oral, face-to-face exchanges, participants must possess excellent public speaking, debating, and language skills. Finally, multilateral diplomacy places a premium on individuals who can balance two contradictory roles: the specialist and the generalist. Over time the need for specialized expertise in diplomacy has grown dramatically, as many issues that are highly technical have moved onto the international agenda. However, these highly technical issues are often interrelated with each other, so effective negotiators need to be able to visualize and build solutions that take advantage of these linkages.

In addition to their multilateral character, the political processes of international organizations have been described by Dean Rusk and others as examples of "parliamentary diplomacy" (as quoted in Appathurai, 1985, p. 98). In such bodies the component parts, the member states, are sovereign actors that rarely afford the organization the level of authority called for in the treaty documents that led to its creation. However, despite their limited authority, many international organizations structure decisionmaking with procedures that are more akin to those of domestic parliaments than those of bilateral diplomacy. For example, many international organizations can make their decisions through voting, often some form of majority rule. In addition, the parliamentary nature of these bodies extends into every aspect of how they operate, including processes for recognizing speakers, mechanisms for organizing debate, and the role of committees in decisionmaking. This complexity makes their political processes more challenging for participants and observers to fully understand.

Given the use of parliamentary rules and procedures in multilateral diplomacy, the process of achieving policy outcomes essentially becomes an exercise in building and managing the coalitions required to secure the necessary number of votes. In some international organizations these coalitions remain relatively stable; however, it is also common for these coalitions to be rebuilt again and again over time, depending on the particular issue or issues under discussion and the number of votes required to pass any new policy agreement. In light of this reality, observers of multilateral diplomacy often describe it as an "art" whose "principal challenge . . . is to design the negotiations in such a way that they encourage the creation of coalitions supporting the agreement and minimize the possibility of coalitions opposing it" (Aviel, 1999, pp. 12–13). In these efforts, hard-and-fast rules, like those associated with scientific processes, are often difficult for both participants and observers to discern. However, there are certain common patterns and rules of thumb that can and should be identified so that scholars, students, and practitioners can better understand how the strategies and tactics that work in one situation can be applied most effectively in other situations.

Participants in international organization decisionmaking face a distinctive challenge, as compared to their bilateral colleagues, because of their need to build and maintain coalitions across a wide range of issues. Not only do they have to be an effective representative of their actor's interests, but they must also learn how to successfully participate in the give-and-take of the organization's political processes (Jacobson, 1979, pp. 122–124). This certainly requires that they have a thorough grasp of the procedures and rules of debate (Hamilton and Langhorne, 1995, p. 199), but it also necessitates an expertise in designing creative "package deals" that offer all participants greater benefits from supporting the agreement than they would enjoy from blocking it. Unfortunately, the strategies that enable participants to pursue their interests are not always the same strategies for facilitating the compromises necessary for building winning coalitions. As a result, all actors involved in international organizations are forced to make tradeoffs, often difficult ones, between the policies that they really want to see adopted and those that realistically can be adopted.

In light of such complexity, it is useful to consider an analogy: the political processes of international organizations like the United Nations can be conceptualized as a global dance. At any particular UN gathering, there are member-state delegates, Secretariat officials, and NGO representatives, each of whom may begin in his or her own little group or clique. Some of the members of the dance troupe naturally assume a role at the center of the dance floor; these lead dancers would include the most powerful member states of the organization and those members who are most directly affected by the issue at hand. Gathered around these lead dancers would be a variety of supporting players: middle power states that serve as brokers, bringing together different key attendees to see if they can dance in the same routine; members of the organization's staff, who serve as the orchestra, offering music and language that have fostered common movements in the past; representatives of civil society, who seek to get the lead dancers and other players to consider new moves and music that has not been used before; and otherwise marginalized members, who lurk as outcasts around the perimeter, able to influence the unfolding dance only by attempting to block or disrupt it.

As the music starts playing and the negotiation process begins, the various members of the troupe must move to form partnerships or be forced to watch from the sideline. What may begin as a dance in which each participant seems to have his or her own moves can gradually evolve into a more scripted routine in which all the dancers start to move in the same direction. However, getting to that point involves understanding both the written and unwritten rules of the dance, knowing which other attendees represent potential dance partners, and pos-

Members of the Security Council gather for a meeting on Iraq on June 8, 2004. These informal contacts among delegates are an essential component of the global dance throughout the decisionmaking process. (UN photo #NICA 7574, by Mark Garten)

sessing the ability to feel the rhythm of the music so that you can tell in what direction the process is moving. As this happens, different members of the troupe have different abilities to shape the unfolding dance. Some can simply rely on their stature and reputation to induce other dancers to follow their lead; others possess the creativity to offer new moves or scarce resources like a particular piece of music. Sometimes the dance may end with an empty dance floor, a frustrated orchestra, and no noticeable progress on the issue at hand. Yet the hope is that the number of participants willing to dance together, and to the same music, will increase over time, so that effective solutions to pressing global problems can be found.

▮ Understanding UN Processes: Where Do We Start?

Scholarly study of international organizations dates back almost as far as the organizations themselves. The creation of the League of Nations and the United Nations was accompanied by a flurry of writings on the origins, structures, and early activities of these new organizations. The best-known of these efforts, such as Inis Claude (1984, first published in 1956), offered a wealth of information about the challenges and opportunities facing international organizations in a world of sovereign states. Unfortunately, reviews of these early writings are mixed. These authors offered important insights into how these organizations interacted with the international political system in which they operated (Martin and Simmons, 2001, p. 440), but such insights were often buried in rich historical detail or thick legal description. These writings tended to focus on what the organizations were rather than on how they functioned.

Over time, a number of scholars have tried to provide the study of international organization with a stronger theoretical footing. In the immediate aftermath of World War II, authors such as David Mitrany (1943) and Ernst Haas (1958) offered theories like functionalism and neofunctionalism, respectively, which focused on how international organizations could be vehicles for solving problems of war and peace. Functionalists saw international organizations as an ad hoc product of technical cooperation between states, designed to promote common economic and social needs. Neofunctionalists adopted a functionalist strategy of cooperation spilling over from one issue area to the next, but with a much more explicit and ambitious goal in mind: regional integration in Europe. Later, in the 1970s, Robert O. Keohane and Joseph S. Nye Jr. (1971; 1977) shifted the focus to transnational relations and complex interdependence, in an effort to push scholars beyond the state-centered and conflict-based realist paradigm; key issues included nonmilitary interaction between states and the increasing presence of nonstate actors (including international organizations) in world politics. While all these theories acknowledged an important, or even central, role for international organizations, they suffered from a number of weaknesses (Archer, 1992, pp. 88–106); for example, they neglected to examine the formal and informal structures and procedures that characterize the decisionmaking processes within these actors.

Across the 1980s and early 1990s, theorizing about international organizations was dominated by regime analysis. In this approach, regimes were defined as "sets of implicit or explicit principles, norms, rules, and decision-making procedures around which actor's expectations converge in a given area of international relations" (Krasner, 1983, p. 2). While not synonymous with international organizations, regime analysis highlighted a number of important dynamics that were instrumental for understanding why states cooperate in international politics and what form that cooperation might take from one issue to the next. As such, international organizations like the United Nations could act as central players in regimes relevant to the different issue areas on their agendas. However, over time regime analysis seemed to lose sight of this early promise, and most dominant approaches to the study of regimes became state centered (Haggard and Simmons, 1987, p. 499). In the 1980s, regime analysis essentially hijacked the study of international organizations, then, without making any contributions to an understanding of how these formal international structures operate.

When the cold war ended in the late 1980s, the United Nations was rather suddenly thrust back into the spotlight of global politics as never before in its tumultuous history. The breakdown in superpower rivalry resulted in a dramatic increase in demands for multilateral management of a growing range of transnational problems, and much of this demand was directed at the institutions of the UN system (Fischer and Galtung, 1991, p. 289). Unfortunately, this increased demand for UN activity came at a time when scholars were only just beginning to move beyond the confines of regime analysis. As reflected in a comprehensive survey by Friedrich Kratochwil and John Ruggie (1986, p. 761), very few articles published in the leading scholarly journal on international organizations across the 1980s actually focused on formal international organizations like the UN. However, soon after this survey, the study of international organization was reinvigorated to some extent by authors who incorporated concepts originally developed in other academic disciplines. For example, Christer Jönsson (1986), Gayl Ness and Steven Brechin (1988), and Ernst Haas (1990) borrowed ideas from organizational sociology to study, respectively, how international organizations work collaboratively across linked policy areas, pursue their goals, and incorporate new areas of knowledge through learning.

Three additional areas of literature potentially relevant to the study of international organizations were developed across the 1990s. The first of these is the study of multilateralism, which focuses on the broad universe of international institutional forms that bring multiple parties together in particular areas of concern. However, the main volume on multilateralism argues that formal international organizations represent only a small part of this broader universe (Ruggie, 1993, pp. 6–7), and as a result international organizations have received limited attention in this research. A second area would be writings on global governance, which explore areas of international activity where relationships that transcend national frontiers are governed without the presence of sovereign authority. In other words, global governance is doing internationally what governments do at home (Finkelstein, 1995). Unfortunately, global governance is typically defined so broadly that the concept appears to include virtually everything, thereby preventing it from offering analytical leverage for examining the internal processes of international organizations. A third area of recent scholarship would be the literature on institutionalism, which borrows extensively from research done on domestic institutional structures. This scholarship examines how institutions can both be caused by state behavior and influence that very same behavior (Martin and Simmons, 2001, p. 451). This is true because formal and informal institutions have the ability to constrain choices, alter preferences, and influence outcomes. However, this focus on the impact of institutions on policy outcomes offers little insight into how the internal political processes of the institutions function.

Despite such efforts to make the study of international organizations more systematic and theoretically grounded, much of this research remains centered on the nature of the decisions made by the actors and on the subsequent effects of the decisions, but little attention is paid to the decisionmaking process itself. This focus is to be expected, since the resolutions and programs of international organizations are often seen as being the goal or culmination of global policymaking. However, even during the UN's adolescence in the 1960s, scholars had begun to realize that these outputs are "hardly ever the most important or meaningful point" of UN decisionmaking (Petersen, 1968, p. 128). As Keith Petersen argued, the dynamics of parliamentary diplomacy are of greater consequence for understanding the UN and its achievements than are the results of specific policymaking victories (1968, p. 131).

Put another way, we need to understand the forces and influences that can move the organization to act if we want to fully understand what it does and why it matters. The study of UN politics provided in this book will demonstrate that Petersen's observations on the importance of process are as relevant today as they were decades ago. After all, if the political process does not move, then no outputs can result.

Given the importance of considering process when one is trying to understand international organizations, it is unfortunate that so much scholarship on these actors has focused on the outputs of global policy-making rather than investigating its underlying dynamics of how and why certain decisions emerge from these efforts. This apparent neglect of process is all the more surprising given the fact that for some four decades scholars have regularly identified a pressing need for systematic studies of decisionmaking in international organizations. Writing in the late 1960s, Robert Keohane (1967, pp. 221–222), David Kay (1969, p. 958), and Chadwick Alger (1970, p. 444) all argued that scholars had neglected the political processes that are central to the functioning of the United Nations. A similar conclusion was reached by J. Martin Rochester (1986, p. 812) and Kratochwil and Ruggie (1986, p. 754) nearly two decades later, when they called for an increased focus on the structure and processes of formal international organizations. Finally, this appeal was repeated after the end of the cold war, when Johan Kaufmann (1994, p. 28), Rochester (1995, p. 199), Kenneth Abbott and Duncan Snidal (1998, pp. 5, 29), Courtney Smith (1999, pp. 173–174), and Alger (2002, p. 218) noted the continued scarcity of scholarship on decisionmaking in international organizations.

While the absence of a theoretical framework for examining the political processes of international organizations represents a serious shortcoming of the literature surveyed above, there are at least three areas of past scholarship that are directly relevant to this effort to investigate United Nations decisionmaking. None of these areas of scholarship led to much accumulation of knowledge over time, since they failed to build a common framework for situating their individual findings. However, despite this shortcoming, their research has important insights to offer this current effort to examine the political processes of the United Nations. A few examples of the many writings in each area will be mentioned here, and their true contributions will become more evident in the chapters that follow.

The first set of relevant research is empirical studies that have addressed certain aspects of the internal workings of the United Nations. While these studies were largely completed decades ago and none of them focused specifically on decisionmaking, they did address related issues such as influence and participation. For example, Alger (1966; 1967) examined how member state delegates to the Fifth (Administrative and Budgetary) Committee of the UN General Assembly interacted as they sought to reach agreement on funding peacekeeping and other issues. He discovered that essentially two processes were happening at the same time in the meetings: a public debate heard by all in the room and numerous private conversations that helped form the building blocks of the subsequent agreements. Another example concerns studies of influence in international organizations by Keohane (1967) and Robert Cox and Harold Jacobson (1973). In both cases, the authors sought to identify factors and mechanisms that enabled certain states to get their way in the UN body being studied. They found that state power was certainly related to influence but that other factors were also important, such as the personality of individual delegates and the use of procedures to manipulate the debate.

A second area of research that offers important insights into how international organizations operate is studies written by experienced UN practitioners. Some of these individuals are former UN staff members, such as C. V. Narasimhan (1988), who served in many senior secretariat positions, including under-secretary-general for special political affairs and chef de cabinet of the secretary-general. Other practitioner writers are former delegates who were posted to the United Nations in New York, Geneva, or both by their governments for many years. One rather prolific example is Kaufmann (1980; 1988), who has written on UN decisionmaking and conference diplomacy more broadly, based on his experiences serving as permanent representative of the Netherlands to the United Nations. The insights and stories offered by these former practitioners are especially illuminating, since they actually participated in the public and private processes observed by Alger (noted in the preceding paragraph).

A third and final type of research that offers a window into the political processes of the UN is detailed studies that focus on one particular institution, usually either the General Assembly or the Security Council. Sydney Bailey (1960) and M. J. Peterson (1986) both address the General Assembly's role in world politics as well as its structures and procedures. The Security Council has received comparatively more attention in this regard, including a number of edited volumes such as Nicol (1981) and Russett (1997). These studies mix a focus on the performance of the Council with a discussion of the mechanisms, both formal and informal, through which it reaches its decisions.

The previous three areas of literature have much to offer; however, they have an additional limitation for the illumination of UN processes beyond their lack of a common framework. Many of them were completed decades ago, when the UN was a very different place than it is today. While some of their insights are just as timely now as when they were first offered, the formal and informal processes used by the UN have evolved over time. Some of this change relates to the end of the cold war, but much of it reflects a longer evolution across the entire life of the organization. For example, studies of UN voting patterns completed in the 1970s found that the nature of group and coalition politics in the General Assembly had changed as its membership increased (Rowe, 1969; 1971; Newcombe, Ross, and Newcombe, 1970). Furthermore, building on this earlier research, studies completed in the 1990s found that many of these blocs were undergoing some degree of realignment and were no longer as unified or cohesive as they once had been (Holloway, 1990). Simultaneous with this change in membership has been a gradual shift from majority voting toward the use of consensus-based procedures in the General Assembly and other UN bodies (Marin-Bosch, 1987; Kaufmann, 1994, pp. 27–28). Given that these procedures structure all subsequent interaction and help to specify how much influence each member will have over the content of the decision, their impact on UN political processes can be significant (Cox and Jacobson, 1973, p. 7).

As a result of these changes, existing scholarship on the political processes of the United Nations and other international organizations needs to be revisited. The goal of this book is to synthesize the insights offered by classic writings on international organizations, such as those surveyed above, into a more systematic framework for understanding how the UN actually works. This synthesis will also draw on more recent examinations, where available, of the actors involved in UN processes and the procedures through which they interact.

However, merely synthesizing existing research would still leave significant gaps in our understanding of UN decisionmaking. These gaps are partly the result of the internal and external changes just discussed, but their roots also lie in the fact that much of the most difficult coalition building in the UN happens out of the spotlight, in private and informal settings. Unfortunately, as the preceding literature review indicates, these are the areas of UN politics most likely to be overlooked in existing scholarship. One mechanism for overcoming this neglect is to draw on the insights of current UN practitioners, both members of the Secretariat and representatives of member states and other actors that play a role in the organization's decisionmaking. When these insights are incorporated into a systematic framework, they can make a significant contribution to our understanding of parliamentary diplomacy, highlighting important processes that would otherwise be ignored and providing real-world examples of the dynamics at play. For this reason, interviews with twenty-five UN practitioners are used to inform the discussion that follows. They are cited in the text and listed with the other references at the end of the book.

■ Understanding UN Processes: The Plan of the Book

The remaining chapters of this book develop a framework for understanding the political dynamics of the United Nations and, at least to some extent, other international organizations. Based on the complex nature of parliamentary diplomacy described above, any effort to divide the many different processes involved into separate chapters necessitates some tradeoffs. The discussion that follows is divided into two rather straightforward parts: a consideration of the actors involved in UN decisionmaking, followed by an investigation of the formal and informal procedures and processes through which these actors can wield influence at the UN. Some mechanisms, such as the role of UN groups and the importance of political leadership, are discussed at key junctures in both parts, since they involve both actors and processes depending on the particular manner in which they are being used.

Part 1, "Members of the Troupe: Actors at the United Nations," discusses the various actors involved in UN processes. Previous international organization scholarship has identified nine distinct participants in UN decisions: representatives of member states, representatives of groups of states functioning as a bloc, representatives of other international organizations, the executive head of the organization, members of the organization's staff, representatives of nongovernmental organizations, private individuals working in their own capacity, representatives of multinational corporations, and the media. The influence of any of these actors on UN decisionmaking certainly varies across issues and over time. Part 1 is divided into four chapters dealing with the following most active UN actors: member states and their delegates, groups of states operating in concert, the organization's staff and its head, and representatives of civil society and the private sector.

Based on their power of vote and their payment of dues, member states represent the most important actors in UN processes, and they are the focus of Chapter 2, "Member States and Delegates." This chapter discusses how member states organize their UN missions to best pursue their interests in light of the power resources they possess within and outside the organization. Differences among these power resources and variations in their international reputations encourage large, middle, and small powers to assume different roles in UN deliberations. Chapter 2 also examines the role of individual state delegates as they seek to balance the often contradictory pressures of representing the interests of their country and participating in the give-and-take of multilateral diplomacy. Key issues in managing this balance are their individual autonomy, or freedom to act, in relationship to their home government and the personal attributes and particular skills that they can bring to bear in the negotiation process.

Chapter 3, "Groups and Blocs," investigates how various collections of UN members function in concert on different issues. Many writings have highlighted the importance of these actors, but they are often treated in an overly simplistic manner, which makes it easy to distort the true implications of this phenomenon for UN decisionmaking. This book differentiates among three dimensions of group politics, each of which has important but distinct influences on the political process. The first dimension is the five geographically based regional groups (Africa, Asia, Latin America and the Caribbean, Eastern Europe, and Western Europe and Other States) that are used for elections to all limited-membership bodies and the selection of candidates for all leadership positions. The second dimension is groups based on common issue positions, ranging in size from the five Nordic countries to the 130-plus members of the Group of 77. This dimension also includes the various regional international organizations, such as the European Union and the Caribbean Community, which often try to speak with one voice in UN debates. The third dimension of group politics in the UN is small negotiating groups used to resolve critical issues that have reached an impasse within larger membership bodies. However, in practice this last type of group politics blurs the line between groups as an actor and groups as a process, so these groups receive attention in Part 2 of the book as well.

Chapter 4, "The Secretariat and the Secretary-General," looks at the role of the UN's staff and its executive head. These individuals constitute the international civil service and are, at least in theory, independent of national influence and loyal to the UN. However, this impartiality does not mean they are without influence in the political processes of the organization. Chapter 4 examines the mechanisms through which the Secretariat has a direct and indirect impact on the decisions that are made, and it also considers various obstacles complicating the Secretariat's work. Additionally, the chapter includes a separate discussion of the political dimensions of the office of secretary-general. Effective incumbents in this difficult job have managed to use their individual style and personal attributes to move the organization in new and exciting directions; however, this can be a daunting task, given the often contradictory pressures they face in promoting and maintaining the UN's role in international politics. In balancing these pressures, the secretary-general can at times have a significant role in UN decision-making.

As the final section in Part 1, Chapter 5 investigates "Civil Society and the Private Sector." The focus is on two additional actors in UN processes: nongovernmental organizations (NGOs) and multinational corporations (MNCs). The relationship between the UN and NGOs dates to the drafting of the UN Charter; however, the mechanisms for this interaction have expanded considerably beyond the consultative arrangements with the Economic and Social Council (ECOSOC), specified in Article 71. These include limited access to other deliberative bodies, NGO liaison offices in nearly every UN department, expanded involvement in UN-sponsored global conferences, and extensive cooperation in the field. Despite this progress, there is still significant frustration on the part of NGOs regarding the obstacles to participation that they face: onerous security procedures, complex processes for accreditation, and a lack of direct access to the General Assembly and Security Council. The situation for MNCs is much less developed. Contact has been sporadic, on an issue-by-issue basis, with many efforts ending in mutual distrust. However, that has changed in recent years, most notably in the form of the Global Compact, which aims to foster partnerships between the UN and the business community. But even with these developments, MNCs still have only limited mechanisms, such as the creation of an affiliated NGO, through which they can have an impact on UN processes.

The second part of the book, "Movements of the Dance: Procedures and Processes," shifts attention from the actors involved in UN decisionmaking to the processes themselves. Across the four chapters of this part, both formal and informal dimensions of UN decisionmaking receive attention. First the structures of the main UN deliberative bodies are discussed, and then the formal procedures through which these bodies operate are examined. Next the book explores the private side of UN processes through which delegates and other players work to build coalitions in a personal and informal manner. The final chapter of this part brings together the key insights from Parts 1 and 2, in search of an understanding of strategies through which actors wield influence based on their attributes and the nature of the arena in which a decision is being made.

Chapter 6, "Formal Arenas: The Structures of Decisionmaking," considers the different forums in which the cast of characters interacts.

These include bodies that encompass all UN members, such as the General Assembly and its main committees, as well as bodies that are based on a more restricted membership, like the Security Council. It also distinguishes between deliberative bodies, including those just mentioned, in which politics is considered a central factor, and those more technical and specialized forums, such as the Economic and Social Council and the Specialized Agencies, where political considerations may be assumed, usually incorrectly, to be less debilitating. Finally, Chapter 6 also discusses ad hoc or temporary forums of decisionmaking, like the numerous issue-specific global conferences held under UN auspices over the last fifteen years. As can be expected, these various structures can result in political processes that are unique to each arena.

Chapter 7, "Decision Rules and Parliamentary Procedures," continues the consideration of UN policymaking arenas by examining the impact of decision rules and procedural tradeoffs on the political processes that ensue. In terms of decision rules, the major distinctions are among simple majority rule, qualified majority rule (including the veto), and consensus. Since each requires different thresholds of support for the UN to act, different dynamics are involved in building winning coalitions. These dynamics are also governed by procedural tradeoffs that must be made. Each UN forum must find an appropriate balance between the broad participation of actors (thereby increasing the legitimacy of its actions) and needs for efficiency and unambiguous statements of preferred behavior. This balance is influenced by a diverse set of procedural considerations that govern how proposals are handled, including the type of leadership provided by the presiding officer, mechanisms for managing debate, and methods through which amendments can be advanced.

After these formal aspects of UN processes are covered in Chapters 6 and 7, Chapter 8, "Informal Networking: The Personal Side," focuses on the informal processes that lie at the heart of UN decisionmaking. A number of UN practitioners have argued that 95 percent or more of decisionmaking in multilateral settings takes place in private, informal exchanges among interested parties. In fact, these informal processes are so important to effective policy outcomes that a rather established vocabulary and set of procedures have been developed regarding them. Unfortunately, this is the aspect of UN processes most likely to be entirely overlooked in the academic literature on international organizations. From "the fine art of corridor sitting" to the roles of delegate personality and ad hoc leadership, Chapter 8 seeks to provide a systematic understanding of what these informal contacts look like and how they affect the formal decisions that are made. It also includes a more detailed examination of how these informal dynamics play an essential role in the work of one particular UN body, the Security Council.

The concluding section of Part 2, Chapter 9, focuses on "Strategies of Influence: Positional, Personal, and Procedural." It brings together many insights from the preceding chapters by investigating how different actors attempt to wield influence in the United Nations based on their interests, their power, their personal attributes, and the arena in which a decision is being made. In general, representatives of different actors can draw on three types of strategies in their effort to influence policy outcomes: strategies that depend on the positional power of the actor they represent (for example, resources or votes), strategies that rest on the personality of the individual representative (for example, charisma or negotiating skill), or strategies that involve manipulating the formal and informal procedures discussed above (for example, premature closure of debate on an issue). Each of these choices has advantages and limitations, and these must be carefully balanced: all the actors involved in the global dance are aware that today's opponent may be tomorrow's dance partner, given the wide range of issues and interests that come before the United Nations.

The concluding chapter of the book, "The United Nations and State Compliance," examines another issue that has been given only limited attention in research on UN processes: do the decisions of the United Nations really matter? Evaluating the UN is fraught with difficulty, since many of its decisions are couched in vague language, subject to interpretation. On top of this, there is serious academic debate regarding exactly what types of outcomes the UN should be realistically expected to achieve. Thus UN observers must be careful when making judgments about the apparent impact of the organization's decisions. Certain considerations can lead us toward more thoughtful arguments regarding the results of UN processes. Chapter 10 addresses the most important of these, including the distinction between implementation and compliance, the differences between binding and nonbinding decisions, the appropriate time horizon for behavioral change, and the relationship between the process by which a decision is made and its ultimate effectiveness.

PART 1

Members of the Troupe:
Actors at the United Nations

2

Member States and Delegates

THE UNITED NATIONS IS A COMPLEX NETWORK OF INTERCONNECTED BOD-
ies: assemblies, councils, committees, commissions, programs, agencies, and funds. This reality is often obscured by journalists and politicians who talk in terms of a single United Nations that either succeeds or fails when it acts. For example, in the first half of 2003 numerous analyses bemoaned the failure of the United Nations to prevent the United States from acting outside the authority of the Security Council when it launched a military campaign against Iraq. Calling the United Nations "irrelevant" or worse, these pundits themselves committed a rather startling failure in their inability to understand that the UN is, first and foremost, an intergovernmental body whose successes and failures, however judged, result from political processes through which its member states interact. Viewing the UN in this manner helps us understand that the Council's inaction against Iraq was not the fault of the United Nations; it resulted directly from the fact that the Council's members could not arrive at a common approach for dealing with continued Iraqi noncompliance with its disarmament obligations.

To clarify what the UN is and is not, and thus allow for more nuanced and accurate assessments of its performance, one eminent international organization scholar has spoken of "two UNs" (Claude, 1996, pp. 290–292). In this conceptualization, the "first UN" is composed primarily of the organization's staff of international civil servants, who are dependent on the organization's members for resources but can act alongside them at times with considerable independence. The "second UN" is a collective entity composed of its member states, who use the organization as a forum for promoting their own interests and preferred outcomes. Sometimes states find that this forum facilitates finding common approaches to pressing issues; however, just as often these efforts can result in stalemate and inaction, as happened in the case of Iraq in March 2003. Naturally, these two UNs operate in very different ways. The "first UN" is mainly concerned with rendering impartial assistance to parties in need through noncoercive, consensual, and neutral mechanisms; the "second UN" by its very nature is essentially judgmental, partisan, and coercive.

Other scholars use a different vocabulary to discuss essentially the same dichotomy. For example, Thomas Weiss, David Forsythe, and Roger Coate describe the UN as both an "actor" and a "framework" (2001, pp. 12–15). At the heart of their discussion of these roles lies the issue of organizational autonomy: when, if ever, is it possible to talk about the UN as an actor that operates independently of the preferences of its members? While there is substantial debate among scholars and practitioners on this point, the consensus view is that the range of issues and tasks in which the UN is an independent actor is necessarily limited. In the great majority of situations, the UN is most accurately viewed as a framework through which its members pursue their goals in international politics, often at the expense of other states. While some examples of how the UN's staff can act independently of its membership will be offered in Chapter 4, "The Secretariat and the Secretary-General," this view of the "second UN" as a framework for its members will dominate the discussion in this chapter and in Part 2 of the book, on UN procedures and processes.

Conceptualizing the UN as an intergovernmental framework is logical, given the fact that its members have two important mechanisms for controlling the organization: the power of vote and the power of the purse. In terms of voting, all authoritative decisions made on behalf of the United Nations are taken by the member states that sit on a particular body. In some cases this involves all 191 members; in other cases it may involve only a small fraction of them (such as the fifteen-member Security Council). As was mentioned in the introduction, there are certainly other actors that play a role in the political processes of the UN and that will be surveyed in the following chapters; however, at the end of the day only the member states have the ability to move the organization to action through their dominance of its structures and procedures for decisionmaking. As if the power of vote were not enough, states also have the ability to dominate the organization by controlling its resources, since all UN funding is provided by its members, either through required assessments for the regular and peacekeeping budgets or through voluntary contributions for specific agencies or funds. A number of proposals for reforming UN financing would modify these arrangements (Mendez, 1997, pp. 297–304), but none of them have achieved much mileage politically, because member states continue to value having two different means of exercising control.

Because of this dominance, any discussion of the participants in the global dance of parliamentary diplomacy must begin with a focus on member states and how they represent their interests at the United Nations. This involves three separate but related areas of concern in this chapter. First, the roles that various types of member states play in the United Nations are examined. These roles vary based on the power capabilities of the state in question and based on its past and future policy priorities at the UN. Second, variations in the permanent missions of member states, in terms of both the size and structure of their delegations, are discussed. Finally, the chapter considers how the personal attributes of individual delegates can have a significant impact on their effectiveness in achieving their state's interests within the give-and-take of the UN's political processes. Variations in delegate autonomy are discussed in this section, and four different general types of UN delegates are described.

▓ State Roles at the United Nations

Article 2, Paragraph 1 of the United Nations Charter says that "the Organization is based on the principle of the sovereign equality of all of its Members." This equality is most directly reflected in the voting formula used in all UN bodies: one state, one vote. While there are some distortions of this equality in voting, such as the great-power veto in the Security Council, one could look at the UN's decisionmaking procedures discussed in Part 2 of this book and conclude that every member state has essentially the same degree of influence over outcomes, since each possess just one of 191 votes in all bodies where the full membership is represented. However, this sovereign equality on paper must be understood in terms of the political realities in which the UN operates; some UN members are clearly more equal than others. The differences in influence among UN members are often attributed to the fact that the international system is composed of states with varying degrees of power, and these power differences translate into corresponding differences in influence within the UN (Keohane, 1967, p. 222). Thus understanding what a state can achieve at the UN has much to do with appreciating the resources and other capabilities it can use to push the organization in the direction it desires.

However, looking solely at state power does not provide a complete picture of the different roles that states can play in the political processes of the United Nations. This is true because, at a very basic level, different members have different visions of what the UN is and what it should be doing. Writing originally in 1961, UN Secretary-General Dag Hammarskjöld identified two distinct ways member states viewed the UN:

> Certain members conceive of the Organization as a static conference machinery for resolving conflicts of interest and ideologies with a view to peaceful coexistence, [whereas] other members have made it clear that they conceive of the Organization primarily as a dynamic instrument of governments through which they, jointly and for the same purpose, should seek such reconciliation but through which they should also try to develop forms of executive action. (Hammarskjöld, 1967, p. 109)

While one could disagree with the exact nature of the two schools that Hammarskjöld identified in the 1960s, his general point is an important one: member states that see the UN in different ways will enjoy distinct advantages and disadvantages in their efforts to influence its decisions. The following paragraphs will seek, then, to arrive at some general observations regarding how two distinct considerations have an impact on a country's role at the UN: its ability to exercise influence and its desire to do so.

From the start, it should be clear that the roles that certain UN members play in the organization have evolved over time. For example, from the founding of the United Nations to the present, the United States has remained one of the most dominant (or, as many would say, the most dominant) of its members. However, over this same period, both the ability and the desire of the United States to influence outcomes at the UN have changed. Over the first two decades of UN activity, the United States was able to draw on its support in Latin America and its large financial contributions to use the UN as a means of legitimizing its desired actions (Karns and Mingst, 1995, p. 412). However, this dominance clearly waned across the 1970s and 1980s, as the membership expanded and the United States lost its long-held voting majority. Though the United States continued to be the largest financial contributor to the UN, its ability to secure preferred policy outcomes was severely diminished (Luck, 1999, pp. 111–114). This, in turn, resulted in a decreased US desire to even try to influence the UN, as it was seen as a "dangerous place" for US interests (Moynihan, 1978). Fortunately, the situation changed in the early 1990s. The US financial contribution remained large, and its control over votes (especially in the General Assembly) remained limited, but its desire to wield influence certainly increased in the aftermath of the successful US-UN partnership during the Gulf War in 1991. However, this euphoria was soon followed by renewed disengagement on the part of the United States (Gregg, 1993, p. 143), a development that marked the beginning of a pattern of rapid and tumultuous changes in the US role in the UN. These changes have persisted through the frustrations associated with how to best handle Iraq in 2003 (see Smith, 2004).

The United States provides a telling example of how changes in a country's ability and desire to influence the UN can significantly affect its role in the UN—and the US experience is far from unique. Other major powers in the United Nations have seen their interests and roles in the organization evolve over time. For example, as Japan moved to the status of one of the UN's largest financial contributors in the 1980s, its desire to wield influence in the political processes of key UN bodies also increased. Such activism had not been apparent in Japan's relationship with the UN in previous decades, and it has clearly resulted in a new set of policy priorities focused on UN reform (Ogata, 1995, pp. 231–232). However, other active UN members have exhibited a greater consistency in the role they have played at the UN. Two middle powers that are often identified in this regard are Canada and the Netherlands. Part of their consistency in the UN may be due to the fact that the ability of these states to wield influence has not undergone much change, as it has for the United States and Japan; however, it also results from the fact that these members have made unwavering support for the UN a cornerstone of their foreign policy (Krause, Knight, and Dewitt, 1995, p. 132; Baehr, 1995, pp. 272–273). Regardless of any changes in their ability to influence UN processes, they have consistently served as an example to other members of how states with a strong desire to work through the UN can use it as an effective instrument to achieve their goals.

Clearly both the ability to influence UN decisionmaking and the desire to do so can cause a particular member state to assume a specific role in the organization (Cox and Jacobson, 1973b, pp. 20–21). This raises an important question: what factors affect whether or not a state will have the ability and desire to exercise influence in the UN? While there are many possibilities, the following pages will discuss four factors that can affect a member state's ability to exercise influence and four separate but related factors that can affect its desire to work through the organization. Factors affecting a state's ability include its position in the international system, its financial resources, its use of voting coalitions, and how vital its participation is in addressing the issue at hand; factors affecting a state's desire include the nature of its political system, its policy history related to the UN, its reputation or status in the organization, and its expertise on salient "niche issues."

Factors Affecting State Ability to Wield Influence

The first factor that affects a state's ability to exert influence in the political process of the United Nations is its relative position in the international system. All international organizations operate within a larger environment that can have a decisive impact on the organization's behavior and performance by acting as both a constraint and determinant of decisions (Cox and Jacobson, 1973b, p. 25; Ness and Brechin, 1988, p. 249). In the case of the United Nations, this environment consists of the entire international state system; when the position of specific countries within this system changes, their ability to wield influence in the United Nations also changes (Haas, 1968, p. 170). As can be expected, much of this interaction between the United Nations and broader dynamics of international politics is based on the coalitions, groups, and blocs that are formed as part of the organization's political processes. These collective actors will receive detailed attention in the following chapter. It is also true that an important relationship exists between the power of individual states in general international affairs and their ability to exercise influence in specific international organizations (Cox and Jacobson, 1973b, pp. 20, 27–28).

Translating power outside an organization into power inside the organization is never an exact science, but it is not surprising that major powers that possess military or economic strength might be accorded special deference or influence in certain decisions. For example, if a member's military power is considered crucial to the success of a particular peacekeeping mission, then that state will enjoy greater leverage in determining the nature and scope of the mission. The efforts of major powers to draw on their international position to increase their influence within an international organization can at times be rather blatant; however, these processes often unfold without resort to explicit threats or pressure (Keohane, 1967, p. 223). In the case of Security Council deliberations on Iraq in February and March 2003, the six undecided members (Angola, Cameroon, Chile, Guinea, Mexico, and Pakistan) came under intense pressure by both the states that favored military action (the United States, Britain, Spain, and Bulgaria) and those that wanted the weapons inspectors to have more time (France, Germany, Syria, Russia, and China). Public discussion of these efforts stressed that neither side was using overt economic leverage on the so-called middle six but that the sizable aid packages and other ties between these states and the various major powers did weigh heavily in the discussions (Weisman and Barringer, 2003).

A second factor that can affect a member state's ability to influence UN decisionmaking is its financial contribution to the organization.

While most UN voting is based on the sovereign equality of the members, UN financing is governed by a formula based on a state's capacity to pay: states with larger economies pay more, while states with weaker economies pay less. Each member is assessed a percentage of the UN's regular operating budget based on its average per capita gross national product (GNP). This basic assessment is modified for the majority of UN members in the case of expenditures for peacekeeping operations; the permanent members of the Security Council pay an extra premium so that states with weaker economies, arranged in eight different groups, get varying amounts of discount.

The results of this system have important implications for the ability of different member states to influence UN decisions. Based on the scale of assessment for the regular budget in 2002, the top seven contributors (who also happen to be the members of the Group of Seven [G7], the world's largest industrialized democracies) are the United States at 22 percent, Japan at 19.7 percent, Germany at 9.9 percent, France at 6.5 percent, the United Kingdom at 5.6 percent, Italy at 5.1 percent, and Canada at 2.6 percent (*United Nations Handbook*, 2002, pp. 360–364). Thus just seven members contribute 71.4 percent of the UN's regular budget, with the 184 other members providing the remaining 28.6 percent. In fact, only eleven other members even break the 1 percent threshold with their contributions, and if their contributions are set with those of the G7, then eighteen UN members provide just under 90 percent of the organization's regular budget. The imbalances found on the regular scale are even more pronounced on the peacekeeping scale, because the G7 countries all pay at the same or even higher rates, and many of the 184 other members receive corresponding discounts.

The major financial contributors to the United Nations have repeatedly demonstrated willingness to use their financial muscle to express displeasure or opposition to certain UN programs and activities. The most dramatic examples of these efforts led to the three major financial crises that have beset the organization (Karns and Mingst, 2002, pp. 273–276). The first of these was in the early 1960s, when France and the Soviet Union questioned whether all members should be required to contribute to new peacekeeping missions in the Middle East and the Congo. The second financial crisis emerged in the mid-1980s, when the United States started withholding part of its dues because the Reagan administration objected to certain UN policies and the politicization of some UN agencies. The United States also sought to force changes in some UN procedures, especially those associated with budgeting, and it was supported by seventeen other UN members that withheld payments for similar reasons. These efforts resulted in new budgeting arrangements that allowed the organization's major financial contributors to have greater influence. The third financial crisis arose in the late 1990s when again the United States used the "withholding tool" in an effort to secure twenty UN reforms contained in the Helms-Biden Agreement, passed by the US Congress in 1999. While the effort to fully resolve this round of arrears remained incomplete as of 2004, two of the most important objectives of the United States were achieved in late 2000 when US assessments for the regular budget and peacekeeping were lowered (see Smith, 2004). All three crises demonstrate that the major financial contributors to the UN have a powerful means of influence that they have been able to use effectively.

The first two factors affecting a state's ability to exercise influence at the United Nations, international position and financial contribution, generally benefit only the most powerful UN members. However, the preceding discussion sheds light on one of the most important mechanisms of influence available to medium and smaller UN members: the fact they represent a majority of UN members. If these states work cooperatively, they can relatively easily command a dominant voting majority in every UN body except the Security Council and forums that rely on consensus decisionmaking. Like-minded states realize that their power is multiplied when they form common negotiating groups (Keohane, 1967, p. 223). Such groups maximize the bargaining power of their members and allow for a division of labor across negotiations that are often detailed and complex (Hong, 1995, p. 280). These groups will be discussed as collective actors in the following chapter; for now it is important to understand that many of the UN's political processes can be understood in terms of members' trying to empower themselves through the use of coalitions and groups (Morphet, 2000, p. 261). Sometimes these groups remain fractured and disjointed; however, they can be a powerful tool for augmenting the ability of small states to pursue their interests through UN processes (Trent, 1995, p. 467). One of the most dramatic examples of the power of a large group of small states working together was seen in the 1970s, when such a group effectively set the agenda of the UN on issues such as the legacies of colonization and demands for a new international economic order (NIEO).

A fourth and final factor that can affect the ability of a member state to get its way in the UN is its role in regard to the specific issue at hand. Some UN members possess sufficient power, money, or allies to exert influence across a wide range of UN issues; however, other members may lack all three of these resources and still be able to change the direction of UN action. This is true even in the case of relatively isolated smaller powers where they are directly involved in either causing or

solving a problem (Keohane, 1967, pp. 228–232). States directly affected by a situation tend to be more committed to seeing their preferred
outcome achieved. More powerful states for which the issue has less
salience may see clear advantages in deferring to the normally less
influential member in this particular case. Even if the more powerful
members remain directly involved, small, isolated members can influence the UN's decisionmaking when it is their behavior that the UN is
addressing. For example, across the 1990s Iraq's sovereignty was
severely circumscribed by the Security Council, as it authorized inspection regimes, no-fly zones, and strict controls on Iraqi oil exports.
However, at least until early 2003, Iraq was able to have a significant
impact on the nature of Council deliberations, since it was Iraq's behavior the Council wanted to change. Iraq repeatedly used this to its advantage by offering last-minute concessions that frequently sidestepped key
issues but created enough disunity among Council members that dire
consequences were avoided. In essence, being a target of UN actions
was itself a source of leverage within the UN's political processes.

Factors Affecting State Desire to Wield Influence

As we turn from factors that affect a state's ability to exercise influence
at the UN to factors that affect its desire to do so, it is important to consider the political processes through which a state determines its policy
at the UN. Classic writings on international organizations often conceptualized this dynamic in terms of different types of domestic political
regimes. A rather obvious focus, given the realities of the cold war, was
on competitive (democratic) versus authoritarian regimes (Cox and
Jacobson, 1973b, pp. 29–32); however, special attention was also paid
to "revolutionary regimes" and how their goals and priorities in international organizations were to a large extent based on their histories of
exploitation (Haas, 1968). An undercurrent in these writings is the
assumption that democratic regimes would desire to play a more active
and supportive role in international organizations, since their domestic
political system is premised on the role that institutions can play in
effective governance. However, the roller-coaster relationship between
the United States and the United Nations over time, discussed above,
suggests that trying to categorize a country's desire to work through the
UN based simply on its regime type is fraught with difficulty.

More recent studies have offered greater detail in conceptualizing
the relationship between a state's domestic political system and its
desired role in the UN. For example, the conclusion of one investigata-
tion of how eight UN members (Algeria, Canada, France, Japan, the

Netherlands, Nigeria, the United Kingdom, and the United States) formed their foreign policy in relation to the organization was that while some states' policy was formed by a small group of political elites in the executive branch, other states' policy was influenced by legislatures and public opinion as well (Trent, 1995, pp. 494). These differences resulted in some states' having a consistent and stable view of their role in the UN, while others, generally those with a more decentralized policy process, moving between UN engagement and UN neglect. The conclusion of a companion study that examined the same issue in regard to a different set of seven UN members (Germany, India, Sweden, Romania, Chile, Jamaica, and Sierra Leone) looked instead at variation in the relationship between the state and civil society (Knight and Krause, 1995, pp. 250–255). In countries with a strong state apparatus, the state's orientation toward multilateralism in general, and the UN in particular, was often influenced by the desires of the top leaders. In some such cases, like Romania and Sierra Leone, there was little desire to work through the UN, but others, like Sweden, developed the opposite orientation. In cases where society was relatively autonomous from the state, like Jamaica, the study found that the country's orientation to the UN was more variable, based on the interests that captured the state at various times.

A second factor that affects a state's desire to exert influence at the UN concerns the state's past history, both within and outside of the organization. In terms of a state's general history, a variety of experiences can cause the state to favor or not favor multilateral venues such as the United Nations: its colonial history (as master or subject), its reputation in terms of protecting the human rights of its people, its traditional allies and enemies, its geographic location, its position in the global economy, and its endowment of natural resources, to name some of the most cited examples (Trent, 1995, pp. 476–479; Knight and Krause, 1995, pp. 248–250). These historical experiences may not apply to all states, and the considerations just mentioned may push the same state in contradictory directions in terms of its orientation toward the UN; in any case, these experiences, where relevant, act as a filter through which a state must decide what role the UN will play in its foreign policy.

A related consideration is the state's past history specifically in relation to the UN. One way to think about this is the state's historical "presence" in the organization (Pentland, 1989, p. 6). This certainly relates to the state's power and financial contribution, but it also involves its level of participation in the organization: is it an active member, and has it provided Secretariat personnel, peacekeeping troops, or leadership in UN bodies? Another aspect of a state's history with the UN concerns any instances when the country has been on the receiving end of UN programs: has it been given assistance for development or decolonization, been the subject of a peacekeeping mission or human rights investigation, or been punished with multilateral sanctions? Finally, both large and small members are likely to calculate the future utility of the UN in light of how useful a tool it has been in the past (Trent, 1995, pp. 472–474). If the state has sought UN approval for a previous course of action, whether or not it received that support will weigh heavily in any future decisions about seeking UN legitimacy for its policies.

A third factor that provides clues for understanding why some states choose to be more active in the UN's political processes than others is their reputation in the organization. If a particular member enjoys a positive reputation in the eyes of its fellow members, its desire to draw on that reputation in order to achieve preferred outcomes can be significantly enhanced. This is especially true for those small and middle powers that over time have come to assume the role of brokers or "bridge-builders" in the United Nations (Kaufmann, 1980, pp. 17–18). These actors will receive additional attention in the following chapter and in Part 2 of the book; at this juncture it is important to stress simply that these states can enjoy a degree of influence in the UN well beyond what their power or financial contribution would suggest.

That certain small and middle powers would play a central role in the UN is not surprising; in fact, certain UN activities like peacekeeping were designed specifically to take advantage of the characteristics of these states (Bennett and Oliver, 2002, p. 157). The most important of these characteristics are, first, their perceived impartiality or neutrality on key issues, which allows them some freedom to maneuver within the complex and shifting coalitions often found in UN bodies, and, second, their high level of consistent support for all UN activities, given that the principles of the UN are seen as forming an integral part of their national interest. The activities of brokers extend to nearly all issues on the UN's agenda. For example, on human rights small and middle powers, especially those who are truly nonaligned with the major powers or offending states, were instrumental in moving the UN from simply drafting standards to actual monitoring and implementation in the 1980s (Forsythe, 1988, p. 254; Egeland, 1984, p. 208). Likewise, on the Law of the Sea negotiations in the late 1970s and again in the early 1990s, small and middle powers were instrumental in building the complex package agreements that were required to create the seabed mining regime and then modify its structure (Sanger, 1987, pp. 194, 210;

Joyner, 1996, p. 46). Member states that have performed this role include Canada, the Nordic countries, the Netherlands, Australia, New Zealand, Senegal, Brazil, Bangladesh, Malaysia, Italy, India, Mexico, the Philippines, Argentina, Fiji, and Indonesia. The influence of brokers has become so important in UN decisionmaking that participants in its political processes are quick to lament their absence where they have chosen not to be active on certain issues, such as the negotiations to reform the Security Council in the mid-1990s (Smith, 1999, p. 191).

The fourth and final factor that can affect a state's desire to influence UN politics is certain areas of specialization or "niche issues" on which some states assume an active and constructive role (Hong, 1995, p. 283). This is especially important in the case of small states that lack the power or resources often associated with influence and whose participation is not required for resolving the problem at hand. In this case, the states want to influence the decisions simply because they find the issue highly salient to them or because they have developed some degree of expertise on technical aspects of the problem. Other members do not *need* to allow these states to wield influence, but they can find it useful to allow them to play an active role due to their passion, knowledge, and willingness to look for innovative solutions. Examples of small and middle states that have developed "niche issues" include Malta on the Law of the Sea and climate change, New Zealand on the safety of UN personnel, Singapore on UN reform, the Nordic countries and Fiji on peacekeeping, Sri Lanka on the Indian Ocean, and Mexico on nuclear disarmament (Hong, 1995, p. 283).

A Typology of State Roles

As was mentioned above, the roles that any state plays in the United Nations are not constant and immutable; they often evolve over time based on changes in the state's ability to wield influence and its desire to do so. However, over the course of UN history, numerous attempts have been made to categorize member states in groups based on the roles they play in the organization. These efforts are most commonly made by former practitioners, but international organization scholars have also offered observations in this regard. The results are often quite illuminating for outsiders who want a basic understanding of the dynamics at play in the UN; unfortunately, the typologies they offer are useful only as long as the constellation of state abilities and desires that they capture remains unchanged. The typology that will be presented here involves eight groups of states identified by Taylor (2000a, pp. 299–304) in the conclusion of a volume evaluating the UN at the turn of the century. His typology is especially useful since his criteria for grouping UN members are very much consistent with the two sets of factors discussed above: "the orientation of their governments towards the organization and their status in the hierarchy of states at the global and regional levels" (ibid., p. 299).

Taylor's first four groups of states are major and middle powers that play an active role in the organization. His first group is status quo powers whose position in the organization is consistent with their status in the international system. The members in this group, the United States, China, and the Russian Federation, are all generally (though not always) willing to work through the organization because it contains certain structural elements (like the veto) that protect their perceived role and interests in international affairs. His second group is composed of status quo powers like Britain and France, whose position in the UN exceeds their status in the international system. These states see the UN as "suiting their interests": their position in the organization enhances their status outside it by enabling them to "punch above [their] weight" (ibid., p. 300). His third group of states is "reformist"; members of this group, Germany, Japan, and Italy, consider their formal status in the organization to fall far below their significant contributions to it and their rising informal status. These states want to reform the organization such that their formal position in it is enhanced to better reflect the actual role that they play. The fourth group identified by Taylor is made up of "system-reinforcing problem-solvers" like Sweden, the Netherlands, Norway, Finland, and Canada. These members are significant contributors to the organization and enjoy a high informal status within it; however, they are relatively unconcerned about obtaining a match between their status in international politics and their formal position in the UN.

Turning to the developing world, Taylor offers four groups in order to capture some great differences between states that are often lumped together in other typologies. His fifth group again consists of "reformist" states, but in this case their claims for increased formal status within the organization are not matched by a corresponding status in the international system or a substantial enough contribution to the organization. For these states, including Brazil, India, and Nigeria, much of their claim for an enhanced status is based on their leadership in their respective regions; however, in each case this leadership has been questioned by other regional powers, like Mexico, Argentina, Pakistan, South Africa, and Egypt. The sixth group is composed of "system loading claimants" from the developing world, including most members of the Group of 77 (G77). These states have little to contribute to the organization but still want to work through it, since they are on the receiving end of UN programs designed to help with their economic and social problems. This group is internally diverse, with some of its members fairly described as developing and other members more accurately seen as being close to collapse. The seventh group is also composed of "claimants"; however, these members (e.g., Yemen, Cuba, Sudan, Malaysia, Indonesia, and sometimes Algeria) believe that the organization is in drastic need of reform before it will be able to fully address their interests. Their focus is on structural reforms and collective action. Taylor's final group consists of pariah states like Libya, Iran, Iraq, and Burma, which see no real positive benefit in their UN membership but remain in the organization solely in order to avoid the added costs they would suffer if they left.

It is certainly possible to disagree with how Taylor has classified certain members, especially those whose role has changed due to new foreign policy priorities and capabilities. One could also question where certain states (like Israel) would fit in his scheme. Nevertheless, his typology is a useful mechanism for thinking about how the membership of states with different resources and different visions of the UN falls into distinct patterns. This in turn sets the stage for considering how member states actually go about representing their interests at the UN. While some of this discussion must wait until UN procedures are examined in Part 2, the next section of this chapter begins the process by exploring how members organize their permanent missions and structure their delegations.

■ Permanent Missions and Delegations

United Nations members have varying priorities and visions for the organization; however, by and large all of them are in the organization because they receive certain tangible and intangible benefits from membership. Every member state has established mechanisms for pursuing its interests at the UN, most often in the form of a permanent mission and delegations. It is common for those unfamiliar with UN processes to lump these two mechanisms together, since their roles and functions are interrelated. Unfortunately, this simplification glosses over some important distinctions (Kaufmann, 1980, p. 103). A permanent mission is essentially a country's embassy to the United Nations; its primary responsibility is to represent the interests of the state in the organization, much as an embassy would in a foreign capital. It is typically headed by an ambassador, staffed by foreign service officers, and functions continuously once established. A delegation, on the other hand, is composed of the personnel who are accredited to represent a country at a particular UN meeting or series of meetings. Their membership is temporary and often more diverse.

A country's permanent mission to the UN and the delegations it sends to UN meetings must work in a complementary fashion (Peterson, 1986, pp. 288–289). For starters, staff from the permanent mission are often included in delegations for specific meetings or conferences. In addition, one of the main functions of the permanent mission is to provide each delegation with the necessary support to effectively represent the country's interests in negotiations. This support can include providing information on past UN efforts to address the issue at hand, analyzing key negotiating texts circulated before the meeting begins, identifying key individuals from other member states who are potential allies or adversaries, communicating with the home government, acting as the institutional memory for the delegation from one meeting to the next, and training new personnel in the dynamics of parliamentary diplomacy if necessary. The importance of this interaction will become evident as the basic features of permanent missions and delegations are discussed in the following paragraphs.

Permanent Missions

The use of permanent missions in multilateral diplomacy is a development that really occurred only after the UN was established. More than forty members of the League of Nations created "permanent delegations" in Geneva; however, scholars have concluded that this development was of "no serious significance" (Walters, 1952, p. 199) and that the League essentially operated without them (Peterson, 1986, p. 288). The UN Charter did not specifically call for member states to create permanent missions in New York. Thus it is rather remarkable that by 1948 permanent missions were an integral feature of the United Nations. Several explanations for this rapid emergence have been offered: the fast-paced tempo of postwar diplomacy, the increase in meeting activity in the UN as compared to the League, and the fact the new organization was not located in a state capital where members might have already had a permanent diplomatic presence (Kay, 1967, p. 93; Appathurai, 1985, pp. 96–97). In addition, Article 28, Paragraph 1 of the UN Charter mandates that "the Security Council shall be so organized as to be able to function continuously. Each member of the Security Council shall for this purpose be represented at all times at the seat of the Organization." It is likely that other states were simply following the example of Council members when they established their own permanent missions (Peterson, 1986, p. 288).

In any case, permanent missions perform a variety of important functions for the member states beyond the services they provide to delegations. In many respects their functions are quite similar to those of any embassy: representing the interests of their country in all negotiations, reporting on developments that have either an immediate or a potential future impact on the country's policy priorities, gathering information about the interests and positions of other participants, disseminating propaganda, and contributing to the process of formulating the country's policy in the first place (Kay, 1967, p. 93; Aggrey-Orleans, 1998, pp. 50–51). However, there are also some functions of permanent missions that set them apart from bilateral embassies (Finger, 1990, pp. 18–22). For example, all the tasks just mentioned do not take place within the context of one other government; they are carried out in an environment where up to 190 other perspectives must be considered when one is drafting policy, designing negotiating strategies, and delivering propaganda. In addition, permanent missions must be aware of how to manipulate UN rules of procedure and be ready to offer specific proposals on a much wider range of issues than bilateral embassies must address.

These differences have led some to suggest that permanent missions can function as if they were mini or shadow foreign ministries, somewhat free of direction from the home government (Finger, 1990, p. 22). The degree to which this is true depends on a number of considerations, including the nature of the issue, the quality of the mission's staff, the size of the foreign policy bureaucracy in the home capital, and the attitude of the government toward the UN. These variations also have much to do with the personal attributes of the diplomats involved, so they will receive detailed attention in the discussion of delegate autonomy in the last section of this chapter. However, one general observation has been offered by several diplomats with experience in both bilateral and multilateral postings: these individuals felt that they enjoyed increased freedom of action in multilateral settings (Jacobson, 1979, p. 110). This conclusion is echoed by Seymour Finger: "The wide range of questions promotes a greater degree of autonomy for the mission, as few governments can keep track of so many details and the government is more dependent on the mission for relevant information" (1990, p. 20).

Clearly permanent missions are an indispensable tool for members that desire to play any type of serious role in the United Nations. In February 2003 there were 191 UN members, 189 of which maintained permanent missions at UN headquarters in New York (United Nations, 2003). The two member states not maintaining permanent missions were Kiribati and Palau; they did send representatives to UN meetings as they deemed necessary. In addition to member states, both the Holy See and Palestine sent observer missions to UN headquarters, the Holy See based on its status as a nonmember state and Palestine based on a standing invitation from the General Assembly to participate in its work. Twelve intergovernmental organizations, mainly regional in scope, and four nongovernmental organizations also sent observer missions to New York based on a standing invitation from the General Assembly. Finally, thirteen UN specialized agencies and related organizations maintained permanent liaison offices at UN headquarters. In addition to this extensive diplomatic presence in New York, most member states had permanent missions in Geneva to deal with the considerable number of UN bodies and meetings located in and around the Palais des Nations, and a number also maintained a permanent presence in Vienna, Austria, where the UN's offices dealing with atomic energy, drugs, and crime are based. Finally, depending on a member state's priorities and resources, it may also send small permanent missions to the offices of different UN programs, funds, regional economic commissions, and specialized agencies based in nearly fifteen other cities around the world.

In spite of these many centers of diplomatic activity, the heart of the UN's political processes lies in New York, and so the permanent missions there are generally staffed with the largest number and highest quality of personnel. Still, there is considerable variation in the size of permanent missions at UN headquarters from one country to the next. The largest mission by far is maintained by the United States, which had 125 diplomatic personnel in 2003 (United Nations, 2003). This size is due in part to the active role played by the United States in nearly every UN body and based on the fact that the US mission must perform a number of unique tasks given its role as host state. Other permanent members of the Security Council also maintain large missions, though not nearly as large as that of the United States. In 2003 the number of diplomatic personnel at the Russian mission was eighty-three, at the Chinese mission sixty-three, at the British mission forty, and at the French mission twenty-eight. Five other members maintained missions of thirty or more diplomatic personnel (Germany at sixty-one, Japan at fifty-two, Cuba at thirty-seven, South Korea at thirty-six, and Brazil at thirty). Nearly all other developed countries have missions in the neighborhood of fifteen to twenty-five, and the missions of a number of developing countries are this large as well. However, the majority of developing states maintain only five to ten diplomatic personnel, and twenty-one members have missions with a staff of three or fewer. In 2003, the Central African Republic, the Marshall Islands, and Timor-Leste (East Timor) had the smallest missions, staffed solely by an ambassador in each case.

Not surprisingly, one of the primary explanations for this variation in the size of permanent missions is the costs associated with maintaining them, both in New York and in Geneva (Aggrey-Orleans, 1998, p. 48). This has always been especially true for newly independent developing states. However, other factors also play a role in determining the size of a country's UN mission. For example, an additional reason developing states tend to have small missions is that these members often have a shortage of trained personnel, based on their colonial experiences (Kay, 1967, p. 96). Nevertheless, many new members have a strong desire to overcome this obstacle and maintain a mission that is larger than one might expect given their limited resources, because they see diplomatic service at the UN as an effective mechanism for increasing the training and experience of their foreign service personnel. Other reasons that small states may desire to have large missions include the common perception that a permanent presence in New York is an important manifestation of newfound independence and the fact that their UN mission is actually the centerpiece of their entire system of foreign representation (Ziring, Riggs, and Plano, 2000, p. 78; Kay, 1967, p. 97). Many developing states find UN headquarters to be an important venue for interacting with a wide range of other member states with whom they cannot afford to maintain a bilateral embassy. Another common practice is for members to have their diplomatic personnel at the UN also handle their country's relationship with the United States, since travel time between Washington, D.C., and New York City is quite brief.

As the figures above indicate, there is also considerable variation in mission size among states that have the financial capacity to send as many personnel as they feel they need. Part of this variation has to do with a country's view of the importance of the United Nations in its foreign policy and the utility the United Nations provides it for reaching its international goals (Ziring, Riggs, and Plano, 2000, p. 76). Further, the UN is only one of many possible international organizations a state may join. If a state is also a member of a cohesive and integrated regional organization, like the European Union, then it may not require as many of its own personnel at the UN, since its positions on key issues will likely be coordinated amongst all the members of the regional organization. A final reason that a member state might increase the size of its mission has to do with a change in its role or position within the organization. For example, when small states serve as elected members of the Security Council, they often increase the size of their UN mission to handle the extra workload for that two-year period. A similar reasoning applies when a diplomat from a particular country is elected to a leadership position. The president of the General Assembly for its 57th Session, from September 2002 to September 2003, was Jan Kavan from the Czech Republic; during that time the Czech mission doubled in size, from ten to twenty diplomatic personnel, to cover both the mission and the president's office (United Nations, 2003).

All missions are headed by a "permanent representative" who enjoys the rank of ambassador. Most mission staff members are foreign service officers stationed at the mission as part of their normal rotation of postings. However, beyond these similarities, there is considerable variation in how permanent missions are structured in terms of their vertical and horizontal patterns of authority. Directly under the permanent representative is usually a deputy permanent representative, who may also enjoy ambassadorial rank, who fills in for the permanent representative when necessary and helps run the mission on a day-to-day basis. Some missions appoint additional representatives with ambassadorial rank for key UN issues. For example, the US permanent representative, deputy permanent representative, alternate representative for special political affairs, and representatives for economic and social affairs and UN management are all ambassadors confirmed by the US Senate.

Directly below the ambassadors in many missions are ministers, counselors, or minister-counselors (the exact title varies) who are often in charge of a general area of UN activity like peace and security, political affairs, economic and social affairs, development, legal affairs, or administration. Below this level the differences across missions increase. Most missions have first secretaries who are in charge of specific issues like terrorism, peacekeeping, human rights, gender, and so on; in fact, the majority of personnel across all missions hold this rank. Missions that are more hierarchical in structure, as in the case of Japan, may also use second secretaries, third secretaries, and even attachés and assistant attachés. Some missions are structured in a more horizontal fashion, where everyone below the rank of minister or counselor is simply given the title of first secretary or adviser, as is the US practice.

Permanent representatives are nearly always "senior diplomats of distinction" (Nicholas, 1975, p. 198); in many countries this posting is considered to be one of the most high-profile and prestigious of the entire diplomatic service. At a minimum the permanent representative is among the handful of top ambassadorships; at a maximum it is a direct stepping-stone to foreign minister or secretary of state, with Madeleine Albright being a recent example of this pattern in the United States. Many permanent representatives in New York already have ambassadorial experience, either in bilateral postings or at the UN's offices in Geneva. Some UN ambassadors also have experience in top positions within the foreign ministry, such as deputy foreign minister, or have worked in the office of the head of state or head of government. Even members who draw their permanent representatives from outside their diplomatic service tend to select senior political figures of great reputation who enjoy close ties to the country's top political leaders (Finger, 1990, p. 15). In the case of the United States, the permanent representative has frequently, though not always, been a member of the president's cabinet alongside the secretary of state. As a result, even though the permanent representative should technically report to the assistant secretary of state in charge of the Bureau of International Organization Affairs in the State Department, she or he often has direct access to the president when important issues are being discussed at the UN. The first term of President George W. Bush marked an exception to this general pattern, since his UN ambassador at the time, John Negroponte, was not a member of the cabinet. However, even with this reduced rank, Negroponte enjoyed a very close relationship to Secretary of State Colin Powell, having served as Powell's deputy on the National Security Council in the late 1980s.

Delegations

Permanent missions serve as the embassies of member states at UN headquarters; however, the job of representing a country's interests at the UN falls to the specific delegations that the country sends to each meeting or series of meetings. In the case of the General Assembly session each year, Article 9, Paragraph 2 of the UN Charter states, "Each member shall have not more than five representatives in the General Assembly," and the travel expenses for these are reimbursed out of the UN budget (Kaufmann, 1980, p. 106). The Assembly's rules of procedure also allow for the appointment of five alternate representatives and "whatever number of experts and advisors a member state cares to send" (Peterson, 1986, p. 284). No matter how many delegates and advisers are sent, each member has one vote in the General Assembly as specified under Article 18, Paragraph 1. Other UN bodies can adopt their own specifications regarding delegation size; however, wherever feasible it is left up to the member states to decide how many delegates to send to a meeting.

UN delegations typically include at least some personnel from the permanent mission (Kaufmann, 1980, p. 103). Nearly always this includes the permanent representative and any other officials in the mission who hold ambassadorial rank. However, these individuals are frequently outranked on the delegation by their foreign minister or secretary of state, or in some cases even by their head of state or head of government (Ziring, Riggs, and Plano, 2000, p. 80). While some states fill their entire delegation with diplomats and senior government officials, other states follow a common practice of including members of their legislature, other government departments, and even private individuals of national importance (Kaufmann, 1980, p. 106). In the case of the United States, the delegation typically includes three or four ambassadors stationed at the US mission, two members of Congress (one from each political party), and four or five others chosen for various reasons: "prominence in politics, industry, labor, the arts, or the sciences; regional balance; payment of political debt; ethnic balance; religious considerations; and the need to have at least one woman" (Finger, 1990, p. 26).

Beyond membership, states also include a more diverse crew of support personnel for a delegation than would typically be stationed at the mission. Again, staff of the mission do serve the delegation, but at a minimum they would be joined by experts from other government agencies and departments appropriate to the issues under debate. One example of this would be sending staff from the US Arms Control and Disarmament Agency to the US mission in preparation for the 1995 Nuclear Non-Proliferation Treaty Review and Extension Conference in New York (S. Williams, 1999, p. 136). Such "reinforcements" are common anytime meetings are in session (Smouts, 2000, p. 33); however, like permanent missions, delegations are most likely to grow larger when the permanent representative or the state itself is performing a leadership role at a particular meeting or session.

Members of a delegation are accredited to the meeting in much the same way that bilateral diplomats are accredited to foreign capitals: through a formal letter of appointment from the head of state. However, in the case of UN meetings, there is no requirement that the secretary-general give prior approval to a permanent representative or to other delegation members, as would typically be the case when a diplomat is posted to another country (Bailey, 1963, p. 42). Member states are usually free to send any persons they choose on their UN delegations. There are two exceptions, however, to this general rule. First, the United States has on rare occasion denied entry visas to delegation members it deemed politically unacceptable; such a decision does provoke serious diplomatic protest, as it violates the spirit of the host-country agreement. Second, the General Assembly's Credentials Committee usually accredits delegation members without much debate or fanfare, but this committee or the Assembly Plenary can at times create problems for some delegations (Smouts, 2000, p. 34). Some examples of complications in accreditation arose with Chinese representation before 1971 and Cambodian representation from the mid-1970s to mid-1980s; examples of rejected credentials include the South African delegation in 1974 and the Israeli delegation in 1975.

The changing composition of member-state delegations to the United Nations means that two elements must be managed carefully if the delegation is to be effective in negotiations. The first of these is the need to make sure that the various members of the delegation are offering a consistent message based on a common strategy and the same set of goals (Peterson, 1986, pp. 287–289). UN negotiations are complex affairs, with many participants discussing multiple issues all at the same time. Large delegations have the advantage of dividing up the work, drawing on more areas of expertise, attending all concurrent sessions, and talking to more allies and adversaries. However, they also face the challenge of avoiding inadvertent contradictions or misleading statements of the country's position by "speaking from different pages." The main vehicle for addressing any problems of coordination is the delegation meeting. While these vary in frequency and formality from one delegation to the next, they are so important to effective negotiation at the UN that most UN meetings do not start until 10:00 or 10:30 a.m. so that delegations have adequate opportunity to coordinate their activities each day.

A second challenge faced by most UN delegations concerns their relationship with their home government. Of necessity, the delegations are operating far from their home ministry, which makes face-to-face direction impossible. Furthermore, it is not uncommon for the home ministry to have a quite different view of how the negotiations are developing from that of the delegation actually at the meetings (Kay, 1967, pp. 93–94; Finger, 1990, pp. 36–37). Of course, for centuries diplomacy has been conducted at a geographical distance, and modern travel and technology make these problems less severe than they once were. But these developments give rise to yet another problem: many members now have bureaucratic structures at home that have capacity to heavily manage how their delegates behave at the UN. This is certainly true in the case of major powers like the United States (Jacobson, 1979, pp. 121–122; Ziring, Riggs, and Plano, 2000, pp. 76–77), and by now the effects of this problem have become pervasive across all missions and delegations to varying degrees. Of various factors that affect the nature of the relationship between the home government and its UN personnel, one of the most important is the "political strength, stature, and personality of the permanent representative" (Finger, 1990, p. 16). For this reason, the last section of this chapter will consider how the personal attributes of individual delegates influence how much autonomy they have and the types of roles they can play in UN politics.

▨ Personal Attributes and Delegate Autonomy

The first section of this chapter considered how both a country's ability and its desire to wield influence in the United Nations can lead it to play certain types of roles in the organization. Yet it is important to remember that these attributes are properties of the member state as a collective whole. As such, they represent only a part of the dynamics at work, given that the actual process of representing a country's interests at the UN falls to that member's permanent mission and the delegations it sends to specific UN meetings. These missions and delegations, in turn, are staffed by individuals who have varying strengths and weaknesses in the art of multilateral diplomacy; some are quite comfortable and skilled at participating in the global dance described in the introduction, but others are not. Many classic studies of member-state influence in international organizations, such as Cox and Jacobson (1973b, p. 20), stress that the personal attributes of individual delegates must be considered alongside the abilities and priorities of the state that they represent.

Variation in attributes among delegates at the UN is made even more challenging to understand, since these individuals are forced to balance the sometimes contradictory challenges of simultaneously representing the interests of their state and participating in the give-and-take of UN politics (Jacobson, 1979, pp. 120–124). The characteristics and behaviors necessary to effectively perform one of these roles may not always match those that are the most beneficial for playing the other role. This final section of Chapter 2 will consider the attributes of individual delegates and how they interact with the dynamics previously discussed, such that members of the organization are able to participate in its decisionmaking. Personal attributes are discussed first, followed by variations in their autonomy and the different roles they can play.

Personal Attributes

Within the writings of academic scholars and former diplomatic practitioners, there are numerous discussions of the role of personal attributes in UN political processes. While authors may highlight different skills and characteristics, there is substantial overlap in their ideas when it comes to identifying the attributes that are most important for effective delegates. Eight such sets of attributes will be discussed here: past experiences, knowledge competencies, charisma, character, perseverance, tolerance, ambition, and negotiating skill. Possession of at least some of these skills can help delegates be more successful at achieving their goals in UN decisionmaking regardless of the attributes of the country they represent.

It is important that delegates have at least some diplomatic experience, whether inside or outside the United Nations. While this usually is the case for personnel of permanent missions, a number of member states include members of legislatures and prominent individuals from the private sector on their UN delegations (Kaufmann, 1980, p. 106). Diplomatic training for these participants can be extremely beneficial to help them understand how multilateral negotiations typically unfold and make sure that they have the basic administrative skills required (Cox and Jacobson, 1973, p. 20). It can be valuable for delegates to have prior experience in multilateral diplomacy, since its dynamics and challenges are somewhat different from those of bilateral diplomacy; however, participants at the UN who have had only bilateral postings previously are often able to be quite active (Alger, 1967, pp. 75–78). Another useful area of experience would involve past service on the particular body in question, both for mission personnel and members of delegations (Keohane, 1969, p. 883; Cox and Jacobson, 1973, p. 20). Such experience is especially useful, since it provides delegates with a better understanding of the rules of procedure used in the body—knowledge that can be critical in contentious negotiations (Nicholas, 1975, p. 106; Mills, 1999, p. 33; Nyerges, 1998, p. 177).

Possessing certain key knowledge competencies is extremely helpful for a UN diplomat. While a number of authors mention intelligence as an important general attribute, given the complex, fluid nature of multilateral diplomacy (e.g., Keohane, 1969, p. 883), others have suggested that high intelligence should be joined with specific areas of knowledge (Cox and Jacobson, 1973, p. 20; Alger, 1989, p. 3). In addition to having an understanding of the particular issues under discussion, delegates should be strong in three skill areas: (1) language versatility, since negotiations may take place in another language or delegates may find it more useful to address a colleague in that individual's native tongue; (2) general knowledge of important academic disciplines such as economics, history, law, and statistics; and (3) the ability to speak and write in a precise, persuasive manner even without the luxuries of preparation time and multiple drafts (Mills, 1999, p. 33; Nyerges, 1998, pp. 175–177; Kaufmann, 1988, pp. 135–140).

Personal charisma is often mentioned as being a vital component of success in all political negotiations, including those in international organizations (Cox and Jacobson, 1973, p. 20). However, charisma is also notoriously difficult to define, due to its subjective character; people are often described as being charismatic only *after* they have influenced others, as if being considered charismatic was a result of their success rather than a cause of it. That being said, certain personal characteristics that are commonly linked with charisma are highlighted in the literature on UN delegates. For example, since UN meetings involve as many as 190 other member states, individual delegates must be extroverted, outgoing, and comfortable mixing with strangers (Mills, 1999, p. 33). Skill at remembering new faces, thoughtfulness to ask about their families, a well-timed sense of humor, and an ability to regale audiences with entertaining stories can all help delegates build a network of contacts and friendships that can benefit future negotiations (Nicholas, 1975, p. 106). Finally, charisma certainly requires that delegates be passionate and engaging in their arguments, so that others might rethink their views, even those that have been rather entrenched.

A fourth set of attributes have to do with the character and reputation of the delegate. Like charisma, the quality of a delegate's character is often determined subjectively (Keohane, 1969, p. 883). A positive reputation can be an invaluable resource for a delegate, who is likely to be interacting with the same group of colleagues on multiple issues over time. Delegates must clearly convey to other participants the underlying ideology of their positions and make sure that these foundations remain consistent over time; this will buttress their perceived legitimacy (Cox and Jacobson, 1973, p. 20). In addition, delegates need to earn the trust and confidence of their colleagues, so that others can be sure that any information offered is accurate and that any promises made will be kept (Alger, 1967, pp. 75–77). Such trust will be built by their honesty over time and their loyalty to other members of negotiating groups, so that politically sensitive compromises are kept private (Kaufmann, 1988, pp. 134, 139).

A fifth set of attributes are those that enable the delegate to persevere in the face of long and difficult negotiations (Cox and Jacobson, 1973, p. 20). On a simple level, this requires that participants be able to avoid boredom despite repetitive and long-winded speeches (Nicholas, 1975, p. 106) and that they remain patient in search of areas of potential agreement in their favor (Kaufmann, 1988, p. 137). However, perseverance also involves a more active component, for delegates must maintain persistence and engagement in the face of slow progress and disappointment (Alger, 1989, p. 3). Several personal qualities can help delegates not only endure long negotiations but actually thrive in them; these include energy and capacity for hard work (Keohane, 1969, p. 883; Alger, 1989, p. 3) and zeal and passion for the material at hand (Kaufmann, 1988, p. 137).

The sixth set of attributes useful for delegate success reflect tolerance in the face of other cultures and preferences (Keohane, 1969, p. 883). Part of this involves having a thick skin, so that delegates do not take needless or unintended offense when legitimate differences of opinion lead to spirited exchanges (Nicholas, 1975, p. 106). The most effective delegates are those with an even temper, who can remain calm in the face of confrontation (Kaufmann, 1988, pp. 136–137). This requires that participants not betray strong emotions to other delegates, except in rare cases where this can be done in a controlled fashion for negotiating effect. Finally, two diplomatic practitioners have observed that one of the best ways to demonstrate tolerance of other viewpoints is to approach negotiations in the posture of a student—in the mode of listening and gathering information rather than immediately seeking to rebut positions advanced by others (Mills, 1999, pp. 32–33; Nyerges, 1998, p. 175).

A seventh, possibly more controversial, set of attributes relate to the issue of ambition. Clearly it is important for delegates to be ambitious about representing the interests of their state, since that is by far their most important task (Keohane, 1969, p. 883). However, some writers have argued that modesty is also an important trait for participants in multilateral diplomacy (Kaufmann, 1988, p. 137). Individual delegates should avoid acting out of vanity, ego, or personal ambition, but they should be as active as possible on behalf of their country's foreign policy goals. Another way to think about this is in terms of courage: delegates must be ready and willing to take advantage of opportunities when they arise (Kaufmann, 1988, p. 140). Courage, when taken to an extreme, can lead to negative outcomes through excessive risk taking. Still, delegates must be ready to carefully exploit any openings that might allow them to mobilize additional resources, persuade other delegates, or shape their own instructions (Cox and Jacobson, 1973, p. 20).

The eighth set of attributes that can enable delegates to be more effective in UN politics have to do with their negotiating ability (Mills, 1999, p. 33, Nyerges, 1998, p. 175; Cox and Jacobson, 1973, p. 20). Of course many of the attributes listed above relate to negotiating ability, but two additional personal characteristics merit special attention under this category. First, effective negotiators must be flexible so they can adapt to the fast pace of multilateral diplomacy, and their various skills must be "mobile," usable in different situations (Alger, 1967, pp. 75–78; Kaufmann, 1988, pp. 138–140). One specific manifestation of these skills is creativity in finding ways around existing or potential roadblocks on the path to agreement (Alger, 1989, p. 3). Second, multilateral diplomacy requires that delegates possess an excellent sense of timing as negotiations are unfolding (Nicholas, 1975, p. 106). Not surprisingly, some individuals are better than others at listening to the music of the global dance and sensing the most appropriate junctures for attempting new initiatives. Unfortunately, this particular skill is a difficult one to learn, requiring years of experience in UN politics to acquire, and even then its use is far from an exact science (Ramaker, 1998). This dynamic will receive additional attention in Part 2 under leadership and informal networking; for now it is important to stress that a delegate who can accurately sense the timing and pace of negotiations can help secure a successful outcome even when it seems that failure is imminent. One oft-cited example is the role of Jayantha Dhanapala of Sri Lanka in the 1995 negotiations that led to an indefinite extension of the Nuclear Non-Proliferation Treaty (S. Williams, 1999, pp. 146–149).

This section has highlighted eight sets of attributes that are beneficial for UN delegates to possess. Needless to say, it is highly unlikely that one individual delegate could possess all of these different, and sometimes opposite, skills and characteristics. The keys to success are to possess as many as possible and, even more important, to recognize one's own limitations. Fortunately, individual delegates only rarely serve on delegations alone; they usually have colleagues or advisers on whom they can depend for the skills they personally lack. Such relationships can be of mutual benefit to delegates and increase their overall effectiveness in pursuing their country's preferred outcome in negotiations (Kaufmann, 1980, p. 106).

Delegate Autonomy

As noted above, delegates to the United Nations must balance two roles: representing the interests of their country and participating in the give-and-take of the organization's political processes (Jacobson, 1979, pp. 120–124; Nicholas, 1975, pp. 136–137). Whatever mix of these roles they perform at any given time, individual delegates have the potential to augment their effectiveness if they possess the right constellation of personal attributes. Therefore, understanding the behavior of any participant in UN decisionmaking requires an exploration of the often contradictory pressures they face in deciding when they need to focus more directly on their country's interests and when they can afford the luxury of engaging in creative thinking about compromise solutions. Part of this decision regarding representation versus participation may be left to the delegate; in these cases, they are able to make strategic calculations regarding whether hard-nosed bargaining or package dealing is the best negotiating route to pursue. However, it is far more common for delegates to have this choice made for them by their home government, which ultimately decides how much autonomy its UN delegates should have. Almost all delegates get some instructions that limit their freedom to act; nevertheless, effective delegates are often able to win a degree of latitude and flexibility in terms of how they meet their goals.

Delegate autonomy is an important consideration. Participants who are forced to advance positions and policies drafted thousands of miles away may not be able to engage in the kind of bargaining that can lead to successful outcomes in UN politics: they will be limited in the types of state resources and personal attributes they can utilize as leverage in negotiations. In addition, if delegates are kept dependent on extensive instructions from home, they can be overtaken by events when decisions must be made but specific guidance from the country's political elites is not available (Kaufmann, 1988, p. 172). Participants who have more room to maneuver can gain influence beyond what their state might normally possess, since they have extra freedom to shape negotiations as they unfold. In the above discussions of permanent missions and delegations, it was observed that delegates in multilateral settings generally enjoy greater autonomy than their colleagues in bilateral postings, due to the greater complexity and faster pace of the negotiations (Jacobson, 1979, p. 110; Finger, 1990, p. 20). Still, even multilateral delegates "are diplomats acting under more or less comprehensive instructions from their governments about the goals that they should seek, the opinions they should express and the general line of conduct they should follow" (Peterson, 1986, p. 284). Furthermore, as technology has increased ease of communication between a home ministry and delegates in the field, it has become possible for instructions to be sent on an almost constant basis in the course of negotiations (Peterson, 1986, p. 286), so that levels of delegate autonomy have decreased among all member states at the United Nations.

Despite this general decrease in autonomy, there is still substantial variation in the instructions received by delegates of different member states across issues and negotiating forums (Ziring, Riggs, and Plano,

2000, p. 80). One former practitioner has indicated that the "ideal instructions" should result from careful study by all relevant departments, be approved by the country's highest political authorities, be specific regarding objectives and degree of activity required, but allow considerable freedom of action if events take an unexpected turn (Kaufmann, 1980, p. 110). Unfortunately, instructions frequently fall short of this ideal. Some delegates are not provided with any instructions at all, even when they ask for them; the home ministry has sent those delegates to New York to "take care of that part of the policy" for the country. At the other extreme is a delegate who, "it is told, not only gets detailed instructions about every vote, but has all of his speeches sent verbatim from his capital with instructions of when to speak with sincerity and when to inject an ironic inflection" (Edvard Hambro, quoted in Peterson, 1986, p. 285). The autonomy of most delegates falls somewhere in between these extremes. Many get instructions on voting, either as to the specific vote that should be cast or in reference to the voting pattern of another state or regional group: for example, to vote either the same as or the opposite of other members, or simply to make sure that their state does not end up in an isolated position (Kaufmann, 1980, p. 110; 1988, p. 171; Peterson, 1986, pp. 285, 287). Some individuals have violated the voting instructions they received; however, this can be done only by delegates of the highest political stature (Jacobson, 1979, p. 109). It is common for all delegates to get instructions at the outset of debate on a particular issue. Once negotiations begin, some delegates proceed without further consultations, while others may get instructions throughout the process, up to the last minute before the vote. While ongoing consultations can create problems when events unfold rapidly, most UN bodies operate in a manner that accommodates last-minute instructions through informal consultations before a formal meeting is held, by setting the agenda in advance of a meeting, or by allowing for a "strategic postponement" so that delegates have time to consult with home ministries before voting commences (Kaufmann, 1980, p. 111; Peterson, 1986, p. 286).

Variations in instructions are never entirely predictable across countries, issues, individuals, or time. However, certain patterns, tendencies, or rules of thumb regarding delegate autonomy have been discerned by practitioners like Johan Kaufmann (1980, pp. 110–111; 1988, pp. 170–172), Seymour Finger (1990, p. 22), and Jaap Ramaker (1998), and scholars like M. J. Peterson (1986, pp. 284–287), Harold Jacobson (1979, pp. 109–110), and Lawrence Ziring, Robert Riggs, and Jack Plano (2000, p. 80). Based on their insights, there are eight possible factors involved in determining how detailed a delegate's instructions will be. First, all of them identified the salience of the issue to the particular member state as the most important influence: the more a country cares about a specific outcome, the more likely it is to give its representatives detailed instructions about how to achieve that outcome. Second, a country's size and the level of its economic development have a direct impact on autonomy. Countries that are larger and more economically developed tend to have larger bureaucracies in the home capital that can micromanage their delegates at the UN. Conversely, smaller and less developed states tend to have a smaller cadre of experts on each issue, and they may in fact be serving as the delegates, which means the home ministry will be more inclined to defer to their judgment. Some writers have observed that delegates from Western states tend to receive the most detailed instructions, while African delegates usually enjoy considerable autonomy and Latin American and Asian delegates fall in between. These first two factors, salience and size, often but not always have complementary effects on delegate autonomy, since larger and more developed states tend also to consider more issues to be salient.

Third, autonomy is influenced by the relationship between the delegate and officials in the home ministry or government. For the permanent representative this involves his or her standing with the foreign minister and head of government; for lower-level delegates this relates to their network of contacts with colleagues in the ministries and departments dealing with the issue under debate. In all cases, the stature or reputation of a delegate rests on his or her expertise and the level of confidence their government has in them; these elements can determine whether they are able to participate in shaping their own instructions before negotiations even begin. Fourth, the role a delegate is playing in the negotiations influences their autonomy: those serving in leadership positions on UN bodies often have more freedom to act, since they need to be able to manage the negotiations in addition to, or sometimes instead of, representing the interests of their state. Fifth, the attitude of the country toward the United Nations can affect delegate autonomy: representatives of states wary of the organization, or targeted by it, will receive more detailed instructions than those from states that are supportive of the UN across the board. This can also vary from one UN body to the next, as delegates may have less autonomy on the Security Council than in the General Assembly, for example. It can also vary based on the state's domestic political structure: democratic systems have more constituencies whose interests must be carefully balanced in the UN policy, and thus more detailed instructions may be required.

Sixth, delegate autonomy is generally higher regarding procedural issues than regarding substantive issues, although this is certainly not always the case. In addition, different types of substantive decisions can result in different degrees of freedom to act, with delegates most likely to be constrained in their voting for any substantive decisions that involve financial commitments. Seventh, as might be expected, delegates often receive more detailed instructions regarding the goals of the state than they do on the tactics for reaching those goals. This means delegates may be able to draw on their personal strengths and their networks of fellow delegates in designing a strategy for building winning coalitions. Eighth, geography has been frequently mentioned as having an impact on autonomy, as delegates from states farther away from UN bodies tend to have more autonomy than those from nearby. However, other observers point out that the impact of this factor has decreased in recent years, as improved communications technologies have made distance much less of an obstacle for a ministry that wants to closely monitor its UN delegates.

Bringing It All Together: Four Types of United Nations Delegates

This chapter has covered a wide range of factors that must be considered when one is trying to understand how member states participate in the UN's political processes: their ability and interests, the structure and composition of their mission and delegations, and the personal attributes and autonomy of their delegates. In each case, various patterns of influence have been identified, but the challenge of thinking about how these interrelated elements work together remains. Conceptualizing these diverse dynamics into a coherent package is certainly a daunting task, but one way to take the first steps in this direction is to think about different types of roles that individual delegates play at the UN based on the state they represent, the structure of the mission or delegation in which they work, their personal attributes, and their autonomy. One especially illuminating typology of delegate roles at the United Nations was developed by Navid Hanif, first secretary in the permanent mission of Pakistan to the United Nations in 1998 (Hanif, 1998). He describes four different types of delegates that bring together the various elements discussed across this chapter: hunters, farmers, traders, and trappers.

Hunters are delegates who represent states that have a very clear goal in mind on the issue in question; they will do whatever they can to make sure that the interests of their state are reflected in the decision that is made. The negotiating strategy favored by hunters tends to be rather crude and blunt; they move like a bulldozer, focused on clearing the path ahead. Such a role is likely to be most necessary for delegates who enjoy very little autonomy in terms of both goals and tactics, and it is likely to be most effective for the representatives of larger states that have the resources and power to throw their weight around at the UN. Personal attributes such as ambition and perseverance are essential, and the mission is likely to be rather hierarchical to maintain a unified focus on the desired outcome. This can be a very effective role; however, this approach to parliamentary diplomacy is heavy-handed and can leave other participants feeling frustrated.

Farmers are essentially at the opposite end of the spectrum from hunters. Where hunters are relentless in pushing for their preferences, farmers are willing to adopt a long-term view of the decisionmaking process and work to build consensus around a package deal that offers significant benefits to all participants. Farmers favor strategies that allow them to act as brokers between different hunters and other delegates. Here too, perseverance is an important attribute, since cultivating consensus can be a difficult task in the face of divergent interests; this role also requires expertise on the issue at hand, tolerance of different viewpoints, the trust and confidence of other delegates, and negotiating skill to build upon areas of potential agreement. This type of role is certainly not available to all delegates, for it requires that their state have a strong reputation in the UN and that they personally enjoy a significant degree of autonomy. Farmers typically represent small and middle powers that are active UN members.

Traders represent a mix between hunters and farmers. Like hunters, they have a clear idea of what they want to achieve; however, their approach to the process involves a mindset closer to that of a farmer. Where hunters prefer to bulldoze and farmers prefer to cultivate, traders adopt strategies that center on bargaining and striking deals between competing interests. These deals may relate to the same issue, or they may stretch across issues and over time. Traders must be charismatic and enjoy the confidence of other delegates. In addition, issue expertise and negotiating skill are important attributes for identifying possible deals. Traders often have little autonomy regarding the goals they need to achieve, but they may enjoy considerable freedom regarding the tactics they can use. They usually represent a developed state, or perhaps a group of developing states, for they must have sufficient resources to deliver on the promises that they make when striking a deal.

Trappers are by far the most conniving of all delegates, but fortunately they are also the rarest at the United Nations. Similar to traders, trappers seek to create deals, securing help from other delegates in achieving their desired goals in exchange for later assistance on another issue. So similar personal attributes can be useful for traders and trappers. However, the similarities end there. The deal offered by trappers is always a false promise that they have no intention of fulfilling; their goal is to secure enough support from other delegates for what they need to accomplish and then feign ignorance or worse when it comes time to reciprocate. This role can be effective only a very limited number of times before the delegate's character becomes so questionable that no other participants will deal with them. Since this role has serious long-term costs, it is likely to be used only as a last resort when a state or delegate has exhausted all other possible avenues of negotiation. It is most common in the case of delegates from so-called pariah regimes that have few resources and are engaging in some type of behavior that other member states want to see changed; the trapper can use the possibility of change as leverage.

It should be clear from this brief discussion that the roles in this typology are not set in stone; individual delegates can take on different roles on different issues over time, depending on the interests of their state and the leverage they possess in relation to the issue at hand. In addition, different states can change roles over time, selecting permanent representatives who have the personal attributes most conducive to one role or another, as the United States did when Madeleine Albright (usually a hunter) was replaced by Richard Holbrooke (closer to a trader) in President Bill Clinton's second term. Furthermore, the typology offered here is not watertight; there are certainly other roles that delegates can play. However, the typology is still helpful for thinking about how member states and their delegates can best achieve their goals at the United Nations. Each constellation of state abilities and interests requires a different type of individual to pursue them, and no single strategy will work in all situations, no matter how powerful or active a member state is. And member states are not operating alone at the UN; the cast of characters in the global dance is diverse, and each type of participant has its own set of resources for exercising influence in the organization's political processes. The following chapters will address the roles of other actors at the United Nations.

3

Groups and Blocs

BUILDING WINNING COALITIONS IN MULTILATERAL DIPLOMACY IS A COM-plicated and challenging process; the cast of characters involved is usually large, with each one pursuing interests that can be quite different from those advanced by other participants. As a result, nearly every discussion of United Nations decisionmaking highlights the role played by collectivities of member states working together as groups or voting blocs. The fact that group politics is considered to be so important in the UN is not that surprising. Most UN bodies include 50 or more states, and many include all 191 members of the organization. Simple common sense suggests that the larger the body becomes, the harder it will be for it to make decisions, since the range of potential interests that must be reconciled will be more diverse and the patterns of interaction between members will likely be more diffuse and complex. Getting 191 different parties to agree on anything, even on relatively benign and uncontroversial matters, can be daunting, and many issues on the UN's agenda are neither benign nor uncontroversial.

However, this straightforward view of the relationship between the size of a decisionmaking body and its difficulty with reaching the necessary agreement to act overlooks important considerations that can facilitate coalition building even in large groups (Kahler, 1993, pp. 297–299, 319). Some of the considerations mentioned by Miles Kahler include the increased benefits that come from having more participants in the group, the willingness of major powers to take a leading role in advancing certain solutions, and the role of smaller groups in building agreement on key issues that can then spread to the decisionmaking body as a whole. Thus, while it might be possible to question whether larger size makes agreement more difficult, it is reasonable to conclude that larger decisionmaking bodies require the use of subgroups if they are to function effectively. The benefits of states' working through groups are not limited to large deliberative bodies. Research on small group decisionmaking in foreign policy has long highlighted that even small committees can have difficulty reaching agreement when competing interests get locked into a bureaucratic stalemate (Hermann, 1993, pp. 180–181). This suggests that group politics can be a potentially useful tool for building agreement in a wide variety of settings in multilateral diplomacy, regardless of the overall size of the decisionmaking body, if the members involved have divergent interests that must be reconciled.

Since most UN bodies, even relatively small ones like the Security Council, are composed of members whose interests are often in conflict, numerous groups and blocs are mentioned in both academic and practitioner writings on the United Nations. Some of these observers have questioned the ultimate impact of these groups on UN outcomes. For example, Hayward Alker Jr. argues, "The suggestion that political conflicts preoccupy members of the United Nations implies that the national interests of UN members, shaped as they are by domestic, regional, political, economic, and ethnic considerations, are more causally determinative of UN policy positions than caucusing-group pressures" (1967, p. 179). There is certainly some merit to Alker's claim; as was discussed in Chapter 2, member states base their UN policy on their capabilities and interests, both of which relate to considerations other than group politics, such as the nature of a state's political system, its colonial history, its level of economic development, the nature of its military power and alliances, and its patterns of trade and foreign aid.

However, other authors have concluded that the existence of groups and blocs at the United Nations affects how states calculate both their capabilities and interests. For example, Sally Morphet argues that "most states [have] found it essential to promote their interests (both political and economic) more effectively at the global level by forming groups that could work both within and, sometimes, outside of the UN system" (2000, p. 224). It is not that states must ignore or overcome political, military, economic, or historical considerations for groups to matter in UN decisionmaking; rather, these groups provide states with certain avenues of action that would not be possible if they were acting individually. Lawrence Finkelstein goes even further: "Decisionmaking in the UN system is strongly influenced, if not determined, by convergence of groups of members to accumulate voting power. . . . The practice has become so well entrenched, and is of such significance, that both scholars and practitioners have referred to some such groupings as political parties" (1988c, pp. 20–21).

While other writers may contend that comparing UN groups to domestic political parties overstates both their cohesiveness and their power, they do echo Finkelstein's view that groups play a central role in the UN's political processes. Like Alker, H. G. Nicholas acknowledges that "where an important political question is at stake a state casts its vote the way its government's assessment of its national interests dictates"; however, he says groups are both "natural" and "indispensable" to the functioning of the UN, since "it is impossible to imagine how the UN could work if there were no groupings of member states to provide elements of stability and predictability" (1975, pp. 133–134). Quite simply, an increasingly diverse membership, an ever-growing agenda, and the fact that each member state has an equal vote mean that groups are a crucial mechanism for making the global dance at the United Nations more fluid and effective (Peterson, 1986, p. 247).

■ The Role of Groups at the United Nations

The use of groups in multilateral diplomacy predates the founding of the United Nations. For all the failings of the League of Nations, one lesson to come out of that experiment was that stable clusters of like-minded states could emerge and persist in an international organization (Peterson, 1986, p. 290). In the case of the league, these groups included the Latin Americans, the United Kingdom and its dominions, the "Little Entente" of Czechoslovakia, Romania, and Yugoslavia, and looser groupings of Balkan states and Central European states (Austria, Hungary, Italy, and Germany). Despite this experience, however, the UN Charter and the rules of procedure for UN bodies like the General Assembly neglected to make any formal provisions for the role of groups (Peterson, 1986, p. 290). The UN's founders realized that consultation and negotiation between members would be required to build sufficient majorities, but they believed that none of these necessary groups would be stable enough to merit explicit mention. Instead, they crafted the language of the Charter and rules of procedure with enough latitude to allow groups to become important players, at least in an ad hoc fashion.

It was not long before member states seized upon this limited opening and began to think in terms of forming groups based on shared experiences and common interests. The first distinct UN group emerged in late 1945, after the Charter was drafted but before the UN had even started to hold meetings (Morphet, 2000, p. 227). Based on the initiative of Eduardo Angel, the Colombian delegate to the Charter-drafting conference in San Francisco, the Latin American states decided to "work together with solidarity" in order to assume leadership positions in the new organization and avoid having to make do with "crumbs" cast off by the great powers. Based on this initiative, these states formed a group that included the votes of twenty-six countries, a majority of the UN's fifty-one members, enough to elect Angel president of the UN Preparatory Commission in 1945.

From this successful beginning, groups have emerged as pervasive and important actors in UN decisionmaking. While there is great diversity in membership and objectives of UN groups (as is discussed below), there are important similarities in terms of how they work: most are based on members' efforts to arrive at some sort of agreement favoring their preferred outcome to a particular UN debate. This agreement is usually achieved through a process of consultation and consensus building, so that all members have a voice in the policy, rather than through majority voting, where individual members of the group could find themselves at odds with the group position (Morphet, 2000, p. 225). Leadership of a group is typically shared among its members, either through a pattern of rotation or through formal elections.

These common processes matter at the UN, since groups perform a number of important and beneficial functions in decisionmaking. However, some scholars have wondered whether certain negative consequences of group politics might not outweigh these positive contributions, at least in regard to certain bodies and issues. Many observers do seem to agree with Kaufmann's assertion that while it is hard to generalize about the benefits and limitations of groups across issues and over time, on balance their overall effect is positive (1988, pp. 156–157). Here we will consider both positive and negative aspects of the functions that groups perform in UN politics.

On the positive side, the use of groups in UN decisionmaking empowers certain states to have a much greater impact on policy outcomes than would otherwise be possible (Morphet, 2000, pp. 260–261; Ziring, Riggs, and Plano, 2000, p. 96; Behnam, 1998, p. 199). This is especially true in the case of like-minded smaller and less developed states, which need a collective voice if they are to take the initiative in UN debates. Acting as a group can enable them to raise new issues on the international agenda, set up new agencies or conferences, push for reform of existing institutions, and advance new norms of international law. A second positive contribution of groups is that they encourage members to begin preliminary discussions on the issue at hand early in the negotiation process (Kay, 1967, pp. 99–100; Ziring, Riggs, and Plano, 2000, p. 96; Behnam, 1998, p. 199). This allows for greater opportunities to exchange information, harmonize policy priorities, and coordinate strategies vis-à-vis other groups. This process of developing common positions is potentially beneficial to all member states—those big and small, and those for and against a particular policy proposal (Kaufmann, 1980, pp. 90–92). The benefits of this policy harmonization within groups are greatest in situations where members hope to reach a consensus that all the different states and groups can support (or at least not block); however, it can also be helpful in majority-rule decisions where any single group lacks sufficient votes to approve policies on its own (Peterson, 1986, p. 248; Behnam, 1998, p. 200).

A third contribution of groups to UN decisionmaking has to do with their comparatively informal mechanisms for doing business. Since members of groups can often interact without cumbersome procedures, simultaneous translation, or a written record, they may be much more willing to talk freely about the issues at hand (Behnam, 1998, p. 199). This, in turn, can allow for greater creativity, more effective brainstorming, and a potential for consultations among groups (Kaufmann, 1988, p. 155). Fourth, groups are a useful mechanism for making sure that all UN bodies function in a manner that draws on the full diversity of the UN's membership. The UN Charter calls for equitable geographic representation in limited-membership bodies, the organization's staff, and the distribution of top leadership positions; the use of groups in UN decisionmaking helps to make sure these Charter principles are reflected in practice (Nicholas, 1975, p. 133; Kay, 1967, p. 99; Kaufmann, 1980, p. 92). A fifth benefit of groups in UN decisionmaking is their ability to serve a "tutorial function" for new member states and new delegates, providing advice on how to pursue their goals, guidance on which issues deserve their focus given limited resources, and generally shortening their period of socialization into the intricacies of multilateral diplomacy (Kay, 1967, p. 100; Peterson, 1986, p. 294; Ziring, Riggs, and Plano, 2000, p. 96). The final contribution of groups to UN politics centers on efficiency; since groups adopt common positions, they often choose to have their ideas presented by just one member. This saves time, avoids unnecessary repetition, and allows more space for other viewpoints to be expressed (Kaufmann, 1988, p. 156; Ziring, Riggs, and Plano, 2000, p. 96).

Despite these positive benefits, there are some drawbacks to the extensive use of groups in UN processes. First, when individual member states choose to act through a group, they are essentially giving up their own voice in favor of a common policy advanced by all (Nicholas, 1975, p. 133). As long as this policy is consistent with the state's interests, the sovereign equality of members reflected in the one-state, one-vote formula is maintained; however, these groups can adopt positions that represent watered-down least-common-denominator solutions or be hijacked by an extremist member (Ziring, Riggs, and Plano, 2000, p. 96; Behnam, 1998, p. 200). In either scenario, the interests of member states in the group are compromised, and any policy outcome that does result is questionable at best. A second negative consequence of group politics is that these dynamics ultimately distort the realities of international power and influence (Nicholas, 1975, pp. 134–145; Ziring, Riggs, and Plano, 2000, p. 96). Groups do empower smaller and less developed members, but this gives certain states the power to move the organization to action (or block it from action) even when they lack the resources to implement the decisions they are making. When states that lack the ability to act push others to do so, or when states that have the ability to act are pressured not to, frustration and recrimination are common results.

Finally, the use of groups can result in a slow and rigid negotiating process (Behnam, 1998, p. 200; Ziring, Riggs, and Plano, 2000, p. 96). All the factors that make groups useful vehicles for building agreement among their members can also make it difficult to build agreement across different groups. Once a group arrives at a common position, changes to that position can become difficult, since they might upset the delicate balance that has been forged (Kaufmann, 1988, p. 157). This is especially true when the process of getting the group to agree has been long and difficult. The result is something of a catch-22: groups make multilateral diplomacy easier by allowing scattered, heterogeneous interests to be narrowed down to a few key issues (Alger, 1989, p. 3); however, they can also make it harder to build a final agreement unless each group remains willing to engage in further compromise. These potential negative consequences of group politics force UN practitioners and observers to make careful judgments about the overall contribution of these actors to UN decisionmaking. But regardless of what judgment is reached, the reality of UN politics is that, for better or worse, groups are central players in the global dance. So their influence must be considered.

◼ Types of Groups and Voting Blocs

Since groups of states acting together are such a pervasive feature at the United Nations, and since these groups perform a wide variety of functions in the organization's political processes, it is not at all surprising that there is considerable variation in their membership and purposes. This variation, in turn, has resulted in some confusion among practitioners and scholars regarding the basic terminology for groups and blocs at the UN. Much of the early research on these actors at the UN focused on using powerful statistical techniques to analyze General Assembly voting records in search of stable patterns across members and issues (Alger, 1970, pp. 433–437). As might be expected, many of these efforts, such as Rowe (1969; 1971), looked for the effects of the cold war in UN politics across the 1950s and 1960s by examining East and West voting blocs. Once the membership of the Assembly expanded to include more developing states, scholars began to uncover a North-South dimension to UN voting blocs as well (Holloway, 1990, p. 280).

However, these inductive studies often found a more complex picture of group voting at the UN than a simple East-West or North-South dichotomy, since each of these blocs was found to have internal divisions. For example, Bruce Russett studied the Eighteenth General Assembly in 1963 and uncovered six voting blocs: the Western Community, Brazzaville Africa (mainly former French colonies), Afro-Asians (cold war "neutralists"), the Communist Bloc, Conservative Arabs, and Iberia (1968, pp. 77–79). Writing a year later, Hanna Newcombe, Michael Ross, and Alan Newcombe analyzed all regular plenary sessions of the Assembly from 1946 to 1963, to see how bloc voting had evolved over the first two decades of the UN (1969, pp. 102–110). Across this time period they discovered that Latin America had moved closer to Western states, while Afro-Asian states had moved closer to the Soviet bloc. Outside of these larger blocs, they also uncovered stable voting patterns for Scandinavian states, pro-Western neutral states, and imperial states. Finally, another study of the General Assembly by Alker during this same period looked at how the internal cohesion of East-West and North-South voting blocs varied across controversial issues such as self-determination, UN membership disputes, peacekeeping finance, apartheid, and so on (1967, pp. 172–177).

Despite the fact that the percentage of General Assembly resolutions that actually come to a vote has substantially decreased over time (Marin-Bosch, 1987), more recent studies have also used voting records to see if these blocs have persisted over time. Based on data through 1985, Steven Holloway (1990, p. 296) concluded that three voting blocs were still present in the Assembly. Most cohesive was a bloc composed of the Warsaw Pact joined with Cuba, Afghanistan, Vietnam, and Syria; second was a still cohesive bloc of nonaligned states held together by the organizational efforts of the Non-Aligned Movement (NAM) and the Group of 77 (G77); and finally, there was a much more internally divided bloc of Western states and other members of the Organization for Economic Cooperation and Development (OECD). However, Holloway also indicated that a major realignment of blocs appeared to be beginning and would certainly have implications for the cohesion of all three groups he uncovered. This expectation is confirmed in a post–cold war analysis of voting records completed by Soo Yeon Kim and Bruce Russett (1997, pp. 33–48), who found that four clusters of UN members in 1983–1985 had diffused into five clusters of members by 1991–1993 and that even groups that remained relatively stable across this period did experience some changes in membership.

These voting studies can provide illuminating pictures of the main lines of conflict within UN bodies; however, they face two shortcomings when it comes to clarifying the actual decisionmaking of these organizations. First, these studies examine votes only after they are taken; they are unable to provide an explanation or underlying logic for the bloc members' choice to favor a particular policy outcome. Second, as the brief summary above has indicated, these blocs have problems with internal cohesion to varying degrees across issues and over time. This results in some conceptual confusion, since the classic definition of a bloc in the UN context is "a group of states which meets regularly in caucus and the members of which are bound in their votes in the General Assembly by the caucus decision" (Hovet, 1960, p. 30). Based on this definition, the only group of states that could reasonably be called a true voting bloc would be the former Soviet bloc (Morphet, 2000, p. 225); the other blocs all faced issues on which they were internally divided. As a result, some scholars have preferred to focus their attention on UN groups more broadly conceived: all collections of states that engage in periodic meetings and have some degree of organizational structure (Kay, 1967, p. 99).

Defining groups in such a broad fashion is important because it captures the great diversity that exists within this type of actor at the United Nations. Many groups active in UN decisionmaking emerge on a temporary or ad hoc basis as part of the negotiation process itself (Hovet, 1960, pp. 45–46; Kay, 1967, p. 99). However, there are also many groups whose functions at UN meetings are so common that they essentially represent permanent fixtures on the UN landscape. Johan Kaufmann has identified four such well-known types of groups (1980, pp. 87–90; 1988, pp. 147–152): (1) regional groups such as African states, Asian states, Latin American states, Nordic states, Eastern European states, and Western European states; (2) political groups like the Commonwealth, the League of Arab States, NATO (North Atlantic Treaty Organization), the Warsaw Pact, and the nonaligned states; (3) groups based on formal international economic agreements like the Council for Mutual Economic Assistance (CMEA), the European Community, and the OECD; and (4) groupings based on a common level of development or some other common interest, like the Group of 77. Rather than focusing on their different origins as Kaufmann has done, Thomas Hovet (1960, pp. 29–46) classifies UN groups according to their composition and function. He identifies forty-six different UN groups as of 1960, including the Soviet bloc and five other general types of UN groups: eight caucusing groups dealing mainly with procedural matters, six geographic distribution groups based on formal and informal agreements in the UN, twenty-one regional groups whose members are "bound" together through regional organizations outside of the UN, seven common-interest groups whose members are not located in close geographic proximity but share a common outlook on key issues, and three temporary groups that have been instrumental in regards to a particular UN issue or debate.

Building on the classification schemes offered by Kaufmann and Hovet, the remainder of this chapter will examine three different dimensions of group politics, each with different implications for the global dance. The first dimension is the five geographically based electoral groups (Africa, Asia, Latin America and the Caribbean, Eastern Europe, and Western Europe and Other States) that are used to select the members of all limited-membership bodies and the candidates for all leadership positions. The second dimension is groups based on common issue positions, ranging in size from as few as three members to as many as 130. This dimension also includes the regional international organizations that often try to speak with one voice in UN debates. The third dimension of group politics in the UN is small, often temporary, negotiating groups used to resolve critical issues that have reached an impasse in larger membership bodies. In practice this last type of group politics blurs the line between groups as actors and groups as a process, so they receive attention in Part 2 of the book as well.

▓ Electoral Groups

A key dimension of group politics that influences the political processes of the United Nations comprises geographically based electoral groups. Currently there are five such groups; their number and composition have evolved as the membership of the UN has expanded. The roots of these groups lie in the need to manage electoral contests in the General Assembly in an efficient and equitable way (Ziring, Riggs, and Plano, 2000, p. 91). Immediately after the UN started meeting in 1946, the Assembly was faced with two controversial tasks: (1) electing its own leadership in the form of a president, seven vice presidents, and chairpersons of its six main committees, and (2) selecting six nonpermanent members for the Security Council, which had eleven total members at the time (Morphet, 2000, pp. 227–228). In order to secure some sort of equitable geographic distribution across these highly contested positions, a "Gentleman's Agreement" (or "London Agreement") reached in 1946 assigned most but not all of the fifty-one original UN members to one of five regional groups: the British Commonwealth, Asia and the Mideast, Latin America, Eastern Europe, and Western Europe. For most purposes the five permanent members of the Security Council (China, France, the Soviet Union, the United Kingdom, and the United States) were treated as a separate category, since nonpermanent Council seats did not apply to them and since an early tradition in UN practice held that each of them would always serve as one of the Assembly vice presidents (Peterson, 1986, p. 291).

These early electoral groupings were an important development in UN decisionmaking; however, a number of factors limited their significance beyond the purposes of elections (Peterson, 1986, pp. 155, 291). First, when the groups were created in 1946, the main political alignments among member states were still not clear, so these geographically based groups emerged simply by reverting to customs that had been in place under the League of Nations. Second, all the groups were rather small, with only the Latin American group having more than ten members. Thus the groups found it relatively easy to reach internal agreement on elections, and preliminary caucusing on other issues was less important when the Assembly had only fifty-one members. Finally, since states were put into these groups somewhat arbitrarily, it was not always clear exactly which states were in each group, and this problem was compounded over time as the membership began to expand. By 1960 the number of UN member states had doubled, and the organization shifted from being predominantly European and Latin American to being predominantly African and Asian.

As a result of these changes, the composition of the electoral groups evolved rather significantly across the 1960s and 1970s. By 1963, there were four electoral groups including Africa and Asia, Eastern Europe, Latin America, and Western Europe and Other States (Bailey and Daws, 1995, p. 38); the Commonwealth was no longer used for electoral purposes, and the Mideast was included in the African and Asian group. In 1971, the number of members from both Africa and Asia had grown so large that each of these two groups began to have its own chairperson, and by the middle of the decade they were treated as separate regions for the allocation of all positions except the nonpermanent seats in the Security Council (Peterson, 1986, p. 294; Bailey and Daws, 1995, p. 38). Since that time, each of these groups has undergone additional changes in internal composition as more and more states have joined the UN; however, the same five basic electoral groups continue to be used. In fact, these geographic distinctions have become deeply rooted in the functioning of the General Assembly: they are seen as an effective mechanism for trying to ensure that the composition of the UN's limited-membership bodies is not dominated solely by the great powers or countries from any one region, as had been the case in the League of Nations (Peterson, 1986, pp. 155–156). The use of electoral groups has fostered broader geographic participation in the work of the UN and provided regions with a vehicle for pushing for changes in the composition of key UN bodies, like the Security Council and the Economic and Social Council (ECOSOC), when changing UN membership warrants a greater voice for certain states.

Though these five geographic groups have become indispensable for managing elections at the United Nations, discussions of their exact composition are fraught with imprecision and occasional contradictions. Several General Assembly resolutions make explicit reference to these five groups: Resolution 1991, which was passed in 1963 and led to the expansion of ECOSOC to twenty-seven members and expansion of the Security Council to fifteen members, Resolution 2847, which was passed in 1971 and led to the further expansion of ECOSOC to fifty-four members, and Resolution 33/138, which was passed in 1978 and expanded the number of vice presidents in the Assembly to twenty-one. In each case, the resolution includes an annex that specifies how the elective seats or positions will be divided among the five regions. However, none of these resolutions actually specifies which member states are in each region; instead, the composition of each is unofficial and is at times subject to interpretation. Nonetheless, the *United Nations Handbook* (2002) provides the following data on the membership of each electoral group.

As of May 31, 2002, there were 53 members of the African group, 52 members of the Asian group, 21 members of the Eastern European group, 33 members of the Latin America and Caribbean group, and 27 members of the Western Europe and Other States group; thus 186 of the UN's 191 members are in one of the five groups. In most cases, group membership is based on simple geography and common sense; however, some clarification is in order. The Arab countries of the Middle East are spread across two of these regional groups, Africa and Asia. The Asian group also includes the Central Asian republics of the former Soviet Union (Kazakhstan, Kyrgyzstan, Tajikistan, Turkmenistan, and Uzbekistan), but the former Soviet republics in the Baltics, Caucasus, and Europe (including Russia) are all part of the Eastern European group. The Western Europe and Other States group includes some Mediterranean countries like Malta but not others like Cyprus, which is in the Asian group. Other states in the Western European group include Canada, Australia, New Zealand, and, as of May 28, 2000, on a temporary basis, Israel. One member state, Turkey, participates fully in two groups, Asia and Western Europe, but for electoral purposes (and for the purposes of the numbers provided above) is considered part of the Western Europe and Other States group. Five UN members are not included in any of these groups. Switzerland and Timor-Leste (East Timor) both joined the UN later in 2002, after these numbers were compiled, and Estonia and Kiribati are not members of any regional group. Finally, the United States is also not a member of any regional group, but it participates in the Western Europe and Other States group as an observer and is considered part of that group for electoral purposes.

These groups play a role in selecting all members of the UN's limited-membership bodies and all candidates for top leadership positions. Some of these elections, such as those for the judges of the International Court of Justice and the secretary-general, are the shared responsibility of the Security Council and the General Assembly. However, most other elections are the province of the Assembly acting alone, as is the case when it selects its own president, vice presidents, and committee chairpersons and when it selects the members of ECOSOC, the nonpermanent members of the Security Council, and the members of the main UN budget body, the Advisory Committee on Administrative and Budgetary Questions (ACABQ). Some important elections, like those for the Commission on Human Rights, are held in ECOSOC rather than in the Assembly as a whole. In the case of all these elections, there is some sort of arrangement, usually a rather formal one, for allocating the seats or positions among different regions. For solitary leadership positions, like the president of the Assembly and the UN secretary-general, regions take turns having a national from one of their states serve in the position. For example, in 2003 for the Fifty-eighth Session of the Assembly, it was Latin America and the Caribbean's turn to hold the office of president, so that regional group nominated Julian Hunte of Saint Lucia for the position, and the rest of the Assembly quickly endorsed the region's choice.

Elections to limited-membership bodies are usually governed by a formula of regional distribution agreed to by the General Assembly as a whole. According to the annex of Assembly Resolution 1991, the ten elected seats in the Security Council are divided as follows: five for Africa and Asia together, two for Latin America, two for Western Europe, and one for Eastern Europe. Likewise, in the case of ECOSOC, the annex to Assembly Resolution 2847 specified that its fifty-four members should include fourteen from Africa, eleven from Asia, ten from Latin America, thirteen from Western Europe, and six from Eastern Europe. A similar system is also used for leadership positions in the Assembly. Five of its twenty-one vice presidents are reserved for the permanent members of the Security Council (who by practice cannot serve as president); the annex to Assembly Resolution 33/138 of 1978 distributes the remaining sixteen positions according to the following formula: six from Africa, five from Asia, one from Eastern Europe, three from Latin America, and two from Western Europe, with the region holding the presidency having its number of vice presidents reduced by one.

While these elections are often rather routine, they do have the potential to be rousing affairs that galvanize the member states (Malone, 2000a, p. 3). The expectation in these elections is that each region will decide which of its members will fill its allotted seats and that the larger UN membership will not challenge its selections (Narasimhan, 1988, p. 327). These types of "agreed slates" are the preferred outcome in UN elections (Malone, 2000a, p. 5); however, the five regional groups have varying levels of success in achieving the desired internal cohesion. All the groups have members that are different from each other in important respects: level of development, language, colonial history, resource needs, and foreign policy orientation (Nicholas, 1975, p. 132; Bailey and Daws, 1995, pp. 39–44). This can give rise to subgroups and other lines of conflict that must be reconciled in trying to arrive at an agreed slate of candidates. In the case of Security Council elections, some groups have set procedures for identifying consensus candidates: the African group usually, though not always, favors a pattern of strict rotation among its members; Latin America and the Caribbean states provide for occasional membership for Central America and the Caribbean but more frequent membership for the larger states in South America like Brazil, Argentina, and Colombia (Malone, 2000a, p. 5). However, the Western European and Other States group has generally adopted a "market-driven" approach: its members can test their chances with the Assembly as a whole rather than on agreeing to an internal slate of candidates.

An additional source of difficulty for electoral groups trying to advance an agreed slate is interference by outside states (often major powers), which may intensely lobby a region to change its candidate. For example, in October 2000, Sudan was the African states' agreed candidate for their only open seat on the Council; however, the United States was strongly opposed to Sudan's Council bid and was able to successfully champion Mauritius for the seat instead (Lynch, 2000). And this is certainly not an isolated incident in regard to Council elections; both David Malone (2000a) and C. V. Narasimhan (1988, p. 327) offer several examples of heated campaigns where "agreed slates" were not possible. Contested elections such as these involve intense jockeying, for members have a strong interest in who serves on these critical, nonuniversal UN bodies (Malone, 2000a, p. 3). The Charter and various Assembly resolutions specify what type of majority is needed (two-thirds for election to the Security Council) and what qualifications, if any, the candidates for various seats should have (Peterson, 1986, p. 153), but they still leave much room to debate exactly which members are most "deserving" of a seat. Which is the stronger motive: keeping a state like Sudan that has a horrible human rights record off the Council or allowing African states the autonomy to select their own representative on the Council?

Such questions are usually resolved through all manner of legitimate and illegitimate means. In the case of Security Council elections, Malone has identified a number of factors that can influence the success or failure of a campaign that is not backed by a cohesive regional group: the state's ability to contribute to maintaining international peace and security, its resources devoted to the campaign (financial and personnel), the personality of its permanent representative, and its reputation at the UN (2000a, pp. 7–18). Common sense suggests that these factors apply in the case of elections to other limited-membership bodies as well. For example, due to resentment over its large UN arrears, the United States lost two elections in a row (1997 and 1998) to ACABQ; the seat was regained only after the United States was able to muscle New Zealand out of the way in 1999 so that it would be unopposed in the election (Laurenti, 1999, p. 17). This example demonstrates the importance of both reputation and raw power.

In a similar example, continued frustration over US policy toward the UN resulted in the loss of the US seat on the UN Commission on Human Rights in May 2001 for the first time since that body was founded in 1947 (Crossette, 2001). In this case, the United States was running against France, Austria, and Sweden for the three open seats allotted to the Western Europe and Other States group, and it finished fourth in the voting. US officials expressed shock at the loss, claiming that they had "locked up" the necessary amount of support in ECOSOC to be reelected. This example illustrates another challenge associated with contested elections at the UN: These votes are conducted through secret balloting (Bailey and Daws, 1995, p. 46). As a result, there is some difficulty within electoral groups with making sure that members will actually vote for the agreed slate, even when one does exist (Peterson, 1986, p. 156). In cases when there is no agreed slate, determining how much support a particular candidate has going into the elections can be even more difficult. A former permanent representative of Italy to the UN, Paolo Fulci, developed a formula for determining how many states would mislead other members regarding their voting intensions: ten percent of written commitments and twenty percent of oral commitments must be discounted (quoted in Malone, 2000a, p. 16). The United States may have been frustrated and disappointed that some other ECOSOC members did not follow through on the voting commitments they had made; however, it should not have been surprised. Needless to say, during the April 2002 election cycle for the Commission on Human Rights the United States made sure that the Western Europe and Other States group fielded the same number of candidates as there were open seats, thus guaranteeing that the United States would regain its seat (United Nations, 2002).

In all the preceding examples, electoral groups played a central role in the success or failure of campaigns for seats on limited-membership UN bodies. However, as heated as these elections may have been, they represent only a small fraction of the organization's political processes. Understanding group politics on UN decisionmaking requires examining two other dimensions: common interest groups and negotiating groups.

◼ Common Interest Groups

The second dimension of group politics at the United Nations relates to collections of member states that are formed when countries have shared interests in the outcomes associated with either general issues or specific negotiations. These groups are fundamentally different from those discussed in the previous section, since the motive is not the need to ensure equitable geographic representation but a desire to successfully adopt preferred policies in UN bodies. This dimension includes several of the types of groups identified by Hovet that were mentioned above: caucusing groups, regional groups, and common interest groups (1960, pp. 31–32, 38–45). In his conceptualization, these groups are similar in the goals they advance (their common positions), but they differ from each other in significant respects. Caucusing groups may or may not be regionally based; they are distinguished by their use of some internal procedures or organizational structure. Regional groups lack this organization but share geographic affinity. Finally, common interest groups have neither structure nor geographic affinity, but they have members with common interests. While these distinctions that Hovet makes are important and will figure in the discussion below, the point that must be stressed in this dimension of group politics is that caucusing and common interest groups (the terms are used interchangeably here) have very different purposes from those of the groups discussed in other sections of this chapter.

There are numerous groups of this type that have an impact on how the global dance unfolds at the United Nations. Some are quite large, others are rather small; some have become permanent fixtures on the UN landscape, others are formed on an ad hoc basis. As a result of this proliferation of caucusing groups, nearly all UN members are active in more than one such group, so each of them enjoys a range of options in their efforts to pursue their interests in cooperation with other states (Kaufmann, 1988, p. 155). Deciding which caucusing groups to use on each issue involves careful consideration of the state's interests, the size of the group, and the preferences of other group members. It also requires a consideration of the power and resources of the group, both within and outside the UN (Peterson, 1986, pp. 58–59), as well as an understanding of how cohesive the group's membership is in general and in regard to the issue at hand (Kim and Russett, 1997, 48–54). Each of these judgments is challenging to make, and they often point in different directions. For instance, states can face a choice of acting through a group that has internal divisions but greater power or a group that is internally united but limited in influence. The group needs to have a means of leveraging the negotiations, but it must also be sure that its members will stay the course with the common position they have adopted.

Understanding variation in the cohesion of caucus groups requires further exploration of some important differences within this dimension of group politics. The first relevant difference concerns the size and geographical basis of the groups. The largest UN group, the Group of 77, has more than 130 members and stretches across three regions of the world; one of the smallest UN groups, CANZ (made up of Canada, Australia, and New Zealand), has only three members but still stretches across two geographic regions. While there are a number of other groups of varying size that cross different regions, a large number of UN groups function within a single region or subregion. These can be as large as the fifty-two-member African Union or as small as the five-member Nordic group. A number of examples of these different types of groups will be considered in the following paragraphs.

Most discussions of groups at the United Nations begin, and many end, with a consideration of the two largest UN groups, the Group of

77, which currently has 133 members, and the Non-Aligned Movement, which currently has 112 members (Ziring, Riggs, and Plano, 2000, pp. 91–95; Narasimhan, 1988, pp. 311–325). Both of these groups are composed almost entirely of developing countries in Africa, Asia, and Latin America, so there is substantial overlap between these two actors in terms of membership and focus. However, there are important differences that are often overlooked when the groups are discussed together. The G77 is larger in membership but narrower in focus, dealing almost exclusively with issues associated with economic development such as trade preferences, multilateral aid, foreign investment, and technical cooperation. The NAM, on the other hand, is slightly smaller in membership but has a broader scope of concern rooted in its members' desire to advance common foreign policy priorities independent of the superpowers. Economic issues have been on its agenda, but these are joined with, and often overshadowed by, concerns dealing with disarmament (particularly nuclear weapons), decolonization, and political issues such as apartheid and conflict in the Middle East.

The origins of the G77 and NAM are distinct, but they do share a common pattern of development. The NAM emerged first at a 1961 conference hosted by the president of Yugoslavia, Josip Broz Tito, in Belgrade. The leaders of India, Ghana, Indonesia, and Egypt, among others, joined him in pushing for an independent path between the dictates of the United States and those of the Soviet Union (Morphet, 2000, p. 238). However, over the ensuing decades the NAM has consistently maintained an anti-Western bias, so that it has had a far more productive relationship with the Soviet Union (later Russia) and China than with the United States. The roots of the G77 are only slightly more recent, dating to the 1964 UN Conference on Trade and Development. This meeting was held at the initiative of developing states, and it provided them with an opportunity to voice their concerns about the structure of the global economic system established after World War II (Morphet, 2000, p. 242). All seventy-seven of the African, Asian, and Latin American states at the conference agreed to form a mechanism through which they could more effectively pursue their economic goals, including trade preferences, foreign assistance, debt relief, commodity stabilization, and reform of the Bretton Woods institutions (the International Monetary Fund and the World Bank).

From these initial meetings, the members of both the G77 and the NAM have worked to coordinate their policies at UN meetings whenever possible. These efforts have been quite successful in a number of cases, such as the Sixth Special Session of the General Assembly in 1974, which called for the establishment of a new international economic order more favorable to developing countries. However, the ultimate effectiveness of the G77 and NAM in UN politics has been limited by two realities. First, no matter how cohesive these groups may be, their only means of leverage within the UN is their voting power. They can certainly pass their preferred policies, but these efforts are often stillborn without the support of states that have the resources to implement them. Second, since these groups are so large in membership, they can have tremendous difficulty securing internal cohesion. The G77 and NAM have worked strenuously to maintain group solidarity (Peterson, 1986, pp. 256–267); however, these efforts are becoming increasingly difficult as the diversity within their membership grows.

The remaining common interest groups at the United Nations are all substantially smaller. Some of these groups have their roots in geographic proximity in addition to shared interests. The membership of these groups can be quite similar to that of the corresponding electoral groups discussed in the last section, as is certainly the case with the fifty-two-member African Union (AU) and the fifty-three-member African electoral group and at least partially true in regards to the thirty-five-member Organization of American States (OAS) and the thirty-three-member Latin America and the Caribbean electoral group. However, in most other cases the caucusing groups that have regional roots include only a subset of the members of that region's electoral group, due to the challenges of finding members that have sufficiently shared interests across the issues of concern to the group.

The fact that common interest regional groups play an active role at the United Nations should not come as a surprise; in fact, the drafters of the UN Charter expected there to be a relationship between regional organizations and the UN (Bailey and Daws, 1995, pp. 35–36). These expectations are most clearly reflected in Articles 52–54 of the Charter, which specify the relationship between regional arrangements and the Security Council in regard to maintaining international peace and security. However, the activity of these common interest regional groups at the UN extends far beyond peace and security issues to include all aspects of the UN's agenda.

Regional and subregional common interest organizations active at the UN are drawn from all continents of the world. Already mentioned are regional-level organizations in Africa (the AU) and Latin America (the OAS); both of these regions also have subregional groups as well in the form of the nineteen-member Rio Group (in Latin America), the fifteen-member Economic Community of West African States (ECOWAS), and the fourteen-member Southern African Development Community (SADC). Asia lacks a regional-level organization, but it does have two subregional groups that advance common positions in UN debates on certain issues: the ten-member Association of South East Asian Nations (ASEAN) and the seven-member South Asian Association for Regional Cooperation (SAARC). There are three other regional and subregional organizations that stand out in terms of their level of coordination at the United Nations: the European Union (EU), the Nordic group, and Caribbean Community (CARICOM). In 2004, the EU expanded from fifteen members (mainly from Western Europe) to twenty-five members, including states from Eastern and Southern Europe. According to a former permanent representative from Belgium to the UN, EU members are committed to advancing a common position on as many UN issues as possible, especially those dealing with economic and social matters (quoted in Grey, 2000, pp. 30–31). However, there is one exception to this pattern: the EU does not attempt to act in a coordinated fashion in regard to the Security Council (Morphet, 2000, p. 245). A second highly cohesive subregional group at the UN is composed of five Nordic countries (Denmark, Finland, Iceland, Norway, and Sweden), which are remarkably unified in their robust levels of support for the organization and the policies they advance (Narasimhan, 1988, pp. 330–331). A final regional group whose level of coordination within the UN is quite high and continues on an upward trajectory is CARICOM, whose fifteen members have been actively trying to use their combined voice to push for greater focus on issues of concern to their region (Drayton, 1998).

In addition to these common interest groups that share geographic ties, there are a number of caucusing groups that regularly participate in UN debates whose membership stretches across different regions. A number of these groups have their roots in economic considerations, including: the Group of 7/Group of 8 (G7/G8), which is composed of the seven advanced industrialized democracies (Canada, France, Germany, Italy, Japan, the United Kingdom, and the United States) and Russia; the thirty-member Organization for Economic Cooperation and Development (OECD), which is mainly European but includes some Asian and Latin American members; the eleven members of the Organization of Petroleum Exporting Countries (OPEC), from Asia, Africa, the Middle East, and Latin America; and finally, the forty-nine states that are classified as least developed countries (LDCs). Some of these groups have common economic concerns but also share a particular geographic disadvantage across regions; these include the thirty Land-Locked Developing States (LLDS) and the forty-five Small Island Developing States (SIDS). Another type of cross-regional caucusing group was the British Commonwealth, but it is no longer possible to identify any real area of shared interest among these former colonies (Narasimhan, 1988, p. 329). However, some former members of the Commonwealth, in particular Canada, Australia, and New Zealand (the CANZ group), do work together on some UN issues and elections (Malone, 2000a, p. 12). Two other caucusing groups are centered on the Middle East and based on shared history, but they both include members from more than one UN region; the twenty-two-member Arab League, which is focused mainly on Palestinian issues, and the fifty-six-member Organization of the Islamic Conference (OIC), which promotes cooperation among Muslim countries (Morphet, 2000, pp. 235–236). The final cross-regional caucusing group at the UN that will be mentioned here is composed of the five permanent members of the Security Council (P5). As will be further discussed in Chapter 8, this group first emerged as a unified actor, at least on certain issues, after the end of the cold war, and its efforts to reach internal agreement, both inside and outside the Council, have intensified in the years since (Morphet, 2000, pp. 252–255).

This diversity in size and geography creates substantial differences in terms of how cohesive these common interest groups are across issues and over time. A related factor that must be considered in this regard is that caucusing groups have different internal mechanisms and procedures for reaching agreement and advancing their interests. These differences stem from both the origins and the duration of the caucusing group. Many of the groups mentioned above were in fact cases where a regional or subregional international organization was attempting to present a unified position in the UN. These organizations have their own charters, staffs, and decisionmaking procedures that can be used to reach agreement and support negotiating efforts. Furthermore, five of the groups mentioned above (the AU, CARICOM, EU, Arab League, and OIC) have received permission from the General Assembly to participate in its work as observers, and as a result they maintain permanent observer missions at UN headquarters (United Nations, 2003). These organizations also have set procedures for selecting the leaders of their group, through either elections or a pattern of rotation. Some of the other groups, like the G77 and NAM, also have procedures for selecting leaders; however, these organizations are not supported by a permanent headquarters or secretariat (Ziring, Riggs, and Plano, 2000, pp. 94–95). Instead, the state serving as chair of the group provides the necessary support services and calls for the creation of committees and working groups as needed. Finally, some of the caucusing groups mentioned above function without any leadership or support staff at all. This is true for some small and long-established groups like the Nordic states, but it is also the case for larger groups composed of underprivileged states that simply have not yet developed a tradition of providing these common resources, like the LDCs, LLDS, and SIDS.

One final point about caucusing groups is in order. It is not uncommon at the UN for temporary caucusing groups to emerge on certain issues (Hovet, 1960, pp. 45–46). These ad hoc interest groups most often arise in response to issues on which the more established caucusing groups mentioned above have not been able to advance common positions. One example of this was reforming the size and composition of the Security Council, a subject that was intensely debated from 1993 to 1997. In this case, the only established caucusing groups that were able to speak with one voice were the Nordic states and CARICOM (Smith, 1999, p. 187). All the other groups suffered from internal divisions, which resulted in the emergence of a variety of ad hoc groups to bring together states with similar preferences regarding Council reform. The two most important of these groups, called the Razali group and the "coffee club," were composed of members that desired a quick expansion of the Council and those that opposed it, respectively. Both of these groups included member states from all regions, with the deciding factor in group membership being whether or not the state supported a Council that would include five new permanent members (Germany, Japan, and one state each from Africa, Asia, and Latin America) and have an overall size of twenty-one to twenty-four members. Many caucusing groups that would usually work together were prevented from doing so on this issue, since their memberships were internally divided as to which states deserved permanent seats. Even with the emergence of temporary caucusing groups, disagreement about how to best reform the Council persisted, and little progress has been made on this issue since 1997. This disappointing outcome was largely due to the fact that the interests of member states on Council reform are simply too divergent to find areas of potential agreement, but it also rests on the fact that a third important dimension of group politics at the United Nations, negotiating groups that build bridges between different common interest groups, was missing in these debates. The final section of this chapter will consider this third dimension of group politics.

Negotiating Groups

Negotiating groups aim to resolve especially contentious areas of disagreement. The caucusing groups discussed in the previous section perform an important function in UN politics: they "permit scattered and heterogeneous interests to be narrowed down to a few key issues"

(Alger, 1989, p. 3). Even once this step has been taken, however, securing multilateral agreement is far from easy, since the few remaining key issues are often those where the disagreements across common interest groups are most intense. Another reason it is important to consider this third dimension of group politics is that the groups' effect on UN decisionmaking is seen as being nearly always positive. In the case of electoral groups and caucusing groups, at least some observers have questioned whether their efforts to increase efficiency are too frequently sidelined by rigidity in the group's negotiating position (Kaufmann, 1988, pp. 156–158). This was seen as being especially problematic in the 1970s and 1980s, when the G77 and NAM were most active and successful at presenting a united front in the General Assembly and other UN bodies. In such cases, group politics resulted in confrontation and stalemate, since these large caucusing groups were advancing policies not supported by the major financial contributors to the UN, and neither side seemed to have much interest in compromise.

However, in the early 1990s, some of these same observers noticed that "the worst period for engaging in group negotiations may be over" (Kaufmann, 1991, p. 133), a conclusion that was based on the decreased cohesion of large caucusing groups and the increased use of negotiating groups in UN processes. Negotiating groups had always been a part of UN decisionmaking, as is reflected by the instrumental roles they played during the creation of the UN Emergency Force to deal with the Suez Crisis in 1956 and during the establishment of the UN Special Fund (a predecessor of the United Nations Development Programme) in 1957 (Kaufmann, 1988, p. 72). In these cases, members such as Canada, Brazil, Denmark, India, Chile, and the Netherlands formed ad hoc groups to search for areas of agreement across traditional lines of cleavage in the UN, including the confrontation between both East and West and North and South. The political processes of the UN continued to evolve as the membership changed, and by the end of the cold war, when consensus increasingly came to replace confrontation as the preferred means of securing outcomes, the use of negotiating groups had proliferated across all UN bodies and issues. This is a positive development at the UN, since these small, ad hoc "contact groups" have consistently demonstrated that they can achieve optimal results in complex multilateral negotiations (Kaufmann, 1991, p. 133). The following pages will consider why this is the case.

In the first place, the goals of negotiating groups are fundamentally different from those of the two dimensions of group politics discussed above. As was the case with electoral and caucusing groups, the large size of many UN bodies gives rise to the need for conducting business through smaller negotiating groups (Peterson, 1986, p. 272). However, electoral and caucusing groups are similar in that their membership is brought together based on a shared desire to elect a particular state or adopt a preferred policy; negotiating groups are instead designed for the explicit purpose of forging agreement across different common interest groups in search of outcomes that can be supported by the entire membership of the organization. These groups have received less attention in scholarship on the United Nations than the two previous dimensions, since their role and membership is determined only on an ad hoc basis, given the needs of each particular negotiation. This makes them hard to examine in a systematic fashion, but it does not detract from the instrumental role they play in promoting the global dance.

One source of confusion regarding these groups stems from terminology; they are often referred to as "contact groups" or "working groups" because the groups are designed to work through key areas of disagreement through intensive negotiation and contact (Peterson, 1986, p. 272). However, Kaufmann uses the more colorful terms "fire brigades" and "bridge builders" to capture the severe nature of the disputes these groups seek to resolve and their need to incorporate at least some of the interests of all parties involved if a widely acceptable package solution is to be found (1980, p. 16; 1988, p. 72; 1991, p. 133). Whatever term is used, the key thing to remember about negotiating groups is that their membership is brought together based on a shared goal of working out the details so that a compromise solution can be found that takes into consideration the preferences of different caucusing groups.

Negotiating groups vary in their origins and structure. Some of these groups are formally constituted and put in place by the chair or presiding officer of the body in which the larger negotiations are taking place. For example, in the General Assembly, the negotiating group might be created by the president or the chairperson of one of its six main committees. In these cases, leadership is provided by the presiding officer or a person that she or he selects. The group will likely have a rather formal character, including a relatively stable membership and a regular meeting schedule. While the procedures used to run the group meetings will be far less formal than those used in the UN's permanent organs, they will involve some sort of agenda and other mechanisms for managing debate. Other negotiating groups are more informal in their origins, structures, and procedures. These groups also emerge on an ad hoc basis, but usually at the initiative of a few member states rather than the presiding officer. Such groups might function during an entire negotiating process, or they might exist only temporarily to deal with one key sticking point. In any case, their membership is likely to be less stable, their meetings will often be more free-wheeling, and their internal leadership might be shared or simply left undefined. Such negotiating groups often represent a bridge between the formal and informal UN procedures that are discussed in Part 2 of the book.

These variations in origins, leadership, structure, and procedures can have an impact on how effective these groups are in the political processes of the UN; however, by far the most important influence on the potential success or failure of negotiating groups is their membership. The work of negotiating groups is both complex and difficult, since often only the most difficult issues make it to these groups. Nonetheless, Kaufmann has concluded that many participants are willing, or even eager, to serve as "bridge builders" on these "fire brigades" because it can give them the opportunity to have a large influence on the decision (1980, pp. 16–17). A state's desire to participate in a negotiating group does not necessarily mean, though, that it will be an effective member of that group. The concern is not so much that a state would join such a group with the intention of obstructing its work (although this certainly does happen) but that the state might not possess the correct set of attributes to contribute to the consensus-building process both within and outside the negotiating group.

In order for these small group encounters to contribute to successful policy outcomes, the membership of the group must include representatives from all common interest groups that are active on the issue that is at stake. Presiding officers and other delegates interested in creating negotiating groups often feel pressure to keep the group as small as possible in order to make negotiations easier; however, a negotiating group that fails to address certain interests because significant members were omitted will only face more difficult negotiations later on, when any agreement reached within the group has to be approved by the entire membership of the body in which the decision is being made. The goal is that agreement within the negotiating group spread to encompass the larger membership of the decisionmaking body (Peterson, 1986, p. 295), but this is impossible—or at least very difficult—when some members of the body feel that their concerns were not addressed within the negotiating group.

A second consideration regarding the membership of negotiating groups concerns the specific countries that are included to represent the interests of each caucusing group. The best-case scenario is for these countries to reflect the attitudes of the entire caucusing group they represent, so that compromises made within the negotiating group will be supported by states not included in the negotiations (Alger, 1989, p.

25). Occasionally participating states are given the authority or latitude to make compromises on behalf of their group; however, it is far more common that each member of the negotiating group must report back to the other states in its caucusing group for approval or acquiescence before each major step in the negotiations (Peterson, 1986, pp. 295–296). One would expect that having a moderate voice speak on behalf of the caucusing group in the negotiating group would be the most effective strategy, since that state is more likely to find areas of agreement with the representatives from other caucusing groups than would a member more extreme in its views, and such is often the case in UN debates (Alger, 1989, pp. 25–27). Yet it is also evident that some negotiating groups have benefited from including more extreme views, even if this did make the process of reaching agreement within the group more difficult, because there was less chance of last-minute obstacles when the eventual agreement was considered by the entire decisionmaking body.

There are no easy answers when it comes to determining the most effective membership for a negotiating group, and a failure to fully consider the tradeoffs involved can make agreement more elusive. This was the case during the UN Special General Assembly Session of 1963, which was focused on financing for peacekeeping. Although agreement was finally achieved during this session, obstacles emerged at several points along the way when it became unclear whether key participants had a mandate to negotiate on behalf of their respective caucusing groups (Alger, 1989, pp. 25–27). Despite this difficulty, some general guidelines have been offered for determining what types of characteristics are beneficial for the delegations of states serving on negotiating groups: each one must have "wide political acceptability, be well informed, enjoy the confidence of countries directly involved in the dispute, be strongly supported by its national government, and in some cases represent a country capable of contributing financially or otherwise to the implementation of UN decisions" (Kaufmann, 1980, p. 17). When a negotiating group is having difficulty reaching an agreement that can be supported by the decisionmaking body as a whole, its membership can be changed; however, this may prove to be a hollow undertaking if the general disposition of the membership is not significantly altered (Alger, 1989, p. 28).

Even though negotiating groups can be challenging to design, they are a ubiquitous phenomenon in UN decisionmaking, appearing in relation to nearly every contentious issue, expect in the notable case of efforts to reform the Security Council discussed at the conclusion of the previous section. For example, during the Third UN Conference on the

Law of the Sea, which stretched from 1973 to 1982, the "Group of Legal Experts" (the Evensen Group) brought together roughly twenty-five states drawn from a range of different common interest groups, including developed states, developing states, coastal states, landlocked states, fishing states, shipping states, and so on (Evensen, 1989, pp. 84–88). In this group responses to some of the most contentious issues regarding ocean use were hammered out, including marine pollution, scientific research, exclusive economic zones, and seabed mining. On a similar note, ad hoc negotiating groups were used in a number of consensus-building efforts at the UN in the 1990s, including compromise language regarding humanitarian assistance in 1991, a renegotiation of the seabed mining regime of the Law of the Sea Treaty in 1994, and the verification regime associated with the Comprehensive Nuclear Test Ban Treaty (CTBT) in 1996 (Smith, 1999, p. 188). In each case, the negotiating groups were carefully composed to represent a wide range of views, which helped produce an overwhelming degree of support when each agreement was eventually considered in the General Assembly: the resolution on humanitarian assistance was unanimous, the Implementing Agreement for the Law of the Sea Treaty had only seven abstentions, and the CTBT had five abstentions and three no votes. Clearly negotiating groups make a substantial contribution to UN decisionmaking.

Two additional benefits of negotiating groups at the UN are present whether or not these groups help achieve successful outcomes. First, ad hoc negotiating groups play a central role in fostering long-term working relationships between states and delegates. Intensive interaction in regard to one particular area of disagreement, if done in an appropriate manner, can lead to progress on a range of other seemingly unrelated issues. This relationship between negotiating groups and the UN's informal processes will be explored in greater detail in Chapter 8. Second, the use of negotiating groups can allow participants other than member states to have a greater impact on the negotiations than might otherwise be the case. For example, Secretariat officials and nongovernmental organizations both have limited formal mechanisms for influencing the internal decisionmaking of many UN bodies; however, they nonetheless can play a significant behind-the-scenes role in regard to some issues. As was mentioned above, intensive negotiations in ad hoc groups often involve a more open and less structured debate, which can allow more opportunities for these other actors to offer their own contributions. The following two chapters examine the direct and indirect means through which these actors participate in the global dance of UN decisionmaking.

4

The Secretariat and
the Secretary-General

MEMBER STATES OF THE UNITED NATIONS TRUST THE ORGANIZATION TO perform a wide variety of tasks in their name: from peacekeeping to economic assistance, from election monitoring to disarmament verification, from drug control to disease eradication, the list is seemingly endless. In order to engage in these diverse functions, member states have provided the organization with a staff, called the Secretariat, which is composed of international civil servants. This staff includes, in the words of the International Court of Justice, all persons who have "been charged by an organ of the Organization with carrying out, or helping to carry out, one of its functions—in short, any person through whom it acts" (quoted in Beigbeder, 1988, p. 5). The staff of an international organization, including the headquarters in which it works and the budget that pays its salaries, provides a long-term, stable presence or identity that distinguishes such organizations from other, more ad hoc manifestations of multilateral diplomacy such as issue-specific global conferences. To say it another way, it is the staff of an international organization that actually makes it an organization.

Thus international civil servants represent half of the apparent dichotomy regarding the United Nations that was discussed at the beginning of Chapter 2. Most often international organizations are viewed simply as frameworks through which member states pursue their interests, either individually or in groups. In this conceptualization, the Secretariat is merely an instrument of the members, providing basic services so that their meetings run smoothly and then working to faithfully implement the policies and programs that they have approved. Like national bureaucracies, UN civil servants "study, compile, report, advise, [and] circulate information . . . but they do not sanction member states nor take decisions enforceable by citizens" as their domestic counterparts often can (Beigbeder, 1988, p. 8). Nonetheless, these administrative roles are absolutely essential, and despite common assumptions to the contrary, they often provide the staff with important opportunities to both directly and indirectly influence the dynamics of the unfolding dance and the content of decisions that emerge from it.

On top of these administrative roles, certain functions performed by the UN Secretariat are more explicitly political in nature. As was mentioned at the beginning of Chapter 2, in some situations it is possible to view the UN and its staff as an independent actor, either because member states have consciously ceded authority in that area to the staff or because member states have neglected to take action in an area where the staff has the potential to contribute. While areas in which the Secretariat enjoys considerable autonomy are necessarily rare, they are sufficiently common that UN observers frequently talk in terms of the successes and failures of the UN and its staff. One notable example is the decision of the Norwegian Nobel Committee to award the Nobel Peace Prize to the United Nations and Secretary-General Kofi Annan in 2001 (Norwegian Nobel Committee, 2001). In making its selection, the committee highlighted the work of the UN and the secretary-general in resolving conflicts, promoting human rights, fighting international terrorism, and combating HIV/AIDS. This is not the first time the Norwegian Nobel Committee has recognized the work of the UN's staff: at least three other UN officials (Ralph Bunche, Lester Pearson, and Dag Hammarskjöld) and three different UN bodies (the Office of the United Nations High Commissioner for Refugees [UNHCR], the United Nations Children's Fund [UNICEF], and United Nations Peacekeeping Forces) have won the Peace Prize. These honors reflect the fact that Secretariat personnel perform important tasks for the effective functioning of the organization. Their role in its decisionmaking will be the focus of the following pages.

◼ The Development of the International Civil Service

That international organizations should have a support staff composed of professional civil servants drawn from all members of the organization is now virtually universally accepted; however, this is in fact a relatively recent development. As multilateral diplomacy became more common through the nineteenth century, nascent traditions regarding the support staff for these conferences and meetings began to emerge. In most cases, the secretariats for these short-term events, except for possibly the most senior positions, came from the national civil service of the host country (Beigbeder, 2000, p. 199). As permanent international organizations like the Rhine and Danube commissions, the Universal Postal Union, and the International Telegraph Union (now the International Telecommunications Union) emerged in the 1800s, permanent staffs were also required. However, these early secretariats typically involved only a small number of personnel who either were from the host country or were seconded to the organization for short periods by member governments with sufficient resources to do so (Bennett and Oliver, 2002, p. 413; Luard and Heater, 1994, p. 102). As a result, these staffs did not reflect the multinational character of the organization's membership.

The creation of a truly international civil service to staff an international organization dates to the creation of the League of Nations in 1920. The covenant of the League was vague, however, in regard to the composition of the staff (Ziring, Riggs, and Plano, 2000, p. 112), simply stating in Article 6, Paragraph 1, that "the Secretariat shall comprise a Secretary-General and such secretaries and staff as may be required." It was largely left up to the candidates who were proposed for the post of the first secretary-general to determine exactly what staff was required and how they would be selected. The position was initially offered to Sir Maurice Hankey, Secretary of the British Cabinet (Luard and Heater, 1994, p. 102), who favored a system of five to nine national delegations (representing the Council members), following existing practice (Beigbeder, 1988, p. 17–18; 2000, p. 199). After Hankey turned down the post, it was offered to a dynamic and prestigious Greek politician, Eleutherious Venizelos, who conceived of the position as that of a chancellor with wide political powers heading a quasi-independent staff of international statesmen (Bennett and Oliver, 2002, p. 413; Beigbeder, 1988, p. 18). However, he too declined the offer, and the Allied powers settled on Sir Eric Drummond, a British civil servant and diplomat, who accepted. The office of secretary-general was then modified to be more nonpolitical and administrative (Beigbeder, 1988, p. 18).

However, that still left the question of the composition of the secretariat unresolved. It was expected that the League's staff's role would be relatively passive and not highly visible. But would it be composed of national delegations (Hankey's view) or organized around an "international civil service" with "each official being supposed to act only on the instructions of the Secretary-General and in the interests of the League, without regard to the policy of his own government" (Drummond's view, quoted in Beigbeder, 1988, p. 18)? Despite some persistent interference on the part of member states regarding certain individual appointments, Drummond's conception of a politically neutral international secretariat prevailed (Jordan, 1988, p. 424). This was reflected in the 1920 Balfour Report, which concluded, "The members of the Secretariat once appointed are no longer the servants of the country of which they are citizens, but become for the time being the servants only of the League of Nations. Their duties are not national, but international" (quoted in Hammarskjöld, 1968, p. 216). Drummond's effort to establish both the international composition and international responsibilities of the League Secretariat has been considered by some observers to be one of the most important developments of the League period (Luard and Heater, 1994, p. 102; Ziring, Riggs, and Plano, 2000, p. 112). However, his successor, Joseph Avenol, clearly had difficulties with maintaining these traditions in the Secretariat, as the League was buffeted by the events leading up to World War II (Jordan, 1988, pp. 424–425).

One frequent point of comparison that sheds light on the early administrative and political roles of the international civil service, especially its top officials, focuses on Drummond and his counterpart at the International Labour Organization (ILO), Director-General Albert Thomas (Jacobson, 1979, p. 99; Bennett and Oliver, 2002, pp. 414–415). These two have often been seen as opposites, with Drummond conceiving of his role as that of a faceless administrator and Thomas acting as a political advocate for policies he supported. While Drummond sought to keep himself and the Secretariat in the background as much as possible, Thomas focused on providing dynamic, even forceful, leadership. Drummond never addressed the Assembly, addressed the Council only as a committee secretary, and kept his annual reports focused on factual summaries (Nicholas, 1975, p. 176). On the other hand, Thomas used his articulate and eloquent style to suggest and defend his policy initiatives before the ILO Conference and Governing Body (Bennett and Oliver, 2002, p. 414). Some of these differences stemmed from their backgrounds: Thomas's experiences in the French labor movement offered a very different conception of the role of an international civil servant from that of the nonpolitical culture Drummond had experienced in Britain (Jacobson, 1979, p. 99). However, these comparisons are often overdone, neglecting to consider the innovative and bold manner in which Drummond guided the creation of a truly international civil service (Nicholas, 1975, p. 176) and that his reputation for discretion allowed him to be quite active as a source of advice and information for League members (Luard and Heater, 1994, p. 102).

The questions on the proper role and composition of the international civil service that surfaced in regard to the League foreshadowed similar debates that have persisted through the history of the United

Nations. This is not surprising, given the fact that there are unmistakable similarities between the UN Secretariat and that of its predecessor. The founders of the UN may have felt that the League Secretariat had some important shortcomings, but they also felt that these "in no way disproved the desirability and practicality of the concept of independent international secretariats" (Ameri, 1996, p. 2). However, the transition from an independent League Secretariat to a similar composition for the UN did not take place without discussion. In fact, the Dumbarton Oaks proposals of 1944 envisioned several parallel secretariats (Beigbeder, 2000, p. 200) headed by an "office manager, not a policymaker" (Jakobson, 1993, p. 155). Fortunately, the small and middle powers that attended the San Francisco Conference in 1945 strongly objected to these proposals, and the principle of an independent and international secretariat was reaffirmed in the UN Charter.

Another subject of discussion when the United Nations was created concerned the executive head of the organization: should this office be primarily administrative, as had been the case under the League, or would that individual be provided with the means to undertake independent political initiatives (Jakobson, 1993, p. 156)? Despite some misgivings, the general sentiment throughout the process of creating the United Nations was that this office would assume broader responsibilities than it had under the League, including a more important political role (Goodrich, 1967, p. 128). Although President Franklin D. Roosevelt's suggestion of "World Moderator" as the title of this position was not adopted (Nicholas, 1975, p. 176), the office of UN secretary-general was endowed with "autonomous political and diplomatic prerogatives," which set the stage for a "recurring tug-of-war between the Secretary-General and the member states for control of the policy-making principal organs, the Security Council and the General Assembly" (Rivlin, 1995, p. 82). The principal differences lie in the powers given to the secretary-general under Articles 98 and 99 of the UN Charter, which will be discussed in the following paragraphs. Their clear expansion of authority beyond the language of the League Covenant is said to have led Drummond to later remark that had these articles been at his disposal, "the position of his office—and, by implication, the influence of the League on events—would have developed differently" (Pérez de Cuéllar, 1993, p. 129). Other observers would certainly question this assertion, arguing that the major powers during the League years would never have tolerated a more activist secretary-general along the lines envisioned in the UN Charter (Bennett and Oliver, 2002, p. 414). While such hypothetical arguments are nearly impossible to resolve, this discussion does highlight a crucial recurring theme regarding the secretary-general and the UN staff: to what extent do their activities involve independent political roles beyond manageri-al and administrative functions?

Most of the rest of this chapter will investigate the balance between politics and administration in the case of both the UN staff and its leader, the secretary-general. Understanding how this balance evolves across issues and over time is crucial for appreciating how these actors can exert both direct and indirect influence in the global dance of UN decisionmaking. However, this consideration must be rooted in the lan-guage of the Charter, which lays out the composition and roles of the Secretariat in Articles 97 to 101. The first three articles deal with the office of the secretary-general, who, according to Article 97, is "appointed by the General Assembly upon the recommendation of the Security Council." Since Article 97 contains no other required qualifi-cations, the veto has loomed large in the selection of each of the UN's secretaries-general. This was anticipated by smaller states when the UN was established; they feared that the Security Council would be drawn to "lowest common denominator" candidates who would "show more talent for tact toward the major powers than common sense and integri-ty" (Jakobson, 1993, p. 156). Later we shall consider the extent to which this concern has been realized.

The roles and responsibilities of the secretary-general are outlined in Articles 97, 98, and 99, which can be seen as a "photograph with double exposure" (ibid.). Article 97 identifies the secretary-general as the "chief administrative officer" of the organization, and Article 98 indicates that the secretary-general "shall act in that capacity" in all meetings of the UN's other principal organs save the International Court of Justice. While the covenant had not included this particular language, the administrative focus of these provisions is very much consistent with the implicit position of the secretary-general under the League (Hammarskjöld, 1968, p. 218). However, the "dual capacity" of the secretary-general emerges as the explicitly political functions of the office are described in Articles 98 and 99 (Pérez de Cuéllar, 1993, p. 127). Article 98 indicates that the secretary-general shall perform func-tions "as are entrusted to him" by the other principal organs and make an "annual report to the General Assembly on the work of the Organization." This last provision is an important one, since "the work of the organization" is a broad phrase that includes at a minimum, "but is not confined to, whatever the organization has done, or had failed to do, or is required to do" (ibid., p. 129); thus the report allows the secre-tary-general an opportunity to initiate new proposals and galvanize the work of the other UN organs (Nicholas, 1975, pp. 176–177). Article 99 goes even further, transforming the office of secretary-general from a "purely administrative" one to "one with an explicit political responsibility" (Hammarskjöld, 1968, p. 219). It empowers the secretary-general to "bring to the attention of the Security Council any matter which in his opinion may threaten the maintenance of international peace and security." Even though Hammarskjöld indicates that this article was hardly debated at the time the Charter was drafted, it has been interpreted to provide the secretary-general with "a broad discretion to conduct inquiries and to engage in informal diplomatic activity" (ibid.). As will be discussed in the following section, this gives the secretary-general a "measure of political initiative" even in cases where Article 99 is not explicitly invoked (Narasimhan, 1988, pp. 272–273).

Articles 100 and 101 of the Charter focus on the Secretariat as a whole, not just the office of secretary-general. The first paragraph of Article 100 articulates the loyalties of the secretary-general and the staff: these individuals "shall not seek or receive instructions from any government or from any other authority external to the organization," for they are "international officials responsible only to the Organization." Paragraph 2 of Article 100 further establishes the independence of the secretary-general and the staff, since member states are obliged to "respect the exclusively international character" of these individuals and refrain from influencing them "in the discharge of their responsibilities." Article 101 raises the issue of staff recruitment and composition. Paragraph 1 indicates that "the staff shall be appointed by the Secretary-General under regulations established by the General Assembly." Since this provides the secretary-general with considerable latitude in managing the organization's staff, it represents an important departure from League practice, where individual appointments actually required the formal approval of the Council (Bailey, 1962, p. 21). Paragraph 3 of Article 101 provides that "the paramount consideration in the employment of the staff . . . shall be the necessity of securing the highest standards of efficiency, competence, and integrity." However, it also indicates that "due regard shall be paid to the importance of recruiting the staff on as wide a geographic basis as possible." These are fundamental principles that provide the Secretariat with the necessary qualities to be active participants in the political processes of the UN; however, they also contain inherent contradictions and areas of potential abuse (Ameri, 1996, pp. 92–93; Narasimhan, 1988, p. 273), which will be discussed in the final section of this chapter.

One final observation regarding these Charter provisions is in order. Article 7 indicates that the Secretariat is one of the six principal organs of the UN. As a result, the Secretariat, and by extension the secretary-general, is "co-responsible with the other organs (the General Assembly, the Security Council, and so on) for achieving the organization's aims and purposes" (Pérez de Cuéllar, 1993, p. 127). Some have interpreted this article even further, arguing that the Secretariat and secretary-general are placed in a position of equality with the Assembly and the UN's Councils, not in a position of "dependence or subservience" (Goodrich, 1967, pp. 132–133). However, because the language in Articles 97 to 101 is not "particularly explicit or detailed" (Rivlin, 1995, p. 83), the exact relationship between the UN's staff and the member states has evolved over time. The Charter is certainly more detailed than the corresponding sections of the League Covenant; still, the specific parameters of Secretariat influence in UN decisionmaking are subject to interpretation and thus vary across issues and individuals. The following discussion will consider various mechanisms these actors use to help shape the rhythm of the dance through which the UN makes its decisions.

◼ The Secretary-General

While the Charter identifies the Secretariat, not the secretary-general, as a principal organ of the United Nations, many discussions of the political roles of the Secretariat begin and end with a consideration of this particular office and the individuals who have occupied it. This is a logical choice, given the fact that the UN Preparatory Commission, meeting in the fall of 1945, concluded that "the Secretary-General, more than anyone else, will stand for the United Nations as a whole. . . . In the eyes of the world, no less than in the eyes of his own staff, he must embody the principles and ideals of the Charter" (quoted in Rivlin, 1993, p. 3). Scholars have held a similar view on the importance of the secretary-general as a symbol of the organization's role in world politics. For example, to return to an issue discussed at the beginning of Chapter 2, Robert Cox concludes that the executive head of an international organization "plays a key role in converting an international organization conceived as a framework for multilateral diplomacy into one which is an autonomous actor in the international system" (1969, p. 229). Likewise, Inis Claude Jr. has argued that, "broadly speaking, a positive correlation exists between the activism of the United Nations and that of the Secretary-General," such that more demands for action on the part of one of these actors leads to more demands for action on the part of the other (Claude, 1993, p. 253).

The office of secretary-general is certainly the most important and visible post in multilateral diplomacy, but it has also been called "the most impossible job in the world" by none other than its first incumbent, Trygve Lie (quoted in Rivlin, 1993, p. 3). While this assessment may be overdone, the secretary-general certainly faces complex and contradictory pressures in the performance of the various tasks explicitly and implicitly entrusted to the office. As was discussed above, the Charter commands the secretary-general to perform tasks specified by the Security Council and General Assembly, but it also empowers the holder of that office to act independently through Article 99. The ability of any particular secretary-general to balance these pressures depends heavily on how developments in world politics affect member states' views of the United Nations and thereby create opportunities and requirements for the secretary-general to act (Claude, 1993, p. 250). On one level, the secretary-general and the organization he or she leads must operate in a world dominated by sovereign member states, which can form a straitjacket with little room to maneuver; however, on another level, the secretary-general is an international player who enjoys independence in regard to services that only he or she can provide (Rivlin, 1993, pp. 9, 17; James, 1993, pp. 25, 27).

Part of the difficulty in understanding this office boils down to the fact that "perceptions as to the proper role of the Secretary-General vary" (Rivlin, 1993, p. 5). Some desire an activist secretary-general, taking initiative and providing powerful moral leadership (the "general" side of the job); others prefer a manager who is only a marginal player in international politics (the "secretary" part of the job). The result is that "the Secretary-General works within a setting of limitations and opportunities that dictate that he, like others with broad political responsibilities, cannot be everything to everybody on all occasions" (Gordenker, 1993, p. 277). This forces incumbents to make difficult choices regarding their goals and priorities and the strategies and behaviors necessary to achieve them. In the words of Secretary-General Kofi Annan, "There are times when I have to be a secretary . . . and there are times when I have to be a general and show leadership" (quoted in Maniatis, 2001, p. 45). Knowing when to adopt a more visible political role, as opposed to a more reserved administrative role is what makes this job particularly challenging.

The Political Roles of the Secretary-General

Considerations of the political roles of the secretary-general often begin with Article 99, since this is where the drafters of the UN Charter were most explicit in their intention to make the office more than that of an administrator. As was mentioned above, since Article 99 allows the secretary-general to "bring to the attention of the Security Council any matter which in his opinion may threaten the maintenance of international peace and security," it has been understood to grant the incumbent the ability to express independent opinions on a wide range of issues, including those where views of the member states do not necessarily coincide (Zyss, 1998, p. 55). This includes the ability to react to an actual crisis and to anticipate potential conflicts by engaging in preventive action (Jakobson, 1993, p. 161). Thus Article 99 puts the secretary-general in the role of an international "watchdog, . . . on guard for situations that might lead to violence or war (as well as those which had already reached this stage), and wake his masters up to them, demanding what action [is] to be taken" (Luard and Heater, 1994, p. 106). This interpretation of Article 99 clearly makes the secretary-general an active participant in the decisionmaking of the Security Council, not just a servant who waits passively outside the chamber until provided with instructions.

Despite this rather strong language in the Charter, the "astonishing fact" surrounding Article 99 is that it has been used only on rare occasions (Jakobson, 1993, p. 161). During the tenure of the first five secre-

UN Secretary-General Kofi Annan (center) participating in a Security Council meeting on Iraq on June 8, 2004. Seated to his left is Ambassador Lauro L. Baja Jr., permanent representative of the Philippines to the United Nations and president of the Security Council for the month of June 2004. (UN photo #NICA 7811, by Sophie Paris)

taries-general (the first forty-five years of the UN), Article 99 was explicitly invoked on only one occasion, in May 1960 by Dag Hammarskjöld, to call the Security Council into session regarding the Congo. Other instances of secretary-general initiative have included some reference to Article 99 after the fact, including Trygve Lie's account of his actions during the Korean crisis of 1950 and Hammarskjöld's revelation that he would have used it to address the Suez crisis in 1956 had the United States not acted first (Nicholas, 1975, p. 177). Beyond these instances, nearly every secretary-general has used the language of Article 99 to convene the Council without specifically invoking its provisions; examples include U Thant during the India-Pakistan War in 1971, Kurt Waldheim during the Iranian hostage crisis in 1979, and Javier Pérez de Cuéllar during the crisis in Lebanon in 1982 (Jakobson, 1993, p. 161). These efforts have often taken the form of a letter to the president of the Security Council expressing concern about a particular situation (Kaufmann, 1980, p. 217). More recent secretaries-general, Boutros Boutros-Ghali and Kofi Annan, have continued this trend of taking political initiatives without explicitly making reference to Article 99. Despite some confusion among scholars and practitioners as to exactly which situations have involved the use of Article 99 (James, 1993, p. 36), the general consensus is that these provisions have been used far less than one might expect given the complex crises the United Nations has faced.

This raises two important questions: why has Article 99 been used so rarely, and what are the implications of this neglect in terms of the secretary-general's role in the global dance of UN decisionmaking? Two possible answers for the first question have been offered. One is that Article 99 has not been explicitly used very often because it has not been needed, since "almost always some member state will raise an issue if it is appropriate for Security Council consideration" (Ziring, Riggs, and Plano, 2000, p. 130). Some observers have indicated that Article 99 may in fact make such action on the part of members, especially those directly involved in a dispute, more likely, provoking them to act when they might otherwise prefer to delay (Kaufmann, 1988, p. 103). The second explanation for the rare use of Article 99 has been most clearly articulated by one of the incumbents, Pérez de Cuéllar (1993, pp. 129–130), who observes that this authority contains three elements: "right, responsibility, and discretion." The Charter clearly gives the secretary-general the right to bring issues before the Council, but this must be done with an eye toward responsibility and discretion. In other words, before invoking Article 99 the secretary-general must carefully consider how well the initiative will fare given the positions of Council members and the parties to the dispute. Pérez de Cuéllar concludes that an ill-advised use of Article 99 could do more harm than good by inflaming the situation and compromising the UN's ability to act in regard to other issues.

Turning to the second question, does the apparent neglect of Article 99 limit the ability of the secretary-general to influence the political processes of the UN, specifically the Security Council? This is an especially important question given that Article 99 gives the secretary-general the power to raise issues but does not diminish the Council's position as the principal organ for matters relating to international peace and security (Bailey, 1962, p. 22). Once an issue is put on the Council's agenda, it is up to the Council to debate it and take any decisions or actions it deems necessary; Article 99 does not provide the secretary-general with any special powers in this regard (Narasimhan, 1988, p. 274). It seems, then, that the quite limited use of Article 99 has not detracted from the political influence of the secretary-general, because Article 99 never was expected to be the only mechanism through which the secretary-general participated in the work of the UN's political bodies. However, the existence of Article 99 and the high visibility of this office can be said to have created an atmosphere at the UN in which member states have felt the need to include the secretary-general in their decisionmaking. The following paragraphs will note some mechanisms through which this process unfolds.

One political function of the secretary-general that has received extensive attention from scholars and practitioners beyond Article 99 relates to quiet diplomacy and conflict resolution. These efforts may be well publicized, conducted under provisions laid out in Article 33 of the UN Charter on the peaceful settlement of disputes, or they can occur entirely behind the scenes, based on the delicate nature of the dispute and the fragile trust enjoyed by the secretary-general (Pérez de Cuéllar, 1993, pp. 132–136; James, 1993, pp. 33–36). These efforts may directly involve the secretary-general or, more often, involve that official's personal representatives; they have been extensively examined by scholars, especially in terms of their role in strengthening the image and stature of the office of secretary-general (Franck and Nolte, 1993; Puchala, 1993). These efforts often result from instructions from policymaking organs like the Security Council and the General Assembly, as specified under Article 98, which calls upon the secretary-general to "perform such other functions as are entrusted to him by these organs" (Bailey, 1962, p. 37). The instructions may be quite explicit, laid out in a UN resolution, or they may remain vague, conveyed to the secretary-general only orally or in an informal written statement, as was often the case under Hammarskjöld's tenure when the phrase "Leave it to Dag" was in vogue (Kaufmann, 1980, p. 217). However, secretaries-general to date have never limited their diplomatic activities solely to issues on which they have received guidance from policymaking organs. Some observers have argued that activities arising from the secretary-general's own diplomatic initiatives represent one of the most important developments in the function of the office (Bailey, 1962, p. 38; Narasimhan, 1988, p. 294).

Quiet diplomacy, with or without the guidance of policymaking organs, is one of the secretary-general's most important political tasks. However, it raises the same question that was considered in regard to Article 99: do these efforts translate into influence in the decisionmaking processes of UN bodies? The answer in this case is clearly affirmative, with two important mechanisms at work. The first is the latitude enjoyed by the secretary-general in implementing these initiatives, even when they result from instructions from policymaking organs (Luard and Heater, 1994, p. 106). This latitude is especially available in regard to peace and security issues, such as the size, composition, and day-to-day control of peacekeeping missions (Ameri, 1996, p. 137; James, 1993, p. 33). Political considerations can create an incentive for the secretary-general to pursue a safe route and avoid difficult choices, but the available latitude can also provide the incumbent with opportunities to expand the responsibilities and authority of the office (Hammarskjöld, 1968, pp. 225–226). But how does this latitude lead to political influence? When the secretary-general is entrusted with tasks by the Security Council and the General Assembly, the instructions often include a reporting function (James, 1993, p. 29). Many such reports are routine and technical; however, some offer the secretary-general an opportunity to raise new issues, frame the debate on existing issues, and offer possible solutions, even controversial ones. Examples include the secretary-general's annual report on the work of the organization and the progress reports required on all peacekeeping missions (Pérez de Cuéllar, 1993, p. 129; James, 1993, p. 29; Rivlin, 1995, p. 92). As a result of this latitude in implementation, the secretary-general may enjoy greater access to scarce information and expertise than the member states; the reporting function then can become a mechanism for influencing the direction of debate in the UN's policymaking bodies.

Another way the secretary-general can influence the political process of the United Nations involves some of the position's administrative responsibilities. This probably holds truer for the executive heads of certain specialized agencies such as the director-general of the United Nations Educational, Scientific, and Cultural Organization

(UNESCO) and the president of the World Bank. In both cases the founding treaties, as well as the accepted policy processes of the organizations, created a powerful leading role for the executive head considerably beyond the administrative powers of the secretary-general (Finkelstein, 1988b, pp. 398–409; Schechter, 1988, pp. 351–353). Yet the secretary-general's performance as a manager is still important for the political processes of the organization, because it has an impact on his or her freedom to engage in the more explicitly political roles discussed above (Sutterlin, 1993, pp. 44, 53). The two spheres of activity, political and administrative (or general and secretary), are inseparable in some respects, for any areas in which the incumbent lacks the confidence and trust of the member states will harm the secretary-general's ability to act in all other areas.

Beyond this general point, certain specific administrative tasks can provide the secretary-general with at least an indirect influence on the political debates that unfold. Some of these include preparing and administering the organization's budget, hiring its staff and organizing its structure, and placing items on the agenda of the UN's policymaking bodies (Beigbeder, 2000, p. 196). It is important to point out that in all three of these areas the secretary-general's responsibilities are shared with the member states, and as can be expected, there is considerable variation in how much discretion each incumbent is able to enjoy. In regard to the budget, the secretary-general operates within some very severe constraints, both financial and political, laid down by the General Assembly (Sutterlin, 1993, p. 50). However, the secretary-general's direct involvement in the appropriation and allocation of resources can help set the organization's priorities and ensure that it has the capacity to meet these goals (Annan, 1993, p. 98). The secretary-general's independence is higher in appointing members of the UN's staff and organizing the overall structure of the Secretariat (Sutterlin, 1993, pp. 48, 50). At least on paper (Article 101 of the Charter) the secretary-general is subject only to the "regulations" of the General Assembly; however, as will be discussed in the section on the Secretariat, both the General Assembly and individual member states have at times limited this independence, especially in the distribution of, and appointments to, high-level posts. Finally, even though the provisions of the Charter only provide for the secretary-general to bring matters of concern before the Security Council, the rules of procedure for both the General Assembly and the Economic and Social Council (ECOSOC) allow the incumbent to place matters on their agendas and to address these bodies regarding any issue under consideration (Luard and Heater, 1994, p. 106; Kaufmann, 1988, p. 104). With these administrative powers, the secretary-general can directly participate in deciding what the policymaking bodies talk about and control, to a considerable extent, how the Secretariat is structured so as to best implement the decisions that are made.

Another means for the secretary-general to influence the political processes of the United Nations lies in the office's placement at the center of a large, informal communications network. This provides the secretary-general with two important resources that can lead to opportunities to provide leadership and exercise political influence: relationships and information (Gordenker, 1993, pp. 270–279). The most important relationships are those with the member states, both at UN headquarters and in state capitals (Bailey, 1962, p. 59). This is especially true in the case of the five permanent members of the Security Council, whose confidence and trust the secretary-general must maintain in order to be effective (or to even keep the job, as the US veto of a second term for Boutros-Ghali in 1996 demonstrated). The secretary-general can benefit from maintaining strong informal relationships with smaller powers as well. After all, they represent a majority of the UN's membership, and their colonial histories often lead them to view the secretary-general as an important voice for them vis-à-vis the developed states (Goodrich, 1967, pp. 135–136). Nearly all secretaries-general to date have appreciated both of these realities (Smith, 2003, p. 145). Finally, beneficial relationships can be formed with other actors, including the heads of other international organizations, members of the UN staff, officials in key domestic political institutions and bureaucracies, representatives of nongovernmental organizations, the media, and the general public (Jacobson, 1979, pp. 129–131; Ziring, Riggs, and Plano, 2000, pp. 128–129). The secretary-general depends on broad support in order to mobilize the UN to action and provide the resources and support necessary to do its work (Gordenker, 1993, p. 278). As will be discussed in Chapter 8, these informal networks can be a powerful tool for exercising influence across a wide range of issues over time.

These relationships provide the secretary-general with opportunities to generate another resource for participating in the global dance: information. As noted earlier, latitude in implementing UN decisions and extensive reporting requirements provide the secretary-general with information that can translate into political influence. Information that reaches the secretary-general through informal patterns of consultation and trust can be useful in the same way (Gordenker, 1993, pp. 270–273). Numerous individuals speak with the secretary-general on delicate issues, and this can provide the secretary-general with opportunities to "advise, encourage, and warn" with "deference and caution"

(James, 1993, p. 28). The first incumbent in the office "acquired considerable reputation as one to whom confidences could be imparted and from whom could be obtained as impartial a summary of a situation as one would be likely to get" (ibid., p. 29). Fortunately, later secretaries-general by and large have maintained this role, and it has become an important mechanism through which the secretary-general can influence the content and tone of debates in the UN's policymaking bodies.

Factors That Influence the Secretary-General's Role

The underlying theme of the preceding pages is that the secretary-general must serve two sets of masters; or, in the words of one incumbent, he must balance a "two-tier constituency" (Pérez de Cuéllar, 1993, p. 140). One of these constituencies is the 191 UN member states, which collectively are the secretary-general's "boss": they control who serves in the position and, to a large degree, specify the parameters of the roles the incumbent can perform. The other constituency is composed of the principles and ideals of the UN Charter, to which the secretary-general must be a faithful servant. Unfortunately for the secretary-general, these two constituencies often exert contradictory pressures that are not easy to reconcile. This creates an environment of "role ambiguity," where the maps toward effective action are unclear and the demands for attention far exceed the resources available (Rivlin, 1995, p. 84). The secretary-general often must make difficult choices, first, between the administrative and political responsibilities of the office (Beigbeder, 2000, p. 205). Additionally, if an activist role has been chosen, the incumbent must be careful to devote the office's limited time and resources to those situations where there is the greatest need for action and the largest opportunity for success (Goodrich, 1967, p. 137).

Two overriding factors strongly influence each secretary-general's efforts to strike a balance between the administrative and political dimensions of the job. These two factors also help explain why some secretaries-general have been able to participate actively in the global dance of UN decisionmaking while others have been more marginal players who either chose or were forced to stay off the dance floor.

The first of these factors is the environment the secretary-general faces while in office (Cox, 1969, pp. 226–229; Schechter, 1987, pp. 197–199; Kaufmann, 1988, pp. 101–103). Some incumbents have been more successful at wielding influence in UN decisions because they have had more opportunities to do so and faced fewer external constraints. One external constraint arises from the organizational position of the secretary-general; while the office has a set of legal powers laid out in the Charter, much of its authority has evolved over time based on the performance of each incumbent. Each secretary-general can face a different set of expectations and limitations, depending on the successes and failures of predecessors.

Another, more important environmental influence on the ability of the secretary-general to participate in the UN's political processes is the incumbent's relationship with member states (Cox, 1969, pp. 226–229; Schechter, 1987, pp. 197–199; Kaufmann, 1988, pp. 101–103). As discussed above, any successful secretary-general must maintain the trust and confidence of the member states, especially the major powers, which have a particularly large say in all aspects of UN activity, including who is selected for the post. Establishing good relationships is a complicated endeavor that may have little to do with the specific characteristics or behaviors of a particular secretary-general. It is influenced by the nature of crises faced by the UN, the international orientations of the member states, the domestic political debates that key members must address, and the distribution of power in the international system (Cox, 1969, pp. 222–226; Ziring, Riggs, and Plano, 2000, p. 132; Smith, 2003, pp. 145–146). If member states are generally in agreement that the United Nations staff should take the lead on a particular issue, then they are more likely to see value in the secretary-general's playing an active political role. However, if UN members are divided on the best course of action to pursue, it will be easy for the secretary-general to do nothing. These more challenging situations, however, also provide the incumbent with opportunities to play an active political role by filling the vacuum left by state inaction (Hammarskjöld, 1968, p. 226).

A second factor that affects the ability of the secretary-general to enlarge "the parameters of his action and influence in expanding executive leadership" is the "personality, philosophy, and diplomatic skills of each incumbent" (Bennett and Oliver, 2002, p. 425). The basic idea is that a secretary-general's character and style shape important dimensions of his behavior in office (Kille and Scully, 2003, p. 176). Harold Jacobson discusses how the executive heads of international organizations vary in personal charisma and that this in turn creates differences in how well they perform within the organizational and political environment they face (1979, pp. 131–132). This is certainly true, but beyond charisma, it involves all the other aspects of personality, individual style, and diplomatic skill discussed in Chapter 2 (Goodrich, 1967, pp. 136–137; Ziring, Riggs, and Plano, 2000, pp. 134–135). Some incumbents have been outgoing and assertive, pushing to expand the role and influence of their office, while others, having a more reserved or less confident personality, have been willing to defer to member states whenever possible. On top of this, the available skill set for each incumbent must be consistent with his or her view of the office; an individual who is assertive but lacks essential skills such as charisma and tact may ultimately be less influential in UN decisionmaking than a more reserved person who nonetheless has the intelligence or negotiating skill to earn the trust of key member states.

The following paragraphs will consider how these two factors, environment and personal attributes, have interacted in the case of each secretary-general, proceeding in chronological order. The focus is on how the interaction of environmental and personal characteristics influenced their ability to expand the scope of the office, wield influence in the UN's policymaking bodies, and otherwise shape the unfolding routines of the global dance.

Trygve Lie of Norway, the first secretary-general, who served from 1946 to 1953, faced imposing environmental constraints: the need to carve out the responsibilities of a new office in the midst of the origins of the cold war. There is considerable variation in how his balance between administrative and political roles is evaluated. Many scholars argue that Lie had an expansionist view of his office, based at least in part on his proposal of a "Twenty-Year Program for Achieving Peace" (Kille and Scully, 2003, 179). This is also reflected in his positions during the crises in Berlin and Korea. However, others have observed that Lie's involvement in the Iranian complaint of 1946 led him to be more cautious throughout his early years in office, when he developed a habit of consulting members before all important political initiatives (Gaglione, 2001, pp. 25, 67). When he did pursue a more activist path, such as the Korean crisis, his efforts ended up having a "shattering effect" on his usefulness, to the extent that the Soviet Union did not even recognize him as secretary-general during his three-year extension of term (Gaglione, 2001, pp. 68, 73). As a result, Lie's ability to play an active role in the political processes was severely restricted.

The second secretary-general, Dag Hammarskjöld, served from 1953 to 1961 and pursued an ambitious path of role expansion. The environment he faced was just as severe as the one faced by Lie, with cold war antagonisms creating frequent periods of stalemate in the Security Council. However, Hammarskjöld clearly viewed these occasions as opportunities to expand the influence of his office. In the words of Peter Heller, he became "a master at playing on the Charter's ambiguities, oxymorons, and silences to try to achieve his goals" (2001, p. 17). Most often these efforts involved quiet diplomacy and behind-the-scenes maneuvering; however, Hammarskjöld was willing to use all means at his disposal, including explicitly invoking Article 99 for the first time in 1960, to try and move the member states to action in places he deemed necessary (ibid., p. 38). The result of these efforts was a dramatic expansion of his office and a demonstration that the UN could act independently in a world of sovereign states. Along the way, Hammarskjöld certainly strained his relationships with some member states; nevertheless, his stature and diplomatic skill allowed him to play an active role in policymaking until he died in office in 1961.

Serving as the third secretary-general, from 1961 to 1971, U Thant clearly departed from the mold of his predecessor, given the absence of any bold initiatives under his watch (Kille and Scully, 2003, p. 180). Thant did possess a desire to make the UN a force on behalf of developing states and was willing to be very blunt in appraising world leaders and their policies (Firestone, 2001, pp. xviii–xiv). However, beneath his placid and composed exterior lay an astute appreciation of the political realities he faced, which resulted in an "honest but unimaginative" secretary-general (ibid., pp. 101, 109). When Thant did try to be more assertive, he quickly ran afoul of major powers (like the United States in regard to Vietnam) and was quick to back down. As a result, Thant was able to maintain the confidence of most members, but his influence on UN decisions remained marginal, if for no other reason than that he was not pushing for much.

The fourth secretary-general, Kurt Waldheim, served from 1972 to 1981, during which time the UN was plagued by hostility between East and West and North and South. Although he came into office with the background of a model diplomat and a desire to be a leading player on the world stage, early in his tenure Waldheim decided to downplay the political roles of his office, choosing instead to focus on consensus issues and implementing the agreements created by others (Ryan, 2001, pp. 16–17, 33, 43). Some have judged Waldheim a success simply because he was able to stay afloat in the midst of turbulent seas; however, he is by far the secretary-general who did the least to expand the role and vision of the office. Waldheim's "yes-man" demeanor did allow him to maintain the trust and confidence of all key member states; however, as for his predecessor, his personal influence on decisions was severely hampered by the fact that he was excessively deferential to member states. His legacy was further stained by allegations, which emerged after he left office, regarding his role in the Austrian military during World War II and its activities in support of Nazi deportations in the Balkans.

Javier Pérez de Cuéllar served as the fifth secretary-general from 1982 to 1991. Some accounts of his tenure conclude that Pérez de Cuéllar continued in the same tradition as his immediate predecessors,

Thant and Waldheim, making little effort to expand the office in which he served (Kille and Scully, 2003, p. 181). This is not at all surprising given his reserved personality, lack of charisma, and dry speaking style (Lankevich, 2001, pp. vii, 113), along with renewed hostility in the cold war during his first term. However, Pérez de Cuéllar did excel as secretary-general in one important area: he was a skilled diplomat, persistent and wholly uninterested in personal glory. He was able to seize the opportunities associated with the end of the cold war and dramatically expand the UN's role in quiet diplomacy and conflict resolution. In the process, he earned the respect of key member states and played a far more active role in UN decisionmaking than any other secretary-general since Hammarskjöld.

At the end of Pérez de Cuéllar's term, member states seemed willing to accept a more activist secretary-general, and that is what they got in the sixth incumbent, Boutros Boutros-Ghali, who served from 1992 to 1996. From the start, Boutros-Ghali was intent on asserting an independent role for the UN, a purpose to which he was so devoted that he refused to back down in the face of apparent limitations of the office (Kille and Scully, 2003, p. 180). Stephen Burgess has argued that Boutros-Ghali surpassed even Hammarskjöld in his desire to "guide the UN toward greater autonomy and power" but that his personality was central to his fortunes as secretary-general (2001, pp. xv, 8). It was expected that his diplomatic skill and administrative experience would serve him well; however, in office he was seen as an "iconoclastic" academic with an uncompromising vision and a combative style. Boutros-Ghali found it difficult to maintain effective working relationships with the major powers, especially the United States. His effectiveness and influence were dramatically reduced by 1994, and he was subsequently denied the customary second term. The differing fortunes of Pérez de Cuéllar and Boutros-Ghali illustrate how the interaction between environment and personality can result in unexpected outcomes: the one who had little desire to expand his role achieved substantial influence in the UN's political process, whereas the one with great ambition arguably left the UN in a more precarious situation than the one he inherited.

Secretary-General Kofi Annan began his tenure in 1997, and definitive assessments of his performance await. However, many preliminary assessments place him as one of the most, if not the most, effective secretaries-general, on a par with or exceeding the role expansion that occurred under Hammarskjöld. There have been difficult moments for Annan, such as questions about the UN's role in Bosnia and Rwanda in the mid-1990s, when he was in charge of UN peacekeeping, the period in 2003 immediately after the United States decided to use force in Iraq without Security Council authorization (Meisler, 2003, p. 37; Henneberger, 2003), and investigations into the oil-for-food program in 2004–2005. However, there have also been significant achievements, such as his mission to Iraq in 1998 (Traub, 1998) and his efforts to provide a vision for the UN through his Millennium Development Goals; these were recognized most dramatically when he received the 2001 Nobel Peace Prize. Most of all, Annan has been credited with restoring dignity and moral authority to the office of secretary-general, an important achievement given the UN's expanding agenda and shrinking resources. Much of his effectiveness derives from his personal attributes; although not known for a formidable intellect, Annan has been praised for his efficiency, evenhandedness, tact, and uncanny ability to follow his instincts correctly in nearly all situations. In the words of Richard Holbrooke, former US ambassador to the UN, Annan is "the international rock star of diplomacy," with "a nearly magical ability to move people through his personal charm and gentle strength" (quoted in Maniatis, 2001, p. 44). These qualities have earned him great credibility and trust and have enabled him to play an active role in the UN's political processes, especially through informal consultations with key member states.

■ The Secretariat

The Secretariat, as one of the six principal organs of the United Nations, extends far beyond the office of secretary-general. However, it was useful to consider the political roles of the secretary-general first because many of the opportunities and constraints of that office can also be said to apply to the members of the Secretariat (Jacobson, 1979, p. 133). The secretary-general depends on the support of his staff to perform many of the functions examined above: he needs their input to design and implement the budget, to write the numerous reports required of the office, and to effectively use the vast array of information that flows through the organization. Now it is possible that a secretary-general and the Secretariat might be inclined to view their roles differently; for example, an activist executive head might be serviced by a more passive staff, or even vice versa (Kaufmann, 1988, p. 101). However, their fortunes are intertwined, if for no other reason than that "the formal structure and the political configuration of the organization" determine whether members of the Secretariat have the capacity for influence in the political processes of the organization in their own right (Jacobson, 1979, p. 133).

Determining the overall size of the UN Secretariat is not as simple as one might expect. Various UN sources offer inconsistent figures, because they include different categories of personnel. However, it is possible to arrive at common parameters regarding three sets of figures for the 1997–1998 period, which are the most recent data available at this point. According to figures released by the Consultative Committee on Administrative Questions, which reports to the former Administrative Committee on Coordination, the overall staff size in 1997–1998 was about 14,100 (Beigbeder, 2000, p. 202). This figure includes all professional and general service staff appointed for one year or more assigned to UN headquarters, other established offices, and special projects. According to *Basic Facts about the United Nations*, however, as of July 1998 the Secretariat's staff was composed of some 8,900 personnel, drawn from more than 170 countries (United Nations, 1998, p. 15). The differences in these figures arise because the lower number includes only those positions covered under the UN's regular budget, whereas the higher number includes personnel "on loan" to the UN from member states to support particular offices, projects, or field missions; in some cases their salary is covered by special UN budgets, but often these personnel remain employees of their home government.

It is not possible for all 9,000 members of the UN's permanent staff to have an impact on the UN's political processes, nor would we expect them to. Roughly two-thirds of these employees are in the general service category, providing essential basic services from housekeeping to security, food preparation to clerical services (Ziring, Riggs, and Plano, 2000, pp. 115–117; Zyss, 1998, p. 57). They are usually hired locally and not subject to the provisions on staff recruitment contained in Articles 100 and 101 of the Charter. The 2,500 or so members of the UN's professional staff—composed of diplomats, lawyers, economists, and other experts—are subject to these provisions, though, since they are the employees most likely to interact with member states and other actors in the course of UN decisionmaking. The professional staff includes several categories of personnel, beginning with the basic professional grades (P1 through P5). At higher levels of authority and responsibility are directors (D1 and D2) and then assistant-secretaries-general and under-secretaries-general. All members of the UN staff take an oath of loyalty to the United Nations, pledging to remain independent of government interference, and the conduct of their service to the UN is governed by staff regulations passed by the General Assembly and staff rules enunciated by the secretary-general (Zyss, 1998, p. 59; Ameri, 1996, pp. 100–104).

The Political Roles of the Secretariat

The primary responsibilities for the UN Secretariat are often seen in a purely administrative light: providing technical services for meetings, translating documents, editing records of meetings, filing, and carrying out various other mechanical tasks. However, "in reality . . . the Secretariat can sometimes influence the course of deliberations and their final outcome substantially. . . . There is no doubt room at every level for an intelligent exercise of initiative and influence" (Ameri, 1996, p. 94–95). Secretariat personnel "are able to exert influence on decisions" due to "their tenure, expertise, and detachment from national roles," much like the staffs of national bureaucracies (Alger, 1968, p. 120). The political roles performed by the Secretariat certainly include assisting the secretary-general as he performs the tasks noted above, but they also extend to mechanisms that allow the organization's rank and file to participate in the UN's political processes in their own right. Furthermore, the political dimensions of the Secretariat's work have increased across all issue areas as member states have asked the organization to engage in an expanding array of responsibilities (Ameri, 1996, p. 132). Three different sets of tasks that allow the Secretariat to play an active role in the global dance of UN decisionmaking will be discussed here.

The first of these tasks concerns the Secretariat's role in servicing the work of the UN's deliberative and policymaking bodies. One responsibility of Secretariat staff is to make sure that the meetings of these bodies run smoothly: translation must be provided, documents must be distributed, and records must be kept (Luard and Heater, 1994, p. 104; Nicholas, 1975, p. 168). However, these administrative tasks are joined with a number of roles that allow members of the Secretariat an opportunity to actually shape the content of the debate that occurs. The Secretariat can provide these organs with an "indispensable institutional memory" (Beigbeder, 2000, p. 196), since its personnel usually work on the same issue and same body for much longer periods than do their counterparts in member-state delegations; in this way they become the "custodians" of the organization rather than simply its clerks (Jacob, Atherton, and Wallenstein, 1972, p. 36). At least one Secretariat official typically sits next to the delegate who is chairing a meeting in order to help provide guidance for the deliberations. On many occasions running the meeting actually becomes a cooperative project between the chair and the committee-secretary, involving consultation on the pace of formal and informal debate, managing the speaker's list (including determining who should be approached to speak at key junctures), and conducting votes when appropriate so that areas of emerging agreement are not lost to further debate (Alger, 1968, p. 118). This is where the civil servant can look much like a politician, persuading, negotiating, debating, gauging the movement of opinion, and sensing pressures before they become explosions (Nicholas, 1975, p. 175).

Even in cases where a cooperative relationship does not emerge between the chair and the committee-secretary, other officials can have an influence on the content of a debate, since UN meetings often center on a discussion of reports prepared by the Secretariat. This is true in regard to all issues on the UN's agenda, and its importance has increased as the UN has moved to consider issues that are increasingly technical in nature, such as economic development, trade, population, and disarmament (Luard and Heater, 1994, pp. 103–104). The need for reports has become so pervasive at the UN that some Secretariat personnel seem to spend all of their time preparing documentation for upcoming meetings on their subject matter (Grey, 2000, p. 41). These reports can take a variety of forms, from studies of emerging issues and trends to basic fact finding regarding areas of dispute (Ameri, 1996, pp. 126–128; Ziring, Riggs, and Plano, 2000, pp. 121–122). They can serve as the basis for a common discussion and sometimes provide Secretariat officials with an opportunity to suggest ways of dealing with the problem at hand (Jacob, Atherton, and Wallenstein, 1972, p. 36).

A second set of tasks that enable the Secretariat to influence the UN's political processes have to do with its responsibilities for implementing decisions of the deliberative bodies. This function emerged within the first few years of UN activity, and its significance has grown as the membership of the UN has expanded to include more and more developing states that are often on the receiving end of UN programs (Bailey, 1962, pp. 23–24). Beyond writing reports, this function dominates much of the day-to-day activity of Secretariat personnel, primarily because "nearly every decision of the General Assembly [and the other policymaking bodies] creates a task for the Secretariat" (Peterson, 1986, p. 166). This is especially true in the case of "operational decisions," which involve the use of resources at the organization's disposal, because these activities "involve a myriad of small decisions" that cannot possibly be resolved by the secretary-general alone or through the complicated machinery of the deliberative bodies (Jacobson, 1979, pp. 133–134). For this reason, "some legislative commands are more specific than others, but nearly all leave room for administrative discretion in the application of rules to particular cases" (Ziring, Riggs, and Plano, 2000, p. 121). On some issues, such as those associated with the UN's economic development programs, the Secretariat's latitude in the efficient implementation of sometimes contradictory instructions can be quite substantial (Ameri, 1996, p. 94; Luard and Heater, 1994, p. 104; Nicholas, 1975, pp. 169–170).

In their effort to prepare reports for policymaking bodies, Secretariat personnel face the challenge of trying to remain neutral before the facts of the situation such that all members will perceive their information to be fair and unbiased. In the case of implementation, Secretariat personnel face the even more delicate task of negotiating with member-state governments to secure behavioral changes. These efforts are especially difficult in quiet diplomacy, where the implementation of peacekeeping missions and peaceful settlement initiatives often must take place with many key political questions left unresolved by the Security Council and General Assembly (Ziring, Riggs, and Plano, 2000, p. 123; Grey, 2000, pp. 46–47). A similar difficulty arises in situations where the Secretariat is mandated to monitor member-state compliance with UN objectives, as with treaties on human rights, the environment, and disarmament (Ameri, 1996, p. 130; Ziring, Riggs, and Plano, 2000, p. 124). Often the Secretariat has only limited access to information in these efforts and must rely on member states to self-report in good faith; Secretariat personnel must exercise careful judgment as to what information meets standards of accuracy and quality so that it can be used to assess performance. While none of the duties associated with implementation are easy, carrying them out effectively, efficiently, and without fanfare can generate more requests for the same (Ziring, Riggs, and Plano, 2000, p. 122), thereby further increasing the political influence of the Secretariat.

The third set of tasks that allow the Secretariat to participate in UN decisionmaking typically remain behind the scenes and have to do with the use of information and advice. The Secretariat's duty to maintain impartiality in preparing official reports for policymaking bodies has already been discussed; however, its role in these areas extends far beyond this public sphere. These activities are so important that H. G. Nicholas concludes, "The collection, ordering, and providing of information at the points where it is most needed and can produce its greatest effect is one of the most important services that UN officials discharge" (1975, p. 169). He goes on to argue that "it is much more than an archivist's or statistician's function; it is political in the highest degree, calling for qualities of political judgment and forethought no less than of accuracy and integrity." Beyond official reports, members of the Secretariat provide private briefings for the secretary-general (Grey, 2000, p. 45) and convey information and advice to delegates (Ameri, 1996, pp. 97, 132). This can include basic clarification, making suggestions, and providing assistance in preparing a speech; such help is of particular use to smaller delegations from developing states or to delegates who do not have a strong expertise or interest in a particular policy area. Much of the time this process of influence occurs through informal exchanges in Secretariat offices, lounges, and corridors and on the margins of official meetings (Alger, 1968, p. 119), so it will receive additional attention in Chapter 8.

On some occasions this type of interaction between Secretariat officials and delegates expands beyond informal channels to involve active and explicit contributions from both parties as a debate unfolds. Often this arises from a conscious decision on the part of delegates to request extensive Secretariat input, based on the expertise and diplomatic skill of key officials (Ameri, 1996, p. 94; Jacob, Atherton, and Wallenstein, 1972, p. 36). One clear example of this occurred in 1991, when the General Assembly was trying to draft a new resolution specifying the conditions under which the United Nations would engage in humanitarian assistance. The compromise language that emerged was largely a product of the efforts of one particular Secretariat official, Ed Tsui, who was brought into the process by the chair of the relevant working group, Jan Eliasson (Khalikov, 1998). In such situations, the service of the Secretariat official extends beyond giving information and advice to include actually drafting the text of a resolution (Ameri, 1996, p. 125; Alger, 1968, p. 119), though national delegates may end up taking public credit for their efforts (Kaufmann, 1988, p. 110).

Challenges Facing the Secretariat

These various contacts allow Secretariat officials to have a rather direct impact on the subsequent policy debates, but in some cases the flow of information between delegates and the Secretariat becomes two-way to the extent that the independence of an official becomes compromised (Ameri, 1996, pp. 97, 132). These and other challenges facing the Secretariat are the subject of the final section of this chapter. There are extensive discussions of the challenges associated with recruiting and managing high-level members of the international civil service (see, e.g., Reymond and Mailick, 1985); only a few of the most pressing issues will be mentioned here, especially in terms of how they affect the ability of Secretariat personnel to perform the functions just discussed.

By far the single greatest difficulty in recruiting professional staff for the UN is the need to balance merit with geography. This has been true ever since the UN staff was first constituted in 1945–1946 (Bailey, 1962, pp. 80–101). To provide some semblance of order to an otherwise chaotic process, a "desirable range" formula was initiated in 1948 to allow each member state to be confident that at least some of its nationals could gain employment with the Secretariat. The range for each member was determined based on its budgetary assessment, which in turn was based on its economic conditions and population (Luard and Heater, 1994, p. 114; Narasimhan, 1988, p. 300). Not all professional posts were included in this arrangement, but these allotments had the effect of radically altering the composition of the Secretariat, so that it was far less dominated by European and American states as the membership of the organization changed (Peterson, 1986, pp. 169–170). Even though the process through which the "desirable ranges" are calculated has been modified periodically (Ameri, 1996, pp. 105–106), this system still serves as a guide for the secretary-general when it comes to selecting personnel for many Secretariat posts.

A result of the "desirable range" formula is that some posts are filled by individuals who have the right nationality rather than the right qualifications (Luard and Heater, 1994, p. 114). This tendency is made worse by two further difficulties associated with recruiting highly qualified Secretariat personnel. The first of these relates to the highest policymaking posts at the under- and assistant-secretary-general level, which have always been seen as the turf of certain members (Bailey, 1962, pp. 68–80). This trend was initiated by the permanent five, which had no expectation of having one of their nationals serve as secretary-general but had a very strong desire to make sure their nationals were employed at the highest levels of the UN (Peterson, 1986, pp. 170–171; Ziring, Riggs, and Plano, 2000, pp. 117–118). In the years since, the number of states seeking to secure high-level posts for their nationals has expanded to include other developed states and regional powers within the developing world (Rivlin, 1993, pp. 9–10).

A second difficulty is that a number of members have compromised the career nature of the international civil service by demanding that their nationals serve in the Secretariat for fixed-term appointments of only three to five years (Kay, 1968, pp. 228–231; Zyss, 1998, p. 62). Some members, in particular developing states, have justified this practice by arguing that they simply cannot afford to have their best and brightest personnel serve at the UN for their entire career when their skills are much needed and scarce back in their home country. Other states, particularly those of the former Soviet bloc, were accused of using fixed-term appointments to limit the independence of their nationals in the Secretariat, since these individuals knew that they would be rotating back to their home government later. There are some positive benefits for the UN in accepting these "secondments," including greater diversity of personnel and a provision of personnel beyond normal staffing levels; however, these arrangements are often criticized since they can compromise the loyalty language of Article 100. Fortunately, the percentage of Secretariat personnel serving in fixed-term appointments has decreased to less than 25 percent in recent years (Ziring, Riggs, and Plano, 2000, p. 118).

These issues related to recruitment can affect the ability of the Secretariat to perform the roles discussed above, because they can result in a less qualified staff than recruitment by merit alone would generate. These practices are especially problematic when governments exert implicit or explicit pressure on the secretary-general as personnel decisions are made (Ameri, 1996, p. 383). Hammarskjöld argued that some assistance from governments in determining the qualifications of their nationals for UN posts can be helpful; however, this role is often abused when governments nominate only one candidate for a post rather than offering the secretary-general a choice among well-qualified individuals (1968, p. 222). Unfortunately, government pressure can take on even more overt forms, as in the 1950s when the US government forced Trygve Lie to dismiss eighteen US citizens who worked at the UN in the wake of Senator Joseph McCarthy's anticommunist hearings (Luard and Heater, 1994, pp. 114–115; Beigbeder, 1988, pp. 48–50; Ameri, 1996, pp. 138–141). This episode, which is far from an isolated case (Ziring, Riggs, and Plano, 2000, p. 120), had a disastrous effect on Secretariat morale and made it far more difficult for its members to perform important political functions once their independence had been compromised and their loyalty questioned. Whenever these pillars are diminished, member states are less likely to view the Secretariat as an impartial source of information, an honest broker in cases of conflict, or a constructive participant in the global dance.

Aside from difficulties in recruitment, some challenges associated with managing an international secretariat can limit the ability of its personnel to influence decisionmaking. The most important of these challenges center on the heterogeneous nature of the organization's staff; not only do they possess different expectations, experiences, and skills, but they also have different cultural backgrounds (Beigbeder, 1988, p. 6; Reymond and Mailick, 1985, pp. 17–19). Problems of leadership style, language, motivation, and accepted behavior, among others, can make the staff hard to manage and coordinate. These problems are made worse by the fact that many top-level Secretariat officials have their own loyalties and constituencies independent of the organization and the secretary-general (Cox, 1969, pp. 218–222). Different members of the UN staff can actually be working toward different outcomes, thereby making an already difficult policy process even more challenging. And of course, general management and coordination problems are to be expected in any large organization that faces complex tasks (Ameri, 1996, pp. 411–412), and overcoming these has been a recurring goal of nearly every secretary-general. Of special concern is to make sure all of the Secretariat's agencies, departments, and offices are speaking with one voice on areas of mutual concern—an undertaking that has fallen under the purview of the former Administrative Committee on Coordination (ACC), now known as the Chief Executives Board for Coordination (White, 2002, pp. 101–105). These efforts represent an ongoing challenge, as many agencies and programs within the UN system try to maintain as much autonomy as possible.

Secretary-General Kofi Annan has made important strides in streamlining and rationalizing some parts of the Secretariat as part of his "quiet revolution" initiated during his first months in office in 1997 (Beigbeder, 2000, pp. 212–219; Ziring, Riggs, and Plano, 2000, pp. 136–138). His efforts have been well regarded by member states, have increased staff morale, and have led to a more efficient and effective Secretariat. A second round of reforms was begun in 2002, early in his second term.

Annan's reforms have helped to ameliorate some persistent management problems, but they cannot ensure that member states will refrain from pressuring members of the Secretariat in the performance of their duties. Problems of recruitment and management will continue as the UN's staff seeks to participate in the work of its political organs. And of course, the Secretariat is not alone in its desire and ability to influence member states at the United Nations; similar issues arise in relation to nongovernmental organizations and other civil society actors, which are the subject of attention in Chapter 5.

5

Civil Society and the Private Sector

THE OPENING LINE OF THE UNITED NATIONS CHARTER, "WE THE PEOPLES," is followed by an inspiring preamble that never limits its focus to governments or states. It serves as a powerful reminder that issues of peace and security and social and economic cooperation are relevant to all global actors, not just the UN's members and its staff. While much of the UN's political machinery is designed to provide its members with forums for debate and action, the UN's work necessitates input and assistance from a wide range of civil society and private sector entities. The most significant of these nonstate actors in the political processes of the United Nations are nongovernmental organizations (NGOs) and multinational corporations (MNCs). The important and growing role played by NGOs and MNCs in the global dance is not surprising: interdependence and globalization have made civil society and private sector actors, along with states, the institutional "pillars" of contemporary global governance (Muldoon, 2004, p. 9). Each of these actors has much to offer the UN, and their efforts to influence outcomes must be considered when one is studying UN decisionmaking.

Understanding the role that civil society and private sector actors play in multilateral diplomacy is complicated by some degree of conceptual confusion as to what these actors actually are. Civil society is often seen as including all organizations and groups that operate in a sphere separate from state control, but there is disagreement as to whether businesses are included in this category. The most common view is that civil society includes "all non-profit, voluntary citizens' groups organized on a local, national, regional or international basis, excluding those defined as the private sector" (Nelson, 2002, pp. 17–18). In this view, civil society and the private sector are distinct entities that pursue different goals and operate based on different rules of the game. However, the lines between these entities are often blurry. While companies may not be considered part of civil society, their trade and industry associations often are, despite the fact that they are funded and directed by corporate interests. Likewise, even though many civil society actors actively campaign against the actions and behaviors of companies, some in fact receive extensive funding from the private sector. These interconnections are further complicated by the fact that both civil society and the private sector encompass a wide range of actors. Civil society includes, among other things, social movements, community-based organizations, trade unions, philanthropic foundations, universities and research institutes, youth organizations, and faith-based groups (Nelson, 2002, p. 18). Likewise, the private sector includes all for-profit enterprises, from local mom-and-pop stores serving a single neighborhood to Fortune 500 companies with a global presence. Fortunately, only a subset of each of these types of actors participates in UN processes, either as NGOs or MNCs, and they will be the focus of the following discussion.

Two fundamental questions must be considered before we begin to investigate the role of nonstate actors in UN decisionmaking. First, why do these actors seek to expend part of their limited resources by targeting or working through the United Nations? This is an important issue, for "contact with and influence on the United Nations system is the raison d'être of many NGO coalitions and a substantial part of the activity of many others" (Ritchie, 1996, p. 180). NGOs are often said to have a more values-based mindset and a longer-term orientation to their work than do states (Sankey, 1996, p. 270), but NGOs can find state-dominated international governmental organizations (IGOs) like the UN to be important venues for pursuing their goals (Cook, 1996, pp. 181–185). This is true for several reasons: (1) the political processes of IGOs can provide the international community with commonly accepted standards of behavior, which NGOs can then use as benchmarks to monitor state behavior; (2) IGOs can offer NGOs a forum to expose violations and confront recalcitrant parties; and (3) IGOs are multilateral meeting spots, allowing NGOs opportunities to interact with many states and other NGOs in one setting. International businesses have been slower to realize the benefits of working with IGOs; however, a growing number are moving in this direction, based on both tangible and intangible benefits (Nelson, 2002, pp. 38–40). Besides viewing the UN as a potential customer due to its procurement needs, some MNCs understand that the norms and treaties created through UN processes can influence their business environment in positive and negative ways. In addition, certain MNCs view their work with and through the United Nations as a way to uncover new market opportunities, enhance their reputation, reduce the risks associated with political instability, and benefit from the UN's development expertise.

These reasons that NGOs and MNCs seek to participate in UN decisionmaking are persuasive and compelling but leave unanswered a second fundamental question: why is the UN—both its member states and its staff—receptive to these efforts? While the enthusiasm for NGOs and MNCs displayed by individual member states and staff officials certainly varies, the UN has become increasingly interested in, and in some cases even dependent upon, the activities of nonstate actors. Michael Edwards says that UN agencies see cooperation with nonstate actors as "good for business" because "operational partnerships and a broader policy dialogue [with these actors] contribute to more efficient project implementation and a lower rate of failure, a better public image, and more political support" (2000, p. 208). In general, involving these actors in UN processes means that they lend greater support for UN values and activities—and they bring different sets of skills and resources from those possessed by the UN, its members, and its staff. In the words of Barbara Adams, "NGOs have been supporters and publicists for the UN, advocates for the UN, critics of the UN, implementers or participants in UN programs; they provide funding, expertise, consultancy and advocacy for equity and justice" (1994, p. 176). While it is certainly premature to say that the same is true for MNCs, the fundamental point of this chapter is that civil society and private sector actors are becoming such active players in the global dance that their influence on the emerging routines of global policymaking must be explored. The following sections will provide background information on NGOs and MNCs, discuss in detail the mechanisms through which they participate in the UN's political processes, and then briefly consider some remaining obstacles they face in their efforts to influence outcomes.

▓ Nongovernmental Organizations

One of the most dramatic transformations in international politics across the last century is the exponential growth in the number of nongovernmental organizations operating both within and across state borders. Citing the *Yearbook of International Organizations* for 1999–2000, A. LeRoy Bennett and James Oliver identify over 5,800 international NGOs and an additional 5,500 domestic NGOs that are internationally oriented (2002, p. 282). These numbers compare to only five international NGOs in 1850, 330 in 1914, 730 in 1939, and 2,300 in 1970 (Jacobson, 1979, p. 11). While there are potentially numerous reasons for this expansion, Leon Gordenker and Thomas Weiss highlight three key changes in the late twentieth century that caused the number of NGOs to more than double in thirty years: the rise of new actors and issues on the international agenda after the end of the cold war, greater ease of information exchange and travel due to technological developments, and the growing resources available to and the increasing professionalism of the NGO community (1996b, pp. 24–25).

While scholars and practitioners agree that NGOs are proliferating on the global scene, there is considerably less agreement on exactly what these organizations are: "confusion or ignorance persists as to the definition of the participants and the nature of their relationship to the UN system and to one another" (ibid., p. 18). Many studies of NGOs lack a strong theoretical footing and a clear analytical focus; as a result there is inconsistency even in the choice of basic terminology. Some observers have described NGOs as "interest groups" or "pressure groups," drawing on the literature regarding similar types of groups operating within a domestic political system (Willetts, 1996c, p. 2; Ziring, Riggs, and Plano, 2000, p. 70). However, the range of supposed synonyms for NGOs is more far reaching, including "grassroots organizations," "private voluntary organizations," "transnational social movements," and the "independent sector" (Gordenker and Weiss, 1996b, p. 18). Compounding these conceptual difficulties is the fact that some writers have offered typologies that subdivide NGOs on the basis of several important distinctions: domestic versus international scope, not-for-profit versus business focus, institutionalized versus ad hoc structure, private associations versus some government involvement, and so on (for example see Willetts, 1996c, p. 8; Ziring, Riggs, and Plano, 2000, p. 70; Gordenker and Weiss, 1996b, pp. 20–21). These persistent differences represent an obstacle to the accumulation of knowledge about the role of NGOs in international politics.

In light of these difficulties, many writers who discuss these actors conclude that the best route is to simply adopt the UN's use of the term "nongovernmental organization" (Gordenker and Weiss, 1996b, p. 18). While this may gloss over important distinctions, it anchors the discussion in the language and definitions found in the UN Charter and subsequent resolutions (more on these below). Scholars have turned to these UN documents in search of guidance as to how the term "nongovernmental organization" can be defined in contradistinction to international governmental organizations on the one hand and other nonstate actors like MNCs, criminal organizations, political parties, and social movements on the other hand (Jacobson, 1979, pp. 5, 10; Gordenker and Weiss, 1996b, pp. 18–20; Willetts, 1996c, pp. 3–5). NGOs are private associations that individuals voluntarily join based on a shared interest in pursuing certain goals; they have a formal structure and procedures for decisionmaking, but they are nonprofit and nonviolent. This conceptualization of NGOs excludes all actors that are ad hoc, commercial, violent, government supported, or intent on gaining political power. The discussion that follows focuses on the functions and activities of NGOs that are international (either through a membership drawn from more than one state or a scope of concern that transcends state borders) and have the desire to influence political debates at the United Nations.

Obviously, a diversity of organizations are included in the definition just offered—and even when our focus is narrowed to international NGOs that seek to participate in the UN's global dance, we still find great diversity. Dimensions of variation include their size, geographic roots, scope of concern, functional goals, organizational structure, and sources of funding (Aviel, 1999b, pp. 156–157; Gordenker and Weiss, 1996b, pp. 40–43; Conca, 1996, pp. 105–107). Some organizations have thousands of members and enjoy a professionalized staff, others are less structured and are serviced solely by volunteers; some are located near centers of policymaking and endowed with substantial resources, others are community based and more limited in their activities; some see their primary mission in terms of providing relief and services, others focus on policy change at the national and international levels; some exclusively address a single issue, others view problems in an interconnected way and search for coordinated solutions. This list of differences is by no means exhaustive, but it does serve to illustrate the point that each NGO has a particular set of strengths and weaknesses when it comes to participating in the political processes of the United Nations.

The present diversity within the NGO community has much to do with how these actors have emerged over time. Creating an NGO is far easier than creating an intergovernmental body, since NGOs require the mobilization of fewer people and can operate with a far smaller budget and staff (Jacobson, 1979, p. 56). Thus NGOs can emerge rather quickly when a critical mass of individuals identifies a shared issue that must be addressed. This helps to explain why NGOs have deep historical roots and why their global presence far exceeds the number of intergovernmental bodies dealing with similar issues. Some observers identify international NGOs as far back as the seventeenth century (Jacobson, 1979, p. 56); however, it was not until the second half of the nineteenth century that a sufficient number of NGOs were active that they could be considered a nascent force in international politics (Seary, 1996, p. 15). These NGOs were concerned primarily with social issues, so it is not surprising that their relationships with intergovernmental bodies began to form as economic and social questions assumed a more prominent place on the agenda of international diplomacy.

Much of this emerging practice was reflected in the relationship between NGOs and the League of Nations. While the League Covenant limited formal recognition of NGOs to a few specific cases, such as Article 25 on the establishment of national Red Cross organizations, the activity of NGOs in regard to issues on the League's agenda was "an established fact" that was recognized at least on an informal level (Seary, 1996, p. 22). NGOs were invited to some League meetings and given the opportunity to share with the League Assembly resolutions that they had prepared. In addition, NGOs were able to maintain "assessors" on some League committees who enjoyed all the privileges of government representatives except the right to vote. Unfortunately, these arrangements were far more common in the early years of the League, as "the interaction between the League and international NGOs changed from one of NGOs supporting and contributing to the policy work of the League to one where the League was less interested in the opinions of NGOs but more willing to provide information for and about them" (Seary, 1996, p. 23). Committees created in the 1930s in an effort to make the League more effective were generally less receptive to NGOs than their predecessors had been.

Given this retrenchment, NGOs had essentially no role in the early discussions on the creation of the United Nations during World War II (Seary, 1996, p. 25). The earliest drafts of what was to become the UN Charter circulated at the Dumbarton Oaks conference of 1944 omitted any reference to the role of nongovernmental organizations in the work of the UN (Stephenson, 2000, pp. 273–275). However, this situation was remedied during the San Francisco conference in 1945, due to two developments. First, the United States, United Kingdom, and Soviet Union were looking for a way out of an impasse regarding the relationship among the International Labour Organization (a UN specialized agency), workers' unions, and the United Nations. Second, the US State Department wanted to build broad public support for the new organization so as to avoid the Senate defeat that had befallen the League; its strategy for doing so involved consultation with numerous citizens' groups, including having representatives from forty-two NGOs serve as members of the US delegation to the Charter drafting conference. The result of these pressures was Article 71 of the Charter, which authorizes the Economic and Social Council (ECOSOC) to form consultative arrangements with international and national NGOs "which are concerned with matters within its competence."

While Article 71 was an important victory for NGOs, it is best viewed as simply a starting point for thinking about the relationship between NGOs and the UN system. As will be discussed later in this chapter, the mechanisms through which NGOs participate in and influence the political processes of the UN have undergone considerable expansion beyond Article 71 since the Charter was written. While the process has been anything but smooth and steady, much of the expansion is due to the fact that NGOs perform a number of important functions in international politics that can benefit and contribute to the work of the United Nations (Grey, 2000, pp. 47–50). These functions occur at all stages of the policy process, from generating policy options to providing for implementation in the field (see for example Gordenker and Weiss, 1996b, pp. 36–40; Bennett and Oliver, 2002, pp. 283–284). This is especially true for large professionalized NGOs like Amnesty International (see Thakur, 2001), but it also applies to NGOs that enjoy only limited resources and capacities.

In the early stages of the UN policy process, NGO activity includes an information and advocacy function. In terms of information, NGOs excel at adding issues to the global agenda, gathering information, disseminating it to relevant parties, raising awareness among otherwise marginalized groups, and framing the subsequent debate (Schechter, 2001a, p. 207). They can assume a consultative role with intergovernmental actors, since NGOs are often recognized as important sources of new insights and alternative policy ideas based on the expertise they possess in their scope of concern (Adams, 1994, p. 179; Uvin, 1996, p. 166). Informational functions can set the stage for effective advocacy programs on the part of NGOs. Even when they are not asked to contribute to policy formulation, NGOs can insert their ideas into policy debates by lobbying governments and helping to broker agreements among divergent positions (Jacobson, 1979, p. 8; Uvin, 1996, p. 166). While an NGO's ability to engage in advocacy at the international level certainly depends on its resources and the nature of the multilateral forum it seeks to influence, such efforts are becoming an increasingly common aspiration within the NGO community as a whole (Gordenker and Weiss, 1996b, p. 39).

The functions of nongovernmental organizations also extend to the later stages of the policy process. For example, NGOs historically have had some responsibilities dealing with treaty implementation (ibid., pp. 37–39; Uvin, 1996, pp. 167–169). These efforts tend to center on monitoring state compliance, whether it be in regard to human rights, the environment, or any other global problem where compliance rests on the good faith of the parties to the treaty. NGOs often work hard at building and maintaining their reputation, since it is the perceived quality of their information that can provide them with access and influence in the political bodies of intergovernmental organizations. In addition, many NGOs have an operational or service function that brings them into close contact with both the people they are trying to help and the field staff of the UN and other IGOs (Uvin, 1996, p. 169). These operational functions can include actually dispersing the resources and funds provided by IGOs or engaging in joint decisionmaking in the field such that the efforts of NGOs and IGOs avoid duplication and waste.

From this brief overview of the functions performed by NGOs in international politics, it is clear that there are many reasons that NGOs would desire to be active participants in the global dance of UN politics. Before turning to a discussion of the mechanisms through which this participation occurs, it is important to consider similar background information regarding multinational corporations.

▥ Multinational Corporations

If the recent growth in the number of NGOs is considered to be a dramatic transformation in international politics, then the global presence of multinational corporations at the beginning of the twenty-first century can only be described as virtually unbelievable. MNCs, also known as transnational corporations (TNCs), are international businesses whose subsidiaries engage in production and marketing activities in more than one state. In other words, these organizations don't merely trade internationally, they operate internationally. By any measure, the global presence of MNCs at the turn of the century is astounding. According to James Muldoon Jr., data from the UN Conference on Trade and Development (UNCTAD) identifies "63,000 parent firms with 630,000 foreign affiliates and multitudes of inter-firm arrangements" (2004, p. 175). In terms of sheer size, as of 1998 there were nine MNCs that had annual revenues in excess of $100 billion each, with the largest (General Motors at $161 billion) exceeding the gross national product of all but twenty-three countries in the world (Bennett and Oliver, 2002, p. 277).

Not only are the largest MNCs massive in size, they are also becoming increasingly international in character. According to UNCTAD's transnationality index, which measures the percentage of total assets, sales, and employment that are foreign, on average the top 100 MNCs increased from 51 percent to 54 percent transnational across the 1990s (Muldoon, 2004, p. 175). It is often assumed that many MNCs, especially the most successful ones, are large companies operating in traditional economic sectors such as banking, energy, automobile manufacturing, and technology. However, this assumption is erroneous in this age of interdependence and globalization (Bennett and Oliver, 2002, pp. 277–278). Despite the overwhelming size of the largest MNCs, the majority of MNCs employ only 250 people or fewer and are concentrated in service industries like real estate, law, insurance, software support, customer service, food retailing, and office cleaning.

As the characteristics of MNCs have evolved, so too has their relationship with international organizations like the United Nations. Prior to World War II the dominant actors in international business had been cartels composed of a number of producers who decided to coordinate their efforts in order to control the price of a particular set of commodities (Muldoon, 2004, pp. 169–174). However, the liberal postwar economic system designed at Bretton Woods in 1944 created an environment in which large companies, mainly from the United States, were well positioned to take advantage of global free trade. What had been essentially national companies whose only previous international activity had been trade began to see benefits in operating on a truly global scale. By the early 1970s, MNCs had emerged as powerful players in the world economy; they were often seen as "highly centralized and exploitative behemoths that entered into decidedly unequal relationships with host countries" (Bennett and Oliver, 2002, p. 278). Various complaints were made about MNCs, from their practice of repatriating profits to the home state to their unwillingness to transfer important technologies and skills to the local workforce. A number of newly independent countries in the 1960s came to view MNCs as a necessary evil: they certainly brought in investment, jobs, technology, and skills, but they did so based on their needs rather than on the development priorities of the host countries.

Two major efforts to give the developing world a greater voice in the global economy, the original UNCTAD meeting in 1964 and the call for a new international economic order (NIEO) ten years later, ended without progress on the issue of MNC behavior. As a result, attention at the United Nations centered on two other mechanisms created in the mid-1970s: an intergovernmental Commission on Transnational Corporations and a Center on Transnational Corporations in the Secretariat (Bennett and Oliver, 2002, pp. 280–281). The first two tasks of the UN Commission on Transnational Corporations were to develop a definition of TNCs and then to draft a code of conduct for regulating their behavior (Rubin, 1977; Haufler, 2002, pp. 164–165). Since there was agreement between developed and developing states that such a code was desirable in general, it was expected that the work of the commission would proceed apace. However, this expectation proved to be incorrect regarding both the definition and the code. In the case of the definition, an intractable dispute emerged between capitalist and socialist states as to whether state-owned industries were TNCs and therefore subject to any regulations that would be drafted by the commission. Despite this disagreement, the commission decided to work on the code, assuming that its provisions would be broadly applicable to most entities involved in the internationalized production of goods and services. At this point, however, disagreement emerged between developed and developing states regarding the content and authority of the code (whether it would be voluntary or binding), and little progress was made in the commission in the late 1970s, other than a few divisive votes on side issues such as investment in South Africa (Bennett and Oliver, 2002, p. 281; Haufler, 2002, p. 165).

By the 1980s feelings about the NIEO were so polarized that it became "unfashionable" to talk about "codes of conduct" for MNCs, at least in certain circles (Sikkink, 1986, p. 815). Yet in this period one surprising breakthrough emerged: a 1984 agreement between Nestlé and the International Nestlé Boycott Committee (an NGO coalition), negotiated by the World Health Organization (WHO) and UNICEF, which created a code of conduct for how Nestlé would market its infant formula in developing countries. This success created some hope that a long-delayed effort to draft a pharmaceutical code of conduct in WHO would gain new momentum, but the unique constellation of actors and timing that lead to the infant formula code was not present in regard to other issues (ibid., p. 837). Work on a broader code in the Commission on Transnational Corporations stalled in 1985, despite agreement on about 80 percent of its contents (Haufler, 2002, p. 165), due to continued substantive differences and procedural mistakes in the negotiations (Dell, 1989, pp. 73–74). By 1992 both the commission and the Center on Transnational Corporations had been disbanded (Bennett and Oliver, 2002, p. 281).

These failed attempts to create a code of conduct for MNCs at the United Nations resulted in some degree of suspicion and mistrust between these actors through the 1990s. However, the unequal effects of globalization, especially noticeable in recent years, have prompted a renewed interest in forming some sort of partnership between the UN and the private sector. There are numerous reasons these partnerships can be positive for both MNCs and the United Nations. As was mentioned in the introduction to this chapter, MNCs can gain a variety of benefits: a new customer based on UN procurement needs, access to new markets with less risk based on UN development expertise, an enhanced reputation based on adherence to UN principles, and greater input into the development of key global norms and treaties drafted in UN bodies (Nelson, 2002, pp. 38–40). On a similar note, the UN can benefit from the involvement of MNCs in both drafting and implementing global standards, since the support of the private sector is just as important as that of governments when it comes to making sure that UN principles are upheld. After all, international businesses can act as both creators and guardians of international regimes related to their sphere of activity (Haufler, 2000).

As is the case with NGOs, these incentives for interaction between the United Nations and the private sector have resulted in various mechanisms that enable MNCs to participate in the political processes of the UN. Some of these efforts are only in the beginning stages, such as the Global Compact Initiative launched by the secretary-general in 1999 (Ruggie, 2003, pp. 309–313; Nelson, 2002, pp. 133–148). Others have become quite institutionalized, such as MNCs' practice of forming international business and trade associations, like the International Chamber of Commerce, which use structures and strategies at the United Nations that are quite similar to those of NGOs (Muldoon, 2004, p. 183; Nelson, 2002, pp. 63–74; Hocking and Kelly, 2002). For this reason the following section of this chapter will discuss the mechanisms of participation for NGOs and MNCs simultaneously, highlighting some differences along the way.

■ Mechanisms of Participation and Influence

The United Nations and its member states are certainly aware of the need to provide mechanisms through which nonstate actors can participate in the organization's political processes. Speaking to the annual conference of NGOs at UN headquarters in 1994, Secretary-General Boutros Boutros-Ghali began, "Dear friends, on behalf of the United Nations and for myself, I welcome you. I want you to consider this your home" (quoted in Alger, 2003, p. 407). This sentiment, while not universally shared, is a result of the developments discussed above: the proliferation of nonstate actors working on UN-related issues and the important functions they perform. These actors certainly operate from a position of disadvantage vis-à-vis member states due to their lack of decisionmaking power; nonetheless, they make both positive and negative contributions to UN activities. As was mentioned before, this participation can occur throughout the policy process, from agenda setting to policy formulation to policy implementation (Willetts, 1996b, pp. 45–49). To put it another way, nonstate actors attempt to influence all types of UN bodies, from the high-profile meetings of "captains and kings" to the "less glamorous committees" that try to make sure "well-meaning declarations are implemented in practice" (Sankey, 1996, p. 273). The following pages will discuss six mechanisms through which this participation and influence operates: Article 71 and consultative status, arrangements in other UN deliberative bodies, offices in the Secretariat, parallel meetings at global conferences, implementation in the field, and informal networking.

Article 71 and Consultative Status
The most explicit, formal, and established mechanism for the participation of NGOs in the work of the United Nations is provided for in Article 71 of the UN Charter, which authorizes the Economic and Social Council to "make suitable arrangements for consultation with non-governmental organizations which are concerned with matters within its competence." This article was included largely based on the role played by some 1,200 voluntary organizations that were present at the founding UN conference in 1945 (Alger, 1999, p. 393). Early in 1946, the General Assembly followed up on the San Francisco conference and recommended that ECOSOC adopt arrangements for this consultation. ECOSOC responded at its first session, setting up a twelve-member Committee on Arrangements for Consultation with NGOs (Stephenson, 2000, p. 275). The committee quickly prepared a report that was passed by ECOSOC in June 1946. It defined which organizations would be accepted into consultative status: those that were concerned with matters under ECOSOC's competence, had goals in conformity with those of the Charter, and represented a substantial proportion of the people and interests in their field (Willetts, 1996b, p. 32). In addition, the report suggested that the NGOs should be international in structure but that national NGOs might be accepted if they were not part of a larger international organization. Thus single-country NGOs have always been part of the system set up by ECOSOC, though they have been fewer in number.

Despite this rapid progress in identifying NGOs eligible for consultative status, it was not until February 1950 that ECOSOC passed Resolution 288B(X), which specified what the consultative arrangements would look like (Stephenson, 2000, p. 276). NGOs were divided into three categories: in category A were those that had "a basic interest in most of the activities of the Council," in category B were those with "a special competence" in a few fields of activity, and in category C were those primarily concerned "with the development of public opinion and with the dissemination of information" (Willetts, 1996b, p. 32). These arrangements failed to anticipate the controversies that emerged regarding the political activities of some category C organizations, so this category was soon replaced by a Registry of NGOs that were "very specialized and might be consulted on an ad hoc basis" (Ibid.); at the same time, organizations whose purpose was to transmit information back to the public were supposed to be serviced by the Department of Public Information (Stephenson, 2000, p. 276).

While this original system of consultation remains largely intact (Alger, 2003, p. 409), there have been some modifications over time. The first of these came at the end of a major review of NGO arrangements in 1968, when ECOSOC passed Resolution 1296 (XLIV). This resolution reaffirmed which types of NGOs would be eligible for consultative status and identified a twofold goal for these arrangements: to provide expertise and to offer a balanced representation of world public opinion (Stephenson, 2000, p. 278). Resolution 1296 also renamed the three categories of consultative status as Category I, Category II, and the Roster: Category I was for NGOs that were concerned with most of the activities of ECOSOC and could make "sustained" contributions to its work, Category II was for NGOs that were "known internationally" in their field but concerned with only a few areas of ECOSOC work, and the Roster was composed of NGOs that could make "occasional and useful contributions" to the activities of ECOSOC. In 1993 ECOSOC began a comprehensive review of consultative arrangements with the goal, at least in the eyes of some participants, of expanding the role of NGOs at the UN (Alger, 2003, p. 409). The result of this process emerged three years later in the form of Resolution 1996/31, which essentially just renamed two of the three existing categories without expanding NGO mechanisms of participation in any significant manner: Category I became "general consultative status," Category II became "special consultative status," and the Roster remained unchanged (Stephenson, 2000, pp. 288–289). This resolution also emphasized that consultative status is not the same as the "participation without vote" that is accorded to nonmember states and specialized agencies, a fact that further disappointed those NGOs that had hoped 1996/31 would strengthen their standing in the UN (Paul, 1999).

Despite these frustrations, Resolutions 1296 and 1996/31 do offer clear guidelines as to the level of participation each category of NGOs is extended in the political processes of ECOSOC and its subsidiary bodies, including the five regional economic commissions and its functional commissions dealing with human rights, population, and women (Gordenker and Weiss, 1996b, p. 22; Stephenson, 2000, pp. 288–289).

NGOs in the general category have the broadest access to these bodies: they can attend all meetings, submit brief written statements, and, with the permission of the Council, make oral presentations. In addition, general category NGOs can propose items for ECOSOC's agenda to the Committee on NGOs (the same group of nineteen member states that decides which NGOs are eligible for each category of consultative status), which in turn can ask the secretary-general to place these suggestions on the provisional agenda. NGOs in the special category enjoy all of these same rights except for the ability to suggest items for ECOSOC's agenda. Finally, the access of Roster organizations is more limited; they can attend meetings related to their field of competence and submit written statements, but only if invited to do so by ECOSOC or the secretary-general.

According to the website of the NGO Section of the UN Department of Economic and Social Affairs, which monitors NGOs in consultative status with ECOSOC (www.un.org/esa/coordination/ngo/about.htm), there were over 2,300 NGOs that enjoyed general, special, or Roster status as of 2004, with the majority of these found in the final category. It is important to point out that private sector organizations have realized the importance of these consultative arrangements with ECOSOC and have formed nonprofit industry and trade associations to qualify for this status in their own right (Nelson, 2002, pp. 64–65). As of August 2001, about 200 of the NGOs with consultative status were business, trade, professional, or industry-related associations, with the majority of them found in the Roster category. A few private sector organizations, including the International Chamber of Commerce, the International Organization of Employers, the International Federation of Business and Professional Women, and the World Economic Forum, enjoyed general consultative status. Many of the NGOs affiliated with ECOSOC, whether business related or not, have a long tradition of trying to bridge their substantive differences in order to form networks to lobby for improvements in the mechanisms of the UN-NGO relationship itself (Stephenson, 2000, p. 277; Nelson, 2002, p. 65). The most important of these efforts is the Conference of NGOs in Consultative Status with the United Nations (CONGO), which dates to 1948 and has been active at each stage of the evolution of consultative status discussed above.

The fact that many NGOs find consultative status to be desirable suggests that these mechanisms provide important avenues of participation and influence in the political processes of ECOSOC and its subsidiary bodies. However, this judgment must be offered with some degree of caution (Jacobson, 1979, p. 127). In at least some respects, the position of representing an NGO with consultative status and that of representing a member state with the rights of full participation are similar: both can attend meetings, make speeches, and offer written proposals. To this extent the ability of NGOs to influence debate, at least on paper, is comparable to that of member states. However, given their lack of electoral and financial power, NGOs have a weaker base for influence. Not only are their rights of written and oral participation easier to restrict, the fact that their opinions cannot be translated into clear support or opposition in decisionmaking means that their speeches and proposals, even when allowed, may receive scant attention (Kaufmann, 1980, p. 93).

As was mentioned above, some NGOs active at the UN work through the Department of Public Information (DPI) rather than ECOSOC, since their main focus is spreading information about the UN to constituencies around the world. As is the case with consultative status, NGO affiliation with DPI began in 1946 and was reviewed as part of Resolution 1296 in 1968 (Stephenson, 2000, p. 279). According to the website of the NGO section of DPI (www.un.org/dpi/ngosection/brochure.htm), 1,400 organizations took part in this arrangement as of 2004. The interaction between NGOs and DPI is managed by an elected eighteen-member DPI/NGO Executive Committee (Alger, 2003, p. 410). However, this relationship can best be characterized as "receiving rather than giving" (Grey, 2000, p. 49), since these NGOs are not seen as having any special expertise to contribute to the policy formulation process as is sometimes true for NGOs active in ECOSOC (Gordenker and Weiss, 1996b, p. 23; Stephenson, 2000, pp. 279–280). Fortunately, as will be discussed in the following sections, there are other mechanisms of participation and influence available to these actors at the UN.

Access to Other Deliberative Bodies

The Economic and Social Council is intended to be the primary point of contact between nongovernmental organizations and the United Nations, mainly because it was expected that most of these actors would be focused on issues under ECOSOC's domain. This expectation is at least partially substantiated by the fact that the number of NGOs in consultative status with ECOSOC nearly doubled between 1992 and 2002 (Bennett and Oliver, 2002, pp. 290–291). Throughout this time, however, there has been a growing desire on the part of NGOs to expand their access to the two main political bodies at UN headquarters, the General Assembly and the Security Council. Their efforts received an important boost in July 1996, when ECOSOC passed

Resolution 1996/297, calling upon the General Assembly to examine "the question of the participation of non-governmental organizations in all areas of the work of the United Nations" (Stephenson, 2000, pp. 290–291). These discussions were centered in the Open-Ended Working Group on Strengthening the UN System, which formed a subgroup focused directly on the role of NGOs. The subgroup suggested some extension of NGO access to the Assembly and asked the secretary-general to prepare a report on, among other things, the financial implications of greater NGO participation. In response, the Executive Office of the Secretary-General released two reports, one in 1998 and one in 1999; unfortunately, only the second one included any NGO input, and even it did not fundamentally address some of the key issues from the point of view of NGOs (Paul, 1999). On top of this, while member states did offer varying views on expanding NGO participation in theory, they were cool to making further changes in practice (Alger, 2003, p. 409). As a result, ECOSOC Resolution 1996/31 (discussed above) remains the basic document governing NGO access to the principal policymaking organs at the UN, with any changes in practice being "largely informal and incremental" (Stephenson, 2000, p. 291).

In spite of these disappointments, there are some signs of limited progress in the ability of NGOs to participate in and even influence debate in the General Assembly and Security Council. For starters, four NGOs have received a standing invitation from the Assembly to participate as observers in its work: the International Committee of the Red Cross, the International Federation of Red Cross and Red Crescent Societies, the Inter-parliamentary Union, and the Sovereign Military Order of Malta (United Nations, 2003). In addition, CONGO was able to push for an expansion of NGOs' access to the committees of the General Assembly in the late 1980s, arguing that there was nothing in the Assembly's rules of procedure that would prevent NGO participation as long as the bureau running the committee approved (Stephenson, 2000, p. 282). This has resulted in NGOs' appearing as petitioners in the Special Political and De-colonization Committees (now consolidated into the Fourth Committee), the Humanitarian and Cultural (Third) Committee, and the Economic and Financial (Second) Committee (Alger, 2003, p. 412). In addition, NGOs were active in the antiapartheid and anticolonization committees, as well as the Tenth and Twelfth Special Sessions of the General Assembly on disarmament (Stephenson, 2000, p. 282). This NGO access to standing Assembly committees has extended to some bodies set up to deal with specific issues of more limited duration, such as the Working Group on

Financing for Development (Alger, 2003, p. 413) and on occasion has also included being able to address "temporarily suspended" sessions of the plenary itself (Paul, 1999). However, due to the past suspicion with which many member states viewed MNCs (Peterson, 1986, pp. 229, 248), similar practices have not emerged for their direct participation in Assembly committees.

Beyond the General Assembly, NGOs have also sought to participate in the work of the Security Council and have seen some limited success in this regard since the mid-1990s. One important example is the NGO Working Group on the Security Council, which brings roughly thirty NGOs concerned with complex emergencies together with Council members, often including the delegation that serves as Council president each month (Stephenson, 2000, pp. 287–288; Alger, 2003, p. 413). Some high-profile NGOs, such as Amnesty International, have been able to formally brief ad hoc meetings of the Council dealing with humanitarian issues; however, interaction between NGOs and the Council most often occurs through informal meetings based on the interests, personal relationships, and interpersonal styles of the Council president and other key permanent representatives. These mechanisms of cooperation have allowed NGOs to form a "well-established" voice on Security Council issues (Alger, 2003, p 413), possibly even exceeding the influence of consultative status in some cases. The fact that these relationships are not formalized, however, means that they are vulnerable to cycles in Council practice and the whims of individual delegates (Stephenson, 2000, pp. 287–288).

Beyond the main policymaking forums at UN headquarters just discussed (the General Assembly, Security Council, and ECOSOC), there are a number of other agencies, programs, and funds across the UN system that have formed some type of relationship with NGOs, MNCs, or both. The most commonly identified example of this is the International Labour Organization, whose tripartite governance structure allows labor unions and business representatives to participate alongside governments in all aspects of decisionmaking, including voting (Ziring, Riggs, and Plano, 2000, p. 71). Other specialized agencies lack these voting arrangements, but they do provide varying opportunities for nonstate actors to influence debate through some type of consultative procedures. The extent of these contacts depends on the issues involved, with the relatively nonpolitical World Meteorological Organization consulting with only fifteen NGOs and the more political UNESCO interacting with nearly 600 (Bennett and Oliver, 2002, p. 291). In some cases this consultation results in only marginal participation with essentially no influence; however, in UNESCO and some other agencies the role of NGOs extends far beyond the consultative status assigned by ECOSOC. "UNESCO offers privileges that would be unthinkable at the UN," including financial support and policymaking influence, to the extent that NGOs are "associated as closely and as regularly as possible with the various stages of planning and execution of UNESCO's activities coming within their particular field" (Hoggart, 1996, pp. 102–103).

Some examinations of the variation in participation granted to non-governmental actors in different UN bodies consider differences in the nature of the intergovernmental organizations, in particular how much they focus on providing services as opposed to how much they act as policy forums for their members (Tussie and Riggirozzi, 2001, pp. 164–174). The expectation is that service organizations will allow greater participation by NGOs and other nonstate actors in both policy formulation and implementation. There is some support for this view: service-providing organizations like the United Nations High Commissioner for Refugees (UNHCR) have long treated NGOs as equal partners, based on decades of mutual support and respect (Penrose and Seaman, 1996, pp. 248–250), whereas the World Trade Organization (WTO), which really has no services to offer other than policy consultation among its member states, remains "relatively closed" to nonstate actors (Williams, 2000, p. 253)—its only arrangements for consulting these actors are "excessively timid and overcautious" (Tussie and Riggirozzi, 2001, p. 174).

Yet there are some policy forums, such as the UN's Commission on Human Rights and its Commission on the Status of Women (both of which are subsidiary organs to ECOSOC), that have been the scene of intense and sometimes effective lobbying by NGOs (Connors, 1996; Cook, 1996). The same can be said on the issue of the environment: the two main intergovernmental bodies, the United Nations Environment Programme (UNEP) and the Commission on Sustainable Development (CSD), have always identified working with NGOs as a central part of their missions (Conca, 1996, pp. 112–114). In the UNEP, the Environmental Liaison Centre International acts as an information clearing house and has provided NGOs with direct access to some inter-governmental negotiations, including those regarding stratospheric ozone. In addition, since 1985 UNEP's Division of Technology, Industry, and Economics has provided thousands of MNCs and NGOs with the opportunity to engage in joint problem-solving with UNEP and other partners to design effective voluntary solutions to environmental problems such as dealing with hazardous chemical emergencies and promoting sustainable tourism (Nelson, 2002, pp. 89–93). The CSD is a far newer body, formed only in 1992; however, in four short years it used consultative procedures less stringent than those of ECOSOC to accredit over 550 NGOs (Conca, 1996, p. 114). These NGOs can attend meetings, make brief written and oral statements, and, at least in the case of general category organizations, propose agenda items.

One final set of intergovernmental institutions that are technically in the UN family have received a considerable amount of attention regarding their relationships with nonstate actors: the World Bank and the International Monetary Fund (IMF). Both of these organizations have received substantial criticism from the NGO community regarding their methods of operation and their lending practices; however, they are slowly becoming more open to the participation of civil society in their programs. The World Bank has come further in this regard. In 1981 a World Bank–NGO Committee was established, and it has served as an important forum for often spirited interaction on a wide range of policy issues (Cleary, 1996, pp. 70–78). This committee became more assertive in the 1990s, a process that has resulted in more bank consultation regarding the content of structural adjustment programs and the extent to which environmental and good governance issues are taken into account when lending decisions are made. One specific example of this concerns the Global Environmental Facility, which brings together the World Bank, the United Nations Development Programme (UNDP), and UNEP with NGOs and MNCs to design and implement environmentally sustainable development projects valued at nearly $3 billion as of 2002 (Nelson, 2002, pp. 98–102). These efforts to interact with nonstate actors can result in important patterns of influence, but progress in the relationship among NGOs, MNCs, and the World Bank remains in the beginning stages, at least in the eyes of the first two of the these actors (Williams, 2000, p. 248; Cleary, 1996, p. 86; Tussie and Riggirozzi, 2001, p. 167). The situation in regard to the IMF is less developed; one executive director of the IMF acknowledged that participation of civil society and private sector actors in the organization remains "in the foothills, and some people want [it] back in the valleys" (quoted in Scholte, 2000, p. 257). There is certainly an increasing range of contacts emerging between these actors, with IMF staff regularly exchanging views with national industrial associations and chambers of commerce. However, the Fund has tried to manage these contacts in unhelpful ways by "educating" and "correcting" its critics rather than truly engaging in a dialogue with them (Scholte, 2000, pp. 258–261). These actors may be participating in the IMF, but they are not influencing its decisionmaking.

Offices in the Secretariat

A third mechanism for participation and influence of nonstate actors in the political processes of the United Nations involves contact with liaison offices spread throughout the different offices and departments of the UN Secretariat. The number of UN offices devoted at least in part to interaction and consultation with these actors, especially NGOs, has proliferated across the history of the UN, especially as the potential contributions of these actors has become clearer to both member states and UN staff. Based on data from a 1990 UN report, Chadwick Alger has identified ninety-two such offices in the UN system, spread across eighteen different cities (1994, pp. 308–309; 1999, pp. 396–398). These include eight general service offices in New York, Geneva, and Vienna; fifty-four liaison offices in substantive departments in these same cities plus Rome and Nairobi; six UNEP regional offices; five offices of the UN's Regional Economic and Social Commissions, which report to ECOSOC; and nine liaison offices in UN specialized agencies such as those discussed in the previous section. These offices are focused on twenty-six different issues on the UN's agenda, including aging, apartheid, children, cooperatives, crime, decolonization, desertification, development, disabilities, disaster relief, disarmament, emergency situations, environment, family, food/hunger, human rights, human settlements, law of the sea, migrant workers, narcotic drugs, Palestinian rights, peace studies, population, refugees, social development, and welfare policies.

While it is certainly not possible to survey all these offices, some of them merit special attention due to their strategic location and critical areas of focus. First on this list would be two NGO sections, one in the office of the Department of Economic and Social Affairs that services ECOSOC and the other in the Department of Public Information (Paul, 1999). These offices both supervise the processes of NGO accreditation discussed above, although the ECOSOC NGO section does so in consultation with ECOSOC's intergovernmental NGO Committee whereas the DPI section does so solely through the Secretariat. Both of these offices can provide valuable services to NGOs: sharing information and documentation related to key policy debates and helping NGOs secure passes to attend the intergovernmental meetings where these debates occur. Unfortunately, these offices face obstacles in their efforts to assist NGOs, including a lack of resources, political pressures from certain member states, cumbersome procedures, a chaotic process of providing documents, and the surprisingly unhelpful attitude of some staff members. A separate but related point of contact between NGOs and the UN Secretariat is the independent Non-Governmental Liaison Service

(NGLS), which was set up in 1975 with the support of a variety of offices and programs (Willetts, 1996a, p. 287; Paul, 1999). The mandate of NGLS is very broad, since it is designed to offer support to NGOs across the entire UN system; however, in practice much of its focus has been on development-related issues. Despite its small staff and limited resources, NGLS has a strong reputation in the NGO community because it has promoted NGO participation in key negotiations and acted as a buffer between NGOs and some of the more intractable rules and practices associated with certain UN offices, such as the two NGO sections just discussed.

Another important source of contact between nonstate actors and the Secretariat lies in the Executive Office of the Secretary-General. Both Boutros Boutros-Ghali and Kofi Annan offered clear statements of support for the activities of NGOs, with Annan especially calling them the UN's "indispensable partners" (Alger, 2003, p. 414; Paul, 1999). Within the Executive Office, an assistant-secretary-general for external affairs, Gillian Sorensen, assumed the role of coordinator for all civil society issues from 1997 to 2003 and also served as the chair of the Inter-departmental Working Group on NGOs. Such high-level contact is extremely desirable for NGOs, but this office is broadly responsible for all UN contacts with the outside world, and this makes it hard for the office to focus on the specific needs of NGOs. The relationship between NGOs and top UN officials is further complicated by the facts that NGOs have only rarely been consulted on key NGO reports and access rules coming out of the Executive Office, Secretary-General Annan has been unable to meet with NGOs when key areas of dispute arose, and NGOs feel they should not be handled through an office dealing with "external relations" since they are very much internal to the UN's activities (Paul, 1999).

Despite these frustrations, there have been some helpful initiatives from the Executive Office dealing with the UN's relations with nonstate actors, in particular the private sector. Most visible in this regard is the Global Compact, which was proposed in 1999 by Secretary-General Annan in an effort to form a partnership between the UN and MNCs in addressing the unequal effects of globalization (Ruggie, 2003, pp. 309–314; Nelson, 2002, pp. 135–148). The Global Compact is a voluntary initiative that asks businesses to work toward "good practices" in regard to ten principles covering human rights, labor, the environment, and anticorruption, drawn from the Universal Declaration on Human Rights, the ILO's Fundamental Principles and Rights at Work, the Rio Declaration on Environment and Development, and the UN Convention Against Corruption. In order to achieve these goals, the Global

Compact relies on three instruments: learning forums, policy dialogues, and partnership projects. While often seen as an effort to get businesses on board with UN goals, these instruments can provide MNCs and other participants with opportunities to shape UN policies regarding both the content of the Compact (including its expansion to cover corruption) and the ways businesses interact with UN agencies on other issues, such as the efforts of the WHO, the WTO, and the pharmaceutical industry to provide developing nations with less expensive access to HIV/AIDS drugs. The Global Compact is still a young initiative, so its overall contribution to the relationship between the UN and MNCs is yet to be determined; however, the performance of the initiative thus far is quite remarkable, with more than 1,200 companies interacting with numerous NGOs and six different operational offices or agencies at the UN: the ILO, the UNEP, the UNDP, the Office of High Commissioner for Human Rights (OHCHR), the United Nations Industrial Development Organization (UNIDO), and the UN Office on Drugs and Crime (see www.unglobalcompact.org).

Achim Stiener, director-general of the World Conservation Union, addresses the closing session of the Global Compact Leaders Summit held in the General Assembly Hall at UN headquarters on June 24, 2004. Seated on the dais from left to right are: John Ruggie, special adviser to the secretary-general; Secretary-General Kofi Annan; and Julian R. Hunte, president of the 58th Session of the General Assembly. (UN photo #NICA 13010, by Mark Garten)

The diversity of NGO offices in the UN Secretariat has resulted in a wide range of modes for interaction between these actors. Alger has identified fourteen different modes of NGO relations with the Secretariat, including representation on committees, consultation regarding reports and policy proposals, joint research, joint implementation or monitoring of a program, joint training, and symposia on key issues (2003, pp. 414–416). This impressive list is based on the fact that these offices perform a number of important functions (Alger, 1999, p. 396), the two most important of which center on sharing information and consultation in policy processes. In terms of information, NGOs and the Secretariat can provide valuable services for each other (Willetts, 1996a, 288; 1996b, pp. 44–45), and the same is becoming true for businesses as well. For starters, information provided by NGOs that have a special expertise or access on the ground to a key population in need can provide Secretariat officials with a greater ability to shape debates in the UN's deliberative bodies through the reports they compile. Complementing this is the way information provided to NGOs by the Secretariat can enable NGOs to take better advantage of other mechanisms of influence, such as consultative status, global conferences, and informal networking. Turning to consultation, NGOs remain frustrated by the absence of consultation in some key policy areas (Paul, 1999); however, the proliferation of points of contact between the Secretariat and NGOs reflects the fact that a large number of UN staff members understand that NGOs can play a key role in building the coalitions that are necessary to draft and implement policy in multilateral settings (Aviel, 1999b, p. 162–164).

Global Conferences

One of the most dramatic developments in the mechanisms of multilateral diplomacy across the existence of the United Nations is the proliferation of global conferences devoted to specific issues. While the roots of these "conclaves" go back to the League of Nations, Jacques Fomerand indicates that this practice gained significant momentum only after the creation of the United Nations (1996, p. 361). Based on data compiled in 1996, Fomerand identifies nearly forty such conferences held during the UN's first fifty years (ibid., pp. 374–375); this list includes periodic meetings devoted to population, food, and the Law of the Sea as well as "world summits" dealing with the environment, children, and social development. At least twelve such events occurred in the first six years after the end of the cold war, and this trend has continued, though at a less intense pace, at the beginning of the twenty-first century. By some accounts the number of ad hoc global conferences is substantially higher; Peter Willetts, for example, has identified more than 150 in a three-decade period (1996b, p. 49). The procedures of these conferences will receive more attention in Part 2 of the book; for the purposes of this chapter it is important to point out that NGOs have become major players at these events, developing several important mechanisms for influencing all phases of the negotiations.

The participation of NGOs in UN global conferences was rather limited before the 1968 conference in Tehran celebrating the twentieth anniversary of the Universal Declaration of Human Rights (Stephenson, 2000, pp. 280–281). However, CONGO organized a separate NGO conference on human rights in Paris, which became somewhat of a prototype for the "parallel conferences" that NGOs now hold alongside nearly all UN-sponsored summits. In addition to these parallel conferences, NGOs have enjoyed varying degrees of access to the intergovernmental meetings themselves. While each conference is free to set its own rules for NGO access (Schechter, 2001a, p. 192), it is standard practice that all NGOs with consultative status in ECOSOC enjoy similar or even greater levels of participation in these conferences as they do in ECOSOC itself (Willetts, 1996b, p. 49; Stephenson, 2000, p. 289). In addition, it has become relatively common to give the same rights of participation to a wider range of NGOs that lack consultative status and yet are engaged in activities related to the issues of the conference. In the case of the UN Conference on Environment and Development (UNCED) in 1992, 1,420 additional NGOs were accredited (Conca, 1996, p. 111); for the Fourth World Conference on Women and Development in 1995, the figure was 1,299 (Fomerand, 1996, p. 363). This activity resulted in over 35,000 participants in each of these conferences, and it can lead to changes in the NGO accreditation procedures used in decisionmaking bodies, as is reflected by the fact that the Commission on Sustainable Development set up at UNCED has less stringent accreditation procedures than its parent body, ECOSOC (Alger, 2003, p. 417).

Sometimes NGOs have failed to capitalize on this access at global conferences, as was the case with the Second Special Session of the General Assembly on Disarmament in 1988 (Alger, 1994, p. 313). Yet on other occasions, such as the negotiations on the Ottawa Treaty, which bans antipersonnel landmines, and the Rome Statute, which established the International Criminal Court, NGOs have been able to become substantial players with an important impact on the outcomes of these events (Alger, 2003, p. 418; Cooper, English, and Thakur, 2002). This raises an important set of questions: why do NGOs seek to influence these meetings, and why are delegates and UN staff receptive, at least at times, to their efforts? The answer lies in the reciprocal relationship between these actors discussed above: NGOs perform essential functions relating to information and services that can greatly assist overburdened intergovernmental bodies, just as intergovernmental bodies provide NGOs with a forum for influencing both national and international policies (Uvin, 1996, pp. 163–165).

Since NGOs are becoming significant players at these conferences, it is important to examine four mechanisms through which they try to influence the policy outcomes. It is also necessary to consider whether or not these mechanisms are available to other nonstate actors such as MNCs. The first mechanism is involvement of NGOs and other actors in preparatory work for a conference. Some have argued that the "best time to wield influence over a world conference is during the preparatory process—at least 60 percent of the final outcome of a UN global conference is determined during the preparatory process" (Aviel, 1999, pp. 159–160). Fortunately, NGOs are often given considerable freedom to participate directly in preparatory committees, due to their expertise and connections with the grassroots.

A second mechanism for influence is direct participation of nonstate actors in intergovernmental negotiations through their consultative status, discussed above (Alger, 1994, p. 312). This is usually limited to attending meetings and offering written and oral proposals, but it can be an important source of influence in certain circumstances: (1) if the nonstate actor is a particularly important player in regard to the issue, such as General Motors, which was an accredited NGO at UNCED even though it is clearly an MNC (Schechter, 2001, p. 184); (2) if the actor is a coalition of NGOs that have key knowledge or expertise on the issue, as is the case with the Climate Action Network on climate change negotiations (Gupta, 2001, pp. 492–493); and (3) if the meeting is not a subject of public attention, there are few delegates present, and few of the delegates are lawyers (Willetts, 1996b, p. 50).

Another way that NGOs and MNCs can directly participate in the political processes of global conferences is by being included on a national delegation to the meeting, a practice that has been on the rise in global conferences (Adams, 1994, p. 184; Donini, 1996, p. 86). Sometimes the extent of this practice at a particular conference is quite remarkable; at UNCED fourteen countries had NGOs on their delegations (Conca, 1996, p. 111), and at the Cairo Conference on Population and Development in 1994, NGO representatives constituted half of the US delegation (Aviel, 1999, p. 160). Even when nonstate actors are unable to join official delegations, they may still form very close relationships with them based on common interest, as has been the case with certain MNCs and like-minded states (such as Canada, Australia, and oil-exporting countries) on the climate change negotiations (Levy and Egan, 2000, p. 143). Finally, representatives from both NGOs and MNCs can assume leadership positions at global conferences; for example, the president of the International Planned Parenthood Federation chaired one of the preparatory meetings for the Cairo conference (Willetts, 1996b, p. 52), and the organizer of the Business Council for Sustainable Development served as a top adviser to the secretary-general of UNCED, Maurice Strong (Levy and Egan, 2000, p. 142).

A third mechanism for nonstate actors to influence UN-sponsored global conferences is through the parallel conferences mentioned above, a process that involves information sharing and networking. Nearly every parallel conference has included a daily newspaper that is circulated to both NGO participants and official delegates (Alger, 1994, p. 312). One of the most famous examples of this practice is the *Earth Negotiations Bulletin*, which was produced by the International Institute for Sustainable Development during and after UNCED (Gupta, 2001, p. 493); however, earlier examples were present at the 1972 Conference on the Human Environment in Stockholm and the 1974 World Population Conference in Bucharest (Willetts, 1996b, p. 52). These forums allow NGOs an opportunity to frame the debate at intergovernmental meetings, even when they are allowed little access to the negotiations. A related pattern of influence emerges when delegates and conference staff attend events at the parallel NGO conference (Alger, 1994, p. 312; Willetts, 1996b, p. 51). Again, these visits expose officials to a wider range of viewpoints than are often present in the intergovernmental meetings, and they can result in changed attitudes and new policies, as is reflected in some initiatives advanced by World Bank president James Wolfensohn in the years after his contacts with NGOs at the Beijing conference in 1995 (Schechter, 2001, p. 196). Essentially, these contacts help build networks and coalitions among like-minded states, NGOs, and MNCs so that innovative solutions are developed and incorporated into negotiations (Aviel, 1999, p. 161).

A fourth and final mechanism of influence available to NGOs and other nonstate actors at global conferences comes in the implementation of the agreements that are reached. Just as NGOs play a role in the preparatory process and during the conferences themselves, they have also been empowered to play significant roles in the follow-up to the conferences (Schechter, 2001a, pp. 185–191). Michael Schechter argues that NGO participation in implementation is one of the most important determinants of the success or failure of any UN conference. This is true for at least two reasons: (1) the UN is being asked to do more by its members without a corresponding increase in resources or authority, and (2) as was indicated above, NGOs have proved themselves in terms of the contributions they can make in information gathering and monitoring state compliance. Thus both member states and conference secretariats have on occasion encouraged direct NGO participation in these conferences (as was true in regards to the World Summit for Social Development in Copenhagen in 1995), and many conferences have built on a pattern established at UNCED, where the documents negotiated in the intergovernmental meetings contain explicit references to the role played by NGOs in implementation. Such active participation in implementation can lead to influence in the policy process in several ways: NGOs are often consulted as implementation provisions are drafted, NGOs can develop information and expertise that can frame the debate in subsequent follow-up conferences, which are often held on a five- or ten-year cycle, and NGOs can lobby governments at the national level to bring their domestic legislation and practices in line with new international agreements.

Implementation in the Field

Beyond their role in the implementation of agreements created at global conferences, nonstate actors can be valuable partners in the UN's effort to carry out policies mandated by its member states, whether these involve implementing treaties or providing services to vulnerable populations. Chapter 4 noted how latitude regarding implementation of vague policy decisions provides the Secretariat with an important means of indirect influence on the policy process. Much of this reasoning also applies to the NGOs that work with the Secretariat in the field. These partnerships are based on UN agencies and programs' providing resources to NGOs, which in turn contribute to the success (or failure) of the relief work undertaken by the UN (Alger, 2003, p. 402). In the heyday of state-centered approaches to development, UN agencies and NGOs tended to operate in separate worlds, with little constructive interaction (Donini, 1996, pp. 92–94). However, when the crises facing the international community became increasingly complex in the late 1980s, the UNDP, the UNHCR, the United Nations Children's Fund, and the World Food Program all began to treat NGOs as "privileged partners."

While UN agencies have significant advantages, such as working in the name of their member governments to negotiate access to conflict areas, NGOs can offer greater expertise, a better-trained staff, and a more effective relationship with the grassroots in important circumstances (Willetts, 1996b, pp. 48–49; Donini, 1996, p. 94). NGOs also provide the UN with opportunities to implement policies that may be sensitive to certain member states, such as gaining the trust of a particular rebel group or dispensing resources for family planning. When member states are highly committed to an issue and willing to devote sufficient resources, NGO influence will be limited; however, when this willingness is missing, NGOs can assume a central place in the relief effort and in discussions about how to make future policies and programs more effective (Willetts, 1996b, p. 48). Each type of actor has its own specialties, so collaboration on an overall relief plan is often seen as a key step toward improving relief services; unfortunately, "this recent UN and NGO marriage is more a relationship of convenience arranged by the press of events and overbearing donor governments than a passionate romance" (Natsios, 1996, pp. 75–76). These actors often pursue different goals and serve different masters, and both jealously guard their autonomy, so effective coordination is an ongoing challenge. However, these difficulties do not diminish the importance of this burgeoning relationship or the mechanisms of influence that it offers to NGOs.

Informal Networking

The final mechanism that enables nonstate actors to participate in the political processes of the United Nations relates to issues of informal networking that will receive more detailed attention in Chapter 8. However, a few preliminary observations are relevant to this discussion, because, in the words of Adams, "formal mechanisms for NGO presence and participation (and assessment of performance) at the UN [in spite of those just discussed] are very limited compared to the breadth and depth of NGO involvement in world affairs" (1994, p. 177). Given this, "formal contacts between nongovernmental organizations and UN bodies are supplemented by a whole range of informal ones [that] are more important" (Peterson, 1986, p. 228). Since much of the most difficult decisionmaking at the UN takes place in small ad hoc groups and other informal contacts, NGOs have seen these forums as a powerful means for expanding their influence vis-à-vis other actors (Aviel, 1999, p. 162). Furthermore, many NGOs actually seem to prefer working through informal channels for two reasons: (1) NGOs often work through informal networks with each other, so they are quite comfortable in these environments (ibid., p. 159), and (2) it allows them to enjoy the benefits of policy input without having to risk compromising their goals and strategies in order to fit into the more formal and rigid consultative arrangements discussed above (Jönsson and Söderholm, 1996, pp. 133–134). MNCs have also realized the value of using informal consultation to influence multilateral negotiations, as is reflected in the 1986 decision by twelve like-minded chief executives to form the ad hoc Intellectual Property Committee in advance of the Uruguay Round of trade negotiations (Sell, 2000, pp. 93–94).

Informal contacts between nonstate actors and other participants in UN decisionmaking are a pervasive phenomenon that can take a variety of forms across different issues and organizations (Gordenker and Weiss, 1996a, p. 213). They typically emerge based on interpersonal ties among people with similar convictions, goals, and interests, so that "informal links among organizational participants congeal alongside formal structures" (Gordenker and Weiss, 1996b, pp. 26, 34–35). Once formed, these relationships can facilitate coalition building (Jönsson and Söderholm, 1996, p. 130) and provide opportunities for ad hoc meetings among nongovernmental actors, delegates, conference officers, and Secretariat officials (Alger, 2003, p. 413). In addition, contacts can occur on an impromptu basis, since consultative status provides NGOs with access to at least some parts of UN headquarters. While the success of these efforts often depends on the receptiveness of the delegate or official involved, NGOs have become adept at making their presence felt in the back of conference rooms and in the halls and lounges in between meetings (Alger, 1994, p. 307; Paul, 1999). It is especially effective when members of well-regarded NGOs operating on the margins of intergovernmental meetings become "nodes of information and advice" based on their informal contacts with a wide range of governmental delegates, as was the case with Rebecca Johnson from the ACRONYM Consortium during the negotiations that led to the Comprehensive (Nuclear) Test Ban Treaty in 1996 (Ramaker, 1998).

▓ Obstacles to Participation and Influence

This chapter has focused on a wide and expanding range of mechanisms that NGOs and MNCs can use to participate in the global dance and influence the policy routines that emerge from it. However, there are obstacles that continue to limit the participation afforded to these actors, most of which have been mentioned above, at least in a passing fashion. For starters, the growing access offered to nonstate actors, and their improving performance in using it, has resulted in some backlash on the part of governments that want to "constrain and even close down" these mechanisms (Bennett and Oliver, 2002, p. 291). Further, it is hard to assess the overall impact of nonstate actors at the UN, since the relationships between these actors vary across issues and organizations and over time (Cook, 1996, p. 184, Ziring, Riggs, and Plano, 2000, p. 73). The "compartmentalization" of the UN creates numerous points of access, but it is also a source of complexity and inconsistency. This reality presents a dilemma for NGOs: how much of their independence and autonomy can legitimately be sacrificed in hopes of being able to work through the institutions of the UN system (Adams, 1994, p. 185)?

The community of nonstate actors seeking to participate in UN processes has also become increasingly diverse. This is a positive development in that previously marginalized groups are now represented through NGOs based in developing states; however, these actors usually lack the resources necessary to take advantage of many of the mechanisms covered in this chapter (Brühl and Rittberger, 2001, p. 35). In addition, greater diversity has resulted in more internal disagreement within and between nonstate actors; not only do NGOs and MNCs often push in different directions in international organizations (Levy and Egan, 2000, pp. 144–145), but NGOs themselves may have competing proposals that can require them to lobby each other as much as they do governments (Morphet, 1996, p. 138; Schechter, 2001, p. 192). NGOs have been called the "conscience of the world" (Willetts, 1996c), since they often pursue policies focused on human betterment through collective solutions to international problems; however, "not all NGOs are moral or have emancipatory goals, much less are they often accountable or democratic in form" (Schechter, 2001, p. 185). There are serious questions about the motives and accountability of certain NGOs (Edwards, 2000, pp. 210–212), and governments (and even Secretariat officials) are able to use this as a reason to place limits upon the access and participation granted to all NGOs.

These obstacles have led some to observe that "the age of innocence is over for NGOs as they relate to the UN system" (Gordenker and Weiss, 1996a, p. 221). However, others have concluded that in recent years "arrangements for consultations with NGOs have been revised, improved, and extended across the UN system, allowing NGOs decisively to influence international political debates" (Brühl and Rittberger, 2001, p. 35). This chapter has shown that NGOs and MNCs have important mechanisms through which they can participate in UN decisionmaking; however, it is also readily apparent that the processes described in this chapter fall far short of the influence wielded by the actors covered in previous chapters, in particular member states. Part 2 of this book, to which we now turn, will consider the formal and informal processes through which these participants interact, given their varying capacities for exercising influence at the United Nations.

PART 2

Movements of the Dance:
Procedures and Processes

6

Formal Arenas: The Structures of Decisionmaking

IT IS COMMONPLACE FOR THE UNITED NATIONS TO BE DISCUSSED AS A UNI-fied, monolithic organization that is structured in a hierarchical fashion and works to pursue its goals through rational decisions and coherent strategies. While this view does contain elements of the truth, UN observers are often quick to point out that the UN is more accurately conceptualized as a *system* of different bodies and organs that are both interrelated and independent at the same time. Some parts of the UN "family" share staff, resources, and facilities in the pursuit of common, or at least complementary, goals; other parts enjoy significant autonomy in their basic structure, strategies, and authority. As a result of this diversity, there is considerable debate regarding the extent to which the bodies operating under the UN umbrella can be considered a single system (for example see White, 2002, pp. 3–11). Some view the UN system as simply a collection of autonomous bodies, each one pursuing its own goals on its own timetable; others see the UN as a strong and effective coordinating mechanism whose component parts function as a complete and coherent system. While examples can be offered to support both these extremes of decentralization and centralization, this book adopts a more nuanced view of the UN as a facilitator or forum that allows the entities operating under its umbrella to form multiple systems of varying cohesion that can work in pursuit of distinct goals with different levels of achievement.

As can be expected, viewing the United Nations system in such a fashion has direct implications for how UN decisionmaking is understood. Since UN bodies differ in their membership, goals, resources, procedures, and authority, they also tend to exhibit political processes that vary. Understanding these dynamics represents the focus of Part 2 of this book. Part 1 found that different actors have different strengths and weaknesses when it comes to exercising influence at the UN; Part 2 will consider how the structure and procedures of different arenas affect the political processes through which the actors covered in Part 1 interact (Feld and Jordan, 1989, pp. 117–120). Across the next four chapters, both the formal and informal dimensions of the global dance will be investigated. Chapters 6 and 7 focus on the formal structures of the UN's main deliberative bodies and the procedures through which they handle political debate and make decisions. Chapter 8 looks at the private and informal side of UN processes, where personal factors play just as important a role in building winning coalitions as do power and procedural advantage. Finally, Chapter 9 brings together the most important insights of Parts 1 and 2 in its discussion of how participants can draw on distinct strategies to wield influence based on their attributes and the nature of the arena in which the decision is being made.

▓ Five Formal Arenas of Decisionmaking

A first step in examining the formal arenas of UN decisionmaking is to refer to the UN Charter, which in Article 7, Paragraph 1 identifies six "principal organs of the United Nations: a General Assembly, a Security Council, an Economic and Social Council (ECOSOC), a Trusteeship Council, an International Court of Justice, and a Secretariat." (See Figure 6.1.) Three of these principal organs will receive attention in this chapter, since they are the deliberative bodies where most political issues are addressed: the General Assembly, Security Council, and ECOSOC. The other three principal organs are not considered here for various reasons. The Secretariat's role in servicing the organization affords it some influence in UN decisionmaking; however, these dynamics were discussed in Chapter 4 and need not be examined again here. Omission of the Trusteeship Council is based on the admission of Palau to the UN in 1994, which left no territories under its domain. While "theoretically colonial territories could still be placed under the Council's auspices" or other uses could be found for the Council, neither of these developments has come to pass; for all practical purposes, its activities have been suspended since the mid-1990s (Groom, 2000, pp. 142, 173). Finally, the International Court of Justice (ICJ) certainly has influence on UN politics through its roles in dispute settlement, treaty implementation, and advisory opinions; however, these roles are carried out primarily based on legal standards and judicial reasoning (see, for example, Ramcharan, 2000; White, 2002, pp. 111–130), not through the political processes and calculations that are the focus of this book.

While the General Assembly, Security Council, and ECOSOC are all principal organs of the UN, each has a unique position within it. Most often the General Assembly is considered to be the heart and soul of the United Nations, based on its universal membership, its broad agenda, the sovereign equality of its members reflected in the one-state, one-vote formula, and the fact that it is "supposed to represent the main currents affecting the planet" and "to ensure a minimal collaboration from all states in the management of complex interdependencies" (Smouts, 2000, p. 21). Article 15 of the UN Charter empowers the General Assembly to receive annual reports from both the Security Council and ECOSOC. In the case of ECOSOC, the need to report on its activities reflects the fact that it operates "under the authority of the General Assembly" (Article 60). This subordinate position is further manifest in Articles 62–66, which indicate that ECOSOC performs functions assigned to it by or approved by the Assembly and that its policy decisions are recommendations requiring further action by the Assembly.

The relationship between the Assembly and the Security Council is more "intricate and fluid" (Bailey and Daws, 1998, p. 281). While the Council submits an annual report to the Assembly, the Assembly never actually discusses this report (as it does in detail for ECOSOC), because "the Security Council is in no sense subordinate to the General Assembly" (Narasimhan, 1988, pp. 55–56). In regard to peace and security, the Charter suggests that the opposite is true, for the Council has "primary responsibility" for these issues and acts on behalf of all members when exercising these duties (Article 24, Paragraph 1). Article 12, Paragraph 1 further specifies that the Assembly "shall not make any recommendations" with regard to any situation or dispute where the Council is currently exercising the functions assigned to it by the Charter. Despite such invocations in the Charter that would seem to prevent the Council and Assembly from addressing the same issue, the Assembly "in practice . . . has not been inclined to countenance any limit on its freedom to debate" (Bailey and Daws, 1995, pp. 25–26). This behavior by the Assembly has been justified in two ways: first on the grounds that the prohibition is against taking action, not debating, and second, that the Council's claim to remain "seized of" a particular matter (the common language in Council resolutions) does not constitute the exercise of function requirement of Article 12. Based on its wider membership and broader agenda, the General Assembly will receive attention first in this chapter.

The Charter allows the General Assembly, Security Council, and ECOSOC to establish subsidiary bodies (Articles 22, 29, and 68,

Figure 6.1 The United Nations System

PRINCIPAL ORGANS OF THE UNITED NATIONS

Security Council[a]	General Assembly[a]	Secretariat[a]
Subsidiary Bodies: Military Staff Committee Standing Committee and ad hoc bodies International Criminal Tribunal for the Former Yugoslavia International Criminal Tribunal for Rwanda UN Monitoring, Verification, and Inspection Commission (Iraq) UN Compensation Commission Peacekeeping Operations and Missions	Subsidiary Bodies: Main committees Other sessional committees Standing committees and ad hoc bodies Other subsidiary organs	Departments and Offices: OSG: Office of the Secretary-General OIOS: Office of Internal Oversight Services OLA: Office of Legal Affairs DPA: Department of Political Affairs DDA: Department for Disarmament Affairs DPKO: Department of Peacekeeping Operations OCHA: Office for the Coordination of Humanitarian Affairs DESA: Department of Economic and Social Affairs DGACM: Department for General Assembly and Conference Management DPI: Department of Public Information DM: Department of Management OHRLLS: Office of the High Representative for the Least Developed Countries, Landlocked Developing Countries, and Small Island Developing States UNSECOORD: Office of the UN Security Coordinator UNODC: UN Office on Drugs and Crime
Programs and Funds: UNCTAD: UN Conference on Trade and Development ITC: International Trade Centre (UNCTAD/WTO) UNDCP: UN Drug Control Programme[b] UNEP: UN Environment Programme UNICEF: UN Children's Fund UNDP: UN Development Programme UNIFEM: UN Development Fund for Women UNV: UN Volunteers UNCDF: UN Capital Development Fund UNFPA: UN Population Fund UNHCR: Office of the UN High Commissioner for Refugees WFP: World Food Programme UNRWA[c]: UN Relief and Works Agency for Palestine Refugees in the Near East UN-HABITAT: UN Human Settlements Programme (UNHSP)	Research and Training Institutes: UNICRI: UN Interregional Crime and Justice Research Institute UNITAR: UN Institute for Training and Research UNRISD: UN Research Institute for Social Development UNIDIR[c]: UN Institute for Disarmament Research INSTRAW: International Research and Training Institute for the Advancement of Women Other UN Entities: OHCHR: Office of the UN High Commissioner for Human Rights UNOPS: UN Office for Project Services UNU: UN University UNSSC: UN System Staff College UNAIDS: Joint UN Programme on HIV/AIDS	UNOG: UN Office at Geneva UNOV: UN Office at Vienna UNON: UN Office at Nairobi

Figure 6.1 The United Nations System

Economic and Social Council[a]

Trusteeship Council

International Court of Justice

Functional Commissions:
Commission on Human Rights
Commission on Narcotic Drugs
Commission on Crime
  Prevention and Criminal
  Justice
Commission on Science and
  Technology for Development
Commission on Sustainable
  Development
Commission on the Status of
  Women
Commission on Population and
  Development
Commission for Social
  Development
Statistical Commission

Regional Commissions:
Economic Commission for
  Africa (ECA)
Economic Commission for
  Europe (ECE)
Economic Commission for
  Latin America and the
  Caribbean (ECLAC)
Economic and Social
  Commission for Asia and the
  Pacific (ESCAP)
Economic and Social
  Commission for Western
  Asia (ESCWA)

Other Bodies:
Permanent Forum on
  Indigenous Issues (PFII)
UN Forum on Forests
Sessional and standing
  committees
Expert, ad hoc, and related bodies

Specialized Agencies[g]:
ILO: International Labour Organization
FAO: Food and Agriculture Organization
UNESCO: UN Educational, Scientific, and Cultural Organization
WHO: World Health Organization
World Bank Group:
  IBRD: International Bank for Reconstruction and Development
  IDA: International Development Association
  IFC: International Finance Corporation
  MIGA: Multilateral Investment Guarantee Agency
  ICSID: International Centre for Settlement of Investment
  Disputes
IMF: International Monetary Fund
ICAO: International Civil Aviation Organization
IMO: International Maritime Organization
ITU: International Telecommunication Union
WMO: World Meteorological Organization
WIPO: World Intellectual Property Organization
IFAD: International Fund for Agricultural Development
UNIDO: UN Industrial Development Organization
WTO[d]: World Tourism Organization

Related Organizations:
WTO[a,d]: World Trade Organization
IAEA[a,e]: International Atomic Energy Agency
CTBTO Prep.Com[f]: PrepCom for the Nuclear-Test-Ban-Treaty
  Organization
OPCW[f]: Organization for the Prohibition of Chemical Weapons

Source: UN Department of Public Information, DPI/2342, March 2004.

Notes: a. Shaded areas indicate a direct reporting relationship, except in the case of the Secretariat, which lists the departments and offices of the Secretariat. Nonsubsidiary relationships include: Security Council—IAEA; General Assembly—IAEA, CTBTO Prep.Com, OPCW; Economic and Social Council—programs and funds, research and training institutes, other UN entities, specialized agencies; the WTO and IAEA—specialized agencies.

b. The UN Drug Control Programme is part of the UN Office on Drugs and Crime.

c. UNRWA and UNIDIR report only to the General Assembly.

d. The World Trade Organization and World Tourism Organization use the same acronym.

e. IAEA reports to the Security Council and the General Assembly.

f. The CTBTO Prep.Com and OPCW report to the General Assembly.

g. Specialized agencies are autonomous organizations working with the UN and each other through the coordinating machinery of ECOSOC at the intergovernmental level, and through the Chief Executives Board for Coordination (CEB) at the intersecretariat level.

respectively), and each of these principal organs has used this power extensively. For example, the General Assembly has created UNICEF, UNHCR, UNCTAD, UNDP, UNEP, and many other bodies; the Security Council has created more than fifty peacekeeping missions, numerous special committees and commissions dealing with sanctions and terrorism, and two criminal tribunals for the former Yugoslavia and Rwanda; ECOSOC has five regional economic commissions (covering Europe, Africa, Asia and the Pacific, Western Asia, and Latin America and the Caribbean) and functional commissions dealing with human rights, women, population, and narcotic drugs, among others. While these subsidiary organs may enjoy some degree of independence and autonomy, they operate under the control of the principal organs that are responsible for creating them, modifying them, and discontinuing them when necessary (White, 2002, pp. 4–5; Tung, 1969, pp. 57–59). The functions of subsidiary organs can cover all dimensions of the activities of their parent bodies. Some are established for a limited duration to address specific issues; others become permanent features of the UN landscape. While governmental representatives attend meetings of the Assembly, Council, and ECOSOC, some of the subsidiary bodies are composed of individual experts acting in their own capacity. As a result of this diversity of composition and purpose, the patterns of decision-making in subsidiary organs may be quite distinct from those of the principal organs that created them. Though a comprehensive investigation of these differences is beyond the scope of this book, some examples of these dynamics will be identified as each principal organ is discussed.

Once the structures of the three principal organs are explored, this chapter will consider two other types of formal arenas of decisionmaking: the specialized agencies and UN-sponsored global conferences. The specialized agencies of the UN system are autonomous bodies established through their own treaty mechanisms, with their own staff, budget, and policymaking bodies. They are independent from the principal organs but nonetheless linked to the rest of the UN system through agreements to coordinate their work with ECOSOC (Wells, 1991, pp. 1–2). Currently there are sixteen such bodies, including the ILO, the WHO, the FAO, the IMF, and the agencies of the World Bank Group. In addition, the International Atomic Energy Agency (IAEA) and the World Trade Organization (WTO) are often treated as part of this group, even though their legal status involves greater independence from the principal organs (White, 2002, p. 100). The specialized agencies are often assumed to be more technical (as opposed to political) in their focus, so that the important services they provide are insulated from the sometimes heated debates carried out in the principal organs. Unfortunately, political questions have become increasingly common in the specialized agencies as their memberships increased and new priorities were advanced (Wells, 1991, p. 8). Thus this chapter will explore several of the specialized agencies, highlighting how their political processes are similar to and different from those found in the UN's principal organs.

The final arena of decisionmaking discussed in this chapter is UN-sponsored global conferences. While these conferences have long been a feature of international politics, "the size, number, and publicity of such conferences have grown, both in the 1970s and again in the early to mid 1990s" (Schechter, 2001b, p. 3). While there is some debate on the usefulness of these conferences (see Fomerand, 1996), their goals have been broad: raising awareness of pressing issues, mobilizing coalitions of like-minded actors, drafting new standards of behavior, and helping to ensure that compliance is obtained. Chapter 5 considered how nongovernmental organizations, and to a lesser extent multinational corporations, have seized upon these conferences as important venues for exercising influence on the interests and policies advanced by governmental representatives. Since these conferences have become centers of UN policymaking, for better or worse, it is necessary to consider how their processes are structured as compared to those of the principal organs and specialized agencies.

Based on this overview, five arenas in which the global dance unfolds are covered in this chapter: the General Assembly, the Security Council, ECOSOC, the specialized agencies, and UN-sponsored global conferences. The procedures for debate and rules of decisionmaking of these bodies will be investigated in Chapter 7; this chapter will focus on their basic institutional and structural features, since these dynamics affect the power of different actors in decisionmaking as well as the authority and effectiveness of the organization (Cox and Jacobson, 1973b, pp. 6–7; White, 2002, p. 79). For each arena, the following discussion will cover composition (including size and terms of membership), scope of concern (including its functions and authority), the conduct of business (including meeting format and agenda setting), patterns of decisionmaking (taking into account subsidiary bodies), and potential proposals for reform.

▓ The General Assembly

The General Assembly can be distinguished from other bodies of multilateral decisionmaking based on its broad scope: both in terms of its universal membership and its nearly all-encompassing agenda. Its role and position in world politics have been aptly captured by Leon Gordenker in describing the Thirty-fourth Session of the Assembly in 1979:

> The United Nations General Assembly represents the organized views of more governments on more subjects than any periodic gathering in the world. . . . Its recommendations make waves—sometimes ripples, sometimes great splashes—in the capitals and the countrysides. Its agenda always contains both the unconquered difficulties of past years and the new issues of recent weeks. . . . The General Assembly pronounces its opinions, whether measured and thoughtful or impulsive and overwrought, on these and a hundred other issues. . . . In both symbolic and practical senses, it presides over the daily difficulties of a world which has little inclination to honor any single conscience or to speak with one voice. (quoted in Kaufmann, 1980, p. 25)

Because of these unique features and its diffuse activities, the Assembly has been called a "global parliament" or "town meeting of the world" (Ziring, Riggs, and Plano, 2000, p. 36). While these catchphrases are certainly an oversimplification (see Luard and Heater, 1994, p. 38), one former diplomatic practitioner has argued that its membership, agenda, supervisory role vis-à-vis other UN bodies, and budget-making powers, and the continued high level of representation at its meetings, make the General Assembly *the* principal organ of the United Nations system (Kaufmann, 1980, p. 25).

While Johan Kaufmann's assessment of the prominence of the General Assembly is far from a solitary view, the Assembly clearly began its work with a less than ideal mandate. Marie-Claude Smouts has argued that the UN General Assembly "is a child of the Assembly of the League of Nations, but it has never entirely benefited from the inheritance of its predecessor" (2000, p. 24). Though the Council and Assembly of the League were similar in both "law and practice," she finds that the founders of the UN established a clear distinction between the powers of the Security Council and the General Assembly by specifying that the "Assembly could discuss, examine, recommend but not act by the means of binding decisions." This distinction has caused the Assembly to undergo cycles of power and influence since its birth, both within and outside the UN system (Luard and Heater, 1994, pp. 51–57; Smouts, 2000, pp. 39–48). The first two decades of UN activity, from 1945 to 1965, are widely viewed as a period of expansion for the Assembly; the Security Council was deadlocked by cold war disagreements, while the Assembly drew on an expanding membership to take the UN in new directions, such as the Uniting for Peace Resolution in 1950. However, as the new majority in the Assembly began to focus on issues of only limited salience to the major Western powers, the Assembly entered a period of stagnation and decline that lasted for two decades, from the mid-1960s to the mid-1980s. Assessments of the Assembly since the 1980s are more mixed. Some observers see further decline, reflected by the continued disillusionment on the part of developing countries and the ongoing hostility of major powers like the United States (Smouts, 2000, pp. 47–48). Conversely, others stress that the Assembly's status as the only forum to which all member states permanently belong means that it remains uniquely suited to address a growing range of issues in an increasingly interdependent world (Luard and Heater, 1994, p. 56).

As Chapter 2 has noted, Article 2, Paragraph 1 of the UN Charter specifies that "the Organization is based on the principle of the sovereign equality of all its Members." Nowhere is this better reflected than in the composition and working methods of the General Assembly, with its "ethos of egalitarianism" (Smouts, 2000, p. 23; Ziring, Riggs, and Plano, 2000, p. 36). Article 9, Paragraph 2 enables each of the 191 UN member states to send five representatives to participate in Assembly deliberations (an additional five more are permitted as alternates), and according to Article 18, Paragraph 1, each member state enjoys equal say, at least on paper, when it comes time for the body to act. This spirit of egalitarianism is further reflected in that fact that, as will be discussed in more detail in the following chapter, Assembly decisions are based on majority rule: a simple majority for most issues except those deemed to be "important questions," for which a two-thirds majority is required (Article 18, Paragraphs 2–3).

Because of the Assembly's size and use of majority rule, the role of group and bloc politics surveyed in Chapter 3 is especially important there, in terms of both procedural and substantive issues (see, for example, Nicholas, 1975, pp. 131–133; Luard and Heater, 1994, pp. 47–49). The size and diverse membership of the Assembly necessitate a high level of support and input from the Secretariat, for the reasons discussed in Chapter 4 (see also Luard and Heater, 1994, p. 44). Finally, the nonstate actors discussed at the end of Part 1 are afforded no official provisions for participating in the work of the Assembly; however, some NGOs have been quite influential (Kaufmann, 1980, p. 32), mainly through the informal mechanisms of decisionmaking that will be discussed in Chapter 8.

In addition to a broad membership of states and an egalitarian ethos, an expansive scope of concern is provided to the General

Assembly in the UN Charter. Article 10 gives the Assembly the right to "discuss any questions or any matters within the scope of the present Charter . . . and, except as provided in Article 12 [discussed above], may make recommendations to the Members of the United Nations or to the Security Council or to both on any such questions or matters." Articles 11, 13, and 15 provide additional guidance on the functions of the Assembly, which include a concern for "the general principles of cooperation in the maintenance of international peace and security," "the principles governing disarmament and the regulation of armaments," "the progressive development of international law and its codification," "promoting international cooperation in the economic, social, cultural, educational, and health fields," "assisting in the realization of human rights and fundamental freedoms for all," and "the peaceful adjustment of any situation . . . which it deems likely to impair the general welfare or friendly relations among nations." These various articles allow the Assembly to address "all aspects of international life" (Smouts, 2000, p. 26), excepting only those issues under active consideration in the Security Council and those that fall within the domestic jurisdiction of member states (Article 2, Paragraph 7).

In addition to these responsibilities involving the role and place of the Assembly in international politics, the Charter confers upon the Assembly a range of powers relating to the functioning of the UN itself. The first of these internal functions concerns the Assembly's supervisory role vis-à-vis all other organs of the United Nations, as specified in Article 15. As noted in the introduction to this chapter, the Assembly takes this role quite seriously, closely examining the reports and recommendations of the other organs except in the case of the Security Council, where the report is most often tabled without discussion (Nicholas, 1975, p. 126; Narasimhan, 1988, pp. 55–56). Despite this apparent deference to the Council, the Assembly has at times drawn on its responsibilities in Article 11 (to recommend, refer, and call attention to the Council situations that threaten peace and security) in order to act as the "conscience" of the Council, even to the point of criticizing its actions and pressuring it for a new approach (White, 2002, p. 96). A second internal function of the Assembly involves approving the budget of the organization and apportioning these expenses among the members, as is discussed in Article 17, Paragraphs 1–2. The draft budget is prepared by the secretary-general, discussed in several Assembly committees (covered below), and then approved by the plenary in a two-thirds vote (based on Article 18, which includes budgetary matters in its list of important questions). However, since 1986 the major financial contributors have insisted that the budget be adopted by consensus, in order to maintain a de facto veto over UN expenditures (Smouts, 2000, p. 49). A third internal function of the Assembly concerns its administrative role in establishing the regulations under which the secretary-general appoints the organization's staff (Article 101, Paragraph 1). This includes standards for promotion and conduct, conditions of work, and the allocation of tasks to different offices and departments within the Secretariat (Peterson, 1986, p. 152).

The fourth and final internal function performed by the Assembly has to do with membership issues, especially in regard to bodies of limited size and various leadership positions (see, for example, Bailey and Daws, 1995, p. 20; Ziring, Riggs, and Plano, 2000, p. 46; Tung, 1969, pp. 78–82). Some membership issues are the sole province of the General Assembly, including elections for the ten nonpermanent seats in the Security Council and the entire membership of ECOSOC. As was discussed in Chapter 3, regional electoral groups play a central role in how these elections are conducted, from the geographic distribution of the seats to the selection of specific candidates for each spot. In addition, there are other membership and elective functions for which the responsibility is shared by the Assembly and the Security Council. In the case of admitting new members to the UN, appointing the secretary-general, and amending the Charter, the Assembly acts (usually very quickly) based on the recommendation of the Council; in the case of selecting judges for the International Court of Justice, the two bodies act independently of each other (Article 8 of the Statute of the Court).

Despite the broad mandate of the Assembly and the important functions it performs internal to the organization, there is still some debate regarding the power and authority enjoyed by the Assembly. While issues of compliance will be the subject of attention in the concluding chapter of this book, it is worth mentioning at this stage that the decisions made by the Assembly are rarely binding in a legal or practical sense. Peterson discusses eight areas in which the Charter gives the Assembly binding authority (1986, pp. 115, 152), all of which relate to internal governance, budgetary, and membership issues. Outside of these limited areas, the near consensus view is that the resolutions of the Assembly "are mere recommendations, without binding authority" and that as a result the Assembly "is not a world legislature" (Smouts, 2000, p. 51). Under this view, the only lawmaking role of the Assembly that extends beyond the confines of the organization involves drafting and approving multilateral treaties and conventions, which remain only recommendations until they are signed and ratified by a sufficient number of states such that they enter into force.

Nevertheless, in the exercise of its broad powers to initiate studies, express opinions, and make recommendations on nearly any international issue, the Assembly has been said to play a "quasi-legislative" role short of drafting formal treaties (see, for example, Peterson, 1986, pp. 136–149; Nicholas, 1975, pp. 115–130). This view is based on the fact that "resolutions directed toward state conduct outside the organization are not binding of themselves, but the rules thus enunciated may have legal force if they are regarded as statements of customary international law or authoritative interpretations of the UN Charter" (Ziring, Riggs, and Plano, 2000, pp. 44–45). Exactly what enables an Assembly resolution to be elevated to the status of customary law remains a subject of debate. Peterson concludes that this is most likely to occur when a resolution reflects state practice over time and the text explicitly includes "language that the states supporting the resolution accept it as binding" (1986, p. 145). Smouts discusses another common argument: repeated approval of similar resolutions by overwhelming majorities can transform their nonbinding language into customary law (2000, p. 51). She concludes that this "illusion" has been swept away by the political and economic realities of the debate between developed and developing countries; still, she says, these resolutions may legitimate certain norms of behavior, thereby creating "a common system of reference that can influence states' practices and lead to the emergence of new principles in international law." The extent to which the Assembly can influence world politics in such a manner varies from one situation to the next, depending on the issue under consideration and the interests that various coalitions have at stake (Peterson, 1986, p. 7). In this conceptualization, the relationship between Assembly decisionmaking and binding authority remains subject to political interpretation.

The General Assembly conducts its business in a large, cavernous hall that mixes the ceremony of a legislative chamber with the functionality of a common auditorium (see the descriptions in Nicholas, 1975, pp. 102–103; Luard and Heater, 1994, p. 42; Narasimhan, 1988, pp. 59–60). At the front of the room is a broad raised platform, which lies underneath a pair of large electronic screens for displaying voting results. From this dais the Assembly president runs its meetings, flanked by the secretary-general (or the secretary-general's representative) to the right and the under-secretary-general for general assembly and conference management to the left. At a slightly lower level lies a massive podium from which diplomats and politicians address their colleagues on issues both vital and mundane. The hall is dominated by a seemingly endless number of desks, arranged in concentric arcs along its sloping floor, at which each member state is able to seat six representatives. The first desk for each session goes to a member state drawn at random by the secretary-general, with the rest following in English alphabetical order. The sides of the hall are interrupted by a series of glass booths from which simultaneous translation is provided, and television footage is recorded, ready to be beamed around the world as needed. The back of the hall includes a small area for the press and a large cantilevered gallery for interested nongovernmental organizations and, on occasion, the general public. While the hall can seem surprisingly empty during routine meetings, it is the center of much commotion and activity when a debate assumes a high level of importance, with a near constant flow of people in and out of the chamber and many informal consultations taking place in its aisles. Soaring above all this activity is a large gold UN emblem and vast domed ceiling.

The General Assembly meets annually in a regular session at UN headquarters in New York. Rule 1 of the Assembly's Rules of Procedure (UN document A/520/Rev.15) specifies that these sessions commence on the third Tuesday of September; however, Assembly Resolution 55/14, adopted on November 9, 2000, amended this rule such that the annual regular session would begin on the "Tuesday following the second Monday in September." The regular session typically lasts for thir-

UN Secretary-General Kofi Annan addresses the General Assembly on December 8, 2004. The meeting was devoted to a discussion of the Report of the High-Level Panel on Threats, Challenges, and Change, which was appointed by the secretary-general in September 2003. (UN photo #NICA 60055, by Ky Chung)

teen or fourteen weeks, closing in late December just before Christmas. The Assembly's rules have always permitted a continuation of the regular session into the spring and summer of the following year, but the meeting schedules of other UN bodies and the press of other international meetings long made this an unattractive option for many member states (Peterson, 1986, p. 265). This reluctance has been overrun by the necessity of a larger membership and an expanding agenda, so that nearly every session since the end of the cold war has involved additional meetings after the end of December, sometimes up to 25 percent of the total for the session (Smouts, 2000, p. 35). Common practice now holds that the official closing of a session occurs the day before the next regular session opens in September of the following year.

Article 20 of the UN Charter specifies that the Assembly can also meet in "special sessions as occasion may require." These sessions are convoked by the secretary-general within fifteen days of such a request by the General Assembly, the Security Council, or any member state with the support of a majority of UN members (Tung, 1969, pp. 98–99). In addition, the Uniting for Peace Resolution adopted in November 1950 provided that the Assembly could meet in emergency special sessions to be held within twenty-four hours of a request by the Security Council or, in the case of a deadlocked Council through use of the veto, a request by a majority of UN members. In order to prevent abuse of these provisions, the agenda of special sessions is closely controlled by the majorities that call for them (Peterson, 1986, p. 46). As of 2003, twenty-seven special sessions and ten emergency special sessions had been held.

The first order of business when a new regular session of the Assembly opens in September is to deal with several procedural issues, including elections for a new president, twenty-one vice presidents, and the chairpersons of its six main committees, discussed below (Narasimhan, 1988, p. 59; Peterson, 1986, p. 267). These individuals are selected through various formulas involving regional rotation. Formulas for selecting the president and the twenty-one vice presidents were covered in Chapter 2. The formula for distributing committee chairs is found in Annex 2 of Assembly Resolution 48/264 of July 1994, which specifies that each of the five geographic regions chairs a committee, with the sixth chair position rotating among three regions (Africa, Asia, and Latin America and the Caribbean) in a complex twenty-year pattern. These twenty-eight elected officers (one president, twenty-one vice presidents, and six committee chairs) constitute the Assembly's General Committee (or Bureau), which will be discussed below; their additional leadership responsibilities will be examined in Chapter 7 in conjunction with other procedural matters.

Once these officers are selected, Assembly work proceeds on several fronts. For the next three weeks or so the plenary holds an annual General Debate, which "is somewhat outside the main flow of Assembly business since it does not lead directly to the adoption of any decisions" (Peterson, 1986, p. 267). Instead, it offers an "opportunity for each delegation to express its government's views on the general state of the world, questions proposed for the Assembly agenda and particular concerns of its own." Traditionally these speeches were presented by foreign ministers rather than by permanent representatives, but a growing number of prime ministers, presidents, and other heads of state have taken it upon themselves to deliver this address on behalf of their population (Narasimhan, 1988, p. 56). Although attendance at the General Debate is actually quite poor unless the speaker is the leader of a major power or enjoys celebrity status, there is intense competition to speak on certain days (Kaufmann, 1980, p. 27). While there is no provision in the Assembly's Rules of Procedure for a General Debate, in the early years of the Assembly a custom developed that the first speech was usually made by Brazil, with at least some of the permanent members of the Security Council also speaking on the first day (Bailey, 1960, pp. 73–74). These patterns remained in effect at the Fifty-eighth session of the Assembly in 2003.

The General Debate has been criticized as an inefficient use of time, given the fact that it rarely includes much actual debate. Evan Luard and Derek Heater describe it as a "leisurely succession of dignified statesmen, reading in measured tones carefully prepared statements" that lack "any continuous thread of discussion at all" (1994, p. 42). Likewise, Kaufmann describes the speeches as "monologues" that rarely inspire enough passion in the audience to spur any request to exercise a "right of reply" (1980, p. 27). In spite of these criticisms, which are certainly justified, the General Debate does perform a number of useful functions for the Assembly (Luard and Heater, 1994, p. 42; Nicholas, 1975, p. 112; Bailey, 1960, p. 74): (1) it provides even the smallest nations a chance to have their voices heard; (2) it can act as a barometer of international opinion on important issues, even those not on the agenda for that particular session; (3) it helps to identify issues on which a significant degree of consensus may be developing such that they might be ripe to solve; (4) it provides members with a opportunity to blow off steam on contentious issues without causing undue damage; (5) it gives delegates, both new and returning, a chance to get used to the proceedings and prepare for the upcoming debates; and (6) it creates an environment especially conducive for the types of informal consultations that will be discussed in Chapter 8.

While the General Debate continues, two important Assembly committees dealing with procedural issues begin their work, interrupting the flow of speakers when plenary approval is required for their recommendations. The Credentials Committee is composed of nine members proposed by the president and appointed by the Assembly at the beginning of each session. Despite the fact that the question of credentials involves political issues associated with recognition and membership, this committee has remained constant in its number of members over time (Smouts, 2000, p. 34), and membership on it is not particularly contested, but the United States, Russia, and China are usually included (Luard and Heater, 1994, p. 44; Kaufmann, 1980, p. 31). In the early years of the Assembly, the Credentials Committee often waited until late in the session to deliver its report to the plenary, since Rule 29 of the Assembly's Rules of Procedure allows delegations not yet formally approved to participate in the Assembly on a provisional basis with the same rights as other representatives while the committee continues its work (Peterson, 1986, pp. 270–271). However, from the 1970s on the issue of credentials became more problematic in some cases, with competing delegations purporting to represent the same state or certain members using objections to the credentials of other members as a tool of embarrassment (as was the case with South Africa, Israel, and Chile, for example). As a result, the work of the Credentials Committee is now typically completed much earlier in the session, usually by mid-October, so that contentious cases can be debated in the full Assembly.

The second procedural committee that meets during the General Debate is the General Committee, whose membership includes the Assembly's leadership, discussed above. While the General Committee is not allowed to decide any political question (*United Nations Handbook*, 2002, p. 24), it nonetheless plays an important steering role in the conduct of Assembly business, since according to Rule 40 of the Assembly's Rules of Procedure, it is responsible for deciding, by a simple majority, which of the many issues on the Assembly's provisional agenda will actually be accepted for debate in the current session (Smouts, 2000, pp. 36–37). While it is rare for the General Committee to reject an item altogether (Nicholas, 1975, p. 109; Peterson, 1986, p. 268), the process of judging whether to include each issue can involve very heated debates that foreshadow arguments, tactics, and lines of conflict that will surface later in the plenary and the six main committees.

Rules 41–44 of the Assembly's Rules of Procedure also empower the General Committee to suggest where each agenda item should be sent for consideration (to the plenary or one of the six main committees), assist the president in setting the agenda for each plenary meeting, coordinate the work of the main committees, and revise resolutions adopted by the Assembly to improve their form (subject to acceptance by the plenary). The General Committee has never fully exploited its power in any of these areas (Peterson, 1986, pp. 268–269). For example, while there is occasionally fierce debate on where a specific issue should be sent for consideration (see Kaufmann, 1980, p. 30), the committee typically has few opportunities to influence this, since the main committees are highly specialized in their focus (see below) and there is often a well-developed tradition of where each issue should be debated. Likewise, as Peterson indicates, the committee has been reluctant to revise the form of resolutions, since the line between merely editing the style and actually changing the substance of the text is blurry and such efforts are often fraught with potential minefields that could lead to the whole resolution's being redrafted from scratch (1986, p. 269). Peterson further observes that the coordinating and planning functions of the committee have been increasingly handled by a more efficient, informal eight-member group composed of the president, the main committee chairs, and the under-secretary-general for General Assembly and conference management, who have been meeting for weekly lunches since 1947.

Evaluations of the effectiveness of the General Committee in managing the agenda of the Assembly often arrive at a negative assessment. For starters, "the number of items listed on the agenda of regular annual sessions has been continually inflated over the years" (Smouts, 2000, p. 35); the first session in 1946 had 46 separate agenda items, whereas the fifty-eighth session in 2003 had 164 (Assembly doc. A/58/251). This can be attributed to the expanding membership of the Assembly and the fact that the membership generally defers to the wishes of states when they request that a particular item be included (Luard and Heater, 1994, p. 47; Kaufmann, 1980, p. 30). The General Committee itself is also to blame, for it "never bothers to revise the agenda by removing redundant items or those that give rise to debates and resolutions that have little connection with reality" (Smouts, 2000, p. 36).

Despite these negative assessments, two considerations suggest that the General Committee's lack of vigilance on the agenda is not as problematic or debilitating as some observers would argue. First, any attempt to ban discussion of an issue by the General Committee would certainly look suspicious and would likely provoke a heated debate about this procedural slight (Nicholas, 1975, p. 110). Then a possibly productive, substantive debate of the issue would almost certainly be replaced by a clearly unproductive procedural debate about whether to debate the issue. Second, as Peterson indicates, the open view of the Assembly's agenda maintained by the General Committee has led to the emergence of several informal mechanisms through which the broad nominal (or provisional) agenda can be made more effective (or prioritized) when it comes time to actually debate the issues in the plenary or main committees (1986, pp. 17–18, 28–41). These mechanisms include allowing the main committees to determine which issues will be debated first and hence receive the most extensive consideration, the use of informal group consultation prior to official committee debate (which will receive more attention in Chapter 8), and referring issues to a specialized agency or subsidiary organ for consideration.

Once the General Committee has completed its work on the agenda, the substantive phase of Assembly decisionmaking begins, where much of the work centers on the main committees (see Peterson, 1986, p. 271). Before 1993 there were seven main committees; however, the unnumbered Special Political Committee and the Fourth Committee (at the time dealing only with decolonization) were merged in Assembly Resolution 47/233 (*United Nations Handbook*, 2002, p. 24). The current six main committees and their area of focus are as follows: the First Committee (Disarmament and International Security), the Second Committee (Economic and Financial), the Third Committee (Social, Humanitarian, and Cultural), the Fourth Committee (Special Political and Decolonization), the Fifth Committee (Administrative and Budgetary), and the Sixth Committee (Legal). Most of the specific substantive issues on the Assembly's agenda are handled in these committees, although some substantive issues of special importance and nearly all procedural matters are handled by the plenary itself without reference to one of the main committees (Kaufmann, 1980, pp. 30–31). In the Fifty-eighth session of the Assembly in 2003, the plenary was allocated sixty-two issues, the First Committee twenty, the Second Committee sixteen, the Third Committee fifteen, the Fourth Committee fourteen, the Fifth Committee thirty-five, and the Sixth Committee seventeen (UN doc. A/58/252).

Each of the main committees operates as a "committee of the whole," meaning that its membership is identical to that of the plenary, reflecting the egalitarian tradition discussed above. As a result, they suffer from some of the same difficulties of engaging in true negotiations that plague the plenary, and any other decisionmaking body of nearly two hundred members for that matter (Smouts, 2000, p. 36;

Nicholas, 1975, p. 111). Still, the committee structure is an improvement over handling all issues in the plenary itself, since work can proceed in a simultaneous fashion and delegates who are specialists in a particular area can focus their attention most effectively. Most of the committees begin their work immediately after agenda items are allocated by the General Committee (usually in late September), which means they have just under three months to complete their work. The exception to this pattern is the First Committee, which by tradition does not begin its work until after the General Debate is complete for two reasons: it used to cover general political questions in addition to disarmament, and heads of delegations (who were involved in the General Debate) usually attended its meetings (Peterson, 1986, p. 271). This means that the plenary and First Committee have slightly less time than the other committees to cover the agenda items allocated to them.

Although the main committees are structured like mini-assemblies, they use less formal procedures than those of the plenary (Bailey and Daws, 1995, p. 19). For example, delegates speak from their desk instead of from a podium at the front of the room, and all voting is by simple majority, even for important questions. Assembly Resolution 52/163 of 1997 specifies that leadership for each committee is provided by a chairperson, three vice chairs, and a rapporteur, all of whom are elected by the committee based on the formula of regional distribution discussed above (*United Nations Handbook*, 2002, p. 24). While their specific functions will be discussed in the following chapter, these leaders, in close consultation with the Secretariat staff assigned to their committee, prepare a provisional agenda and "work programme" that specifies the order in which the issues allocated to the committee will be covered and how much time will be spent on each (Luard and Heater, 1994, pp. 44–45). This agenda is usually adopted by the committee without dispute, but it remains a provisional agenda since new issues can be added to the committee's agenda by the General Committee at any point in the session. In practice, the "work programme" prepared by the committee leadership often becomes no more than a "theoretical document," for "no committee has even been known to keep to it," given the tendency of every delegate to speak on every issue "even if they have nothing new to say" (ibid.). This is especially problematic late in the session, when many issues still require discussion and yet the list of delegations wishing to speak, even on unimportant matters, is seemingly endless.

The nature of proceedings varies considerably from one committee to the next, since their different issue domains give rise to different lines of conflict and require different types of winning coalitions

(Peterson, 1986, pp. 29, 271–278; Luard and Heater, 1994, p. 45; Kaufmann, 1980, pp. 32–40). The main line of conflict in the First Committee has traditionally not been East and West or North and South, but between those states that want to prevent horizontal nuclear proliferation (the current nuclear powers) and those that focus more attention on the need for vertical arms control (virtually everyone else). The Second and Third committees have always been plagued to some extent by the presence of too many issues to debate in any depth, some of which usually overlap between the two committees and the work of ECOSOC as well (see below). The Third Committee spends more time than the Second drafting standards of behavior, usually on human rights issues, but both are important forums for the debate between developed and developing states. The focus of the Fourth Committee has evolved from being solely on decolonization to include consideration of other political questions that require prompt attention yet fall outside the scope of the First Committee. The lines of conflict in its discussions shift from one issue to the next, depending on which specific political disputes are under debate.

The Fifth Committee covers the UN budget and all other administrative issues; thus its main line of conflict is between developing states that desire larger UN budgets and developed states that prefer zero-growth budgets. It is assisted by two committees that were established during the first session of the Assembly in 1946 and are composed of individual experts (as opposed to state representatives): the sixteen-member Advisory Committee on Administrative and Budgetary Questions (ACABQ) and the eighteen-member Committee on Contributions (*United Nations Handbook*, 2002, pp. 25–26). In both cases the membership is selected by the General Assembly on the recommendation of the Fifth Committee, based on the criteria of broad geographic representation, personal qualifications, and experience. Issues of budget and dues assessment are handled through a three-way negotiation among state representatives of the Fifth Committee, the experts on ACABQ and the Committee on Contributions, and the Secretariat staff that prepares the budget and staffs these committees (Peterson, 1986, p. 277). The final committee, the Sixth, is a rather underutilized committee composed of international lawyers who draft legally binding conventions for later ratification or review those drafted elsewhere. Its debate is more subdued than that of the other committees, but controversy is nonetheless present. It is assisted in its efforts by the International Law Commission, an expert body composed of thirty-four members.

There are more than thirty other subsidiary bodies created by the

General Assembly (*United Nations Handbook*, 2002, pp. 27–56): some are intergovernmental in membership like the main committees, others are composed of experts like ACABQ; some are permanent structures, like the Committee on Relations with the Host Country, others are ad hoc bodies dealing with a finite issue, such as the Open-Ended Working Group on the Question of Equitable Representation and Increase in the Membership of the Security Council; some are designed to address specific substantive issues, like the Committee on the Peaceful Uses of Outer Space, others assist in the administration of the UN, such as the UN Administrative Tribunal. While this proliferation of bodies has resulted in a complex set of decisionmaking machinery, it does allow for the Assembly to do more work through a helpful, although far from perfect, division of labor (Peterson, 1986, pp. 160–165). The membership of each body is distributed across regional groups, either by formal agreements or according to informal custom. This creates patterns of debate that can be more or less similar to those found in the Assembly plenary, and member states have been quick to learn that they can enjoy more or less success in pursuing their goals depending on the arena in which they raise a particular concern (Manno, 1968b, pp. 368–369, 382–383).

Reports and resolutions prepared by the six main committees, as well as many of the Assembly's other subsidiary bodies, must be approved in the plenary before they are considered to be official documents of the United Nations (Kaufmann, 1980, p. 41). Some of these reports and resolutions are ready early in the regular session, but most are presented to the plenary in a flurry of activity in the final days, or even hours, of the session in late December each year (for example, see Narasimhan, 1988, p. 56). This can be a confusing time for even the most informed delegate, with resolution after resolution coming up for a vote—some with amendment after amendment—in rapid succession; in fact some delegates have unfortunately voted for the wrong one and had to explain their error when the official record of the Assembly is prepared (Luard and Heater, 1994, p. 50). Debate on many of these items in the plenary "will often be perfunctory and sometimes non-existent" (Nicholas, 1975, p. 111), but on rare occasions "an intense backstage campaign can sometimes manage to shift votes from the moment a project has been adopted by a committee and the moment it comes up for a vote in the plenary" (Smouts, 2000, p. 36). The pace of activity in the final hours of the Assembly's fall session leaves most delegations exhausted and in need of a vacation.

As one might imagine from this overview of how the General Assembly conducts its business, reform in the name of greater efficiency has been a recurring theme for decades (Smouts, 2000, pp. 52–54; Ziring, Riggs, and Plano, 2000, p. 48). Numerous committees have been charged with offering proposals to reform the Assembly, but these have almost always involved basic procedural tinkering, and even at that they have only rarely been implemented to any positive effect. Luard and Heater recount how one ambassador, frustrated with the amount of speechmaking, proposed replacing simultaneous translation with simultaneous oration, with all speeches given at different microphones at the same time; since no one ever listens to the other speakers, nothing would be lost and much time and money would be saved (1994, p. 57). More serious proposals, based on a similar frustration with the amount of time devoted to empty debate, have suggested that the annual General Debate be eliminated, shortened, or at least oriented toward a specific theme. On a similar note, the work of each main committee could be focused on a particular theme each year, or, even better, their agendas could be lightened (either by considering issues on alternating years or by removing those that are merely placeholders from one year to the next) to allow for more detailed discussion of the issues that really matter. Further, the work of both the Assembly and the Secretariat could be more efficient if the traditional practice of having the secretary-general prepare a report on nearly every issue each session could be abandoned in favor of a more rational and focused work program. Unfortunately, these reforms face two seemingly immovable obstacles: every practice that is wasteful in the eyes of one delegation is seen as being of vital importance by another, and most UN members are currently more focused on the need to reform the UN's other main political organ, the Security Council, to which we now turn.

▓ The Security Council

Despite the many reasons discussed above that place the General Assembly at the center of the United Nations system, it is the Security Council that is most often identified as the "apex body" of the organization (Knight, 2002, p. 19). This is true for two rather straightforward reasons. First, of the many purposes and objectives identified for the UN in the Preamble and Article 1 of the Charter, the organization's primary responsibility is to "maintain international peace and security." Since this task requires the active participation of the great powers, the organization needed a forum in which these powers could meet to address any threat that might disrupt the territorial integrity or political independence of any member state. The logic behind the Council's role in this regard was "generally accepted . . . in both the planning and writing of the UN Charter" (Ziring, Riggs, and Plano, 2000, p. 48). Second, the Security Council was endowed with a set of "specific and detailed powers through the UN Charter to carry this out" (Knight, 2002, p. 19). The most important of these powers (discussed in more detail below) is the ability to make decisions under Chapter 7 that are binding on the entire membership of the UN, not just the members of the Council itself; as a result, it acts as the "pre-eminent authoritative body within the UN system" (ibid.).

Like the General Assembly, the Security Council is very much a child of the League of Nations, mainly in the sense that UN planners identified several problems with the League Council that needed to be avoided (Sutterlin, 1997, p. 2; Luard and Heater, 1994, p. 10). These weaknesses included: (1) the requirement of unanimity that gave every member a veto over action, making it difficult for the League Council to make decisions; (2) the lack of differentiation between the role of the League's Council and Assembly in dealing with security issues; (3) the provisions for enforcement available to the League Council, which were inadequate and ineffective; and (4) the membership of the League Council, which never included all major powers and was therefore unrepresentative. The gradual process of designing the new institution in a series of conferences during World War II gave the great powers an opportunity to address these weaknesses in the UN Charter (see Dedring, 2000, pp. 62–69; Kirgis, 1995, pp. 506–509): the veto was limited to the five permanent members (Article 27, Paragraph 3); the respective roles of the General Assembly and Security Council were clearly defined, with the Council having primary responsibility for peace and security (Article 24, Paragraph 1); the Council was given a broad set of powers in this regard, both nonbinding (Chapter 6) and binding (Chapter 7); and the membership included the five major powers that triumphed in World War II, along with a number of nonpermanent members (more below) that could contribute to the Council's work (Article 23, Paragraph 1).

Based on these differences, it was expected that the UN's Council would perform differently from the League's Council: it would have a clear set of functions, it would operate independent from Assembly authority, and it would be controlled and managed by the great powers working collectively (Chase, 1950, p. 169). There was a sense of euphoria at the conclusion of the San Francisco Conference in 1945 when the UN Charter was complete; members of the US delegation (among others) indicated that the Council was "without precedent in international relations" and that its "powers are thus equivalent, in substance, to those of a supreme war-making organization" (Nicholas,

1975, p. 76). While such pronouncements seem foolishly naive for seasoned statesmen, these hopes and dreams clearly rested on the assumption that great power unity would continue in the years after World War II. Because of the central role played by the great powers in its functioning, the Security Council was deeply affected by the cold war rivalry between the United States and the Soviet Union; rhetoric and posturing replaced unity, and many problems of peace and security were handled outside its deliberations from the 1950s until the end of the cold war (Luard and Heater, 1994, pp. 13–15; Knight, 2002, p. 21). While some exceptions to this pattern are certainly evident, such as the important peacekeeping missions mounted during this period, the effect of the cold war "was that the Council was far weaker than many had hoped" (Luard and Heater, 1994, p. 13).

When the cold war ended at the beginning of the 1990s, the Security Council experienced a dramatic rebirth. As the East-West ideological rivalry faded, the permanent members of the Council were able to act with a degree of unity not unlike that which had been hoped for forty years earlier (Dedring, 2000, p. 61). The use of the veto was reduced, while the number of meetings (both formal and informal), agenda items, resolutions, and peacekeeping missions all increased "literally overnight" (Knight, 2002, p. 22). The impact of these changes on the Council's role in international politics was "momentous" and "massive"; its involvement in nearly all regional conflicts was transformed as it assumed a more proactive and instrumental role in promoting international peace and security (Malone, 2000b, pp. 22–23; Dedring, 2000, p. 81).

As might be expected, the Council experienced a number of growing pains during this process of rebirth. The most challenging of these was the Council's inability in early 2003 to find a common approach to handling continued Iraqi noncompliance with the disarmament obligations required of it. Some have observed that the Council's "failure" in this case has caused the "collapse" of the entire system of promoting peace and security envisioned by the UN Charter, necessitating that we "return to the drawing board" to create a new institution better engineered to an international environment now dominated by the United States (Glennon, 2003). However, other UN observers have responded that talk of the Council's demise is premature, since the Council never was intended to block or sign off on the military actions of the great powers, given the veto power provided in the Charter (see, for example, Luck, Slaughter, and Hurd, 2003). In this view, the Security Council's role in international politics may have suffered during the Iraqi crisis, but it remains a vital forum for debating issues of peace and security in an increasingly complex world.

The basic composition of the Security Council is provided for in Article 23 of the United Nations Charter. Originally the Council was composed of eleven members, but this was expanded to fifteen as a result of a Charter amendment approved by the General Assembly (Resolution 1991A, Eighteenth Session, 1963) that came into effect after being ratified by two-thirds of the UN's membership in 1965. Of these fifteen members, five states are identified in Article 23 as permanent members: the Republic of China, France, the Soviet Union, the United Kingdom, and the United States. Even though these names in the Charter have not been amended, two changes have been made regarding exactly which states occupy these permanent seats (Bailey and Daws, 1998, p. 137): the seat for China was held by the Nationalist regime in Taiwan from the Chinese Revolution until 1971, when it was replaced by the People's Republic of China, and the seat for the Soviet Union was assumed by the Russian Federation in 1991, after the USSR dissolved into fifteen separate states.

The remaining ten seats are for UN members elected to serve on the Council for staggered two-year terms, with five new members coming on the Council on January 1 of each calendar year. The Charter specifies that these states be selected with "due regard being specially paid, in the first instance to the contribution of Members of the United Nations to the maintenance of international peace and security . . . and also to equitable geographic distribution." The result of these provisions is an election process where geography is often the decisive factor (Nicol, 1981b, p. 6) and states engage in a campaign of intense jockeying for seats (see Chapter 3 and Malone, 2000a). General Assembly Resolution 1991A, which expanded the size of the Council, also specified that the ten elected seats should be distributed five to Asia and Africa, two to Western Europe and Other, two to Latin America and the Caribbean, and one to Eastern Europe. Informal practice usually distributes the five seats for Asia and Africa as two Asian states, two African states, and one Arab state, but this allocation is subject to significant variation (Luard and Heater, 1994, p. 16). The Charter's final requirement for the ten elected seats is that "a retiring member shall not be eligible for immediate re-election," in order to prevent the dominance of these seats by middle powers to the exclusion of small states, as happened under the League of Nations (Ziring, Riggs, and Plano, 2000, p. 49). Based on these procedures, as of the 2002–2003 election cycle, 108 states of the 186 eligible members (191 total members minus the permanent five) had served at least one term on the Security Council, which means that 78 states had remained excluded from this opportunity (*United Nations Handbook*, 2002, pp. 60–63).

In the early years of the United Nations, the Security Council included nearly 22 percent of UN members (eleven of fifty-one total members). As UN membership increased, this percentage decreased. Although Council expansion in 1965 was designed to counteract this trend, an expanding UN membership has caused the problem to worsen. With the current 191 members, the Council represents less than 8 percent of total UN membership, which more than anything else has prompted calls for Council expansion (White, 2002, p. 84). While an increase in permanent or nonpermanent membership would likely decrease the power of individual elected members (see O'Neill, 1997), it would make the Council more representative of the UN's overall membership and increase its legitimacy. While these efforts remained stalemated into 2004 (more below), the working methods of the Council make it possible for nonmember states and other actors to participate in its discussions, thereby ameliorating to a small degree the exclusive nature of Council membership.

One avenue for nonmember participation comes in the form of informal consultations under the so-called Arria and Somavia formulas (Dedring, 2000, p. 92; Bailey and Daws, 1998, pp. 73–75), which will be discussed in more detail in Chapter 8. Other mechanisms provide for access to formal Council debate. For example, Articles 31–32 of the Charter indicate that any UN member may be invited to participate without vote in any Council discussions if its interests are affected by the issue under debate and that any state, whether UN member or not, must be invited to participate, again without vote, if it is party to a dispute under consideration by the Council. These practices are reflected in Rules 37–39 of the Council's Provisional Rules of Procedure (UN doc. S/96/Rev.7), which enable these nonmember states to submit proposals but require that such proposals be put to vote only by a Council member (Bailey and Daws, 1995, p. 21). In addition to parties to disputes before the Council, the states most often claiming their rights under these rules have been those that contribute troops to UN peacekeeping operations (troop-contributing nations, or TCNs), which have consistently demanded greater access to the Council as the number and complexity of missions have increased (Malone, 2000b, p. 30; 2002, p. 40).

In addition to nonmember states, some other actors covered in Part 1 of this book can play a role, sometimes an active one, in the Council. The first of these is the secretary-general and the Secretariat, who participate in both formal and informal deliberations of the Council (Nicol, 1981b, pp. 23–27; Bailey and Daws, 1998, pp. 110–124). As was discussed in Chapter 4, the role of the secretary-general and Secretariat staff can involve considerable initiative, such as bringing issues before the Council under Article 99 of the Charter, or be more routine, as under Rule 39 of the Council's Provisional Rules of Procedure, which enables the Council to invite members of the Secretariat to supply it with information. Various UN groups, as discussed in Chapter 3, may also be involved in Council deliberations. While group politics is not nearly as pervasive in the Council as it is in the much larger General Assembly, they do play a role, especially for elected members from the Non-Aligned Movement, who often feel some degree of obligation to represent the interests of their larger group in an effort to counteract as much as possible the dominance of the permanent members (Bailey and Daws, 1998, pp. 70–71; Nicol, 1981b, pp. 16–17). The final set of additional actors considered here are NGOs, which have been "clamoring" for access to the Council with increasing urgency and volume (Malone, 2000b, pp. 32–33; 2002, p. 40). While these demands have been partially met through informal mechanisms that will be covered in Chapter 8, Rule 39 of the Council's Provisional Rules of Procedure does allow for the Council to invite "other persons, whom it considers competent for the purpose, to supply it with information or to give it other assistance in examining matters," and the Appendix to the Provisional Rules of Procedure specifies how communications from these actors should be distributed to Council members. While these mechanisms had often been used to permit the participation of national liberation movements (such as the Palestine Liberation Organization) in the past (Richard, 1981, p. 250), some NGOs have also been able to address the Council under Rule 39 in more recent years (Bailey and Daws, 1998, pp. 320–321).

The functions of the Security Council are all oriented toward its "primary responsibility," the maintenance of international peace and security (Article 24 of the Charter). As noted earlier in this chapter, Article 12 specifies that "the General Assembly shall not make any recommendations" with regard to a dispute that is currently under consideration by the Council. In practice, though, the Assembly and Council have to some extent shared this responsibility, since the Assembly has regularly discussed "other aspects" of peace and security issues on the agenda of the Council (Narasimhan, 1988, p. 71). Because of its important focus, the Council is given little to do with UN administration (Nicholas, 1975, p. 85), except for specific elective functions that it shares with the Assembly (discussed earlier) where the voice of the great powers was seen as being especially relevant, including the selection of the secretary-general, elections for the judges of the ICJ, and the admission of new members (Ziring, Riggs, and Plano, 2000, p. 50). The Charter provides two additional functions for the Council that are no longer actively on its agenda. In Article 26 the Council is called upon to develop plans "for the establishment of a system for the regulation of armaments." The Council shared this responsibility with one of its subsidiary organs, the Military Staff Committee, which, as will be discussed below, has never been able to fulfill its intended mandate, especially after the advent of nuclear weapons made this issue far more challenging from what the Charter had envisioned (Nicholas, 1975, p. 88; Kaufmann, 1980, p. 50). The other obsolete function involved the administration of UN trust territories that were considered to be of strategic importance, a responsibility that effectively ended when the last trust territory, Palau, was admitted to the UN in 1994.

Within its focus on peace and security, the Charter gives the Council two main functions: to settle disputes peacefully (Chapter 6) and to meet threats to peace with collective military action on the part of the entire organization (Chapter 7). The Council has frequently tried to address issues as simple disputes as much as possible, even in situations where both sides were engaging in extensive military hostilities (Ziring, Riggs, and Plano, 2000, p. 50). Nevertheless, there has been a noticeable increase in the use of Chapter 7 procedures since the end of the cold war (Malone, 2000b, pp. 24–25; 2002, p. 41). In order to exercise these functions, Chapters 6–7 of the Charter provide for a range of techniques that can be used, depending on a number of political considerations: who is involved in the dispute, whether or not the Council is unified on the issue, and the wishes of the parties in question (see Nicholas, 1975, pp. 85–94; Luard and Heater, 1994, pp. 22–29, for an overview of this issue). For Chapter 6, Articles 34–38 give the Council authority to investigate any dispute to see if it endangers international peace and security and to make recommendations regarding any dispute brought to its attention by any state (both UN members and nonmembers). In exercising this function, the Council can draw on a variety of "third-party" conflict resolution techniques specified in Article 33: negotiation, enquiry, mediation, conciliation, arbitration, judicial settlement, and referring the dispute to a regional arrangement. For Chapter 7, Articles 39–40 empower the Council to determine whether any situation constitutes a "threat to the peace, breach of the peace, or act of aggression," and if so, it can call on parties to apply measures that it deems "necessary or desirable." If these efforts prove inadequate, Articles 41–42 further empower the Council to use various kinds of sanctions against the parties and, as a last resort, authorize it to "take such action by air, sea, or land forces as may be necessary to maintain or restore international peace and security."

Cold war hostilities made it difficult for the Council to carry out many of its responsibilities under Chapters 6 and 7; only two enforcement actions were completed during the UN's first fifty years (Korea in 1950–1953 and Iraq/Kuwait in 1990–1991), and they came forty years apart and both involved a "coalition of the willing" rather than UN forces as the Charter requires. However, the manner in which the Council has conceptualized the provisions of Chapters 6–7 has evolved over time. One early innovation that allowed the Council to remain active in cases where Chapter 6 peaceful settlement had failed and Chapter 7 collective security was blocked by cold war tensions was the use of neutral, lightly armed peacekeepers to police borders, act as buffers, and monitor troop withdrawals and ceasefires (Luard and Heater, 1994, pp. 27–29). The success of early peacekeeping efforts prompted the Council to considerably expand their role, with decidedly mixed results, through the 1990s. In addition, this period marked a further expansion in how the Council conceptualized its responsibilities regarding international peace and security, incorporating issues such as intrastate conflicts, refugees, complex humanitarian emergencies, human rights, and democracy, to name but a few examples (Malone, 2000b, pp. 23–30). Critics have argued that this broadening scope of concern has led the Council to increasingly violate the domestic jurisdiction of member states provided for in Article 2, Paragraph 7 (which in fact exempts Chapter 7 matters from its provisions). Malone more accurately concludes, however, that the Council has "sharply redefined in practice our conception of what can constitute a threat to international peace and security and a proper subject for international intervention" (2000b, p. 33).

The expanding scope of Council activity has sparked a renewed focus on the limits of its authority. Part of the debate stems from the fact that the Charter provides for different levels of Council authority across Chapters 6–7 (for example, see Bailey and Daws, 1998, pp. 18–20): quite simply, Assembly decisions made under Chapter 6 are never more than recommendations to the parties involved, whereas Chapter 7 decisions can be legally binding on the entire UN membership. In the early years of the United Nations, the enforcement mechanisms of Chapter 7 remained inoperable, mainly due to cold war tensions (Nicholas, 1975, p. 90; Caradon, 1981, p. 81). It was seen as a major achievement of the Council when it acted under Chapter 7 against a member state in 1977 (South Africa, due to its apartheid policies) for the first time, a full thirty-two years after the founding of the UN (Kaufmann, 1980, pp. 48–49). The rarity with which these provisions were used during the cold war makes it easy to understand why some UN observers have concluded that the Council is best viewed as a "bargaining mechanism" through which compromise decisions are pursued that ultimately depend on the political will of the member states for implementation (Luard and Heater, 1994, p. 32).

However, examining the record of the Council in recent years can lead one to the opposite conclusion: that the Council is hamstrung not by too little authority but by too much. David Caron argues that the Council "legislates in that its decisions potentially bind all states—both members of the United Nations and . . . states that do not belong to the United Nations at all. In short, the Council has substantial authority" (1993, p. 562). The primary reason for this assessment is that the Council has recently shown itself much more willing to make Chapter 7 decisions than at any other time in its history (Malone, 2000b, pp. 24–25; 2002, p. 41). Frederic Kirgis Jr. used the fiftieth anniversary of the UN as a starting point for investigating some of the most dramatic ways the Council had expanded its repertoire of quasi-legislative and quasi-judicial acts, from its handling of the Iraq/Kuwait conflict to its growing number of sanctions regimes, from its creation of criminal tribunals for the former Yugoslavia and Rwanda to its greater willingness to authorize humanitarian intervention (1995, pp. 520–532). He concludes that the Council has demonstrated a tendency to act under Chapter 7 without clearly indicating what the threat to international peace actually is (ibid., p. 538). This is a troubling pattern, since the Council should ascertain that its power is being used judiciously and with accountability to the larger UN membership if it is to remain a legitimate institution in the eyes of the international community (White, 2002, p. 94; Kirgis, 1995, p. 516; Caron, 1993, p. 562).

The Security Council meets in a moderate-sized room dominated in the center by a large horseshoe-shaped semicircle of connected tables. At the top of the horseshoe sits the representative from the member state that holds the Council's one-month rotating presidency. To the president's right sits the secretary-general (or secretary-general's representative), and to the left sits the under-secretary-general for political affairs or another senior member of the Secretariat offices that service the Council. One representative from each member state is also provided with a seat at the table, with two concentric rows of blue chairs behind this allowing room for a few advisers. At each tip of the horseshoe are two chairs reserved for nonmember states, Secretariat officials, or other individuals who have been invited to address the Council. On either side of the horseshoe at the front of the room are two sets of red chairs for additional support staff from Council members and the Secretariat. Above and behind these chairs, a series of glass booths are set into the walls; from them translation is provided and television footage is filmed. Just past the opening to the horseshoe, the floor of the Council chamber begins to slope upward at a steep angle toward the back of the room. The effect of this gallery is to make the chamber resemble a sort of well or pit (Nicholas, 1975, p. 98). The front half of the gallery is filled with red chairs reserved for delegates from member states that are not currently serving on the Council but that wish to attend the meeting. The second half is filled with green chairs for members of the press and NGO representatives. At the front of the room, soaring above the horseshoe, is a large mural that depicts a phoenix rising from the ashes of destruction of World War II (see photograph on page 209).

Article 28 of the UN Charter specifies that the "Security Council shall be so organized as to be able to function continuously," which requires that all members of the Council keep a representative at the seat of the organization at all times. The Council's Provisional Rules of Procedure further indicate that the Council meets at any time the Council president deems necessary and that the "interval between meetings shall not exceed fourteen days" (Rule 1). The president is instructed to call for a Council meeting when requested by any member of the Council (Rule 2) or when any dispute or situation is brought before the body by parties to the dispute, the secretary-general, the General Assembly, or any individual UN member as specified in the Charter (Rule 3). The president usually honors requests for a meeting within twenty-four hours, but problems can arise that necessitate delaying the meeting while consultations are held regarding the best way to address a particular issue (Nicol, 1981b, p. 14; Luard and Heater, 1994, p. 19; Bailey and Daws, 1998, p. 23). These consultations can cover issues such as whether the Council meeting should be closed (for Council members only) or open so that other interested parties can attend and, if an open meeting is going to be held, which additional actors should be invited to participate. Article 28, Paragraph 2 of the Charter also indicates that "periodic meetings" of the Council can be held, and Rule 4 of the Council's Provisional Rules of Procedure further specifies that two such meetings shall be held each year. These were designed to give the Council an opportunity to examine larger issues that extend beyond any single dispute, but only a few such meetings have been held (Narasimhan, 1988, p. 77; Bailey and Daws, 1998, pp. 45–50).

The procedures by which the Council conducts its business are considered provisional, but they have assumed a high degree of permanence (Sutterlin, 1997, p. 8). The mechanisms for running the meetings, setting the agenda, and voting have remained relatively constant through the UN's existence; these will be briefly considered below and will receive more detailed discussion in Chapter 7. Two ways in which the Council has evolved over time have had a direct impact on the nature of its debate. The first is in the interpretation of statements made in the Council. Originally the Council required that all statements be interpreted both simultaneously and consecutively (for greater accuracy) into all the UN's official and working languages (Bailey and Daws, 1998, pp. 91–92). This resulted in a very leisurely, even tedious, process of debate, so in 1972 the Council dropped consecutive interpretation by general consent and now relies exclusively on simultaneous interpretation. This change was especially necessary and welcome since the number of non–Council members wishing to participate in Council debates had grown to the point that some public meetings became virtual "mini-Assemblies" (Kaufmann, 1980, p. 49).

The second of these concerns the relative frequency of public versus private meetings. Before the 1970s, private meetings were usually held only to address very sensitive subjects, such as deciding the Council's choice for secretary-general (Sutterlin, 1997, p. 8, Narasimhan, 1988, p. 75). This was largely a result of Rule 48, which specifies that "unless it decides otherwise, the Security Council shall meet in public." This general pattern persisted even though the number of meetings held by the Council each year has increased rather steadily from the 1950s to the 1990s (Bailey and Daws, 1998, p. 35). But this pattern obscures the fact that a third type of meeting, informal consultation, has become a central way the Council conducts its business. Nicholas has observed that there have always been in fact two Councils, one that meets before the public and one that meets informally in delegates' lounges, dining rooms, and missions (1975, pp. 97–98). The use of this second, more informal Council became so important in the 1970s that a separate consultation room was established solely for this purpose (Sutterlin, 1997, p. 8; Nicol, 1981b, p. 14). In the time since, the frequency and importance of these informal consultations have continued to grow; this was most evident in the resurgent Council of the early 1990s (Kirgis, 1995, pp. 518–519). A wide range of Council activities are now grouped under the general heading of informal consultations (Bailey and Daws, 1998, p. 60), and these will be discussed in Chapter 8.

The specific procedural mechanisms used by the Council are the subject of the following chapter; however, a few preliminary comments about leadership, agenda setting, and voting are appropriate in this discussion of the Council's structure. Leadership on the Council is provided by the president, a position that rotates every month among the fifteen Council members in English alphabetical order. The position is held by the member state, not any one particular delegate or individual as is the case with the General Assembly presidency. This system of rotation was put in place to prevent any abuse of power by any Council member, but it has also made it difficult for any one president to impose a degree of rationality on the proceedings of the Council, since each has only a short time to make the attempt (Nicholas, 1975, p. 100; Nicol, 1981b, p. 7; Ziring, Riggs, and Plano, 2000, p. 51). The president of the Council has limited powers regarding calling meetings, setting the agenda, and engaging in informal consultations (Kaufmann, 1980, pp. 45–46; Bailey and Daws, 1998, pp. 130–132).

Once a decision has been taken to hold a meeting of the Council, the Provisional Rules of Procedure specify that a provisional agenda for the meeting should be drawn up by the secretary-general and approved by the president (Rule 7). This provisional agenda can include all matters communicated to the secretary-general that require consideration by the Council, unfinished business from the previous meeting, and any agenda items the Council had previously decided to defer. Rule 8 provides that the provisional agenda be communicated to Council members at least three days before the meeting, "but in urgent circumstances it may be communicated simultaneously with the notice of the meeting." In practice, the nature of the issues considered by the Council are often considered urgent, and the Council has usually been willing to dispense with the three days' notice requirement (Bailey and Daws, 1998, p. 37). There is another important way the actual process of creating the provisional agenda differs from the formal rules just discussed: the use of informal consultations to inform members that a meeting on a particular issue is being considered and to discuss how that issue should best be handled if the meeting is held (Bailey and Daws, 1998, p. 395; Nicol, 1981a, pp. 17–18).

Once an actual meeting begins, the first order of business is to formally accept the provisional agenda as the agenda for the meeting (Rule 9), a process that usually is relatively straightforward, even for contentious issues, because informal consultations have been carried out ahead of time. Once an issue makes it to the agenda of the Council, the body is said to be "seized of" the matter, which, as discussed above, technically means the issue is off limits to the General Assembly. Furthermore, when the Council becomes "seized" with a particular issue, it is almost never removed from the agenda, which would require a separate decision of the Council (Narasimhan, 1988, p. 71).

Resolutions are introduced and debated through a process that combines elements of public speechmaking and private negotiation (see Luard and Heater, 1994, pp. 19–20), dynamics that will be subjects of attention in the following two chapters. As this process unfolds, motions regarding the conduct of debate and resolutions (sometimes more than one for each issue, with amendments) regarding the course of Council action must be decided through voting procedures specified in Article 27 of the UN Charter as amended in 1965. Each member of the Council has one vote, and decisions require a qualified majority of nine (as opposed to eight) votes to be approved. Article 27 further specifies that for procedural matters the affirmative votes of any nine members are sufficient but for substantive issues the nine votes must include the "concurring votes of the permanent members" (except for those states party to a dispute before the Council, which must abstain). While the "concurring votes" terminology suggests that permanent members must vote affirmatively for a substantive resolution to pass, in practice permanent members that abstain or are absent are seen as concurring; they must vote against a resolution to block Council action (Bailey and Daws, 1995, p. 22; Kirgis, 1995, p. 537; Kaufmann, 1980, pp. 43–44). This veto power came under criticism from the start based on its violation of the sovereign equality of members (Chase, 1950, p. 177); however, it is clearly a more flexible procedure than the unanimity required in the League Council (Tung, 1969, p. 104), and it is based on the compelling logic that the Council was designed to act "at the behest of the permanent members," not against a permanent member (Knight, 2002, p. 28). In other words, the veto was designed to keep the permanent members in the United Nations, since all the great powers could be assured that the organization would not overextend itself by acting directly against their interests or the interests of their peers.

The Charter is silent on the question of which issues are substantive and which are procedural. During the San Francisco Conference, which drafted the UN Charter, the major powers agreed that any disagreement on whether an issue was substantive or procedural was itself a substantive question where the veto would apply (Kirgis, 1995, p. 510; Ziring, Riggs, and Plano, 2000, pp. 51–52). As a result, the permanent members enjoy a "double veto": they have the opportunity to veto treating an issue as a procedural question and then the opportunity to veto the resolution itself. While use of the double veto did create some difficulties in the early years of the Council (Tung, 1969, p. 105), there has always been some confusion as to how it operates due to its "obscure" nature (Nicol, 1981b, p 19), and its use was later reduced such that it is no longer considered to be a problem (Ziring, Riggs, and Plano, 2000, p. 52). In addition, over time the Council has resolved some of the ambiguities associated with determining whether an issue is substantive or procedural simply through the process of creating precedents as it has conducted its business (Tung, 1969, pp. 105–107).

Article 29 of the Charter empowers the Security Council to "establish such subsidiary organs as it deems necessary for the performance of its functions." Like the General Assembly, the Council has used this power extensively (see the overviews in Bailey and Daws, 1998, pp. 274–281, 333–378; *United Nations Handbook*, 2002, pp. 64–84). The Charter itself calls for one of these subsidiary bodies, the Military Staff Committee, which is composed of the chiefs of staff (or their representatives) of the permanent members in order "to advise and assist the Security Council on all questions relating to [its] military requirements for the maintenance of international peace and security" (Article 27). The Committee was designed to assist the Council in the command of any armed forces placed at its disposal through the agreements specified in Article 43. However, since none of these agreements were ever completed, on July 2, 1948, the Committee informed the Council that it would be unable to achieve its mandate, and it has had only token meetings of low-level representatives every fourteen days since that time (Bailey and Daws, 1998, p. 274). Other subsidiary bodies have been more active. For procedural matters, the Council is assisted by standing committees dealing with its rules of procedure, meetings away from headquarters, and the admission of new members, as well as ad hoc working groups dealing with its working methods and documentation.

The Council also has numerous subsidiary bodies dealing with substantive issues. One of the newest is the Counter Terrorism Committee, established to assist member states in their efforts to implement the requirements of Council Resolution 1373, passed shortly after the terrorist attacks of September 11, 2001. Another set of subsidiary bodies are sanctions committees created by the Council to monitor various binding sanction regimes the Council has imposed; as of 2002 there were eight such committees (covering Iraq, Libya, Somalia, Angola, Rwanda, Liberia, Sierra Leone, and Afghanistan), each of which functions as a committee of the whole and meets in private. In addition to these various committees, the Council has established fifty-six peace-keeping operations since 1948, with thirteen in place at the end of 2003, stretching across Africa, Asia, Europe, and the Middle East. Finally, the Council has established specific commissions and tribunals to deal with the legacy of threats to peace from the 1990s; these include the UN Monitoring, Verification, and Inspection Commission (UNMOVIC), which investigated Iraqi compliance with its required disarmament provisions; the UN Compensation Commission, which oversees the payment of compensation from Iraq to those negatively affected by its invasion of Kuwait; and the Criminal Tribunals for the Former Yugoslavia and Rwanda, which are charged with prosecuting persons accused of committing genocide in these two conflicts. All these committees, operations, commissions, and tribunals are required to submit periodic reports on their activities to the full Security Council.

The beginning of this discussion of the Security Council highlighted its position at the "apex" of the United Nations, a perception that has only increased once the Council became more active after the end of the cold war. This development served to accentuate existing dissatisfaction among some UN members regarding the size, composition, and working methods of the Council; this was most apparent in the case of aspiring permanent members, like Germany and Japan, and in the case of the developing world, which felt the Council was dominated by rich Western states (McCarthy, 1997). In response, on December 11, 1992, the General Assembly passed Resolution 46/62, which invited member states to submit written comments on the "Question of Equitable Representation on and Increase in the Membership of the Security Council." Over 100 member states jumped at this opportunity over the next few years, and an open-ended working group (OEWG) to address this issue, open to all UN members and chaired by the president of the Assembly, was created. The work of the OEWG was divided into two clusters: the first focused on the size and composition of the Council and the veto, and the second concerned the working methods of the Council, specifically efforts to increase transparency (Dedring, 2000, p. 88). The OEWG first turned its attention to cluster one and immediately found itself facing a wide range of proposals with very different ideas as to the overall size of the Council, what types of seats should be added (permanent versus nonpermanent), who would hold the new permanent seats, and whether new permanent members would enjoy the veto (see Knight, 2002, pp. 30–32, for an overview of the main proposals).

The intensity of the competing interests and desires that supported these divergent plans quickly resulted in a logjam regarding Council reform (Russett, O'Neill, and Sutterlin, 1996). During the Fifty-first Session of the Assembly in 1996–1997, the president, Razali Ismail of Malaysia, advanced a reform proposal that called for a total Council of twenty-one to twenty-six members, with five new permanent members: Germany, Japan, and one each from Asia, Africa, and Latin America—the regions would select who should hold the seat. While this package received some wide support, including that of the current permanent members and those states likely to get new permanent seats (like Brazil and India), it was opposed by those states that felt deserving of a permanent seat but were not seen as the regional frontrunners, such as Italy, Pakistan, and Mexico (Malone, 2000b, pp. 39–40). After Razali pushed his proposal in the face of this opposition, the debate over Council expansion descended into procedural bickering regarding the necessary majority for Charter amendment (two-thirds of the UN membership versus two-thirds of the states "present and voting"), and cluster one became fatally stalled (Smith, 1999). In the years since, some significant gains have been made regarding transparency, such as the increased consultation with troop-contributing nations discussed above (Dedring, 2000, p. 92); however, after more than a decade of debate on Council reform, this issue remains "controversial well into the new millennium" (Malone, 2000b, p. 40).

▓ Other Formal Arenas: ECOSOC, the Specialized Agencies, and Global Conferences

While the activities of the Security Council often are the subject of global headlines, nearly every introductory textbook on the United Nations highlights that over three-fourths of the organization's budget is devoted to economic and social activities (see, for example, Bennett and Oliver, 2002, p. 297). While some of these are the province of the General Assembly, a large portion of this activity takes place through the Economic and Social Council, the specialized agencies, and UN-sponsored global conferences. The focus here will not be on the diverse and important activities of these actors, however, but on their roles as arenas of formal UN decisionmaking. The roots of the UN's economic and social activities, and of ECOSOC itself, can be found in the work of the League of Nations (Luard and Heater, 1994, p. 62; Taylor, 2000b, pp. 101–102). In the twilight of the League in 1939, the Special Committee on the Development of International Cooperation in Economic and Social Affairs (the Bruce Committee) suggested that one way to strengthen the organization would be to expand upon its successful work in the less political areas of social and economic cooperation. While these ideas were never implemented in the League due to the outbreak of World War II, they were incorporated into the new United Nations after the war. Though the structure of ECOSOC fell short of the rather centralized system the Bruce Committee had in mind, its placement as a principal organ designed to oversee the economic and social activities of the entire UN system was seen as a clear statement that the UN would be much more than a peace and security organization.

ECOSOC was originally composed of eighteen members, with one-third of the membership elected by the General Assembly each year for staggered three-year terms (Article 61 of the Charter). As the membership of the UN grew in size and diversity, the composition of ECOSOC was expanded twice through Charter amendment, first to twenty-seven members in 1965 (as a result of General Assembly Resolution 1991B (XVIII) of 1963) and then to fifty-four members in 1973 (as a result of Assembly Resolution 2847 (XXVI) of 1971). The fifty-four seats on ECOSOC are distributed geographically, based on a formula established when the expansion was approved: fourteen from Africa, eleven from Asia, six from Eastern Europe, ten from Latin America and the Caribbean, and thirteen from Western Europe and Other States (*United Nations Handbook*, 2002, p. 87). Retiring members are eligible for immediate reelection, and member states that are not currently serving on ECOSOC are able "to participate, without vote, in its deliberations on any matter of particular concern to that member" (Articles 61 and 69).

Based on its role at the center of the UN's economic and social activities, the work of ECOSOC and its subsidiary organs has always been relatively more open to the participation of a wide range of actors. Due to its large size, an agenda that often puts developed and developing states at odds, and the need to provide membership for its many subsidiary bodies, all three of the types of groups discussed in Chapter 3 play a role in ECOSOC (for example, see Tolley, 1983, for the Commission on Human Rights). Article 71 of the Charter explicitly specifies that ECOSOC serves as the primary point of contact for nongovernmental organizations in the UN's decisionmaking machinery (as was discussed in Chapter 5), and ECOSOC's procedures allow for these actors to participate in debate by receiving documents, attending meetings, and on occasion submitting written and oral statements (Bailey and Daws, 1995, p. 23). The Charter also instructs ECOSOC to make arrangements for the reciprocal participation of representatives from the specialized agencies in its debates (Article 70), a responsibility that has been problematic at best, as will be discussed below. Finally, the Secretariat plays a twofold role in ECOSOC: it provides reports on issues under discussion in ECOSOC, and it assists the leaders of ECOSOC in running the meetings (Kaufmann, 1980, p. 55).

ECOSOC enjoys a wide mandate emanating from its responsibility, under the authority of the General Assembly, for the discharge of the very broad objectives identified in Article 55 of the Charter: promoting higher standards of living, full employment, economic and social development, health, education, and human rights (see also Article 60).

Nicholas has observed that these provisions of the Charter are far more vague and diffuse than those dealing with the Security Council, mainly because they suffered from a lack of attention and close examination in the drafting process (1975, pp. 138–139). As a result, the Charter positions ECOSOC as something of a catchall organization for the "residue" of the UN's economic and social activities. It is designed to perform its own work in the form of studies, reports, recommendations, draft conventions, and conferences, all of which must be approved by the General Assembly (Articles 62 and 66). At the same time it is given the responsibility, but little actual authority, to coordinate the work of other UN bodies, including the rather autonomous specialized agencies, which are active on issues under ECOSOC's purview (Articles 57–58, 63–64). The "modest" and "tentative" language of these articles has made it difficult for ECOSOC to play its "dual role" as both a coordinator and part of that which is to be coordinated (Nicholas, 1975, pp. 139–140). These problems of mandate and authority are made worse by the fact that many of ECOSOC's functions and issues have been assumed by other organizations, most often a specialized agency or one of the main committees of the General Assembly (see Kaufmann, 1980, pp. 55–57; Narasimhan, 1988, p. 187; Ziring, Riggs, and Plano, 2000, p. 52). Part of the problem, according to one US representative on ECOSOC, was that the body never had the operational capacity to address all the issues placed before it, so it was forced to pass on much of its work to other bodies (quoted in Grey, 2000, p. 39). This has led one UN observer to conclude that "total confusion reigns," since "there is no division of tasks" between the Assembly and ECOSOC; the Assembly has become increasingly overburdened, and ECOSOC functions as a mini-Assembly (Smouts, 2000, p. 49).

Originally ECOSOC held two meetings each year: one in New York in the spring and one in Geneva in the summer. In 1991, General Assembly Resolution 45/264 changed this practice to one meeting a year between May and July, alternating between New York and Geneva (*United Nations Handbook*, 2002, p. 93). Further changes to the structure of ECOSOC meetings were contained in Assembly Resolutions 48/162 of 1993 and 50/227 of 1996 (Taylor, 2000b, pp. 125–129). The substantive session is now limited to four weeks in July of each year, with the session divided into four primary segments called High-Level, Coordination, Operational, and General. The four-day High-Level segment is open to all member states and devoted to general questions of policy on one or more social or economic themes. These discussions are held at the ministerial level and result in a set of "agreed conclusions." The Coordination segment examines common themes across global conferences and ECOSOC's functional commissions (more below), in an effort to identify specific proposals for action to pass on to one of the main committees of the General Assembly. The Operational segment deals with the activities of ECOSOC's subsidiary bodies and the specialized agencies, making sure that General Assembly and ECOSOC policies are appropriately implemented. The final segment used to be devoted to simultaneous work by two of ECOSOC's three sessional committees, the Economic Committee and the Social Committee (the Policy and Programme Committee was the third); however, since 1996 this committee segment was replaced by the current General segment, where all issues are debated in the plenary. The overriding theme of these reforms was an effort to rationalize, as much as possible, the work of ECOSOC in relation to its subsidiary bodies and the General Assembly, in order to avoid having different deliberative bodies repeat the same debates (Taylor, 2000b, p. 128).

Planning for the annual substantive session begins in January or February of each year, when a short organizational session is held (*United Nations Handbook*, 2002, p. 93). Elections for ECOSOC's leadership positions (a president and four vice presidents, one from each geographic region) and membership in its subsidiary bodies are held at a resumed organizational session in late April or early May. The annual substantive sessions operate in much the same way as the General Assembly and its main committees: each member can send whatever individuals it desires to represent its interests, each member has one vote, and decisions are taken by simple majority. However, ECOSOC has been plagued by at least two problems with this process of debate. The first concerns the types of delegates who have traditionally been sent to ECOSOC: "its tasks may be too broad for specialists and too specialized for many members of permanent missions" (Kaufmann, 1980, p. 58). As a result, ECOSOC meetings often have lower-level representation than does the General Assembly; given this, the High-Level segment was shortened to just four days so that higher-level representatives might be sent for a focused discussion (Taylor, 2000b, p. 125). The second problem concerns the quality of debate: many of the governments represented on ECOSOC are not all that interested in its work, so it is not uncommon for only a fraction of delegates to be in the room listening to speeches while the rest are having their coffee (Narasimhan, 1988, p. 195). Even early assessments of ECOSOC concluded that its debates were best characterized as an "airing of views" without any actual discussion or interaction (Nicholas, 1975, p. 148). These tendencies are made worse by the relaxed and easy atmosphere that characterizes the body: meetings almost never start on time, and issues are frequently postponed for later consideration (Narasimhan, 1988, p. 195). The reforms in ECOSOC's methods discussed in the previous paragraph have helped to ameliorate some of these problems (Taylor, 2000b, p. 128), but difficulties still remain.

One challenge that has faced ECOSOC throughout its existence is its responsibility for coordinating the work of numerous subsidiary bodies, the specialized agencies, and many of the global conferences that have been held on specific economic and social issues. Of these various arenas, those that come most directly under ECOSOC's purview are its own subsidiary bodies, beginning with five regional economic commissions: the Economic Commission for Africa, the Economic and Social Commission for Asia and the Pacific, the Economic Commission for Europe, the Economic Commission for Latin America and the Caribbean, and the Economic and Social Commission for Western Asia. They vary in membership from thirteen members in the one for Western Asia to fifty-five in the one for Europe (*United Nations Handbook*, 2002, pp. 130–136) and were established "to encourage the regional sharing of expertise regarding common problems, the cooperative study of regional economic issues, and the preparation of action on the regional level" (Kaufmann, 1980, p. 59). This decentralization of concern for economic and social issues received strong support from regional groups, especially as these bodies moved beyond simply studying problems to actually coming up with plans to address them (Luard and Heater, 1994, p. 64).

ECOSOC also has functional commissions dealing with social development, crime prevention and criminal justice, human rights, narcotic drugs, population and development, science and technology for development, sustainable development, status of women, and statistics. They are composed of anywhere from twenty-four to fifty-three members, who, in spite of some early argument that they should be individual experts (Nicholas, 1975, p. 139), are representatives of member states distributed by a geographic formula agreed upon in ECOSOC (*United Nations Handbook*, 2002, pp. 94–128). Some of these commissions have their own subsidiary bodies; in the case of human rights there is a Sub-Commission on the Promotion and Protection of Human Rights, at least seven other issue-focused working groups that report to the commission, and five working groups that report to the subcommission. The subcommission for human rights departs from its parent body in that it is composed of individuals who are selected by a geographic formula but who serve in an individual capacity, not as representatives of governments. This use of experts is also found in a number of other ECOSOC working groups and standing committees (*United Nations*

Handbook, 2002, pp. 140–148) and does enable these bodies to be less prone to the very political debates often aired in the functional commissions and the ECOSOC parent body.

More removed from the direct oversight of ECOSOC and yet very important in the economic and social activities of the United Nations is the work of the specialized agencies. As was mentioned earlier in this chapter, these bodies cover a wide range of UN activities and, according to Articles 57 and 63 of the UN Charter, are subject to the coordinating oversight of ECOSOC. Some of these bodies—the Universal Postal Union, the International Telegraph (now Telecommunication) Union, and the International Labour Organization—predate the United Nations but quickly entered into "relationship agreements" with the new organization and thereby became "specialized agencies" (Luard and Heater, 1994, p. 76). These early "relationship agreements" then became a pattern on which subsequent ones were based, although some significant modifications were required in the case of the IMF and World Bank, to provide them with greater autonomy, and minor simplifications were made for the smallest, most technical specialized agencies (Taylor, 2000b, p. 104). Such relationship agreements typically involve recognition of the fact that the organization in question is a specialized agency, an indication that membership in the agency is somehow linked to membership in the United Nations, the establishment of reciprocal representation (without vote) at some (but not all) of each other's meetings, the right to propose agenda items for each other's consideration, provisions for an exchange of information through annual reports to ECOSOC or the General Assembly, and a recognition of the desirability of common standards regarding their international civil service employees (Sands and Klein, 2001, pp. 79–83). In theory these provisions were to enable ECOSOC to coordinate (but not control) the work of these diverse agencies (Luard and Heater, 1994, p. 76); however, in practice this coordination has been sporadic and largely ineffectual, which has led to various proposals for reform, discussed below.

The specialized agencies are often seen as the embodiment of "functionalist" thinking (see, for example, Luard and Heater, 1994, p. 62; Sands and Klein, 2001, p. 78): cooperation to solve the common economic and social problems that these agencies address would contribute to building "peace by pieces" (Wells, 1991) as general welfare improved, interdependence between states increased, and friendships emerged across traditional lines of conflict. The goal was to decentralize these economic and social activities in order to better insulate them from the intense political debates that were likely to plague the General Assembly, Security Council, and other deliberative bodies of the UN system. This would allow these agencies to better perform their primary tasks of promoting information exchange, designing programs to assist member states in the agency's area of competence, and drafting common standards and rules to facilitate economic and social interaction (Ziring, Riggs, and Plano, 2000, pp. 325–326). The nonpolitical and technical work of these agencies was to be one of the most important features of the UN. Unfortunately, the illusion on which these hopes rested became all too apparent when the work of many specialized agencies became "politicized" in the 1970s. The process of politicization occurs when "highly controversial issues not always relevant to the agency's work are introduced by nations to further their political interests" (Lyons, Baldwin, and McNemar, 1977, p. 81), and it results in a dysfunction of the agency in question because it becomes unable to discharge its intended activities (Ghebali, 1991, p. 20). This occurred primarily due to disagreements between developed and developing states regarding the global economy and colonialism, cold war rivalries between the East and West, and the persistent problems in South Africa and the Middle East. While these issues did not plague all the specialized agencies to the same degree (Lyons, Baldwin, and McNemar, 1977, p. 88), they have made the general challenges of ECOSOC's coordination far more difficult to overcome.

The specialized agencies have an institutional structure that is broadly similar in most cases: a plenary organ composed of all member states, a small council of limited membership vested with some degree of separate power, and a secretariat composed of international civil servants (Sands and Klein, 2001, p. 83). In many of the specialized agencies the plenary is entrusted with greater powers than those of the limited-membership council, which typically assumes a position of subordination. However, comparative studies of the political processes of various specialized agencies (see, for example, Cox and Jacobson, 1973a and 1973b; Wells, 1991) have found some important areas of variation that can make the dynamics of each agency unique. For example, Cox and Jacobson (1973a, pp. 371–436) highlight a number of institutional factors that affect the nature of decisionmaking and the degree of politicization that results: the degree to which the agency functions as a forum for member-state debate as opposed to a provider of services to its members; the type of decision activities typically on an agency's agenda; the type of actors able to participate in the agency's processes, through either voting or simple consultation; the procedures used for managing debate and making decisions (the subject of Chapter 7); and the degree to which lines of cleavage in world politics intrude upon the workings of the agency.

While a survey of these issues in regard to all the specialized agencies is beyond the scope of this chapter, it is important to offer a few examples of how basic institutional structures influence the work of various specialized agencies. First, many of the specialized agencies have arrangements whereby the member states most affected by their activities enjoy a special role in their political processes, usually through guaranteed representation on the limited-membership body that handles decisionmaking in between the meetings of the plenary. One such example is the International Civil Aviation Organization (ICAO), which provides for adequate representation for states "of chief importance in air transport" and states "which make the largest contribution to the provision of facilities for international civil air navigation" (White, 2002, p. 84). Second, some of the agencies have similar privileged roles for the member states that contribute the most money or other resources for the organization's operation. The IMF and World Bank are two well-known examples, where the donor countries effectively decide lending policy. The International Fund for Agricultural Development (IFAD) enjoys a similar but distinctive arrangement, as "contributing developed countries" (members of the Organization of Economic Cooperation and Development) and "contributing developing countries" (members of the Organization of Petroleum Exporting Countries) have both opted for a system of weighted voting (Talbot and Moyer, 1997, pp. 279–282; Gregg, 1977, pp. 77–78). A third structural consideration that affects the political processes of these agencies concerns the actors that participate in their decisionmaking bodies. While many limit this to whatever delegates a member state chooses to send, the ILO specifies that its members be represented by a tripartite delegation that includes representatives from government and the national workers' and employers' associations. A perceived erosion of the tripartite arrangement led the United States to temporarily leave the ILO in the late 1970s (Allen, 1991, p. 187–190). In spite of this controversy, the ILO structure has created a distinctive forum where the interests of various communities within a state are represented in addition to, or alongside of, the interests of the state (Sands and Klein, 2001, p. 98).

One of the disadvantages of the decentralized system of specialized agencies just discussed is the frequent emergence of separate, sector-oriented plans for addressing issues that would more appropriately be handled through interdisciplinary and "multi-organizational" forms of cooperation (Kaufmann, 1980, p. 79). In theory ECOSOC is responsible for playing this role, but its organizational and procedural weaknesses have necessitated a search for alternate forums of decisionmaking, and UN-sponsored global issue conferences have filled this void. The basic features of these conferences were discussed in Chapter 5, since they represent an important venue for nongovernmental organizations and multinational corporations to seek to wield influence in the UN system. Here we will briefly consider how the ad hoc structure of these conferences leads to patterns of decisionmaking that are both similar to and different from those considered above. Global conferences share some essential features with the General Assembly: both are characterized by near universal participation and voting by the representatives of member states. Global conferences can be seen, then, as "political events par excellence that remain subject to the vicissitudes of the political process be they bureaucratic disputes, personality conflicts, or underlying tectonic movements" (Fomerand, 1996, p. 371). If sufficient political will is present and the issue under consideration is ripe for resolution, then the conferences can have dramatic results; when these conditions are lacking, though, the conference can actually leave the international response to a pressing issue more fragmented than it was when the debate started.

While the success or failure of a conference can rest on many things, basic structural elements of conferences can have an important impact on the political debates that ensue. One important consideration is the objectives of the conference, which can include sharing information, exchanging views, pledging money or other resources for a situation of need, generating nonbinding recommendations or voluntary commitments, drafting binding international treaties, and reviewing progress toward implementing an earlier agreement (Kaufmann, 1988, pp. 6–11; Rittberger, 1998, pp. 21–22). As common sense would expect, the more ambitious the goals of the conference, the more likely it is that its political processes will come to resemble the most difficult political debates held in formal arenas of decisionmaking such as the General Assembly and Security Council. Nevertheless, some observers have suggested that the ad hoc nature of global conferences can result in more agreement-friendly processes of debate, even where there are intense negotiations (Rittberger, 1998, pp. 24–25). This is true for several reasons: conferences usually include a lengthy preparatory phase in which the most contentious issues can be hammered out; they often take place in a setting more isolated from day-to-day distractions, thereby allowing for more focused negotiation; they often allow for greater participation on the part of civil society actors, which, as was discussed in Chapter 5, can create more pressure for agreement on state delegates; they typically offer ideal opportunities for package dealing and other strategies that will be discussed in Chapter 9; and they are often structured with a pivotal role for the types of negotiating groups and brokers discussed in Chapter 3. As a result of these features, global conferences can on occasion achieve results that the General Assembly, ECOSOC, and the specialized agencies cannot.

Given the fact that ECOSOC has such an expansive agenda, manages numerous subsidiary bodies, and addresses issues also considered in the General Assembly, the specialized agencies, and global conferences, it is hard to overstate both the importance of and the difficulty of providing effective coordination. All these forums consider too many issues, often the same ones, and each has developed what can be called a "sovereign equality complex" (Kaufmann, 1980, p. 64), being intent on protecting its own autonomy and turf even while paying lip service to the importance of effective coordination. Numerous attempts have been made to overcome these problems, both by changing ECOSOC's internal structure and procedures (as was discussed above) and by creating interagency bodies for planning and coordination (Taylor, 2000b).

One of the most cited, and criticized, examples is the Administrative Committee on Coordination (ACC), which was originally created in 1946 to bring together the secretary-general and the heads of the specialized agencies (White, 2002, pp. 101–105). Unfortunately, this mechanism was long seen as simply giving the various agency heads a venue for asserting their autonomy and independence from UN headquarters. There are some signs that the ACC has become more proactive and dynamic in its work. Most promising is the fact that a chain of authority from the General Assembly to ECOSOC to the ACC to the agencies has been "operating in a more pragmatic and results oriented fashion" (White, 2002, p. 105). While in 2001 ECOSOC changed the name of the ACC to the Chief Executives Board for Coordination (CEB; ECOSOC decision 2001/321), it did not change the existing ACC mandate (*United Nations Handbook*, 2002, pp. 148–150). Like the ACC, the CEB is chaired by the secretary-general and meets twice annually. It is now assisted as well by two high-level committees with narrower mandates: one addresses coordination on UN administration and management, and the other focuses exclusively on the program work of the twenty-seven organizations and agencies included in the CEB. The degree to which these efforts are successful will have a direct impact on the UN's political processes in the future. These reforms have the potential to change the procedures through which each body conducts its debates and makes its decisions, which is the subject of the following chapter.

7

Decision Rules and Parliamentary Procedures

INTERNATIONAL ORGANIZATIONS ARE CALLED UPON TO PERFORM A WIDE range of functions and tasks in international politics. This is especially true for the organs, bodies, programs, and funds within the United Nations system, given their broad purposes and near universal membership. In light of this diversity, Cox and Jacobson found it helpful to distinguish between two different categories of international organizations: those that are established to provide a forum or framework for negotiations and those that are intended to provide specific services (1973b, pp. 5–6). Organizations in the first category are primarily concerned with allowing member states to exchange views, seek collective legitimization for their actions, or negotiate binding legal instruments. Organizations in the second category may collect, analyze, and disseminate information or engage in other concrete activities that are designed to provide a direct service to a population in need. While many international organizations perform functions and tasks in both categories, the distinction does offer a useful opportunity to think about different patterns of decisionmaking across the two categories. For example, Cox and Jacobson suggest that more service-oriented organizations are likely to have larger, more powerful bureaucracies that play a direct and influential role in decisionmaking. In the case of forum or framework organizations, they expect member states and groups to be the central actors.

The primary mechanism through which forum and service organizations carry out their functions and tasks is decisions (Cox and Jacobson, 1973b, pp. 14–15). Some of these decisions cover "issues of great import that receive wide attention"; most, however, "are made on questions that are of minor consequence" (Alger, 1973, p. 205). But even those of minor consequence can have a significant impact on the organization's decisionmaking over time, since they "help create the context in which occasional decisions recognized to be highly important are made" (ibid.). Scholars have concluded, then, that it is more fruitful to differentiate among decisions based on the nature of the issues involved rather than based on perceived importance. Cox and Jacobson offer a taxonomy of seven types of international organization decisions in their comparison of eight agencies within the UN system: representational decisions dealing with membership, symbolic decisions designed to test how opinions are aligned, boundary decisions concerning the organization's relationship with other actors, programmatic decisions that strategically allocate the organization's resources, rule-creating decisions that define acceptable behavior in regard to an issue, rule-supervisory decisions that monitor and judge compliance with accepted rules and norms, and operational decisions regarding the use of the organization's resources to provide services (1973b, pp. 9–11). In a similar vein, Alger identifies five types of decisions based on different subjects covered within the United Nations and three of its specialized agencies: administrative decisions dealing with the Secretariat, budget and finance decisions including assessments, elections and appointments decisions encompassing both membership and leadership, procedural decisions regarding how the organization functions, and program decisions concerning the future direction of the organization's activities (1973, pp. 209–211).

One underlying issue in both of these typologies is that different types of decisions will necessarily involve distinct patterns of interaction (Cox and Jacobson, 1973b, p. 14; Alger, 1973, pp. 211–214). This is true because different decisions are made in different contexts based on each organization's functions, structure, procedures, and history (Cox and Jacobson, 1973b, p. 5). In a more detailed examination of the same dynamic, Alger identifies six factors that affect the way decisionmaking on a specific issue is handled:

1. the intensity with which participants desire to reach a consensus;
2. the degree to which relevant national policies are different;
3. the manner in which regional caucus groups (and other groups) unify portions of the membership behind common positions;
4. the abilities, experiences, and personalities of individual participants;
5. interrelationships between the issue being debated and other agenda items, past and present;
6. the organizational milieu created by such factors as the cultural setting of the organization, the secretariat, and the kind of social structure linking participants that has been created by past activities. (1973, p. 208)

Many of the factors suggested by these authors have received attention in other chapters; however, one area that clearly merits additional examination is the parliamentary procedures and decision rules that are used to debate and decide between competing proposals for UN action. Some of these rules of procedure, such as those covering membership and agenda setting, were covered in Chapter 6. This chapter will expand on that discussion to consider how the music and routines of the global dance are shaped by the procedures for managing debate, providing leadership, and conducting votes. To set the context for this discussion, a few preliminary observations about rules of procedure in international organizations are in order.

Rules of procedure are a nearly universal feature of international conferences. They include "all the rules and practices which determine the status of each of the participants in an international conference and the conduct of the discussions until the conference adopts its final decision" (Sabel, 1997, p. 1). As such, they can cover all aspects of how the conference is managed, such as the participation of delegates, the responsibilities of the presiding officer, the manner in which delegates can address the conference, the process through which proposals are submitted and amended, the mechanisms for conducting voting on both procedural and substantive issues, and the role of committees in the decisionmaking process (see Sabel, 1997, table of contents; Kaufmann, 1988, p. 39). The rules of procedure are equally important, if not even more so, in international organizations, since one of their principal differences from conferences is the degree to which these rules and other structures of decisionmaking are institutionalized. However, such differences are narrowing: "the rules of procedure and their interpretation follow remarkably consistent patterns [such that the] conferences and assemblies of different organizations tend to reach similar conclusions on procedural issues" (Sabel, 1997, p. 1). Understanding the impact of rules of procedure on multilateral decisionmaking is important in the case of all types of institutionalized settings; this chapter focuses on those found in the UN's main political bodies, the General Assembly and Security Council.

International organizations by definition work by a specific and established set of procedural rules; these may be quite comprehensive or more modest in scope (Chrispeels, 1998, p. 119). The rules of procedure in many international organizations are surprisingly constant, yet they do evolve over time through custom and practice (Bailey and Daws, 1998, pp. 13, 17–18). No matter how detailed and stable they are, rules of procedure enable international organizations to act as "catalysts for agreement" (Keohane, 1984, p. 90). Cooperation is said to be easier within an international organization than outside one, based on efficiency: rules reduce the costs of transacting business, since "establishing the rules and principles at the outset makes it unnecessary to renegotiate them each time a specific question arises" (ibid.). The rules "specify in advance how much influence each member has over decisions, the procedures by which proposals will be considered and the amount of support necessary to turn proposals into decisions" (Peterson, 1986, p. 54). Rules of procedure help to legitimate whatever decisions are made by ensuring that all competing proposals were properly considered.

Having set rules of procedure does not, of course, remove all potential for conflict regarding the way debate is conducted. After all, the rules and the procedural decisions that result from them "are often only a reflection of the political reality at an assembly or conference" (Sabel, 1997, p. 4). If an organization or conference is to have significant authority in regard to a particular area of concern, then those actors most affected by this authority will likely push for "structural and procedural devices to ensure for themselves the means of exerting special influence" over the decisionmaking (Cox and Jacobson, 1973b, p. 7). However, "states nevertheless tend to follow precedents in procedural matters," especially if they "are accompanied by a reasoned decision of an experienced presiding officer" (Sabel, 1997, p. 4). These competing conceptualizations reflect an inherent tension regarding the role of procedures in international organizations: they can be an important tool for managing difficult negotiations in a fair and unbiased manner, but they can also become a subject of intense dispute and manipulation. The first of these dynamics will be explored in this chapter; the latter will be covered in Chapter 9.

◼ The Consideration of Proposals

Debate in the political bodies of the United Nations can be used in the pursuit of a wide range of objectives. Those that often receive the most attention are unfortunately not the ones most consistent with the reasoned consideration of competing proposals. Such objectives include scoring debating points and reaching audiences beyond the actors actually participating in debate (Petersen, 1968, pp. 131–134). In terms of scoring debating points, participants in UN politics may see public discussion as an opportunity to embarrass their opponents, either by directly challenging policies that appear to violate international law or common norms of behavior or by making reference to inconsistencies in behavior over time or inconsistencies between word and deed in regard to a particular issue. In terms of outside audiences, diplomatic rhetoric at the UN is "more usually designed to convince third parties, or to appeal to people over the heads of government, or to win the approbation of public opinion at home, or to ensure that a point of view is on record" (Bailey, 1960, p. 111). While these objectives can be very satisfying to the initiator and represent important "achievements" in their own right, they rarely play a constructive role in building agreement on the substance of debate (Petersen, 1968, p. 134). In fact, since the parliamentary nature of UN diplomacy has "altered the nature of this verbal combat," it can in some instances have the opposite effect by increasing tension and hostility (Bailey, 1960, p. 111).

The United Nations is intended to serve as a vehicle for promoting international cooperation. As such, it is really useful to governments only if it can "devise procedures and practices which can resolve rather than expose differences" (Bailey, 1960, p. 147). The following paragraphs will consider the procedures and processes through which competing proposals are advanced and debated within the UN's main political bodies. On some occasions these dynamics involve no formal debate of specific proposals before a decision is taken; more commonly, they may simply include interested delegations' offering carefully worded comments about proposals they support or oppose in formal meetings so their position will be on the record (for example, see Bailey, 1960, pp. 152–157; Alger, 1973, pp. 211–214). In these cases the "debate" is really only a series of prepared speeches delivered without any pretense of persuading other parties. However, it is possible for these discussions to become much more animated and intense, with delegates arguing about differing approaches, alternate language, or even "the significance of a single comma" (Kaufmann, 1988, p. 12). Depending on the salience of the issue and the procedures that are being used to manage debate, these exchanges typically include a mix of public and private interaction (Peterson, 1986, pp. 91–92). While informal politics will be the subject of Chapter 8, it is important to point out here that they are an undercurrent that can significantly affect how the public debate unfolds at the United Nations. Some observers have characterized this interaction with the analogy of an iceberg: public debate is simply the visible tip of the political process, while much of the give-and-take required in effective multilateral diplomacy remains beneath the surface (Alger, 1972, p. 296).

At the United Nations, decisionmaking involves consideration of various proposals for action, most often in the form of resolutions. UN resolutions typically contain two interrelated parts. The first is a preamble that situates the resolution in the context of the problem at hand and makes reference to previous efforts to address the problem or relevant internationally accepted norms of behavior. The second is an operative part in which the UN body adopting the resolution either requests action on the part of certain relevant actors or provides a statement of opinion about the problem.

The initial drafting of a resolution may be a group process involving representatives from several delegations; for practical reasons, however, the effort is usually led by a specific member state. This may be the state that originally proposed the agenda item, but it can in fact be any interested member that wants to advance a particular approach to the problem or issue at hand (Luard and Heater, 1994, p. 47; Nicol, 1981b, p. 20). There may be several states interested in a particular agenda item, in which case these potential sponsors may take turns with the drafting, especially if the agenda item recurs from one year to the next (for example, see Terpstra, 1999, pp. 215–216). The ultimate identity of the state taking the lead on the drafting can be of crucial importance in decisionmaking, because the character and tone of the original proposal will to some extent set the stage for all future debate on the issue (Luard and Heater, 1994, p. 48). The process of actually writing a draft often involves an interactive exchange between a state's UN mission and personnel in the foreign ministry back home (Kaufmann, 1980, p. 119). The degree to which the mission or ministry takes the lead depends on the perceived importance of the issue, and either of these parties may find it helpful to quietly consult members of the Secretariat for their knowledge of the language used in previous texts on the same issue. Other than a deadline for the submission of new proposals (called the "closing date"), there are relatively few restrictions on the freedom of delegations to submit draft resolutions in UN bodies (Kaufmann, 1988, p. 13). However, there are certain practices at the drafting stage that delegates can find helpful when it comes time to actually debate their proposals, such as drawing on language similar to that already approved in other UN bodies whenever possible (Tolley, 1983, p. 43).

Once a delegation has a draft proposal that they would like to pursue, the first step is to quietly circulate it among their close friends and allies. Typically, this is done as the drafting process continues so that others' reactions can be addressed in the text to ensure that the new proposal will have the basic endorsement of a key group of supporters (Kaufmann, 1980, p. 120). The new and improved draft proposal is then circulated to a larger group of interested parties, based on either regional affiliations or common interest groups, as discussed in Chapter 3 (Nicol, 1981b, p. 20; Luard and Heater, 1994, p. 48). This process of consultation allows negotiations to get under way before public debate of specific proposals even begins (Alger, 1972, p. 296). These negotiations can involve informal conversations as well as the circulation of "working papers" on behalf of the original drafters. On some occasions the drafters may want to offer a politically uncertain proposal without explicitly identifying their role in writing it, in which case it is circulated without any sponsors as a "non-paper" (Kaufmann, 1988, p. 13). These proposals, which are sometimes said to have been found "lying on the floor," allow states to offer "trial balloons" whose content can later be denied, since the drafters are not formally linked to the document in any way (even though most parties will have a strong idea as to the identity of the authors).

The process of building support for various working papers continues as general discussion of the agenda item proceeds in the formal meetings of the UN body (Peterson, 1986, p. 104; Bailey and Daws, 1998, p. 201). Efforts to draft and adjust the proposals are typically influenced by the Secretariat report prepared to serve as background on the agenda item and by public statements made in the general discussion by both potential supporters and opponents (Kaufmann, 1988, p. 13; Tolley, 1983, pp. 44–45). Depending on the nature of the issue and how far apart the interests of the relevant member states are, the interactive process of drafting and building support for a particular proposal can be as short as a few hours or as long as several months (Luard and Heater, 1994, pp. 19–20). The duration of this process is also partially governed by how much support the original drafters of the proposal desire to secure before their working paper is officially introduced into debate. While fewer sponsors for each proposal was the norm in the UN's early years (the more important need was winning the support of the great powers), this soon gave way to drafters' frequent attempts to secure as many sponsors as possible in order to increase the chances that their proposal would be adopted (Bailey, 1960, pp. 147–148) and to demonstrate exactly how strong opinion was regarding a particular problem (Luard and Heater, 1994, p. 48). Even more significant than the sheer number of sponsors is securing sponsors from as wide a range of members as possible, since broad-based support, even if it is from a smaller total number of states, can provide much more momentum toward the successful adoption of a particular proposal (Kaufmann, 1980, p. 122). It is also important to realize, however, that extensive or broad-based sponsorship can severely reduce the original drafter's room to maneuver, so some delegations intentionally limit the number of parties that become sponsors to their proposals.

After a draft proposal has achieved the desired number of sponsors, it is officially introduced into debate. As this happens, discussion of the agenda item moves from a preliminary or general phase to a period of more intense examination of the specific proposal or proposals that are ready for formal action by the decisionmaking body (Peterson, 1986, p. 104; Bailey and Daws, 1998, p. 201). Although this shift in the nature of debate may not be sharply differentiated in practice, having specific proposals on the table does signify that the discussions are entering a critical period. When proposals are officially introduced into debate, the sponsors provide a copy to the Secretariat, which assigns the document an official UN symbol (a combination of identifying letters and numbers) and then distributes copies to all members participating in the meeting. The rules of procedure for most UN organs and UN-sponsored global conferences require that all proposals be circulated in writing no later than the day preceding the meeting at which the proposals are to be considered (Sabel, 1997, p. 126; Chrispeels, 1998, p. 130); however, it is common for many of these bodies (including the General Assembly and Security Council) to waive this requirement, allowing proposals to be introduced orally first or to be circulated the same day as the meeting is being held, so long as the membership is willing to go along with these modifications (Kaufmann, 1988, p. 14; Bailey and Daws, 1998, p. 200).

Often the original drafters will provide a brief oral introduction of the resolution in order to frame its content and clarify "any wording that could give rise to misunderstanding" (Kaufmann, 1988, p. 15). These comments may be offered by one delegation, or they may involve a coordinated division of labor among several members, with each speaking on a specific part of the draft. In some cases the original authors may "wish to remain in the background" for political reasons and therefore defer the task of introducing the proposal to more politically acceptable sponsors (ibid., p. 14). Once the proposal is formally introduced, the floor is open for other delegations to discuss its relative merits. If the proposal has been circulated among only a small circle of states or formally introduced on short notice, then the other members are likely to be initially unprepared to respond in a formal setting, and debate may proceed on another topic while the proposal is scrutinized.

United Nations bodies typically permit more than one proposal to be formally introduced into debate in relation to the same issue. During the 1950s and 1960s it was in fact common practice for "contending clusters of sponsors to prepare drafts on a question and formally present them early in the proceedings" (Peterson, 1986, p. 93). This was especially true in regard to highly political questions, and it required that the negotiation process include formal rules about the order in which competing proposals would be considered and brought to a vote. In the

Security Council, the standard practice is to handle proposals in the order they are submitted, but on occasion agreement is reached to bring a later draft to a vote first (Bailey and Daws, 1998, p. 200). In many cases where multiple proposals have been introduced, only one will ultimately come up for a vote: "it is usually known by all how much support there will be for each" through formal and informal debate, and as a result "all except one will be withdrawn" (Luard and Heater, 1994, p. 20).

While competing proposals still appear on many issues, since the 1970s it has been quite rare that more than one proposal would be formally introduced on the same agenda item. As UN organs increased in membership and the number of sponsors for the typical draft soared, it became far more difficult to make the changes necessary to reconcile competing formal proposals (Peterson, 1986, p. 97). Instead, an alternate process of considering proposals came into vogue, where competing approaches were debated through informal consultations with the goal of developing as much consensus as possible on one compromise proposal that would be formally introduced into debate only toward the end of discussions on the relevant agenda item. This development has had several implications for UN decisionmaking: (1) the process of debate has been streamlined in overworked UN bodies (ibid., p. 108); (2) group politics (as discussed in Chapter 3) and the informal mechanisms of debate that will be discussed in Chapter 8 now have a significant impact on decisionmaking throughout the process, not simply during the drafting phase; and (3) the public and private processes that are unfolding simultaneously may in fact be going in different directions or even addressing entirely different issues altogether (Alger, 1966, p. 147). Both public and private processes can contribute to effective decisionmaking, so it is important to briefly consider the rules of procedure that govern how public debate is conducted.

The rules of procedure for UN bodies maintain that no participant "may address a meeting without having previously obtained the permission of the presiding officer" (Chrispeels, 1998, p. 128). The typical practice is for the presiding officer to call on speakers "in the order in which they signify their desire to speak." Participants signify their desire to speak by placing their name on a "speakers' list," which has "always been used to regulate the order in which the presiding officers [call] on delegates" (Peterson, 1986, p. 107). In some UN bodies the speakers' list is maintained by the presiding officer (Tolley, 1983, p. 41); however, it is far more common for the Secretariat official who serves as the secretary of the particular assembly or committee in question to maintain the list (Chrispeels, 1998, p. 128). In the General

Assembly and its related bodies, securing a prime position on the speakers' list can involve intense jockeying among delegations (Narasimhan, 1988, p. 66). The most desirable spot is second on the list, since the first speaker often must address a room that is only partially full as the discussion begins. Once the first speaker begins, the room will quickly fill, and delegates will usually pay close attention to at least one speaker before engaging in informal caucusing or leaving for another meeting. Thus participants who desire the largest audience will try to move as close as possible to the second spot; once names are inscribed on the list, however, positions can be changed only through mutual consent. In the Security Council the situation is somewhat different, since certain customs have developed regarding the order in which participants will usually appear on the speakers' list (Bailey and Daws, 1998, pp. 189–191). Typically the Council member requesting the meeting will speak first, followed by states or other actors directly involved in the question or dispute. Then each remaining member of the Council will speak according to their place on the speakers' list, with the Council president (speaking as her or his state's delegate) taking the final spot. Nonmembers who are not party to the dispute may also be inscribed on the list, but their turn comes only after all Council members who desire to speak have finished.

The rules of procedure for the General Assembly and most other UN bodies empower members to limit the time allowed to each speaker (Sabel, 1997, pp. 93–94). While these rules have been used in the case of some specialized agencies and other committees, they are rarely applied to debates in the UN's main political bodies, such as the plenary of the Assembly or the Security Council. If they are applied at all, it is more common to find them used late in the annual session of a particular body, when time is scarce but remaining business is not (Tolley, 1983, p. 54). Rules for setting limits on the number of times a particular participant may be permitted to address a meeting are also seldom applied (Chrispeels, 1998, p. 128), although commonly accepted practice has limited each state to one speech during the Assembly's General Debate. The reason behind the scarce use of these procedures that are potentially helpful to manage an often unwieldy process of debate is that most delegations "feared partisan use of any [such] rules," so they have been willing only "to adopt those devices that appeared to impinge equally on all" (Peterson, 1986, p. 107). The modest increases in efficiency that have been possible within the UN system in recent decades owe their realization to the tireless efforts of some presiding officers to respond to the pressures of a growing membership and agenda by exhorting their colleagues to be succinct. Nearly every UN meeting features at least one appeal by the chair for speakers "to remain mindful of the length of the speaker's list and the lateness of the hour."

Once a speaker has the floor, it is rare that his or her comments would be interrupted by the chair or another participant. Early in the practice of the General Assembly it was decided that presiding officers have the power, but not an obligation, to call speakers to order based on three grounds of objection: that their remarks were irrelevant, needlessly repetitive, or abusive to another participant (Bailey, 1960, pp. 128–130). All three of these grounds have been difficult to apply in a consistent fashion, and thus they are infrequently used. Presiding officers often find themselves walking a fine line between keeping the meeting moving toward substantive progress and respecting the desire of participants to use their floor time in the manner they consider most appropriate. If a participant feels that the presiding officer needs to call a speaker to order or has any other question or concern regarding how the meeting is being conducted, she or he can raise a "point of order" to the chair (Chrispeels, 1998, p. 127–128). A point of order may be raised between speakers or, if necessary, be used to interrupt the speaker; in any case, they take precedence over all other matters and require immediate attention by the chair once raised. As can be expected, the privileged position of points of order in UN rules can invite abuse. This problem is compounded by the lack of a clear definition of what constitutes a legitimate point of order (Bailey and Daws, 1998, p. 192). Requests for information or clarification about the procedures of debate are always permitted; however, using a point of order to jump the speakers' list by discussing the substance of the issue under debate is not. Likewise, identifying a problem with the interpretation is certainly acceptable, but using repeated points of order to fluster speakers or question the content of their remarks is rarely permitted and creates an environment of ill will.

Some United Nations bodies make it possible for a participant to discuss the substance of the issue at hand even if they are not on the speakers' list through the use of a "right of reply." The right of reply is intended to permit delegates "whose country, government, or government's policy is the target of rude remarks" or who believe that their own remarks were misrepresented to respond after the speakers' list has been closed (Peterson, 1986, p. 105). Like points of order, the right of reply has been subject to considerable abuse at the UN, for two reasons. First, most rules of procedure neglect to define exactly what a right of reply is or to specify the circumstances under which it should be granted (Chrispeels, 1998, p. 128). When delegates have acted as if they were entitled to a right of reply, presiding officers have nearly always been willing to grant it (Sabel, 1997, p. 101). Participants seem to have forgotten that it is "a privilege and not a right to speak out of turn" (Bailey, 1960, p. 133). Second, the right of reply can allow members to jump to the front of the speakers' list when the reply takes place immediately after the remarks that prompted the request (Peterson, 1986, pp. 105–106). From the very beginning of UN practice, participants started requesting an immediate right of reply even when the speakers' list was still open, and then frequently the speaker whose comments prompted the original right of reply would also request a short response. Thus the process of debate could easily be hijacked by a narrow dispute between two states, with each side focused on scoring debating points. Fortunately, these problems were never as acute in the Security Council, where the president can permit delegates "to make a further statement" (Bailey and Daws, 1998, p. 197) and most other UN bodies have placed limits on how many times a member can exercise a right of reply (usually just one or two per issue or meeting), how long she or he can speak for each one (typically from three to ten minutes), and when the rights of reply are conducted (generally at the end of the meeting or the end of that agenda item, whichever comes first (Sabel, 1997, pp. 103–109).

As debate unfolds, two types of discussions occur simultaneously: those regarding the substance of the issue at hand and those regarding the nature of the procedures through which the substantive debate will be managed. Although not specifically required by all rules of procedure, it is common practice in UN bodies that discussion of procedural motions takes precedence over discussion of substantive proposals (ibid., p. 242). After all, it simply makes sense to decide on the ground rules of debate first and then actually get to the business at hand. However, procedural disagreements can arise throughout the process of considering various substantive proposals. This creates an environment where both substance and procedure serve as instruments that participants can use to push for outcomes they favor and to obstruct those they oppose (Chrispeels, 1998, p. 127; Luard and Heater, 1994, pp. 20–21).

While the tradeoffs involved in choosing between substantive and procedural strategies will be considered in Chapter 9, that discussion rests on an understanding of the order of priority among different types of business that UN bodies conduct. As was mentioned above, points of order take precedence over all other business, including procedural motions, since points of order are decided by the chair (usually without discussion) whereas procedural motions are discussed and decided by the body as a whole through debate and voting (Sabel, 1997, p. 222).

Procedural motions are handled in the order they are proposed; however, motions to suspend the meeting, adjourn the meeting, adjourn debate on the item under discussion, and close the debate on the item under discussion take precedence over all other procedural motions in that order (Chrispeels, 1998, p. 127; Sabel, 1997, p. 244). While successful use of these "priority motions" is rare in both the General Assembly (Peterson, 1986, pp. 109–112) and the Security Council (Bailey and Daws, 1998, pp. 201–212), the interplay between other procedural motions and the conduct of substantive discussion is often quite opaque to the observer but instrumental in decisionmaking outcomes.

One clear example of how procedure and substance interact arises in the process of amending proposals after they have been officially introduced into debate. One point of contention involves determining whether a separate proposal is simply an amendment to an earlier proposal or a new proposal altogether. Most UN bodies follow the General Assembly's lead in defining an amendment as a proposal that "merely adds to, deletes from, or revises" part of another proposal (Sabel, 1997, p. 175). Amendments can seek to change the spirit of a proposal by adjusting its preamble or to change its intended effect by adding, deleting, or modifying its operative paragraphs (Tolley, 1983, p. 47). Deciding whether a proposal qualifies as an amendment or not is typically left up to the presiding officer, who need not provide a reason for the decision (Sabel, 1997, p. 185). At times, though, significant disagreement over the correct status of a proposal has resulted in a process through which the body as a whole decided the issue in a procedural motion (Kaufmann, 1980, p. 123).

Short amendments can be introduced orally, but written submission is always the preferred route. If an amendment is to become part of an existing proposal, then all of the original sponsors must agree that the amendment is a "friendly" one (Peterson, 1986, p. 97). If it is not acceptable to all original sponsors, then the amendment is discussed separately from and before the proposal itself. In the case of multiple amendments, priority is given to the one "furthest removed in substance from the original proposal" (Kaufmann, 1988, p. 17). Before the 1970s, the political processes of both the General Assembly and the Security Council were characterized by an extensive use of amendments to support or derail competing proposals (see Bailey, 1969, p. 10; Peterson, 1986, p. 96). Since then, an increased use of consensus decisionmaking, as will be discussed in the final section of this chapter, has resulted in a corresponding decrease in efforts to formally amend substantive proposals after they have been officially introduced. Instead, it is far more common for the original sponsors and those offering amendments to meet informally in search of a friendly compromise solution, so that debate can focus on a single text (Kaufmann, 1988, p. 16).

▓ Managing Debate Through Leadership

The roles and functions performed by presiding officers in United Nations bodies surfaced on numerous occasions in the preceding discussion on the consideration of proposals. There are differences of opinion among scholars and UN observers regarding the significance of these roles and functions for the decisions that get made. For example, Philip Jacob, Alexine Atherton, and Arthur Wallenstein argue that "what is at stake [in the selection of presiding officers] is prestige, not authority, as the president or chairman of a body has no more power than any other delegate; in no circumstances can he presume to act for the organ unless he is explicitly instructed to do so by it" (1972, p. 23). While these authors are certainly correct regarding the limited autonomy of the presiding officer vis-à-vis the body itself, they neglect the potential importance of the presiding officer as an effective manager of debate. Sydney Bailey has argued that "it is difficult to exaggerate the extent to which good chairmanship can facilitate, and bad chairmanship can obstruct, the work of the Assembly" and other UN bodies (1960, p. 121). He notes that while strong leadership does not guarantee success, "an incompetent presiding officer can, single-handedly, create procedural chaos if he does not understand the Rules, or does not enforce them, or acts in a dictatorial or partisan manner" (ibid.).

Understanding the challenges that presiding officers face in exercising their limited powers in the absence of true authority can be made easier with the use of several helpful analogies. One former UN ambassador from France, Jacques Kosciusko-Morizet, has described his experience as president of the Security Council as being like that of "the conductor of an orchestra" who is hamstrung by the fact that "his musicians have a tendency to think that each is a soloist and are not loath to indulge in squawks and cacophony" (1981, p. 169). Another former permanent representative from Malaysia, Razali Ismail, used a chemistry analogy to describe his tenure as president of the General Assembly: "Being a Chairman at the UN requires infinite patience. You have to broker some kind of consensus. . . . You have to create some kind of chemistry . . . broaden the parameters of agreement. The Chair is the catalyst" (quoted in Grey, 2000, p. 26). These analogies share the basic idea that presiding officers at the UN are not endowed with power to command, demand, or require but simply with the responsibility to push, prod, and inspire to the extent feasible. Yet even this modest conceptualization of the role of presiding officers allows opportunities for tremendous influence, since their leadership is essential to get the decision process moving and keep it running smoothly (Alger, 1989, pp. 3–4; Smith, 1999, p. 179).

Presiding officers at the United Nations "are chosen so that every state may feel it has received a fair share of the positions of honor and responsibility" (Jacob, Atherton, and Wallenstein, 1972, p. 23). In order to accomplish this, a system of rotation is typically used (Chrispeels, 1998, p. 124). In the case of the Security Council, where the presidency is held by a state, not a person, the position rotates on a monthly basis among all Council members in English alphabetical order (Narasimhan, 1988, p. 70; Kaufmann, 1980, p. 49). Any discussion of how to select the most effective leaders is somewhat meaningless, since it is up to each state to send the individual it chooses—whether that be its permanent representative, foreign minister, or even head of state—to run the Council meetings during its presidency. In the General Assembly, most presiding officers (including the president and chairs of the six main committees) are elected based on their individual qualifications. However, even in these cases a system of regional rotation is used (as discussed in Chapters 3 and 6), where the "personal qualities of a particular delegate are sometimes taken into account" but these concerns "are a secondary consideration to what country he represents" (Jacob, Atherton, and Wallenstein, 1972, p. 23). Despite the importance of regional balance, the dangers associated with having an ineffective presiding officer (vividly described by Bailey above) have meant that these "political considerations" (geography) have become joined with a "tacit understanding among delegations to appoint competent individuals" (Sabel, 1997, p. 52).

Presiding officers are certainly important sources of leadership in managing UN debates, but they are not the only actors who can play this role. They may be assisted by an "inner circle" of other delegates with whom they have strong working relationships and whose assistance and insights they value and trust (Kaufmann, 1988, pp. 71–72). The presiding officer may even designate certain members of this circle as the leaders of the small negotiating groups—the "fire brigades"—discussed in Chapter 3. However, leadership can also arise at the UN in an ad hoc manner from sources totally unrelated to the presiding officer. Often cited reasons for this alternate leadership are that the existing formal leadership either is proving to be ineffective or has adopted a path that some participants perceive as being biased in favor of a particular approach to the question at hand (Smith, 1999, pp. 183, 194–195). This is a crucial issue, since the rules of procedure for most international organizations and conferences maintain an obligation of impartiality for the presiding officer so as to best maintain her or his effectiveness in managing the debate (Sabel, 1997, pp. 56–57).

Another occasion in which ad hoc leadership may emerge arises when a particular delegation that is not serving in an official position of leadership decides to guide a particular initiative through a UN body (Kaufmann, 1988, pp. 69–70). Such efforts are typically an uphill struggle, but they can be facilitated if the delegation in question possesses two sets of important attributes. First, the delegation must have an established track record as an active member of the body where the initiative is being made. This is necessary so that the delegation can draw on their previously established networks of interaction in search of support for their chosen initiative (Alger, 1966). Second, the delegation must be able to draw on several types of leadership in their effort to persuade other member states to support their proposal (Kaufmann, 1988, p. 70). Oran Young (1991) has identified three types of leadership that are particularly relevant in multilateral settings: structural leadership based on the material resources of the state the delegate represents, entrepreneurial leadership based on the delegate's negotiating skills, and intellectual leadership based on the persuasiveness of the delegate's ideas. While a mix of these types of leadership can be helpful for any actor playing a leadership role at the United Nations, they are particularly important for ad hoc leaders, since these lack the institutional mandate (even if it is only a weak one) that presiding officers enjoy.

The roles and functions performed by presiding officers generally fall into two categories: those dealing with the procedures of debate and those dealing with the substance of debate (Chrispeels, 1998, p. 125; Kaufmann, 1988, pp. 81–99; Sabel, 1997, pp. 57–77). In terms of procedures, the presiding officer has the duty to declare meetings open and closed, accord the right to speak to delegates and other participants, rule on points of order, conduct votes, announce decisions, ensure observance of the rules, and maintain order throughout the discussions. In exercising these duties, the presiding officer remains under the authority of the body, and its members may challenge a ruling if they so desire (Chrispeels, 1998, p. 125). In addition to these duties, the presiding officer shares with the other delegates the ability to propose changes in how the body is conducting its business by opening or closing the speakers' list, limiting the time available to each speaker, moving between items on the agenda, ending a meeting, or closing debate. In the case of these changes, proposals from the presiding officer take effect only if approved by the body's membership. Finally, as was discussed above, the presiding officer can call a delegate to order if his or her comments are irrelevant, repetitious, or abusive; however, presiding officers rarely call speakers to order on their own initiative, preferring to resort to this action only if pushed to do so through a point of order on the part of one or more delegates (Kaufmann, 1988, p. 88).

These many procedural functions of presiding officers often consume much of their time (ibid., p. 95). An effective president or chair must possess the experience and intelligence to "give rapid and correct rulings on procedural questions" (ibid., p. 78). Presiding officers also must have good negotiating skills, accurate political instincts, and be a good judge of character, since their substantive functions require them to appoint the members of certain committees and to play a role in mediating between conflicting views (ibid., pp. 95–99). This last function is arguably the most difficult to perform and yet potentially the most important in terms of securing effective outcomes. It can include simply allowing time for states to engage in informal consultations by adjusting the meeting schedule, or it can necessitate more direct involvement in managing the informal contacts and actually drafting a compromise text that captures the "points of crystallization" on a particular issue (ibid., p. 97). The processes through which the presiding officer can facilitate these informal contacts (especially in the context of the Security Council) will receive more attention in the following chapter.

The two most important presiding-officer positions at the United Nations are the presidency of the General Assembly and the presidency of the Security Council. Despite the identical titles, the two positions are in fact quite different (Narasimhan, 1988, p. 70; Kaufmann, 1980, p. 49). As has already been mentioned, the General Assembly president is an individual elected by the entire membership of the Assembly, based on personal stature and a system of regional rotation among the UN's five geographic groups (covered in Chapter 3). Assembly presidents serve in office for one year, from September to September, during which time they perform no other functions; another person must represent their state in the Assembly. The presidency of the Security Council is a member state, not a person, that serves for one month, after which the position rotates to another member state in English alphabetical order. During its turn, a state may have several different people serve as Council president, each of whom can run the Council meetings and then, usually at the end of the speakers' list, also address the Council on behalf of their state, as long as they make it clear they are doing so at the outset of their remarks.

The presidency of the General Assembly, according to Smouts, was intended to be a "prestigious, global-level function" whose incumbent would be "the incarnation of the United Nations Organization" (2000, p. 37). As a result, the goal was to find an individual "of experience, a shrewd strategist and diplomat, universally accepted and independent." Unfortunately, the practice of the UN evolved differently; the Assembly president was never granted substantial authority, and what little authority the position did have was rather quickly eroded through the 1950s due to several developments (Bailey, 1960, p. 121). First, due to the performance of Dag Hammarskjöld, the office of secretary-general, not Assembly president, came to be the symbol of the organization to the outside world (Smouts, 2000, p. 37). Second, Assembly presidents have always found themselves walking a fine line between their limited authority and the need to respect the sovereignty of member states (Peterson, 1986, p. 279). Member states realize they need a president with some authority to facilitate a fair and efficient functioning of the Assembly, but they remain wary of granting any power that could be taken too far. Third, over time the Assembly's rules of procedure and customary practices became sufficiently established such that the president lost significant latitude on ad hoc procedural questions (Bailey, 1960, p. 122). Finally, Assembly presidents frequently lack sufficient resources to carry out their many responsibilities, since they are "mostly dependent on the staff and support granted them by their own government" (Smouts, 2000, p. 38).

These limitations aside, the Assembly president has become an important actor on both the procedural and substantive matters discussed above. This has fostered some debate as to the proper balance between the procedural and substantive responsibilities of the position (Bailey, 1960, p. 148). It is certainly helpful for the president to initiate substantive proposals, but too much of this activity can endanger his or her ability to be seen as an impartial arbiter of the rules of procedure. The success of presidents in managing this balance often rests on individual personal qualities, especially their courtesy, tolerance, and fair-mindedness, as well as their ability to command respect and inspire confidence (ibid., p. 123; Smouts, 2000, p. 38). While the president can try to impose her or his will on an often fractious Assembly, most choose not to push too hard because they don't want to risk rebuff, create dangerous precedents, or compromise their potential usefulness in informal consultations (Peterson, 1986, p. 281). This tendency toward light-handed approaches has allowed the Assembly presidency to become a more active position over the years, despite its limited and decreasing authority. The growing use of informal consultations and consensus decisionmaking (discussed in the next section of this chapter) in the work of the Assembly has accelerated this trend (ibid., pp. 282–283).

The president of the Security Council faces many of the same challenges as the president of the General Assembly in terms of trying to promote the efficient work of the body with only limited authority. Yet two additional obstacles faced by the Council president can make the job especially challenging. The first of these is the one-month term of office, which can necessitate a change in leadership just as an individual "finds their grove" as president or right in the middle of an ongoing crisis (Narasimhan, 1988, p. 72; Nicol, 1981b, p. 7). Some expected this to cause the work of the Council to suffer, and longer terms of office were considered, but they were rejected by the permanent five "on the grounds that the role of the presidency of the Security Council is an important one and it would be unwise to entrust such a political role to one person, no matter how able and impartial he were to be" (Chai, 1981b, p. 85). Fortunately, the officials sent by Council members to serve as president have generally been seasoned diplomats who are often (though not always) able to adjust to running the Council rather quickly, and the practice of rotation has not been a serious problem (Narasimhan, 1988, p. 72). The only adjustments made to the rotation process occurred at the end of 1946, when the term of the United States was extended by two weeks so that the presidency would be coterminous with the calendar month, thereby preventing an elected member from rotating off the Council in the middle of their presidency (Bailey and Daws, 1998, p. 125).

A second potential obstacle faced by Council presidents is the fact that they are simultaneously a representative of the entire Council and a representative of their state. The president is charged with running the meetings in an efficient and impartial manner, with the assistance of the Secretariat personnel who are responsible for servicing the Council (Chai, 1981b, pp. 91–93). The Secretariat can provide advice on the operation of the Council, generate reports to serve as background for its debates, and even offer guidance when the president represents the Council in public or at a meeting of another UN body. However, at all times the president must remember that he or she can act in the capacity of president only under the authority of the Council itself (Nicol, 1981b, pp. 10–11). When speaking on behalf of the Council, they must be careful to focus as much as possible on matters where the Council has achieved widespread agreement (Kosciusko-Morizet, 1981, p. 166). At other times the president will need to articulate the views of her or his state in the Council; most presidents have explicitly indicated that they are "now speaking as the representative of their state," or something to that effect, when they switch between these dual roles (Nicol, 1981b, p. 11; Bailey and Daws, 1998, p. 399).

Despite this practice, there is some debate among former Council presidents as to which of the two roles (representing the Council or representing their state) should receive priority. Ambassador Yakov Malik of the Soviet Union has observed that he was at all times a representative of his state and never made any effort to separate the two roles (1981, p. 174); however, Ambassador Senjin Tsuruoka of Japan has argued that "the President should attach more importance to his role as President than as the representative of his government" (1981, p. 304). Given this debate, "it is surprising that this practice [the dual roles of the president] so rarely leads to difficulty" (Bailey and Daws, 1998, p. 128). One reason this is rarely a problem is Rule 20 of the Council's Provisional Rules of Procedure, which allows the president to cede the position to the next member in the rotation "during consideration of a particular question with which the member he represents is directly connected" (Bailey and Daws, 1998, p. 125). Typically it is left to the president to voluntarily invoke this rule; however, other member states have at times used points of order or informal consultations to push the president in this direction, sometimes successfully (Nicol, 1981b, p. 13; Bailey and Daws, 1998, pp. 126–128, 399–400). Uncovering patterns on the issue of ceding the presidency is problematic, since it is often difficult to define the words "directly concerned" (Chai, 1981b, p. 86); however, Sydney Bailey and Sam Daws have observed, "It appears that it is more likely for a President to cede the chair when criticizing than when criticized" (1998, p. 128). In any case, differences of opinion on the practice persist. One former president who served in the position eleven times from the 1950s to the 1970s concluded that he did not remember "any instance when [he] should have surrendered the presidency in a difficult situation" (Malik, 1981, p. 174). Due at least in part to this type of thinking, the "invocation of this rule has been less and less frequent" over time (Chai, 1981b, p. 86).

While the powers of the Council president are undoubtedly limited, incumbents are charged with a number of important procedural functions: setting the agenda, deciding when the Council should meet, managing the pace of debate to avoid both a rush to judgment and excessive filibustering, and ruling on points of order and other procedural questions quickly and correctly (Kosciusko-Morizet, 1981, pp. 165–166; Nicol, 1981b, p. 9). The president has "no express power to call a speaker to order" if that person wanders from the agenda, repeats what others have said, or uses abusive language, but he or she can urge delegates to keep their comments concise and diplomatic in tone (Bailey and Daws, 1998, p. 132). Managing a body of fifteen members dis-cussing the most contentious issues of the day with little authority is a delicate but indispensable task. Over time, these procedural duties have been increasingly joined with substantive responsibilities regarding informal consultations and quiet diplomacy (Chai, 1981b, p. 86–88; Bailey and Daws, 1998, pp. 133–135). This evolution has made it more important that the Council president maintain a close relationship with the secretary-general, since the two positions involve similar peace and security functions (Chai, 1981b, pp. 88–91). It has also required that incumbents bring a greater range of personal attributes to the presiden-cy if they hope to be effective (Nicol, 1981b, pp. 31–32). Skills as a procedural technician remain necessary but insufficient; they must be joined with the experience, patience, and sound political judgment required to balance the "muscle of the presidency" (such as it is) with the need to accurately sense how momentum in the Council is unfolding (Richard, 1981, pp. 242–244).

■ Making Decisions Through Voting

There is a rich tradition of studying voting patterns at the United Nations. One survey of international organization scholarship complet-ed decades ago argued that "voting studies reflect the most sustained and integrated research activity" to date and that "knowledge of voting has advanced as scholars have built on the work of others" (Alger, 1970, p. 433). Research on voting patterns continued as the UN's mem-bership expanded with decolonization and the environment in which the UN operated became less hostile with the end of the cold war (for example, see Holloway, 1990; Kim and Russett, 1997). This research (which was surveyed in Chapter 3) has focused on the stability of and evolution in the composition of different voting groups and blocs over time. The discussion of voting here, however, looks at the procedures and processes that determine how voting is conducted rather than exam-ining the patterns and blocs that emerge once voting is complete. Voting procedures and processes can have a direct impact on the behaviors and activities of the United Nations, since they govern how decisions get made. While not necessarily every decision involves a formal vote, and not necessarily every vote leads to a substantive decision (Bailey, 1969, p. 7), the process of voting often represents the final phase of UN deci-sionmaking. Furthermore, the specific rules in place for this final stage can affect the types of strategies that are necessary to build sufficient agreement throughout the decisionmaking process (Peterson, 1986, p. 53).

The procedures used for voting and making decisions in international organizations have always been a "peculiarly difficult problem," given the need to maintain state sovereignty and yet allow for some degree of efficiency (Jacob, Atherton, and Wallenstein, 1972, p. 27). In the League of Nations and its predecessors, the balance between sovereignty and efficiency was clearly tipped toward sovereignty; decisions taken by an international body or conference generally required the unanimous consent of all parties (Sabel, 1997, p. 282). However, during this time the need for unanimity gradually gave way to majority decisionmaking, at least for procedural matters such as setting the agenda and questions that were primarily technical in nature (Sands and Klein, 2001, pp. 263–264). Substantive decisions still formally required unanimity in the League, until some exceptions began to emerge with the practice of allowing members to abstain from a decision without disrupting the requirement of unanimity in cases where a "substantial majority" of states favored action and when "vital national interests were not at issue" (Bennett and Oliver, 2002, p. 91).

The UN Charter in 1945 represented "a fairly radical break with tradition," as majority voting, not unanimity, became the primary voting rule for both procedural and substantive issues (Sands and Klein, 2001, pp. 264–265). This development marked the acceleration of a trend away from unanimity across many IGOs in the post–World War II period (Feld and Jordan, 1989, p. 125), which in turn "led to the factual decline of sovereign equality, in that decisions can be adopted over a minority of states" (White, 2002, p. 85). This decline in sovereign equality may be seen as less precipitous given that most UN decisions are merely recommendations (ibid.), that some type of unanimity is still required in many international organizations that are endowed with the power to make binding decisions (Sabel, 1997, p. 284), and that many UN bodies have moved in the direction of consensus decisionmaking in recent decades (Smith, 1999, p. 173). Nonetheless, the move to majority voting represents an important milestone in the evolution of decisionmaking in international organizations.

The following pages will discuss the merits of majority voting at the UN, consider how these concerns are modified in the case of the Security Council veto, and explore the particular challenges associated with consensus decisionmaking. First, though, it is important to give a brief overview of the different methods of voting that are used at the United Nations. While quorum requirements for UN meetings are rarely enforced, the quorum requirements for voting are strictly followed; in the case of the General Assembly a majority of members must be present to conduct any voting on proposals (Kaufmann, 1988, p. 20). Once voting begins, there are essentially three common methods that can be used: a show of hands or nonrecorded vote, a roll-call or recorded vote, and a secret ballot (Kaufmann, 1980, pp. 124–125; Chrispeels, 1998, p. 131; Lydon, 1998, pp. 156–157). The first of these, a show of hands, is used on procedural motions and many substantive votes, including those in the Security Council, where the delegates often raise a thin yellow pencil (Nicol, 1981b, p. 22). The chair asks for all those in favor of a resolution to raise their hands, followed by all those opposed, and a member of the Secretariat tallies the vote, which is announced to the body and included in the minutes of the meeting. This method is valued for its efficiency, but it makes it difficult to determine who actually participated in the vote and which way they voted, especially in large bodies. This problem is avoided in the second type of voting, through a roll call, but the process can take considerable time, as the chair must begin with a randomly selected member and go one by one in English alphabetical order, asking whether the member votes yes, no, or abstain. A roll-call vote provides a clear record of who voted and how they voted, which makes it an attractive choice when sponsors expect a close vote (Kaufmann, 1988, p. 23). In UN bodies the "accepted practice" is that

Members of the Security Council vote, by a show of hands, on Resolution 1546 on June 8, 2004. The resolution, which was approved unanimously, endorsed the new leadership of Iraq and paved the way for the country to assume full sovereignty and authority for itself. (UN photo #NICA 7572, by Mark Garten)

any state can call for a roll-call vote and such a request will be honored (Sabel, 1997, p. 260). The third type of voting, by secret ballot, is reserved for elections of individuals or member states to particular positions, but it can be waived by general agreement, especially in the case of elections where an agreed slate of candidates from a region matches the number of open seats (Kaufmann, 1980, p. 125; Lydon, 1998, p. 156).

Voting at the United Nations has evolved over time to include additional options beyond the three traditional types of voting just discussed. For example, most UN meeting rooms are equipped with electronic voting systems, which make it possible to conduct both recorded and nonrecorded votes more quickly and accurately (Sabel, 1997, p. 259). In addition, the growing use of consensus at the United Nations (discussed in more detail below) has resulted in a process of adopting decisions by acclamation (in the case of elections) or by acquiescence (in the case of substantive proposals). Technically an official vote is not held in these cases, since the chair simply indicates that the proposal will be adopted unless a member specifically objects (Bailey, 1960, p. 161; Sabel, 1997, p. 269). Yet since acclamation or acquiescence allows the UN to act, these must be counted as a method of making decisions even if they do not involve voting. Two other options relating to the method of conducting voting involve dividing votes such that different sections of a proposal are voted on separately (Kaufmann, 1988, pp. 17–18; Sabel, 1997, pp. 314–317; Bailey and Daws, 1998, pp. 222–223) and whether or not member states are permitted to explain their vote, either before or after the vote is held (Sabel, 1997, pp. 110–118). A request for separate votes can be made by any member state, and such a request is honored unless an objection is made, in which case the motion for a divided vote itself is voted on by the entire body. A request for an explanation of vote can also be made by any member of the body, usually subject to the approval of the presiding officer; in practice such approval is nearly always granted.

The United Nations has utilized two different decision rules that govern how much support a particular motion or proposal must enjoy before it can pass: majority rule and consensus (Peterson, 1986, pp. 54–55). The formal rules of procedure for UN bodies call for majority rule; the informal practices of these bodies often work toward consensus. As will be discussed further in Chapter 9, member states that prefer confrontation or are unwilling to take the time and effort to build consensus will use their superior numbers to push for majority decisions. Conversely, since consensus requires that all members support or at least acquiesce to a proposal, this will be the preferred decision rule in cases where a broad statement of opinion is sought or the support of a wide range of members is required. The advantages and disadvantages of majority rule will be considered first, including qualified majority voting arrangements like the veto, followed by the challenges associated with consensus decisionmaking.

According to Article 2, Paragraph 1 of the UN Charter, the organization is based on the sovereign equality of all its members. As was discussed above, the move away from unanimity toward majority rule in the UN Charter was seen as an infringement on the sovereignty part of this principle; however, the practice that every state has one and only one vote in any UN body of which it is a member serves to reinforce the equality part of the principle (ibid., p. 55). After all, if states are being morally or legally bound by the resolutions adopted in UN bodies, then they should all have equal say in what is decided. However, the one-state, one-vote formula has been criticized because it ignores the political realities in which the UN operates (see, for example, Claude, 1984, pp. 124–127; White, 2002, pp. 86–87). For one thing, one-state, one-vote neglects the power of states outside of the UN, since it enables a group of numerous yet small states to push their preferred policies through majority voting even though they have only a fraction of the world's population, material resources, or military power. Furthermore, when this type of behavior persists over time, it can do much to undermine the perceived legitimacy of the UN in the eyes of the frustrated minority, even though majority rule, at least in principle, is said to enhance that legitimacy.

In light of this disconnect between the principle of equality and the realities of power, there have been repeated proposals during the UN's existence to modify the one-state, one-vote formula with some sort of weighted voting, where influence would be allocated based on a set of predetermined relevant criteria (Sands and Klein, 2001, p. 267). This has always been the practice at the World Bank and International Monetary Fund, where votes are allocated based on financial support for the organizations. Proposals that have suggested weighted voting for the General Assembly have also focused on financial contribution as a potential criterion, or possibly population, or a combination of both (Tung, 1969, p. 101). Over time such proposals have proliferated and received much attention in terms of their probable impact on the functioning of the Assembly (see, for example, Dixon, 1989). However, all efforts to modify the one-state, one-vote formula are doomed to failure for two reasons: (1) it is impossible to reach agreement on what factors should serve as the basis for the weighting of votes (White, 2002, p. 87), and (2) even if agreement on the factors was possible, the need to secure support from two-thirds of the membership as required for Charter amendment would be daunting at best (Peterson, 1986, p. 56). As a result, the one-state, on-vote formula lives on at the United Nations.

Majority voting at the UN can involve a simple majority or some sort of qualified majority. The decision rule can vary across bodies or even within the same body across different issues (Sand and Klein, 2001, p. 269). A simple majority requires that a proposal receive more affirmative votes than negative votes in order to pass (50 percent plus one of those voting must vote yes); a qualified majority requires a higher numerical threshold of support. Article 18, Paragraph 3 of the UN Charter specifies that the General Assembly uses a simple majority of those states "present and voting" to decide all issues other than those deemed to be an "important question," for which a two-thirds majority of those members "present and voting" is required. Article 18, Paragraph 2 indicates that "important questions" include recommendations dealing with international peace and security; the election of members to the Security Council, ECOSOC, and the Trusteeship Council; the admission or suspension of members; and budgetary questions. In addition, some cases specified by the Charter require a two-thirds majority of all UN members, not just those "present and voting"; these include elections for the International Court of Justice, amendments to the Charter, and calling for a general review conference under the provisions of Article 109 (Bennett and Oliver, 2002, p. 95). Voting on amendments to any proposed resolutions dealing with important questions also requires a two-thirds majority (Kaufmann, 1980, p. 125).

Two aspects of these voting procedures for the General Assembly found in the Charter have provoked some degree of debate: the meaning of "present and voting" and the scope of issues included as "important questions" (Peterson, 1986, pp. 62–68). First, "present and voting" refers to those states attending the meeting and casting either an affirmative or a negative vote; states that are absent, answer "not participating," or abstain are not counted as "present and voting," and the necessary level of support must be recalculated accordingly (Chrispeels, 1998, p. 132). Controversy can arise when a decision to miss a meeting or abstain from a vote directly affects the support a controversial proposal needs to obtain in order to be adopted. Likewise, the issue of determining "important questions" appears to be straightforward on paper; the Charter provides a list of qualifying subjects and specifies that a simple majority of the Assembly can determine that other categories of issues are "important questions." There is widespread agreement that procedural matters never qualify as "important questions" and are thus subject to a simple majority vote (Sabel, 1997, p. 287). However, the Assembly has sparked controversy by declaring specific issues to be "important questions," because it has often done so on an ad hoc and case-by-case basis rather than by defining whole categories of questions as important, as the Charter would seem to require (Sands and Klein, 2001, p. 271; Peterson, 1986, pp. 65–66).

All of the issues that come before the Security Council are assumed to be important questions, given its focus on peace and security. As a result, the Council uses a system of qualified majority voting that was agreed upon by the United States, United Kingdom, and Soviet Union at the Yalta Conference in February 1945 and subsequently included in the UN Charter in Article 27 (Bailey, 1969, p. 12). As amended in 1965, when the Council was expanded from eleven to fifteen members, Article 27 provides that each member of the Council will have one vote, that decisions on procedural matters require the affirmative votes of any nine members, and that decisions on "all other matters" (usually referred to as substantive matters) require the affirmative votes of nine members, "including the concurring votes of the permanent members," providing that a party to a dispute before the Council will abstain from voting.

It is the last clause on the "concurring votes" of the permanent members that has provoked the greatest debate regarding Council voting. The great power veto is certainly a less burdensome requirement than the unanimity rule in the Council of the League of Nations (Tung, 1969, p. 104); however, it still sparked controversy among small and medium powers, which feared that the veto would be used to maintain great power domination (Bailey, 1969, p. 13). In practice, it was not great power domination but great power disunity that caused the Council to be "virtually impotent" during the early years of the cold war (Jacob, Atherton, and Wallenstein, 1972, p. 29). This problem was amplified since the permanent members are not required to explain why when the veto has been exercised (Bailey, 1969, p. 26), and therefore its use has often appeared inconsistent and arbitrary. Likewise, there have been concerns regarding the fairness of the veto, since it effectively allows the five permanent members to escape being governed by the Council (Caron, 1993, pp. 565–566). Regardless of whether one feels that the veto has made the Council too powerful or too weak, it is important to remember that the veto was put in place to make sure the UN did not face the same fate as the League—it gave the most powerful states a means of protecting their vital interests so that they would stay in the organization (Jacob, Atherton, and Wallenstein, 1972, p. 29). The veto can be seen as a "fuse" that prevents the UN from acting in cases where conflict could escalate into another world war (Claude, 1984, p. 156) and as a "useful brake" that "imposes a certain restraint on those who would otherwise attempt to push through extreme resolutions" (Crowe, 1981, p. 95). Putting aside for the moment these general arguments over the relative merits of the veto power, let us consider a number of debates regarding exactly how the veto has been used in practice over the last sixty years.

The first debate regarding the use of the veto concerns the meaning of "concurring votes." Does this require that the permanent five all vote in favor of a proposal? What happens if one or more of them abstains, does not vote, or misses a meeting altogether? When the UN Charter was drafted, the permanent five gave the impression that "concurring votes" meant affirmative votes, and a strict reading of the Charter would seem to support this view. However, some of the permanent members had second thoughts, and no explicit statement on this issue was ever approved (Bailey and Daws, 1998, pp. 250–251). Situations soon emerged in which permanent members wished to abstain but not veto, and this practice was not questioned by other members. As a result, the "generally accepted" procedure of the Council, according to the International Court of Justice, is that only a negative vote constitutes a veto. Debates regarding these so-called voluntary abstentions have also been joined with some controversy surrounding the "obligatory abstentions" that are required by Article 27 of the Charter when Council members are party to a dispute before the Council. Determining exactly when a state is or is not a "party" to a "dispute" has been the subject of sometimes intense debate. Bailey indicates that the "general view" in the early practice of the Council was that these were questions to be determined by the Council, not the individual parties (1969, p. 63). However, the Council has been reluctant to make formal conclusions about the existence of a "dispute" in a particular situation. In order to sidestep this controversy, governments have usually avoided the term *dispute* in favor of simply bringing "situations" to the attention of the Council (Kaufmann, 1980, p. 44), so that all members can participate in the voting if they so desire.

A third debate concerning the use of the veto has to do with the distinction between procedural and substantive issues. As was briefly discussed in Chapter 6, it was decided by the permanent members in the San Francisco Statement of 1945 that any disagreements regarding whether an issue is procedural or substantive would itself be a substantive matter subject to the veto (Bailey, 1969, p. 18). This was done because it was possible to envision a chain of events in which a meeting that began by dealing with the procedural matter of whether an issue should be included on the Council's agenda could rather quickly move into a substantive debate on possible courses of action (Bailey and Daws, 1998, pp. 240–241); at what point in this chain would the veto start to apply? However, the language from the San Francisco Statement contained internal inconsistencies, and it was not included in the Charter. Significant disagreements have emerged over time, since this practice in effect gives the permanent members a "double veto": they can first veto a decision to treat an issue as a procedural question and then veto the substantive proposal itself (Sands and Klein, 2001, p. 272).

According to Bailey (1969, pp. 19–24) and Bailey and Daws (1998, pp. 242–247), the question of the double veto emerged in at least eight cases during the first fifteen years of Security Council practice. While these authors have concluded that these cases are sufficiently confused and inconclusive to reveal clear patterns in the use of the double veto, other authors have observed that the Council "over the years has gotten over such procedural hurdles as the double veto" (Kirgis, 1995, p. 537). This has been possible because the precedent developed that the exercise of the double veto could be limited by a ruling of the Council president and because Council practice has gradually established clearer guidelines as to what issues are procedural as opposed to substantive (Sands and Klein, 2001, p. 272; Tung, 1969, pp. 105–107; Bailey and Daws, 1998, p. 226). Matters commonly accepted as procedural include decisions taken in regards to Articles 28–32 of the UN Charter, dealing with the internal organization of the Council, including the establishment of subsidiary bodies; decisions to change the Council's Provisional Rules of Procedure, including the method of selecting its president; decisions to invite nonmembers of the Council to participate in its deliberations; decisions involving the election of judges for the International Court of Justice; and decisions regarding the conduct of a meeting or the content of its agenda. On the other hand, practice holds that decisions on the content of the list of matters of which the Council is seized and recommendations to the General Assembly on the admission of new members are both treated as substantive matters. Finally, decisions to amend the Charter are procedural; however, the veto still applies, since Article 108 of the Charter specifies that amendments enter into force only once they are ratified by two-thirds of UN members, including the permanent five.

A fourth debate regarding the veto concerns the extent to which its use has harmed the effectiveness of the Council over time. Studies of voting power in the Council have confirmed the conventional wisdom that possession of the veto power gives the permanent members a sig-

nificantly higher degree of influence over the outcome of Council decisionmaking than the elected members that lack the veto power (O'Neill,
1997, p. 79). When the veto is exercised, it reflects a situation in which
the Council was otherwise willing to act but was prevented from doing
so by a permanent member; thus it is important to consider how often
this happens. The UN itself does not keep an official list on the use of
the veto, but researchers have attempted to compile this data.
Unfortunately, there are inconsistencies in their findings, since some
proposals have been vetoed by more than one permanent member and
because some vetoes have been cast at private meetings but were not
included in the official records of these meetings (Bailey and Daws,
1998, p. 230). One study covering data from 1946 to 1990 identified
279 instances when the veto had been exercised (Thalakada, 1997, p.
84); however, another study covering the period from 1946 until August
1997 identified only 273 vetoes, including those "said to have been
cast" in private meetings (Bailey and Daws, 1998, p. 230).

These inconsistencies aside, it is possible to identify different phases in the use of the veto over time. From 1946 to 1965, the Soviet
Union cast over 90 percent of all vetoes; many of these dealt with membership issues, but they covered nearly all types of substantive matters
before the Council (Bennett and Oliver, 2002, p. 93; Bailey and Daws,
1998, p. 239; Bailey, 1969, pp. 58–59). While the predominant use of
the veto by a single member created some intense feelings that the veto
was a problem to be overcome, these fears are considered to be exaggerated by some, given the isolated voting position of the Soviet Union
at the time and the fact that its use of the veto had declined dramatically
by the end of the 1960s (Claude, 1984, p. 150). In the 1970s and 1980s,
it was the United States that most frequently used the veto, as it found
itself increasingly at odds with the expanding membership of the UN
and the Council (Bailey and Daws, 1998, p. 239). A third phase
emerged in 1990, after the end of the cold war. Since this time, the
"overt" use of the veto has decreased dramatically; from May 1990 to
May 1993 no vetoes were cast, and only three were cast from May 1993
to the beginning of 1997 (ibid., pp. 18, 237). While the veto continues
to be used on occasion, the period since 1997 reflects a continuation of
this pattern of infrequent overt use.

While this is certainly a promising trend in terms of Council effectiveness, two caveats must be mentioned. First, the influence provided
through the overt use of the veto has always been joined with the influence provided through the "threatened or anticipated" use of the veto
(Claude, 1984, p. 149), and this avenue continues to be exploited by the
permanent members in spite of their apparent recent restraint in using

the veto (Russett, O'Neill, and Sutterlin, 1996, pp. 69–70). Second, the more assertive nature of the post–cold war Security Council has created a situation where states have the opportunity not only to veto the initiation of Council action but also to veto its alteration or termination (Caron, 1993, pp. 577, 582–588). This "reverse veto" makes the initial decision to act all that more important, because it increases the power of the permanent members and makes it difficult to adjust Council policy even in the face of a changing environment—a problem that is clearly illustrated by the Council's handling of Iraq through the 1990s.

Given these many debates regarding the veto, it comes as no surprise that proposals for reforming the veto have been advanced on a regular basis. Many of these have been included in the discussions on reforming the size and composition of the Council, discussed in Chapter 6; they often address the issue of whether any new permanent members that might be added would enjoy the existing veto power, some sort of modified veto power, or no veto at all (Russett, O'Neill, and Sutterlin, 1996, p. 75). Reform proposals have also considered making changes to the veto power currently enjoyed by the permanent members, regardless of whether new permanent members are added. Eliminating the veto altogether is an attractive option for the entire membership of the UN other than the five permanent members, who would certainly oppose any such change and have the power to block it through their effective veto regarding Charter amendments (Caron, 1993, pp. 569–570). However, other reform proposals have been offered that would serve to limit, but not eliminate, the use of the veto. Early examples of these proposals included limiting the use of the veto on the admission of new members and recommendations regarding the peaceful settlement of disputes (Jacob, Atherton, and Wallenstein, 1972, p. 29); more recent suggestions have focused on limiting the veto to only those decisions taken under Chapter 7 of the Charter (those that are legally binding on the entire UN membership) or at least eliminating its use in regard to the selection of the secretary-general (Sutterlin, 1997, p. 7; Russett, O'Neill, and Sutterlin, 1996, p. 77). Even these more modest proposals to limit the scope of the veto have been met with vigorous resistance on the part of the current permanent members, and the veto is likely to remain unchanged for the foreseeable future.

In addition to the various forms of majority voting just discussed, Peterson observes that United Nations bodies like the General Assembly have used consensus as a second type of decision rule (1986, p. 54). Kaufmann has argued that the UN has "become an experimental laboratory for new decisionmaking procedures," in that "methods of consensus are increasingly replacing or at least complementing more automatic majority vote related procedures" (1994, p. 27). The following paragraphs will consider the meaning of consensus, the reasons for the growth in its use, the mechanisms by which it operates, and the implications of this development.

In the context of multilateral diplomacy, the term *consensus* has been used to refer to both a method of negotiation and a method of decisionmaking (Chrispeels, 1998, p. 133). Consensus as a method of negotiation relates to issues that will be considered in Chapter 9; consensus as a method of decisionmaking is the focus of this discussion. In this second conceptualization, consensus as practiced at the United Nations stands somewhere in between unanimity and majority rule in the degree of agreement it reflects (Peterson, 1986, p. 84). It is a "technique of adoption of institutional acts by which the president of the organ concerned, after consultations, reports that there is general agreement between the members on the proposal before them, and declares the act to be adopted" (Sands and Klein, 2001, p. 266). Thus *consensus* refers "to a decision being made without objection from any voting member of the body in question" (Smith, 1999, p. 174). Put another way, it means that the decision was supported by, or at least not objectionable to, all parties involved. *Consensus* has often been used interchangeably with *unanimity*; however, unanimity requires that all parties actively support the proposal through an affirmative vote, whereas consensus simply means that no party found the proposal sufficiently problematic to merit attempting to block the "general agreement" surrounding it (Sabel, 1997, pp. 285, 303). Consensus allows a "substantial positive majority" to act "without the divisive consequences of a vote or the barriers to efficiency posed by a formal unanimity rule" (Kahler, 1993, p. 318).

Consensus as an approach to decisionmaking has grown in popularity at the United Nations; "both the General Assembly and the Security Council in recent years have frequently used the technique of announcing the adoption of resolutions by consensus" (Bennett and Oliver, 2002, p. 95). Yet it is important to realize that its use is not a sudden development but the culmination of a gradual move away from sometimes confrontational majority voting. In the Security Council, consensus, at least among the permanent five, had been more or less attainable over time, depending on the vicissitudes of the cold war, but the Council has historically demonstrated a return to consensus-building methods when possible (Kaufmann, 1980, p. 49). In the General Assembly, consensus first emerged in the 1960s in some of its more technically oriented subsidiary bodies and then spread rather quickly in the 1970s throughout its main committees (Peterson, 1986, pp. 82–83).

In the Assembly plenary, the use of consensus has fluctuated over time (Marin-Bosch, 1987, p. 708), but in recent years as many as three-fourths of its decisions have been made in this manner (Bennett and Oliver, 2002, p. 95).

The primary reason for the growing use of consensus at the United Nations is the disconnect between voting power within the organization and the realities of material power outside the organization. By the late 1960s, the UN's membership was composed primarily of developing states with new and different priorities that they were willing to pursue using their newfound voting power, even over the strenuous objections of the minority of developed states (Manno, 1968a, pp. 249–256, 261–262; Gregg, 1977, p. 72). This practice put the General Assembly "in the unenviable position of having made a decision it has neither the power nor the authority to enforce as law on states that object" (Jacob, Atherton, and Wallenstein, 1972, p. 30). Without the support of developed states, passing confrontational resolutions "turned out to be a fool's game that was just as dangerous as unproductive" (Smouts, 2000, p. 31); it rendered "majority voting increasingly useless for lawmaking decisions because of the danger of powerful alienated minorities" (Buzan, 1981, p. 326). Consensus decisionmaking was seen as a way of overcoming this problem, since it necessitates compromise between the developing states that enjoy the power of vote and developed states that possess the material resources to actually implement UN policies. This demand for consensus decisionmaking was also joined with certain developments in the UN's political processes that made consensus more feasible to achieve (Peterson, 1986, p. 82); these included the increased use of group politics and informal consultations, as discussed in Chapters 3 and 8.

One difficulty with exploring this approach to decisionmaking at the United Nations is that the terminology associated with consensus can vary across bodies or even within the same body across issues or over time (Smith, 1999, p. 174). For example, in the General Assembly the common distinction is between adoption "by consensus" and adoption "without a vote or without objection" (Peterson, 1986, p. 86; Smouts, 2000, p. 31). The first of these involves an inclusive process of negotiation in which all members participate and come to identify positively, at least to some extent, with the outcome. The second refers to a less inclusive process, where some states remain ambivalent in regard to the proposal; they do not support it, but they will not block it either. Kaufmann uses a different vocabulary to make a similar distinction between cases of "consensus," where a proposal "commands general support," and cases of "pseudo-consensus," where that level of support is not present but the text is adopted anyway (1980, p. 128). Another possible variation is between "consensus with a resolution," which is typically reserved for relatively noncontroversial matters, and "consensus without a resolution," where the issue is important and controversial to the point that delegates prefer to avoid both debate and the adoption of a specific text (Kaufmann, 1988, pp. 25–28). A final distinction regarding consensus concerns whether the possibility of voting is permitted (Sabel, 1997, pp. 310–312). In the General Assembly and its subsidiary bodies, consensus is usually seen as a substitute for voting; in the Security Council, a proposal adopted by consensus may or may not come to a formal vote (Chai, 1981a, p. 49).

There is some degree of debate among scholars regarding the importance of the distinctions just mentioned. Smouts concludes that "no one outside of the Delegates' Lounge could care less about this sort of subtlety" (2000, p. 31); however, Peterson argues that these nuances allow delegates to "indicate the seriousness of disagreement relatively precisely," which allows for more careful judgments when it comes to implementing the agreements (1986, p. 86)—an issue that will receive more attention in Chapter 10. Miles Kahler would appear to agree with Peterson regarding the importance of these distinctions, because "under the opaque exterior of consensus undoubtedly lie rules of thumb not only concerning the degree of consensus that must be achieved but also concerning which of the parties must be included" (1993, p. 319). In fact, he concludes that most multilateral institutions seem to have a "tip point" at which a large majority becomes a consensus (see also Hopmann, 1996, p. 248).

But how is this "tip point" reached? A number of factors have been identified that can facilitate the processes of reaching a consensus. The first of these concerns the quality of the presiding officer, since much trust and discretion must be delegated to the consensus builder if the process is to work effectively (Kahler, 1993, p. 319). For example, it is crucial that the chair provide an accurate summation of the presumed consensus so as to avoid prolonged procedural wrangling (Bailey, 1969, p. 76–82; Chai, 1981a, pp. 56–62; Kaufmann, 1988, p. 27). A second factor that facilitates consensus is extensive use of informal consultations before a formal public debate is held in the main decisionmaking body (Bailey and Daws, 1998, p. 259). These can be conducted through "fire brigades," regional groups, extensive negotiation in subsidiary organs, or consultations of committees of the whole (Grey, 2000, p. 20; Peterson, 1986, pp. 87–91); the key issue is that all interests must be consulted, since any one actor can block a consensus if it is determined to do so. These dynamics of consensus building will receive further attention in Chapters 8 and 9.

The growing use of consensus in UN bodies is criticized on three grounds. First, since consensus requires that all parties go along with the proposal, the language is often weakened or watered down in search of purposeful vagueness (Tolley, 1983, p. 49; Narasimhan, 1988, p. 75). While this can also be a problem with proposals adopted by majority rule, Barry Buzan concludes that the "large amount of negative power implicit in consensus procedures" results in the likelihood that "their product might contain more than the usual amount of vague and ambiguous drafting" (1981, p. 345). Second, the fact that every state can block a consensus means that there are many opportunities for delay and obstruction (ibid., p. 344). As a result, consensus building can drag on and on until the end of a meeting or session is near and the resulting time pressures cause contentious points to be overlooked in a mad rush for agreement (Gregg, 1977, p. 72; Crowe, 1981, p. 95). Third, proposals that are ambiguous and drafted in haste are more likely to be subsequently disavowed by participants even after they are adopted, through a process of articulating "reservations" to key provisions (Gregg, 1977, p. 72; Crowe, 1981, p. 96; Bennett and Oliver, 2002, p. 95). These reservations may be offered immediately after the consensus is approved, or they may come in a later debate on the same issue (Righter, 1995, p. 138). As a result of these difficulties, Colin Crowe has concluded that consensus-based resolutions mean less than majority-based resolutions (1981, p. 96). Rosemary Righter is more damning and colorful in her conclusions, arguing that consensus is a "ruse for disagreement" because resolutions adopted in this manner include "linguistic subterfuge" to the point that they are deprived of "all real meaning"; in essence, consensus "resembles an enormously elaborate mating ritual that ends with the pretense of a consummation that has not taken place" (1995, pp. 69, 138).

In spite of these criticisms, many assessments of the overall impact of consensus on the UN's political processes are positive. For one thing, the protracted negotiations that are required to build consensus allow more time for participants to understand and adjust to the compromises that are necessary along the way (Buzan, 1981, p. 344); put another way, it gives them more time to learn and appreciate the music and rhythm of the emerging routine of the global dance. Furthermore, this process largely occurs behind the scenes, which allows participants who decide to make politically difficult changes in policy to avoid some of the embarrassment that can accompany public scrutiny (Bennett and

Oliver, 2002, p. 95). Finally, some scholars and UN observers have disputed the claim that consensus leads to "least common denominator" outcomes by avoiding difficult decisions (Childers and Urquhart, 1991, p. 4). Instead, they argue, consensus decisions can deal with crucial issues in a concrete and decisive manner. Furthermore, some of the most significant UN resolutions have been adopted by consensus, and "this has not prevented them from enjoying a very high degree of authority, both politically and legally" (Sands and Klein, 2001, p. 266). This authority is most likely a result of the fact that consensus-based resolutions project unity and are therefore seen as being stronger statements of collective public opinion (Crowe, 1981, p. 95). These potential relationships between the processes of decisionmaking and the subsequent effects of the decisions that are made will be further investigated in Chapter 10.

8

Informal Networking: The Personal Side

MULTILATERAL NEGOTIATIONS IN INTERNATIONAL ORGANIZATIONS SUCH as the United Nations are typically a curious affair. Participants in the process, whether they be member states, Secretariat officials, or representatives from civil society, often begin the negotiations with entrenched positions far removed from each other. It is not uncommon for delegates to offer uncompromising proposals whose intended audience is domestic rather than international, all the while talking past each other in endless debates of questionable value. Press coverage of the meetings and conferences where these negotiations take place frequently stresses the degree of divergence in views, indicating that the chance for agreement is marginal at best. While some of these efforts eventually end in an unsurprising failure, multilateral negotiations often do achieve some sort of positive outcome; these can range from vague "agreements to disagree" or "general statements of principles" to rather ambitious plans of action or concrete international treaties. The degree of agreement that results can appear both dramatic and sudden in the eyes of those not directly involved in the negotiations. What makes it possible for these agreements to emerge seemingly out of nowhere so late in the negotiations when failure appeared certain?

Such puzzling questions are certainly not unique to the study of the United Nations or any other international organization; they are likely shared by students of almost any political process where interested parties pursue apparently conflicting goals with scarce resources. However, developing a better understanding of how these dynamics unfold at the UN is especially challenging due to two imposing obstacles. The first is the existing deficiencies in the international organizations literature, discussed in the introduction to this volume: the vast majority of this scholarship centers on the nature of the decisions these actors make and

223

on the subsequent effects of their decisions, while little attention has been paid to the political processes through which the decisions are reached in the first place. There have been repeated calls to correct this problem. Writing in the late 1960s, Keohane (1967, pp. 221–222), Kay (1969, p. 958), and Alger (1970, p. 444) all argued that scholars had neglected the political processes that are central to the functioning of the UN. A similar conclusion was reached by Rochester (1986, p. 812) and Kratochwil and Ruggie (1986, p. 754) nearly two decades later, when they called for an increased focus on the structure and processes of formal international organizations. And this appeal has been repeated since the end of the cold war: Kaufmann (1994, p. 28), Rochester (1995, p. 199), Smith (1999, p. 173), and Alger (2002, p. 218) have observed the continued need for systematic exploration of UN decisionmaking.

Unfortunately, this general neglect of the UN's political processes is compounded by a second obstacle to understanding how multilateral agreements are formed: much of the negotiation process takes place in private and informal settings closed to all but those directly involved. Nearly every account of UN decisionmaking authored by former practitioners and members of the press is replete with situations in which "behind-the-scenes" negotiations provided a catalyst for the formal decisions that were made (for example see Meisler, 1995). Private negotiations and informal consultations have always played an important role at the United Nations, but their use has increased dramatically in the years since the end of the cold war (Kostakos, 1995, p. 66) for two straightforward reasons: (1) the UN is being asked to address a growing range of transnational problems, necessitating the use of every available means of building agreement in the face of overcrowded agendas, and (2) the UN is no longer captive to the East-West rivalry, and this has opened the door to new avenues of coalition building, a process that is clearly facilitated by informal contacts among delegates.

The use of informal contacts pervades all the formal arenas of decisionmaking at the UN, covered in Chapter 6. Smouts describes how "General Assembly resolutions spark off a flurry of backstage activity not unlike parliamentary activity, with its caucuses, permanent groups, ad hoc coalitions, clientelism and influence peddling. Off-the-record meetings, caucus deliberations, rumours, prognostications, dramatization, suspense . . . such are the delegates' delights" (2000, p. 31). In a footnote on the same page she credits a French diplomat with an analogy to American football: "The ball disappears beneath the pack of players, there is a chaotic scramble, no one knows what is going on, then the ball appears somewhere and everyone starts running." These colorful descriptions of informal networking clearly show how these dynamics can shape all aspects of the global dance, from the tone and pace of the music of negotiation to the cast of characters included in any emerging routines of agreement.

The primary reason these informal consultations are so important in UN bodies relates to the need for individual delegates to pursue the interests of their state while still participating in the give-and-take required to build winning coalitions. As was discussed in Chapter 2, these twin responsibilities require a delicate balance, since they can place competing demands on delegates (see for example Jacobson, 1979, pp. 120–124; Nicholas, 1975, pp. 136–137; Cox and Jacobson, 1973b, pp. 17–19). Each member state is likely to be pursuing a policy based at least to some extent on compromises made at the domestic level, which can make further compromise at the international level politically difficult (see Putnam, 1988). Yet, if widespread agreement is to be reached in a multilateral setting, then a process of give-and-take designed to reconcile divergent national positions is required (Ziring, Riggs, and Plano, 2000, p. 90; Bailey, 1969, p. 11). This is most likely to happen in a private setting, away from the glare of public scrutiny in formal meetings—perhaps in a vacant conference room, at a delegation office, over lunch, or even in the corridors of UN headquarters. Unfortunately, the very characteristics of informality and privacy that make these settings particularly conducive to difficult compromises have the additional effect of making them very challenging for scholars to study in anything more than a descriptive fashion.

With its focus on the actors and processes in United Nations decisionmaking, this book as a whole is designed to address the first obstacle mentioned above: the apparent neglect of research on the formal structures and procedures of international organizations. The goal of this particular chapter is both more modest and more difficult: to overcome the second obstacle by providing a systematic understanding of how the private and informal side of the UN's political processes influences the formal decisions that get made. In order to accomplish this goal, the following pages will build upon existing descriptive accounts of informal consultations at the UN with insights gained from open-ended interviews with nearly fifty UN delegates and officials. The discussion will be divided into two parts. The first will provide a detailed picture of the scope and nature of these informal contacts by addressing the following questions: What types of informal contacts are used at the UN? How are they established? What actors use them? And how do they matter within and outside of the UN? The second section will look more closely at the role played by informal contacts in one particular arena of decisionmaking, the UN Security Council.

▓ The Scope and Nature of Informal Contacts

The processes of multilateral diplomacy can be conducted through a wide range of meetings: public versus private, official versus unofficial, and formal versus informal, to name some of the most common trade-offs that are available (Lydon, 1998, pp. 152–154). These different types of meetings are set up and conducted in various ways: some are announced well in advance, others emerge on an ad hoc basis as circumstances permit; some are held in large meeting facilities with a specified seating arrangement and established procedures of debate, others are held in small rooms or in the corridors where delegates interact in a less constrained manner; some involve both interpretation and official records, others lack one or both of these mechanisms, which means that a much smaller range of participants will actually know what transpired.

While there are differences in the terminology used to describe various types of meetings, Anthony Lydon has provided a helpful guide (1998, pp. 153–154). *Public meetings* are those open to states that are not members of the body in question, to representatives from civil society and the press, and even to the general public if space and security practices permit; verbatim records are prepared and made available for public consumption. *Private meetings* differ in that they are open only to the direct participants in debate (with some rare exceptions), and records, if they are kept at all, are usually released only in a summary fashion or are available only to those who participated in the meeting. *Official meetings* are held by the "duly constituted bodies of the organ concerned," are announced well in advance of the meeting, and are often held in public, whereas *unofficial meetings* are typically "working groups" or "study groups" of limited composition that meet in an ad hoc fashion as needed. Finally, *formal meetings* are those whose conduct follows established rules of procedure (from the seating arrangements to the mechanisms of debate and voting), whereas *informal meetings* are those where the processes of discussion unfold in a more free-wheeling and unscripted manner. While other combinations are possible, most meetings are either public, official, and formal or private, unofficial, and informal. The first category was the subject of attention in Chapters 6 and 7, and the second category is the focus of this chapter.

Before we consider the specific characteristics of private, unofficial, and informal meetings, it is important to point out that these mechanisms are often used in tandem with more public, official, and formal meetings. In other words, as UN processes unfold, decisionmaking typically moves between formal and informal mechanisms in order to facilitate (or obstruct) efforts to build winning coalitions to address the issue at hand (see, for example, Peterson, 1986, pp. 92–103). This can be thought of as a two-level phenomenon: both public and private exchanges occur simultaneously and are influenced by each other (Alger, 1967, p. 52; 1972, p. 279). On the one hand, committee chairs understand that public meetings provide important opportunities for informal consultations, and they may endeavor to keep the formal debate going, not because they "believe that yet another public speech will help the committee reach consensus, but [because] they do believe that, while the committee is in session, private lines of communication are established and members are encouraged to work on committee problems" (Alger, 1967, p. 52). On the other hand, the public debate is certainly shaped by the informal conversations, because they can act as an important and relatively quick feedback mechanism regarding the ideas that are being discussed (ibid., p. 83).

Evidence of the reinforcing nature of public and private processes can be found in the fact that the patterns of informal interaction that take place in the back of meeting halls and during brief adjournments in formal debate can be "remarkably different than the patterns of participation in public debate" (Alger, 1972, p. 279), with countries that are seeking agreement (as opposed to dissenting) being more likely to engage in informal consultations than public speeches (Alger, 1966, p. 157). Formal procedures are typically more conducive to obstructionist tactics and majority voting among competing proposals, whereas informal processes provide those states seeking agreement with additional avenues for building consensus around a single proposal (Peterson, 1986, pp. 92–96; Alger, 1966, p. 158).

Types of Informal Contacts

References to the use of informal contacts are not uncommon in the literature on United Nations decisionmaking, since much of the give-and-take of multilateral diplomacy occurs through these processes. However, these dynamics are often discussed simply within a catchall category, which obscures the wide range of informal contacts that play a role in the organization's political processes. Interviews with participants allow for a deeper examination of how different types of informal contacts can be used in different types of situations. Overall, these interviews indicate that the use of informal contacts is becoming so ubiquitous that it is now common to distinguish between "informals" and "informal-informals" (Darmanin, 1998; Shestack, 1998; Khalikov, 1998; Tsui, 1998). While different participants have defined these distinctions in slightly different terms, it is possible to derive a basic picture of what "informals" and "informal-informals" look like in the global dance.

The exact use of "informals" varies from one committee to the next, but they are fairly well established in UN decisionmaking, with a number of common features similar to those discussed by Lydon in regard to informal, unofficial, and private meetings (1998, pp. 152–154). They tend to be unofficial meetings of working groups and other ad hoc bodies, open only to a select group of participants, who interact without the cumbersome rules of procedure discussed in the preceding two chapters. Generally no records are kept, but translation may be provided, and there is likely to be one delegate who chairs the meetings in the sense of bringing the group together and making sure it stays focused on the task at hand (Darmanin, 1998; Shestack, 1998; Khalikov, 1998; Tsui, 1998). These groups may meet in member-state missions as a means of removing, as much as possible, the distractions associated with UN headquarters; however, there is a general preference that "informals" be conducted in UN facilities if possible (Kaufmann, 1980, pp. 113–114). This saves time for delegates who are moving from one meeting to the next throughout the day, and it allows for a more open and comfortable discussion for those delegates who perceive the UN as a neutral and less partisan meeting place. In addition to the location of the "informals," the size and layout of the room in which they are conducted can affect their effectiveness (Kaufmann, 1988, p. 45). It is best if the room is organized such that delegates face one another and that it contains sufficient space for the delegates and their advisers (preferably no more than one each) along with any support staff from the Secretariat provided to assist the "informals." If delegates have to climb over or squeeze by each other, or if they have trouble hearing the arguments of their colleagues, then the "informals" are less likely to help foster agreement.

One common example of the use of "informals" in UN decisionmaking is the negotiating groups or "fire brigades" (Kaufmann, 1980, p. 16) discussed at the end of Chapter 3. These groups negotiate some of the most contentious issues facing large decisionmaking bodies in an effort to build agreement within a small group of states first and then have the agreement spread through the UN membership as a whole (Peterson, 1986, p. 295). Thus it is imperative that the negotiating group be composed of states that can speak on behalf of their larger common-interest caucusing groups and hopefully deliver their support for whatever agreement is reached (Alger, 1989, pp. 25–27). In some situations participants have called these groups "friends of the chair," since they are often composed of experienced delegates who enjoy the confidence of the presiding officer of the decisionmaking body and its membership as a whole. Each member of the group may take ownership of building agreement on one contentious issue, or they may address issues one by one in a collective fashion (Ramaker, 1998; Tsui, 1998). In either case, this "group of friends" can assist the chair in determining when each issue is sufficiently ripe for agreement and it is time to share the proposals worked out in "informals" with the rest of the member states. If this is done at the appropriate time, states will agree that "convergence has reached its peak" and that the package completed in the negotiating group deserves the support of the entire membership. Because of the difficult compromises that are required in order to get to this point, it is helpful if the negotiating groups operate in a private, unofficial, and informal manner, free of the posturing and rhetoric that often characterize large public meetings at the United Nations.

The use of "informals" is not limited to situations where the primary goal is to arrive at political compromises on UN programs and policies. Research by Jochen Prantl and Jean Krasno on the use of ad hoc informal groupings of states at the United Nations has uncovered that they can have dimensions of activity—both within and outside the UN—that deal primarily with implementation (2002, p. 21), not decisionmaking. These ad hoc groupings, which have been called "contact groups" or "groups of friends of the Secretary-General," are composed of about five states that have a special competence for addressing a particular situation of conflict on the UN agenda based on shared history, past involvement, regional status, available resources, or a strong reputation. They function as needed by the secretary-general, helping to limit his vulnerability to criticism in the General Assembly or Security Council and helping to increase the success of his efforts to create and implement peace agreements among parties to the conflict (ibid., p. 39). They are active both at UN headquarters and in the field, occasionally through public pronouncements but more often through private initiatives developed in informal consultations (ibid., pp. 45–46). These ad hoc "groups of friends" are prone to some of the same difficulties in membership as those facing negotiating groups (ibid., p. 48), but they have made significant contributions to the peaceful settlement work of the United Nations (ibid., p. 57).

Over time various "informals" have become increasingly formal, both in the way they operate and in their expected role in the political process. As a result, practitioners have talked about the importance of "informal-informals," where interested parties come together in a rather spontaneous manner to address key sticking points in regard to the issue at hand (Darmanin, 1998; Shestack, 1998; Khalikov, 1998; Tsui, 1998). These encounters have been a feature of UN decisionmaking from the San Francisco Conference onward. They are characterized by the absence of nearly every feature associated with formal meetings: no records are kept, no interpretation is provided, leadership is entirely ad hoc (if it is present at all), there is no set agenda, and participants can vary from one "informal-informal" to the next, even when the same issue or sticking point is being addressed.

"Informal-informals" can take on many forms, three of which will be used as examples here. The first involves extensive use of small group caucusing during brief adjournments in formal meetings or even as formal meetings are under way. One of the most striking features for nonparticipants observing UN meetings is the level of commotion present in the moments before and after a meeting; individual delegates try to consult with as many of their colleagues as possible before the session is called to order or before the delegates escape the room after the speakers' list is exhausted for the day. Even more surprising to nonparticipants is the fact that much of this commotion continues after the meeting has begun, with delegates frequently moving around the room to consult with one another or stepping out into the hall for a more lively debate. While some might consider such practices undiplomatic and disrespectful to the speaker, they are nonetheless vital to the effective functioning of nearly all UN bodies, since it is practically impossible for even rather small decisionmaking bodies to engage in useful drafting simply through a process of formal speechmaking (Kaufmann, 1980, p. 114).

These informal interactions are difficult to study in a systematic way; however, Alger carried out nine months of intensive observation of the General Assembly's Fifth (Administrative and Budgetary) Committee during 1962–1963 in an effort to understand how these dynamics affected UN decisionmaking (1966, 1967, 1972, 1989). He found that informal exchanges can involve something as simple as a discussion between seatmates or a casual conversation at the back of the hall, or they can involve a more intentional effort of one or more delegates to circulate around the perimeter of a meeting, looking for specific participants whose input is desired (Alger, 1966, p. 147; 1967, pp. 56–59). Needless to say, the number and form of these informal contacts varies across different issues, actors, and arenas, and Alger uncov-

Delegates attending the General Assembly's Resumed 10th Emergency Special Session on the Middle East engage in caucusing on July 20, 2004. These informal processes helped to build agreement around a draft resolution that overwhelmingly called for Israel to heed the June 2004 advisory opinion of the International Court of Justice, which declared the construction of a security barrier in and around the West Bank to be illegal. (UN photo #NICA 17631, by Sophia Paris)

ered several factors that might explain these patterns: the interest of states in resolving an issue, the degree of divergence among national positions on the issue at the start of debate, the past working relationships established between key delegates, and the personal characteristics of participants, including their interpersonal skills, knowledge, and UN experience (1967, pp. 63, 82).

A second example of "informal-informals" is the extensive delegate interaction that occurs in social settings within and around the UN. Both Alger (1961, pp. 131–132; 1976, pp. 59–60) and Kaufmann (1980, pp. 115–117) highlight how meals, receptions, and bars can be effective forums for consulting the views of other delegates in a relaxed and off-the-record atmosphere (especially those delegates it would be politically difficult to meet with elsewhere), for trying to gently persuade others to see a particular issue from a different point of view, or for making arrangements for a more extensive consultation at a later time. Alger's vivid description of the Delegates' Lounge (1976, pp. 59–60) notes numerous occasions where delegates are essentially forced to interact with each other: in line for food or drinks, rummaging through the overflowing rack provided for briefcases and coats, or sharing space at the limited number of available tables. Similar scenes are repeated in the restaurants and bars around UN headquarters; many of the participants interviewed for this project underlined the importance of what many of them called "cocktail napkin diplomacy" (in fact, some of these interviews themselves were completed in these venues). As useful as these social settings are for "informal-informals," delegates must be cognizant of each other's mood, since some of them may be at the bar or restaurant in search of a much-needed respite from the UN's political processes (Kaufmann, 1980, p. 116).

The final example of "informal-informals" considered here is a practice that Kaufmann has termed "the fine art of corridor sitting" (1980, p. 113). It involves a delegate's positioning himself or herself at a strategic location in UN headquarters in an effort to either connect with a specific participant (or participants) or to just keep in touch with the flow of events on that day. In many respects this resembles the period in between classes at any American high school, when students gather near the locker or classroom of a close friend or try to use an "accidental" hallway encounter as a means of breaking the ice with a member of the opposite sex. Fortunately, UN headquarters in New York is designed in a manner that facilitates this practice (Kaufmann, 1980, pp. 113–114; 1988, pp. 45–46): most delegates lack private office space in which to hide, buildings join together in a few key hallways, most meeting rooms are located in close proximity to each other, and the wait for elevators in the delegates' section can be considerable. One location particularly conducive to "corridor sitting" at UN headquarters is a small coffee and pastry bar located in a moderate-sized room where the basements of the General Assembly building and conference building join. At least three conference rooms open directly into this café, and one entrance to the UN's parking garage is close by. Thus it represents a sort of "choke point" through which a large volume of UN traffic must pass. This is a perfect location for delegates to "hold court," and some transact an amazing amount of business in a short period of time: sharing briefing papers, exchanging ideas, setting up further meetings, and building the friendships and working relationships that can facilitate future decisionmaking (Drayton, 1998).

The Establishment and Use of Informal Contacts

The important role played by informal contacts is not limited to any one arena of decisionmaking at the United Nations; the dynamics just described can have an impact on every political body, from those with universal participation to those with restricted membership (Kaufmann, 1980, p. 114). Comparative studies of multilateral diplomacy across bodies within and outside the UN system have found that informal contacts are nearly always present in cases of successful consensus building and that agreement is essentially impossible in their absence (see Smith, 1999, p. 193, and the case study chapters in Kaufmann, 1989). Furthermore, the growing range of participants in the "new diplomacy" of efforts to design mechanisms of global governance within and outside the UN system has only served to increase the importance of informal contacts (see the edited volume by Cooper, English, and Thakur, 2002). They have been one of the primary mechanisms through which "like-minded states" (mainly small and middle powers) and nongovernmental organizations have built their winning coalitions for the international campaign to ban landmines and the establishment of the International Criminal Court. On complex negotiations regarding specific provisions of treaty language, members of the Secretariat have been instrumental in using informal consultations for suggesting language that would bridge contentious areas of disagreement (Khalikov, 1998). NGOs too have used informal contacts to wield influence, even on issues of national security, as is reflected by the effective use of corridor sitting by Rebecca Johnson of the ACRONYM Consortium during the comprehensive nuclear test ban negotiations in the Geneva-based Conference on Disarmament in 1996 (Ramaker, 1998). As these few examples illustrate, the use of informal contacts extends to all arenas and actors involved in UN decisionmaking. Based on their frequent and significant impact on the UN's political processes, the participants interviewed for this project seemed to assume that informal contacts would and should be used in all possible situations.

The ad hoc nature of informal contacts often makes it unclear to all but those directly involved exactly who initiated their use in a given situation. The spontaneous and temporary nature of "informal-informals" means that identifying who played what role is likely to be an effort in futility; however, this is far from true in the case of "informals," where the legitimacy of the effort typically rests on the origins and composition of the negotiating group (Kulyk, 1998; Bisogniero, 1998). While informal contacts may be a first step in the negotiating process, designed to see if there is support for holding formal meetings on a particular topic (this is frequently done in the Security Council, as will be discussed in the final section of this chapter), it is more common for the informal consultations to emerge parallel to a process of formal negotiations (Kondo, 1998). In such cases, the informal contacts are typically established in one of three ways (Kulyk, 1998). The first is for the presiding officer of a particular body (whether this position is elected or rotating) to either initiate the informal consultations or select a well-regarded delegate to do it (see, for example, Grey, 2000, p. 19; Khalikov, 1998). A second possible route is for the secretary-general or another senior Secretariat official to either initiate the informal consultations or approach a particular delegate in the hopes that she or he might do so (Kulyk, 1998; Kondo, 1998). Finally, in the absence of action on the part of the presiding officer or secretary-general, any delegate without direct interests at stake who enjoys a strong reputation may initiate informal consultations; however, this route is the most likely to encounter problems of legitimacy (Kulyk, 1998; Bisogniero, 1998). Examples of all three routes will be included in the following section of this chapter.

The previous paragraphs have established that just about any participant in any United Nations arena can initiate and use "informals" and "informal-informals" in an effort to secure policy objectives. Often participants are strongly tempted to engage in informals, for they can allow individuals an opportunity to shape the negotiations in a substantial way, giving certain actors (like small states and NGOs) avenues of influence they otherwise would have lacked and indicating that they are considered part of the "in-group" whose contributions are desired in regard to the issue at hand. Unfortunately these same three reasons, and especially the last, have also led to strong criticisms from actors whose influence is effectively marginalized when they are excluded from informal consultations. These debates have been most intense regarding the informal consultations used by the Security Council, so they will receive more detailed attention below. Nonetheless, whether actors view informal consultations as basically inclusive or inherently exclusive, they are likely to want to be included in them when they are used.

Yet the fact that delegates can use informal consultations or might want to use them does not always mean they *should* use them. Alger has found that countries seeking to block agreement (dissenters) are less likely to participate in informal consultations, since it is easier to be obstructionist in formal meetings (1966, p. 157). Donald Puchala has offered a similar observation: "The weakest members shout the loudest, the most radical seek the most attention, and the most paranoid are the most critical" (1982–1983, p. 572). Clearly participants who plan to obstruct agreement, bring few resources to the table, and advance extreme positions are not the type that should be included in informal consultations; instead, it is important to select participants who are active on the issue (whether or not they have direct interests at stake) and who possess a particular expertise or resource that can contribute to addressing the issue (Darmanin, 1998; Hanif, 1998). Exactly which participants will meet these criteria depends on a number of factors that are quite similar to those discussed in regard to state roles and delegate personality in Chapter 2 and negotiating groups in Chapter 3: the specific issue at stake, the desire of an individual participant or the actor he or she represents to assume an ad hoc leadership role in the negotiations, and the set of personal attributes that an individual participant brings to the table, such as experience and charisma.

The Impact of Informal Contacts

Given the fact that informal contacts are so pervasive in UN politics, one would expect that they have a significant and valuable impact on decisionmaking; otherwise why would they be used? These expectations are certainly borne out across comparative case studies, which have found that informal contacts have two distinct types of influence on the political process: one regarding the substance of debate, the other regarding the environment in which the debate occurs. In regard to substance, Luard and Heater have observed that informal consultations play a central role in building agreement in large negotiations, usually in a step-by-step fashion (1994, p. 48). First, informal consultations are often used to build agreement within the various regional and common interest caucusing groups discussed in Chapter 3; then informal consultations may also be used to build agreement across these groups. The first step is absolutely necessary to get sufficient votes to pass a resolution through majority voting; this may not be true for the second step, but it nonetheless frequently takes place, since sponsors of the resolution are likely to desire as much support as possible for their approach. This dynamic was consistently highlighted in participant interviews, mainly because (as was discussed in the previous chapter) it is increasingly common for UN decisions to be made by consensus rather than simple majority voting. One participant has defined consensus as a situation where "the most interested parties have reached a livable agreement and the middle has been dragged along" (Drayton, 1998). Informal contacts can help with both of these requirements: building agreement between the most interested parties and getting those in the middle to go along.

Informal contacts foster a number of processes that can help participants work through the substance of competing proposals: they provide opportunities to plan strategies, exchange ideas, seek out sponsors, resolve otherwise vague communications, and make the necessary adjustments to draft proposals in order to bring more parties on board

(Kaufmann, 1980, pp. 113–117; 1988, pp. 173–174; Luard and Heater, 1994, p. 48). Evidence of all these processes was uncovered in a comparative analysis of three relatively successful cases of consensus building in the General Assembly in the 1990s (Smith, 1999, p. 193). In regard to the 1991 debate on the coordination of responses to humanitarian emergencies (Resolution 46/182, adopted on December 19, 1991), informal consultations were initiated through a "breakfast group" that was ultimately responsible for drafting compromise language that balanced the competing interests of donor and recipient states. On the efforts to renegotiate the seabed mining provisions of the UN Convention on the Law of the Sea from 1990 to 1994, informal contacts were used by the secretary-general and the "boat group" to first determine if there was sufficient interest to reopen the discussions and then to develop proposals regarding the content of the new agreement. Finally, during the negotiations on the Comprehensive (Nuclear) Test Ban Treaty, a group of "friends of the chair" used informal consultations among nuclear weapons states, threshold states (India, Pakistan, and Israel), and non–nuclear weapons states to work out specific details on the scope of the ban, the requirements for entry into force, and the verification procedures that would be used. In each of these cases, the use of informal contacts contributed to, but did not determine, the degree of consensus that was reached (ibid., pp. 196–197).

Despite these successful cases, it is not uncommon for informal contacts to be used and yet have little discernible impact on the substance of debate; after all, they are often used to address some of the most difficult sticking points in multilateral negotiations. However, even when stalemate occurs, scholars should not rush to conclude that the informal contacts were of no value. Kaufmann has observed that "seldom are delegation positions changed by personal relations, because individuals, unless very senior, have little influence on national policies." However, he concludes that these contacts can "foster a better understanding and appreciation of national positions . . . and sometimes affect subsequent formal exchanges and long-term voting patterns" (1980, p. 117). In other words, the use of informal contacts can improve the environment in which decisionmaking takes place even when they do not change the substance of decisions that are made. Furthermore, these positive results can persist even in the case of very difficult and contentious negotiations, especially when the participants involved have already built strong working relationships through the use of "informal-informals" in previous negotiations. For example, during the often tense and heated debates regarding Security Council expansion held in an open-ended working group of the General Assembly through the 1990s, delegates with conflicting goals still began their statements with "My good friends" due to their strong personal friendships. The result was a situation in which other participants "did not want to get caught in the crossfire of bouquets" (Bisogniero, 1998). Informal contacts can be used to change the negotiating environment as a first step toward substantive progress at a later date. Such a strategy of "informal-informals" was used by the US ambassador to the UN, Richard Holbrooke, during late 1999 and early 2000 when he faced an extremely hostile environment at the UN regarding the long-standing US arrears (Smith, 2004, p. 204). He visited many other permanent representatives one on one in their offices, which helped to create a more favorable environment when new scales of assessment for the regular budget and peacekeeping were successfully negotiated in the fall of 2000.

Informal contacts that help create strong friendships and positive working relationships may also have a long-term benefit or byproduct for future negotiations on other issues or in other international organizations (Kaufmann, 1989, p. 300). In Alger's investigation of the "non-resolution consequences" of UN activity, he concludes that "the sustained interaction of the delegates as well as the variety of the occasions on which they confront each other provides opportunities for the development of friendships across national boundaries that surpass those of normal diplomatic intercourse" (1961, p. 134) and that these networks of contacts can have effects outside the United Nations (1963, p. 420). Quite simply, they provide opportunities for more flexible interaction than is possible through formal diplomatic channels, permitting delegates to explore areas of potential agreement or cooperation even where there are official government policies to the contrary. In some cases, governments have specifically instructed their UN delegates to cultivate friendships and informal contacts as vehicles for interacting with unfriendly countries even when their bilateral diplomats are being told to maintain the status quo (Alger, 1965, p. 283; 1968, p. 110). Daily interaction between friendly delegates can plant the seeds for formal diplomatic initiatives in bilateral settings or in other international organizations where participants lack these networks of contacts.

While the impact of informal consultations is generally seen as being positive, there are some disadvantages to their use and even some situations where they can backfire, making agreement more difficult rather than easier. In terms of disadvantages, Kaufmann has observed that informal contacts and other social functions are so common and important at the UN that they can require "a heavy expenditure of time and energy" (1980, p. 117). While the preceding paragraphs would suggest that this is often time and energy well spent, it does have a negative impact on delegates' ability to engage in other important aspects of their work. A more serious problem can arise when informal contacts actually promote disagreement and tension rather than helping to resolve them. Such an outcome occurred in regard to Security Council reform in 1996–1997, when General Assembly president Razali Ismail used a series of informal consultations to build support for a quick-fix approach to Council expansion that was opposed by a large number of member states (Bisogniero, 1998). The Assembly president is most effective when she or he is viewed as being impartial, but Razali compromised his reputation and the office of president by appearing to take sides during the process of informal consultations. As a result, his use of informal contacts generated considerable suspicion, for it prevented all interested parties from playing an active role in the discussions, and ultimately it made further use of informal contacts on this issue impossible (Smith, 1999, p. 193). At least one participant interviewed on the issue of Council reform stressed the importance of making sure that informal contacts are only used alongside a more open and transparent process of discussion, so that a degree of transparency is maintained (Kulyk, 1998). Similar arguments have been made regarding the controversial use of informal consultations in the work of the Security Council, an issue to which we now turn.

▨ Informal Consultations in the Security Council

Like other United Nations bodies, the Security Council can conduct its business through several different types of meetings (see Bailey and Daws, 1998, pp. 21–22, for an overview). As was discussed in Chapter 6, Rule 48 of the Council's Provisional Rules of Procedure (UN doc. S/96/Rev.7) specifies that the Council should meet in public unless it decides otherwise. These public meetings are held in the Council's chambers and are open to nonmember states (which can participate without vote) and representatives of interested media and nongovernmental organizations (who can watch from the gallery). During the cold war, the Council conducted much of its business in public, reserving its private meetings for particularly sensitive subjects like the appointment of the secretary-general (Sutterlin, 1997, p. 8; Narasimhan, 1988, p. 75). This trend continued even as the number of meetings held by the Council underwent a rather steady increase through the UN's first fifty years (Bailey and Daws, 1998, p. 35). Private meetings, when held, differ in that they are open only to Council members and access to the records of these meetings is often, though not always, limited to those states and Secretariat officials who actually participated in the meetings (ibid., p. 21).

Despite this apparent preference for meeting in public, there have always been two different Councils at work in the UN: one that meets in formal and often public meetings and one that meets informally in delegates' lounges, dining rooms, and missions (Nicholas, 1975, pp. 97–98). These informal consultations became increasingly important during the height of the cold war and the growing conflict between developed and developing states for one simple reason: they provided an avenue to escape the rhetoric and posturing that often distorted the work of the Council by placing drama ahead of progress in public meetings (Sutterlin, 1997, p. 8; Luard and Heater, 1994, p. 18). While a variety of means have been developed to convey information about these informal consultations to nonmembers and the public (Bailey and Daws, 1998, p. 22; Sutterlin, 1997, p. 9), some observers have argued that it is their relative secrecy and off-the-record, noncommitting character that has made them fruitful (Luard and Heater, 1994, p. 35). These informal consultations were initially held in the crowded office of the Council president in an ad hoc fashion; however, by the 1970s they had become so frequent, crowded, and in need of orderly procedure that they were held in Conference Room 5 until a permanent consultation room adjacent to the Council chamber was provided by West Germany (Sutterlin, 1997, p. 8; Nicol, 1981b, p. 14). In this format, informal consultations have essentially become replicas of the formal Council (simultaneous interpretation is available, and there is sufficient room for advisers and Secretariat personnel), except for the fact that the proceedings are confidential and open only to Council members.

The end of the cold war resulted in a resurgent Security Council in the 1990s. In order to better handle an unprecedented amount of work, the Council began to carry out most of its work in its informal consultation room (Kirgis, 1995, p. 518). Public meetings often had predetermined outcomes, since they were used primarily to officially approve resolutions already drafted in private and to allow Council members (and occasionally other states) an opportunity to publicly comment on the content of the new policy. Furthermore, the resurgent Council in the 1990s also witnessed an increase in the use of "informal-informals," especially between the permanent members and the Secretary-General, among the members of the Non-Aligned Movement serving on the Council, and on occasion between Council members and states whose opinion they value but that are not currently on the Council (Lavrov, 1999, pp. 35–38). These developments have meant that certain states without a permanent or nonpermanent seat on the Council effectively enjoy "a kind of de facto membership by virtue of their informal consultations with members" (Hurd, 1997, pp. 136, 143–147). This is especially true for members of the Non-Aligned Movement and those states that contribute troops and other material support to peacekeeping operations.

Types of Informal Consultations in the Security Council

The use of informal consultations in the Security Council is "an essential element of UN diplomacy [but] almost by definition [they] are hard to define and precisely categorize" (Bailey and Daws, 1998, p. 60). Nevertheless, this section will distinguish among four different types of informal consultations in the Security Council: informal "consultations of the whole," informal consultations involving a subset of Council members, informal consultations between Council members and nonmember states or other actors, and informal consultations conducted by the Council president.

In practice, the distinction between private meetings of the Council and informal "consultations of the whole" are fuzzy at best; participants in these meetings have been known to use either term to characterize the same meeting (Bailey and Daws, 1998, p. 56). In recent years the use of "consultations of the whole" has become so common and structured (in the consultation room mentioned above) that they have essentially replaced private meetings, except for those required by Rule 48 of the Council's Provisional Rules of Procedure regarding the appointment of the secretary-general. These "consultations of the whole" are private gatherings of all fifteen Council members and presided over by the Council president (see the overview in Bailey and Daws, 1998, pp. 60–68). They appear on the Programme of Work for the Council prepared by the president for each month, but they are not "meetings" of the Council according to the UN Charter or the Council's Provisional Rules of Procedure. They are instead considered to be "meetings of the members of the Council," since nonmembers are excluded and no official records are kept. They have been used to address all types of issues on the Council's agenda, from peacekeeping reports to sanctions updates to briefings by special representatives of the secretary-general. The degree to which nonmembers of the Council are briefed on the work conducted in "consultations of the whole" varies according to which member holds the presidency in any given month; however, recent practice holds that these briefings occur on a daily basis when "consultations of the whole" are used and that the draft resolutions under consideration in these informal consultations should be made available to all member states.

A second type of informal consultations in the Security Council involves the efforts of a subset of Council members to coordinate their positions in Council debates or coordinate their responses to a particular problem faced by the Council (Bailey and Daws, 1998, pp. 68–72). While almost any interaction of Council members could qualify as this type of informal consultation, a number of possibilities have been institutionalized in the sense that they are recognized by the diplomatic community at the UN. The most important of these consultations are those among the permanent members of the Council (the P5) that were initiated in 1986 and expanded after the end of the cold war. These meetings can be held in a room at the UN or in one of the missions and may include the secretary-general or his representative. The "coordinator" for these consultations rotates every three months among the P5, and the meetings can take place at any diplomatic level, from permanent representatives to lower-level issue experts. It is now common for agreements to be initially worked out by the P5 and then shared with the rest of the Council in a "consultation of the whole" before having the Council formally approve the draft resolution in a short public meeting. Although arguably less important than consultations among the P5, similar meetings are held by the Western permanent members (France, Britain, and the United States, the P3), the four to seven members of the Non-Aligned Movement serving on the Council, and the members of the European Union serving on the Council. In addition to these established informal consultations, ad hoc "contact groups" and "groups of friends" can emerge to address particular issues. The activities of these groups are basically similar to that of their counterparts discussed under "informals" above, but they are composed entirely of Council members.

A third category of informal consultations in the Security Council comprises three types of meetings held between Council members and nonmember states or even other actors. First are meetings held under the "Arria formula" (named for the Venezuelan ambassador who initiated the practice), which bring members of the Council together with eminent international personalities, often visiting dignitaries of states not on the Council, but they can also include representatives from nonstate parties involved in a dispute of concern to the Council (Bailey and Daws, 1998, p. 73; Dedring, 2000, p. 92). These meetings are normally attended by all Council members, but they differ from other Council meetings in four ways: they are held away from the Council's chambers, they are convened and chaired by a member other than the Council president, notification of the meeting comes from the convener rather than the secretary-general, and aside from interpreters, members of the Secretariat do not attend. A second and related type of meeting involves the "Somavia formula" (named for the Chilean ambassador who suggested the practice), which would bring members of the Council together with representatives from nongovernmental organizations. One such effort was made in 1997, but it was not done under the auspices of the Council, so the Somavia formula has yet to be used (Bailey and Daws, 1998, 75; Dedring, 2000, p. 92). A final type of informal consultation between Council members and nonmember states involves those states that contribute troops and other resources to UN peacekeeping operations (Bailey and Daws, 1998, p. 74; Hurd, 1997, pp. 145–146). These meetings were formalized in 1994 and typically focus on mission mandates; however, they are not meetings of the Council itself, given their tripartite participation of Council members, troop-contributing countries, and the Secretariat. These developments illustrate that "in small and unofficial ways" the Council has used informal consultations to open itself to greater participation on the part of nonmembers (Dedring, 2000, p. 92).

The final manner in which informal consultations are used in the Security Council involves some activities of the Council president not covered in Chapter 7. In order to effectively run the Council, the president needs to consult with a variety of other actors: the secretary-general, one or more of the permanent members, certain nonpermanent members (especially those from the Non-Aligned Movement), the parties to a conflict, nonmembers of the Council who can play a special role in relation to the issue at hand, and regional groups that have a common position on the issue (Kaufmann, 1980, pp. 45–46; Nicol, 1981b, pp. 14–15). These consultations help the president judge whether or not to convene a meeting on a particular issue; at least one Council president has observed that most of his time was spent handling issues that needed to be addressed but did not require that the Council actually meet to discuss them (Jakobson, 1981, pp. 160–161). Sometimes this behind-the-scenes work will indicate that further discussion is necessary. Often this will be conducted through additional informal consultations, since it is much easier to understand policy preferences in face-to-face discussions free of any distractions that can make participants more reserved (Malik, 1981, p. 176). Based on the information gathered, the president can plan a course of formal and informal meetings designed to draft a resolution to address the issue; however, these meetings should include the full membership of the Council "sitting around a table" only once the agreement has begun to crystallize through informal consultations (Richard, 1981, p. 247).

Assessment of Informal Consultations in the Security Council

The preceding discussion has highlighted both advantages and disadvantages of the use of informal consultations across different bodies of the United Nations, focusing in particular on the Security Council. Nearly all UN observers who discuss the role of informal contacts would agree that they are "an essential part of diplomacy and the negotiation process" (Bailey and Daws, 1998, p. 393) and that their use "has unquestionably facilitated the process of compromise and agreement," even for smaller decisionmaking bodies like the Security Council (Sutterlin, 1997, p. 9). The reasons behind these views are discussed above, but some are worth repeating: they avoid the tendency toward rhetoric and spectacle in public meetings (Grey, 2000, p. 22); they allow UN bodies such as the Security Council to play a more effective role as peacemaker and peacekeeper, since careful exchanges can be held in an environment free of debilitating distractions (Dedring, 2000, p. 78); they can provide a flexible mechanism through which limited-membership bodies can consult with nonmembers and other actors deemed relevant to their work on a case-by-case basis (Hurd, 1997, p. 148); they have provided leading member states, such as the permanent five, with a means for reconciling their interests so that the Council can play a more proactive role in world events (Malone, 2000b, p. 22); and they have allowed the Council and other UN bodies to cope with their expanded workload in the post–cold war world (Dedring, 2000, p. 92).

These positive benefits of informal consultations must be balanced against one major shortcoming: these processes unfold behind closed doors and as a result may lack sufficient transparency to allow their decisions to be perceived as legitimate. This concern is voiced most often in regard to the Security Council, since it is vested by the UN Charter with the authority to act on behalf of the entire membership of the organization, not just its own membership (Bailey and Daws, 1998, p. 393). The use of informal consultations is not addressed in the Charter or the Council's Provisional Rules of Procedure; in fact these documents indicate that the Council should usually meet in public and should make its meetings open to those states affected by issues on its agenda (Rule 48 of the Provisional Rules of Procedure and Articles 31–32 of the Charter). Even UN observers who accept the positive benefits of informal consultations have expressed some reservations about their use. Informal consultations have allowed the Council to consult with nonmembers such as troop-contributing countries, but they have also been used by the permanent five in order to present ready-made agreements to the Council as a whole without consulting the nonpermanent members in advance (Malone, 2000, p. 22). In other words, informal consultations in the Security Council have empowered some UN members and marginalized others. Even those states that have been given "a kind of de facto" membership on the Council through these informal consultations have remained unsatisfied, since they desire permanent membership for both its practical and symbolic value (Hurd, 1997, p. 148).

The brief discussion of Security Council reform in Chapter 6 highlighted how this debate has centered on two related clusters of issues: the composition of the Council and its working methods. Both of these areas need to be addressed for the Council to become more representative of the UN membership and for its actions to be more legitimate in their eyes. The growing use of informal consultations has increased calls for enlargement even as the working methods of the Council have been modified in an effort to make sure nonmembers are able to contribute to and stay abreast of Council discussions. For example, the contents of informal discussions are "seldom kept secret very long," due to briefings by the president and members of regional groups as well as the willingness of some participants to talk with the press (Sutterlin, 1997, p. 9). Even on extremely contentious issues, such as the debate on Iraq in 2003, the Council maintained a mix of public meetings where numerous nonmembers could weigh in and informal consultations where the actual resolutions were drafted when possible. These practices certainly fall short of the changes envisioned by nonmembers; however, they have led some UN observers to wonder whether the real issue for nonmembers is frustration with the procedures of decision-making (as is often the claim) or simply disagreement with the substance of what has been decided (Bailey and Daws, 1998, p. 393). These different possibilities will receive more attention in the following chapter, which examines the tradeoffs participants must consider in the use of different substantive and procedural strategies of influence at the United Nations.

So what do these advantages and disadvantages mean for the future use of informal contacts in the Security Council and other UN bodies in which the global dance unfolds? It is likely that the current practice of mixing public meetings with informal consultations will continue, for the simple reason that both forums have useful and distinct attributes and purposes. Different participants will prefer different processes based on their interests regarding the issue at hand and their relative influence in the arena in which the decision is being made. While "informals" and "informal-informals" have long been part of the UN landscape, their role and visibility increased through the 1990s. This development sparked what some might see as a backlash on the part of some member states at the end of the decade, especially in regard to the Security Council. Since then there has been a modest renewed commitment—certainly in rhetoric, maybe also in action—to the transparency that only public meetings can provide. However, since ongoing disagreement on Council reform makes dramatic changes in the UN's political processes seem unlikely, UN decisionmaking will continue to occur through both formal and informal mechanisms, operating in a parallel but interrelated fashion.

9

Strategies of Influence: Positional, Personal, and Procedural

DIPLOMACY AND NEGOTIATION AT THE UNITED NATIONS INVOLVE A WIDE range of actors, arenas, and processes. Even in a traditional bilateral context it is common to describe diplomacy and negotiation as constituting just as much "art" as "science" (Nicolson, 1988, pp. 4–5). This is true because diplomacy and negotiation are difficult and challenging endeavors that change and evolve from one situation to the next. While one can speak of patterns or tendencies, it is not possible to specify clear and consistent rules of the game for these processes. Instead, participants are forced to feel their way as best they can given the resources at their disposal, the personal attributes and experiences they possess, and the situations in which they find themselves. These difficulties are often significantly compounded in the case of multilateral negotiations such as those at the United Nations, due to the greater complexity of the negotiating environment: more actors are involved, multiple decision rules are possible, outcomes from one debate can blur into the next debate, coalition building is required on contentious issues, and crosscutting cleavages are common (Hopmann, 1996, pp. 245–258). Each participant in United Nations decisionmaking faces the daunting task of designing strategies to secure their preferred outcome, with the awareness that up to 190 other member states, not to mention actors from the Secretariat, civil society, and the private sector, are all trying to do the same thing.

Part 1 of this book examined a wide range of UN actors: member states, groups, the Secretariat, nongovernmental organizations, and multinational corporations. Of special concern were the characteristics of each actor and the various mechanisms through which they participate in UN decisionmaking. Part 2 has explored the various arenas and procedures that provide the structure and context in which these actors engage in political debate and make decisions to act; both formal and informal processes have been considered. This chapter seeks to bridge the material covered in these two parts by focusing on the strategies of influence that are available to each actor in the global dance, given its own characteristics and the dynamics of the arena in which a decision is being made.

For the purposes of this discussion, influence "is defined in terms of effect on outcomes rather than control over individual states" (Keohane, 1967, p. 222). While changing the behavior of one other actor may be a significant achievement, exercising influence can be far more challenging, for it requires a participant to "affect the decisions of the [body in question] so that they accord with its wishes." As was discussed in Chapter 2 and elsewhere in Part 1, authors such as Cox and Jacobson (1973b, pp. 18–222) have argued that an actor's capacity to exercise influence in an international organization hinges on several factors: the position it occupies in the organization and international politics more broadly, the personal attributes of its representatives in the debate, and the salience of the issue in question. In other words, wielding influence requires that an actor have both the capacity and the desire to achieve a preferred outcome in a given situation. While these arguments certainly ring true, they leave unanswered the question of *how* an actor exercises influence in light of its abilities and interests. Here one must first consider which specific strategies and behaviors are available and then decide which ones are most likely to produce the desired result.

Unfortunately, neither of these questions lends itself to easy answers. The list of available strategies is seemingly endless; at a basic level they can be either reciprocal or one way (Keohane, 1967, p. 222). Reciprocal strategies can include, for example, compromise on a single issue, a package deal among related issues, "logrolling" across artificially linked issues, or even "mutual understandings" or "patterns of cooperation" covering a broad range of UN business. On the other hand, one-way strategies involve efforts by one actor to change the behavior of other actors, but not vice versa, through persuasive arguments, positive inducements, and even pressure, threats, or sanctions if necessary. These strategies that specifically target other actors can be joined with those that seek to alter, at least to some extent, the environment in which negotiations are being conducted, either by drawing on the personal attributes of the participants or by adjusting, in both favorable and unfavorable ways, the rules of procedure that are being used to structure debate.

Once at least a partial list of available strategies has been generated, actors face the task of engaging in a cost-benefit calculation for each so that the most effective one can be identified. Ideally, this would involve a rational decision on how to best cope with the strategic environment they face; however, it is often clouded by the fact that the actors involved are individually autonomous, pursuing different goals, and operating in an environment of uncertainty regarding the interests and behaviors of the other participants (Martin and Simmons, 2001, p. 448). While the complexity typically associated with multilateral negotiations can provide more opportunities for successful reciprocal strategies such as those mentioned above, it is more common for this complexity to complicate the tradeoffs each actor faces (Hopmann, 1996, p. 257). Even basic questions about how far apart the participants are, how many interest groups are involved, what decision rule is being used, who your potential friends and enemies are, and who is managing the negotiating process can be difficult to answer (ibid., pp. 249–272). As a result, actors must often rely on instinct, intuition, and experience when selecting strategies.

Furthermore, judgments regarding the tradeoffs between different strategies must be made in light of the salience and satisfaction each actor feels vis-à-vis the different possible outcomes of UN policymaking. Lawrence Finkelstein has explored various hypotheses regarding the relationship between the salience of the issue and the degree to which an actor will favor centralized versus decentralized processes and outcomes (1988a, pp. 465–468). For him, *salience* refers to "the intensity of the importance to members [and other actors] of the stakes involved in decisions and actions of UN agencies" (ibid., p. 465). He argues that salience is not an easy concept to grapple with, since it is not always clear exactly which issues will be perceived as salient and since these perceptions can change over time. However, he finds that perceptions of salience can affect the strategies an actor is willing to use and the compromises it will accept domestically. It is common to assume that actors associate salience with those outcomes likely to further their power; however, Barry O'Neill has argued that increased power is not always synonymous with greater satisfaction (1997, pp. 66–67). Actors may be satisfied (or not) that a particular outcome is consistent with their perceived interests regardless of whether they actually had the power or capacity to do anything about it. Therefore, the choice of strategies for participants in UN decisionmaking will be based on their power and capabilities as well as the salience and satisfaction they associate with various possible outcomes. Low salience may cause an actor to shy away from rocking the boat with confrontational strategies; however, if these strategies are seen as being necessary to reach a satisfactory outcome on an important issue, then they may be used despite the risks.

Some scholars, journalists, and practitioners have observed that the political processes of the United Nations are geared toward positive outcomes in negotiations. For example, Kay finds that "negotiations are strongly influenced by the orientation of most activity towards the ultimate adoption of a resolution" (1967, p. 105). Likewise, Righter quotes a Swiss diplomat who argues that "considerable atmospheric pressure . . . builds up at all meetings in favor of producing 'an outcome'" (1995, p. 135). Those in favor of a particular policy option often desire to build as much support as possible, just as those opposed to that policy "would prefer, in most cases, not to be forced to take a public stand against the majority of the United Nations"; both preferences produce "an inherent bias toward compromise in the negotiation process of the Organization" (Kay, 1967, p. 105). Still, building agreement in the face of conflicting interests is not a simple or easy undertaking. Successful multilateral negotiations require that considerable resources, energy, and determination be invested in order to identify issues that are ripe for agreement and push for action by as many participants as possible. The presence of multiple arenas of decisionmaking, a wide range of actors, linkages between issues, and the desire for widespread support create numerous opportunities for those who oppose a policy or action to block its adoption in multilateral settings. Given this, it is necessary to further investigate the strategies available to participants with different resources and goals in the negotiations.

The following pages will explore three types of strategies: those that depend on the positional power of the actor in question (for example, votes, resources, or reputation), those that rest on the personal attributes of individual representatives (for example, their charisma, negotiating skill, autonomy, or public speaking ability), and those that involve manipulating the formal and informal procedures discussed in Chapters 6–8 (for example, breaking for informal caucusing or a premature closure of debate on an issue). As each type of strategy is discussed, examples of how they have been used in several different issue areas and UN bodies will be offered in order to illustrate the tradeoffs involved.

One final introductory comment should be offered. In his discussion of institutional bargaining and the formation of international regimes, Young concludes that the presence of multiple types of leadership is required for a successful outcome: structural leadership based on power and resources, entrepreneurial leadership based on persuasion and negotiation, and intellectual leadership based on vision and ideas can each play a vital role in multilateral diplomacy, depending on the requirements of each situation (1991, pp. 303–305). The same can be said for the three types of strategies just mentioned; each type has advantages and limitations that must be carefully balanced. All the actors involved in the global dance are aware that today's opponent may be tomorrow's partner, given the wide range of issues and interests that come before the United Nations. However, drawing on multiple strategies does not always ensure that an actor will achieve a successful outcome in UN negotiations; its delegates may find themselves frustrated and stymied at every turn and may decide to pursue policy in another setting outside the United Nations (see Cooper, English, and Thakur, 2002). Such efforts are referred to as "new diplomacy" since they involve a greater range of actors, a broader scope of issues, a less structured set of forums, a higher intensity of interaction, and quicker results as compared to traditional UN negotiations. Like-minded states and interested NGOs have been particularly willing to use this "new diplomacy" to draft global policy on issues such as the Ottawa Treaty, which bans antipersonnel landmines, and the Rome Statute of the International Criminal Court.

▓ Strategies Based on Positional Power

Early studies of UN decisionmaking have offered important insights into the range of actors involved in the organization's political processes and the potential sources of influence that each enjoys (for example, see Cox and Jacobson, 1973a, pp. 393–402). More recent studies have echoed at least some of these earlier findings (such as Smith, 1999), and Part 1 of this book provided a more detailed examination of these dynamics for five types of actors: member states, groups, the Secretariat, NGOs, and MNCs. This discussion will build on this existing material to explore three different types of strategies participants can use based on the positional power of the actor they represent: majority-based strategies, minority-based strategies, and broker strategies. Majority-based strategies are most attractive to states that share a common position or goal with a large number of other members, such that they can control the direction and behavior of the organization in a one-state, one-vote environment. In some situations civil society actors can also use the public pressure associated with large numbers to move debate in a particular direction. Minority-based strategies are those that can be used by a small group of actors (or even by one actor single-handedly) when these particular actors enjoy power and resources outside the organization that can be translated into leverage inside it despite their inferior numbers. Such actors certainly include the major powers; however, they may also include relatively isolated smaller powers when it is their behavior the UN is trying to address (see Keohane, 1967, pp. 228–232; Taylor, 2000a, pp. 301–302), and in the future it might even include MNCs in cases where their participation is required to address a particular issue (such as the need for cheaper generic drugs in the global fight against HIV/AIDS). Finally, broker strategies are available only to those actors that enjoy the confidence and trust of other actors based on their strong reputation and impartial previous behavior; this is most likely to be true in the case of middle powers, NGOs, and members of the Secretariat.

Given the sovereign equality of members and the use of egalitarian voting procedures, majority-based strategies have always been a powerful tool at the United Nations, especially in decisionmaking bodies composed of the organization's full membership like the General Assembly. If a majority of the membership of a UN body desires the same outcome, they need not strategize to build support for its adoption; rather they can simply hold a majority vote, and their preferred outcome becomes UN policy (Luard and Heater, 1994, p. 48). During the early years of the United Nations, these practices were primarily an instrument of the West, led by the United States and its allies in Europe and Latin America, who used their dominance of the General Assembly to counter Soviet intransigence in the Security Council (Peterson, 1986, pp. 60–61). However, by the 1960s the dominant majority at the United Nations was composed of developing states that were willing to use their superior numbers to push through new policies regarding colonialism, the international economy, and pariah regimes like South Africa and Israel. These states realized they could get more out of the UN by working together than they could by working alone; as a result, delegates from these states formed positive orientations toward the organization (Vincent, 1968, p. 930) and used it to actively promote their agenda.

However, the voting strength of the developing states at this time was "out of all proportion to their populations, contributions, and responsibilities in the UN." It became common to use the analogy of a "wildly tipping seesaw" to describe the overstated influence of UN majorities (Manno, 1968a, p. 263). One can argue that developing states effectively hijacked the General Assembly through their domination of its procedures and voting. Furthermore, when these states found it difficult to push their demands in the Assembly (which did happen on occasion), they were more than willing to use other forums of UN-affiliated conference diplomacy to pursue their goals. These included global issue conferences, special sessions of the General Assembly, and existing or newly created specialized agencies or subsidiary bodies if needed (Feld and Jordan, 1989, pp. 128–129). Majority-based strategies were the vehicle that enabled developing states to use UN venues as a means toward the end of legitimating their concerns and priorities. However, these efforts frequently encountered the determined opposition of UN members that were individually powerful outside the UN yet lacked the formal voting power to ensure that their concerns would be taken into account.

As was discussed in Chapter 7, this imbalance gave way to an increased use of consensus decisionmaking in UN bodies through the 1970s. The developing states maintained their formal control of the General Assembly and other full membership bodies, since majority voting could be substituted for consensus at any time if over half of the membership so desired (Peterson, 1986, p. 57). However, the ability and willingness of developing states to go this route using majority-based strategies decreased due to two emerging realities. First, the unity of the developing world, which could essentially be taken for granted before the 1970s, increasingly had to "be created and then defended on particular issues" by the 1980s (Peterson, 1986, p. 61). In the Group of 77 and other interest groups composed primarily of developing states, it became harder to maintain a common minimum position across arenas or over time (Pathmarajah, 1998, p. 115). Second, developing states realized that simply passing a majority-driven resolution over the objection of some of the UN's most influential members was of only limited utility if their goal was in fact to legitimize actions and demonstrate strong opinion on a particular issue or situation (Luard and Heater, 1994, p. 48). Therefore, the developing world has come to realize that majority-based strategies have important limitations and that consensus can better serve their interests on many occasions. Figures from both the General Assembly and Security Council reflect this change: 76 percent of Assembly resolutions and 86 percent of Council resolutions were adopted by consensus in 2000 (Fasulo, 2004, p. 146).

So what does this mean for the future of majority-based strategies? While they are still used on occasion by a unified group of developing states to overcome the resistance of developed states, it is far more common for them to be used to target the actions of a relatively isolated state that refuses to go along with the wishes of the vast majority of other UN members. Examples of this in the General Assembly include the annual resolution condemning the unilateral embargo imposed on Cuba by the United States and regular efforts to criticize Israeli treatment of the Palestinians in the Occupied Territories. In addition, as was mentioned above, a new type of majority-based strategy has emerged in multilateral diplomacy within and outside the UN system: a coalition of like-minded states and NGOs that have pushed for strong international instruments in the areas of human security and human rights, even where achieving them requires abandoning official UN forums and bypassing the consensus of major powers (see the essays in Cooper, English, and Thakur, 2002). Whether or not the success of this "new diplomacy" is limited to exceptional issues like the landmine ban and the International Criminal Court or is a broadly applicable harbinger of things to come is the subject of considerable ongoing debate; however, the use of unprecedented majority-based strategies in these cases suggests they remain relevant in UN decisionmaking.

While majority-based strategies embody the power of numerical dominance, minority-based strategies reflect the fact that certain actors in United Nations politics enjoy a privileged position based on the unique resources and behaviors that they control. One extreme example of this would be where a hegemonic power within an international organization can simply specify the policy or decision that will be adopted since other members are in no position to oppose this course of action (Young, 1991, p. 290). While such absolute control by one actor is rare, there are numerous occasions at the UN where a single key member state or other participant can make its power and influence felt unilaterally (Cox and Jacobson, 1973a, p. 394). It is not hard to envision a major power using its sheer economic or political strength to get its way, but less obvious actors can also effectively use minority-based strategies at times. The key issue is leverage; this leverage can come from the possession of material resources, or it can emerge when the cooperation of a specific actor is required in order to implement a particular decision (Keohane, 1967, pp. 222–223). If an actor is engaging in a behavior that needs to be changed or controls resources that could assist others in addressing a pressing issue, then it is more likely to play a role, for better or worse, in how the political process unfolds. This leverage can be utilized in a concrete and explicit fashion through "arm twisting and bribery" (Young, 1991, p. 289); however, it is far more common that the threats and pressure in minority-based strategies remain implicit, vague, and behind the scenes (Keohane, 1967, p. 223).

There are numerous sources of power that can serve as the foundation of a minority-based strategy. Each one will be more or less successful depending on how effectively it can be translated into bargaining leverage within the situation that the minority faces (Young, 1991, p. 289). The most important source of leverage for powerful actors is their control over resources that the organization needs to act, since "these assets carry prestige" (Cox and Jacobson, 1973a, p. 393). In some cases this prestige is reflected in the procedures used in key UN bodies. One example of this that dates back to the UN's founding is the great-power veto in the Security Council: these particular members alone were seen as having the military capability to enforce the peace and security provisions of the UN Charter. A similar (albeit weaker) procedural protection for the most powerful UN members that was added in the 1980s is the use of consensus procedures in the UN's budgetary process (Karns and Mingst, 2002, p. 275). Before this change the UN had faced several financial crises when states with large assessments would not pay for programs that were passed by majority-based strategies over their objections (Finkelstein, 1988c, pp. 23–24). This form of "opting out" has unfortunately been a consistently effective tool for wealthy states in the minority at the UN to extract changes that they desire, even after the budgetary reforms of the 1980s; one example of a member state's using this withholding tool was the US effort to get its assessments for both the regular and peace-keeping budgets reduced in 2000 before it would settle nearly one billion dollars in arrears to the organization (Smith, 2004). In addition to "opting out" of paying for programs they have not approved, powerful members enjoy more freedom when it comes to "opting out" or offering reservations regarding resolutions and treaties they do not support, even when they are overtly dissenting from a near consensus policy (Finkelstein, 1988c, pp. 23, 25). This has been particularly true in the case of the United States after the end of the cold war, including its refusal to ratify a number of treaties that the United States initially played a major role in drafting (Smith, 2004, pp. 197–199).

The preceding paragraph might lead one to conclude that the key ingredient of an effective minority-based strategy is power and that a state that enjoys power can be heavy-handed and direct in exercising influence at the United Nations. Actually, there are many situations in which even major powers face constraints in terms of the strategies that they can use. This is true because "every exercise of influence creates a corresponding political liability: a political debt that must be discharged in the future, a commitment of one sort or another" (Keohane, 1967, p. 232). These debts and commitments are especially common for major powers because other members are more likely to be envious of the privileged position of these states and want as much as possible in return for being willing to put up with having policies imposed on them. Major powers that use minority-based strategies must rely on more than just muscle to have long-term success at the United Nations.

One additional set of benefits for major powers at the UN is that they have the largest delegations, substantial bureaucracies at home, and a foreign service with a global presence, which gives them access to a wider range of information and allows for more effective lobbying at the UN and in national capitals around the world (Cox and Jacobson, 1973a, p. 393). This system of support means that large states can simply outwork or outflank smaller states, but only if the policies and strategies they are pursuing in UN bodies and national capitals are closely coordinated so that they all build to the same outcome (Manley, 1998). In the absence of such coordination, a powerful state can harm its own chance of success if it ends up pushing in different directions in different settings. These problems can be compounded if major powers are democratic, as is often the case, since they will also have to win the support of a domestic legislature, interest groups, and public opinion (Peterson, 1986, p. 214). If constructed successfully, this support can lead to more effective strategies at the global level, but this is a delicate processes even for powerful states, because it requires that international and domestic interests be carefully reconciled (Putnam, 1988).

So what does an effective minority-based strategy look like when a state or other actor decides to "turn it on" at the United Nations? Ziring, Riggs, and Plano's mini–case study of the US effort to get the 1975 General Assembly resolution that equated Zionism with racism repealed in December 1991 offers many clues regarding an effective minority-based strategy (2000, p. 97). Since the United States did not have the support of an "instant majority" of UN members on this issue, months of lobbying, pressure, and persistence were required. The campaign occurred at the UN and in national capitals in every region of the world, and the US was careful to enlist other states to support its efforts so that the repeal would not be identified solely as a US and Israeli goal. Nine years later the United States followed a similar strategy when it sought to secure new scales of assessment for the regular budget and peacekeeping in December 2002 (Smith, 2004). The United States had been using the "withholding tool" to demand these changes for several years, but it was not successful until a more proactive strategy of engaging other member states at the UN and around the world was adopted well in advance of the final push in the negotiations. This strategy required the United States to replace its demands for change "or else" with support for symbolic initiatives important to other UN members and increased contact between members of the US Congress (which controlled the payment of the sizable US arrears) and other UN member states (Hayes, 2000; Orr, 2000). The strategy also hinged on the effective use of brokers and the personal attributes of US permanent representative Richard Holbrooke, two issues that will receive more attention in the following pages.

These cases illustrate that major powers like the United States can achieve successful outcomes at the UN when their vested interests are at stake, even in cases where they are pushing other member states in directions they might not be eager to go (Ziring, Riggs, and Plano, 2000, pp. 102–103). Another important lesson from these cases, however, is that minority-based strategies can rarely rely on heavy-handed demands alone. In the period of diplomacy at the United Nations immediately preceding the war in Iraq in March 2003, the United States failed to secure Security Council support for its military action. The United States had succeeded at getting the scales of assessment reformed just three years earlier in the midst of an extremely hostile environment at the UN, but it was not successful in the case of Iraq. Both were salient issues for the United States, and in both cases the United States was the dominant player involved, with the most resources to offer the UN. So why did it succeed in one case and fail in another? The answer lies in how the minority-based strategies were designed in each situation (Smith, 2004, pp. 211–213). In 2000, as in 1991, the United States supplemented its power with an effective strategy of active participation, lobbying, and engagement; in 2003 it abandoned these tested strategies in favor of lackluster (or even nonexistent) diplomacy and heavy-handed demands, warning of the UN's impending "irrelevance" if the Council failed to take action.

The third type of strategies based on positional power is available to those actors at the United Nations who have the ability to act as brokers by building agreement among conflicting groups and coalitions. While potentially any participant in UN decisionmaking could act as a broker, it is most common for this role to be played by middle or small states (Smith, 1999, p. 181). As was discussed in Chapters 4 and 5, there are also certain situations in which Secretariat officials and representatives of NGOs can act as brokers in contentious negotiations. Some practitioners who are deeply familiar with the UN's political process have argued that brokers are frequently indispensable for successful negotiations (Kaufmann, 1980, p. 16; Rosenstock, 1998). They can be referred to by many names: "bridge builders" to illustrate their efforts to forge agreements across competing interests, "fire brigades" to highlight that their work is essential to resolve the most contentious issues, "like-minded states" to capture their internal cohesion and commitment, or simply "the good guys" since their efforts make the UN more successful than it would otherwise be.

These actors have always been present in the work of the United Nations (Keohane, 1967, p. 223), but their efforts have grown in scope and attention since the end of the cold war (Cooper, 2002, pp. 5–6). The end of superpower polarization at the UN has increased the number of actors that can serve as brokers, and it has also increased their freedom to act. This in turn has forced many long-time brokers to become more focused and specialized as niche players rather than trying to be active on every negotiation that comes their way. These developments are most noticeable in the case of large UN bodies like the General Assembly. In the Security Council some have actually observed the opposite trend—with increased great power cooperation, countries that excelled as "helpful fixers" in the Council in earlier decades suddenly find themselves marginalized as the permanent five work things out among themselves (Malone, 2002, p. 39). However, as some examples below will indicate, brokers still have valuable contributions to make at the United Nations, even in small decisionmaking arenas like the Council.

Brokers perform a number of functions that can allow them to help salvage agreement in the face of failure such as providing leadership, bridging differences, and guiding the work of the negotiating groups discussed in Chapter 3 (Smith, 2004, p. 207). They can be instrumental in pushing the process along by sidestepping or overcoming procedural roadblocks that majority or minority groups might try to use (Smith, 1999, p. 191). At the same time, they can contribute to the substance of debate by quietly sounding out different parties regarding possible compromise language in draft resolutions and other proposals (Kunita, 1998). One common way they influence the substance of debate is by managing the "rolling text" or "single negotiating text" that serves as the basis of the negotiations. These texts are typically prepared by the chair or a small group of interested parties; they include all language that has been finalized as well as areas of continued disagreement marked off by brackets, which brokers can then work to remove over time (Kaufmann, 1988, p. 168; Feld and Jordan, 1989, p. 130).

Though serving as a broker at the United Nations is "a time-consuming and often thankless task" (Kaufmann, 1980, p. 17), there are actors that are willing and even eager to serve in this role because it can lead to increased stature in the organization and it allows them to have a greater impact on decisionmaking than would be the case if they were to rely on majority- or minority-based strategies. However, in order to be an effective broker, actors should meet a number of criteria (Keohane, 1967, p. 222; Kaufmann, 1980, p. 17; Young, 1991, pp. 294–295). First, they must have wide political acceptability in the eyes of the entire UN membership. They should not have any interests at stake on the issue, they should maintain a reputation for neutrality and impartiality over time, and they must enjoy the confidence of the parties directly involved in the dispute. Second, they are frequently actors whose goals and objectives at the international level are very much consistent or congruent with UN principles and ideals. This blesses them with a certain moral authority to push parties to make compromises that they would not be willing to consider if they were suggested by any other actor. Third, they should enjoy strong support from their home ministry or other constituencies, so that they have the necessary freedom and autonomy to build package deals and make what could be politically difficult compromises. Finally, it is helpful (but not necessary) that they be able to back up their role as brokers with the ability to contribute financially or otherwise to the implementation of the agreement they are helping to make.

There are many United Nations decisions that can be used as examples of situations in which the activity of brokers was an essential component of the political process, some of which have been mentioned in other chapters of this book. Three good examples come from the 1990s: the drafting of General Assembly Resolution 46/182 on humanitarian assistance in December 1991, the renegotiation of the seabed mining provisions of the UN Convention on the Law of the Sea from 1990 to 1994, and the completion of the Comprehensive (Nuclear) Test Ban Treaty (CTBT) in September 1996 (Smith, 1999). Brokers in the first case included donor states and representatives of the Group of 77: the Netherlands, Canada, Sweden, India, Mexico, Brazil, and the Philippines. These states were instrumental in drafting the ultimate compromise language that balanced state sovereignty and humanitarian intervention. In the second case, Fiji, Brazil, Argentina, and Indonesia were instrumental in forging agreement on adjusting and delaying the implementation of the seabed mining provisions, first among developing states and then between this group and the developed states. Finally, on the CTBT negotiations Australia, New Zealand, Mexico, and Sweden served as brokers to draft working papers and push the process along by overcoming procedural roadblocks, as will be discussed in greater detail in the last section of this chapter. Another more recent case where brokers played an important role in the negotiations involved the US effort to reform the UN scales of assessment for the regular budget and peacekeeping in December 2000 (Smith, 2004, pp. 207–208; Chandra, 2001). Several Latin American states, led by Colombia, were the primary architects of a plan to move from two large discount groups on the old peacekeeping scale to a more nuanced scale with eight discount groups that required many members to increase their financial commitment. This helped to create the impression that a wide group of states, not just one, was pushing for reform. It also made it easier for another group of brokers, composed of South Africa and other members of the caucus of the Non-Aligned Movement, to prevent states like Cuba and Libya from disrupting the agreement at the last minute just to spite the United States.

The fact that brokers can be so instrumental in building agreement at the United Nations makes their absence especially obvious and lamented when they are not active. One clear example of this occurred with the issue of reforming the size and composition of the Security Council in the mid-1990s. The General Assembly's open-ended working group (OEWG) dealing with this issue included more than 100 active members. Representatives from the five veto powers, all of whom generally favored expansion, hoped that "the good guys" would be able to broker agreement between the competing proposals being offered (Rosenstock, 1998; Manley, 1998). However, the states most likely to play this role, the Nordic countries, made a conscious decision not to do so for this particular negotiation; they realized their chances of success were minimal given the entrenched and conflicting positions emerging out of each region. Why should they risk their future ability to act as brokers by getting dragged into a no-win situation (Kooijmans, 1998; Thoresson, 1998)? A similar dynamic emerged in the polarizing diplomacy in the Security Council in early 2003 as the United States pushed for action against Iraq. The six undecided members of the Council (Angola, Cameroon, Chile, Guinea, Mexico, and Pakistan) were not able to act as brokers between those favoring force (the United Sates, Britain, Spain, and Bulgaria) and those that wanted more time for inspections (France, Germany, Syria, Russia, and China) because they became the targets of intense and sometimes hostile pressure from both sides (Weisman and Barringer, 2003). It was not until the following fall, during the discussions on Council Resolution 1511 in October 2003, that brokers (in this case China) reemerged in the Council in regard to the issue of Iraq (Barringer, 2003).

■ Strategies Based on Personal Attributes

Participants in United Nations decisionmaking are represented by individuals, so it is not surprising that individual attributes can have an effect on which strategies are used and how effective they are. In the 1960s and 1970s, however, it was more common for scholars to explore other directions of influence, such as how participation at the UN affected delegate attitudes and behaviors in general (Alger, 1963 and 1968; Riggs, 1977) or how the national attributes of the states they represented affected delegate attitudes and behaviors within the organization (Vincent, 1968). These studies found that participation at the UN had a generally but not exclusively positive effect on delegate attitudes and that distinctions between the attributes of developed and developing states were an important source of divergent behavior on the part of delegates from these different states at the United Nations. What was not explored at the time was the opposite effect: how the attributes and attitudes of individual participants can affect both the strategies used by the actors they represent and the manor in which the UN's political processes ultimately unfold.

Fortunately, as scholars and former practitioners began to examine UN decisionmaking more closely, they soon discovered that the personal attributes of individual participants must be taken into account when one is seeking to understand how and why different outcomes are achieved. It is not so much that delegate personality will cause national policies to change as that they can make these policies more or less effective, since it is up to delegates directly involved at the UN to sell them to the other actors whose support is required for a particular policy to succeed (Peterson, 1986, p. 215). It is often assumed that personal attributes are most important in the case of delegates from smaller states, since these states have less positional power on which to draw and since their delegates often enjoy greater freedom to use their individual skills and abilities in any manner possible (Cox and Jacobson, 1973a, p. 394). A similar logic might be applied to other actors that also lack positional power, such as NGO representatives and, on occasion, members of the Secretariat. However, the "tendencies and biases of those participating in the [UN's] process" must also be taken into account if we are to understand the substantive goals and procedural approach of even the major powers (Vincent, 1968, p. 931). One case in which delegate personality mattered a great deal for a major power was Richard Holbrooke's success as US permanent representative in building widespread support for reforming the UN's scales of assessment. His predecessors had failed in this same task because they lacked his charisma and engaging one-on-one style, which was ultimately the key to selling a policy that had been initially unpopular with many other members (Smith, 2004, p. 204; see also Mwakawago, 2000; Chandra, 2001; Eldon, 2001).

Strategies based on personal attributes have the potential to be very effective at the United Nations, since the organization in many respects represents a "village" that has its own customs, languages, culture, and way of life (Fasulo, 2004, pp. 90–93). David Malone, a former Canadian UN diplomat, has observed that within this village "people really matter . . . anything that happens at the UN happens because of certain individuals" (quoted in ibid., p. 90). He goes on to argue that "at any given time . . . about thirty-five [participants] control the game. So, if you know those thirty-five key people, you can do anything. And if you don't, forget it" (ibid., p. 91). These key people include delegates from large and small states as well officials in the Secretariat. What makes them key is not only the actor or office they represent but also the personal attributes and skills they bring to the table.

Chapter 2 surveyed a number of personal attributes that can enable participants in UN decisionmaking to be especially effective at representing the interests of their actor and engaging in the give-and-take required to build winning coalitions. These include past experiences, knowledge competencies, charisma, character, perseverance, tolerance, ambition, and negotiating skill. It is virtually impossible for any one participant to possess all of these different, and sometimes contradictory, skills and attributes. Successful personal strategies require that participants understand their own strengths and weaknesses. A mix of attributes is essential, as is a strong match between the goals and resources of the actor and the abilities of its representatives. Again, this is true even in the case of major powers like the United States, for the comparative effectiveness of different American ambassadors at the UN has hinged on the fit between the quality of their skills and the nature of the policy they were being asked to pursue (Finger, 1990, pp. 338–345).

Participants' ability to use personal strategies to augment the positional power of the actor they represent depends on more than having the right set of skills and attributes; they must also have the freedom to use them as the situation requires. The successful use of personal strategies is related to another issue already discussed in Chapter 2: participant autonomy. Some delegates receive specific instructions covering all substantive and procedural aspects of the negotiations, whereas others are given free rein on methods and even goals; the autonomy of most participants falls somewhere in between. Chapter 2 identified numerous factors that can affect participant autonomy: issue salience, actor size, their role in the negotiations, and whether the instructions concern procedural versus substantive matters. It can also hinge, especially in the case of the United States and other countries in the Security Council, on the domestic political stature of the representative (Finger, 1990, pp. 345–348; Fasulo, 2004, pp. 33–36; Ignatieff, 1981, p. 137; Nicol, 1981a, pp. 313–314). The key point from this discussion that bears repeating here is that participants who receive overly detailed instructions will not be able to go beyond the positional strategies already available to them, whereas those with freedom to maneuver can draw on their charisma, their expertise, their entrepreneurship, and their own ideas to augment the positional power of the actor they represent.

Participants can also draw on the quality of their working relationships with their colleagues when designing personal strategies. As was mentioned before, the UN is in many respects its own village, and participants who have lived together in that village for long periods of time will have numerous opportunities to form friendships. These friendships can even predate their arrival at the UN through common service in another multilateral body, repeated meetings at global conferences, foreign service assignments in the same country, or attendance at the same university or professional training institute (Smith, 1999, p. 183). Common practices of tact and courtesy in diplomacy can facilitate the emergence of these friendships, as diplomats are often careful not to make offense even in the case of intense disagreement (Pathmarajah, 1998, p. 115–116). Working relationships are most relevant for actors that are playing the role of farmers and traders, to use the typology from Chapter 2 (Hanif, 1998). Since farmers and traders both seek to build agreement and form package deals, they must enjoy the respect and confidence of their colleagues. On the other hand, working relationships are less relevant to hunters and trappers. Hunters enjoy strong positional power to pursue their goals regardless of the opposition they face, while any personal goodwill trappers have accumulated will be sacrificed the moment they spring their trap.

Working relationships are seldom strong enough to have direct influence on national policies, but they can "affect subsequent formal exchanges and long-term voting patterns" such that consensus is facilitated (Kaufmann, 1980, p. 117). They provide participants with avenues for clarifying national policies that are poorly understood, they enable participants to keep lines of communication open even when their actors are working for different outcomes, and they create a level of accessibility between participants that can be instrumental when a crisis arises that requires immediate attention. Furthermore, these working relationships are a key component of the informal networking discussed in Chapter 8, since they allow participants to sound out other actors regarding new policy directions in a private and off-the-record fashion.

Based on their attributes, autonomy, and working relationships, participants will have a variety of personal strategies they can use to complement the positional power of the actor they represent. One of the most important means of influencing other actors is offering persuasive arguments in UN debates. Delivering an effective speech at the United Nations requires certain abilities and much practice (Pathmarajah, 1998, p. 116). There are many potential obstacles to overcome, ranging from basic linguistic difficulties to the use of complex, culturally rooted concepts that may not be broadly applicable (Kaufmann, 1988, pp. 173–174). Comments must be carefully tailored to meet the intended purpose of the speech and be delivered in a style that is conducive to persuading other parties of the correctness of one's position. Speeches that are too fast, too slow, too long, too short, too vague, or too repetitive will allow other participants to let their minds drift to other concerns rather than focusing on the ideas the speaker is trying to convey. Even the most terrific proposal can encounter problems if it is presented in a boring, disorganized, long-winded speech. Conversely, a logical, well-supported argument presented with a relevant story or anecdote can cause other actors to pay attention to an approach they might otherwise have dismissed out of hand.

It is not just the manner of speaking but also the content of the speech that can be instrumental in building support for a preferred policy option. While the substantive goals of an actor are likely to be determined through a deliberative process, individual participants in multilateral negotiations can provide leadership by developing linkages across issues or by offering new ways of conceptualizing old issues and problems. Young has used the terms "entrepreneurial leadership" and "intellectual leadership" to capture how individuals can draw on their negotiating skill and intellectual insights to offer solutions that their structural (or positional) power alone would not have made possible (1991, pp. 293–302). One often-cited example of a speech in which an actor with few positional strategies at his disposal used the power of ideas to move the UN action was delivered by Arvid Pardo of Malta to the General Assembly in 1967. It linked the concept of the common heritage of humankind to the need to provide management for the oceans, and a more than two decades long process of drafting the Law of the Sea treaty was born.

■ Strategies Based on Procedural Manipulation

A third set of strategies available to participants in United Nations decisionmaking involves manipulating the formal and informal procedures through which the political processes of the organization unfold. These can be both powerful and tempting strategies. Keohane quotes an experienced permanent representative who observed, "It is a general principle that whoever can take advantage of the rules of procedure will do so." Keohane concludes that "votes on procedural questions are frequently more crucial than votes on the substantive issues with which they are associated" (1967, p. 233). This claim is just as fitting today as it was decades ago. However, as will be discussed in the following pages, procedural manipulation has some potentially negative side effects, so its use must be carefully balanced with strategies dealing with the substance of the issue if one is to be effective, especially in the long term. Thus participants in UN decisionmaking face an important choice when deciding how to interact with other participants: do they focus the substance of the issue through package dealing, logrolling, and related approaches; or do they attempt to change the rules of the game as the debate unfolds, so that certain proposals are prevented from receiving full consideration (Smith, 1999, p. 182)?

Exactly what the balance between substance and procedure should look like for maximum effectiveness can hinge on several factors. First, actors must be cognizant of the goals they are pursuing and how those relate to both domestic and foreign interests: do they feel so strongly about achieving a particular outcome that they are willing to burn some bridges along the way to get it (Keohane, 1967, pp. 224, 236)? Put another way, are short-term needs valued more highly than long-term patterns of cooperation? Second, the nature of the issue under consideration may be more or less conducive to procedural manipulation versus substantive compromise. Young has argued that issues are more amenable to substantive compromise (and therefore procedural manipulation is likely to be less fruitful) when all parties see a need for some type of change in the status quo, when arrangements that are seen as equitable to all sides can be designed, when easily identifiable salient solutions are present that can serve as the focal points of debate, and when exogenous shocks or crises help to create a sense of urgency (1989, pp. 366–374). When these conditions are absent, the debate is likely to be more protracted and contentious, thereby increasing the number of participants willing to consider manipulating the procedures in order to protect their interests.

Third, the most effective balance between substance and procedure is also influenced by the positional and personal strategies discussed above, since they lead some participants to be more able and willing to fall back on procedural manipulation if they perceive it as potentially helpful. For example, some practitioners from developing states have found that large states are more apt to throw their weight around by manipulating the procedures than are small states (Darmanin, 1998); however, diplomats from developed states have countered that developing states are far more likely to be represented by their procedural experts who can effectively seize upon any carelessness or reluctance on the part of developed states to use procedures when necessary (quoted in Righter, 1995, p. 135). In the same vein, participants with strong personalities are more able to manipulate procedures than are those lacking this particular attribute (Millar, 1998), and states that fall outside of traditional coalitions and thus become pivotal undecided players can have a disproportionate influence on procedures used to manage debate (Keohane, 1967, p. 224).

The rules of procedure for most international organizations and global conferences make a clear distinction between substance and procedure: substance is the content of what is debated, whereas procedure is the mechanisms through which it is debated. The organs of the United Nations share this tendency toward keeping substance and procedure separate; nowhere is this truer than in the Security Council, where Article 27 of the UN Charter specifies that the veto applies only to substantive decisions. However, as our discussion of the scope of the veto in Chapter 7 indicated, the line between substantive and procedural matters can be fuzzy and controversial. Kaufmann has found that this confusion is not limited to the Council, since across UN bodies "procedural devices [can be] used to obtain a substantive result and procedural debates often turn out to be debates on substance" (1980, p. 131).

In his discussion of strategy in the UN Commission on Human Rights, Tolley paints a picture of member states moving back and forth between procedural and substantive strategies depending on where they fall in the shifting coalitions that evolve during debate (1983, pp. 47–48). This is so common in UN bodies that the present discussion may risk artificially separating what are in practice interwoven dynamics. While this is an important caveat, there is considerable evidence that states and other actors see substance and procedure as being sufficiently distinct that they make judgments about how to design strategies that effectively encompass both elements. For example, "states frequently choose to contest an issue through use of procedural motions rather than contesting the substance of the issue . . . when a state estimates that it is easier to garner support for its position on an ostensibly neutral procedural issue" (Sabel, 1997, pp. 3–4). Other observant participants certainly realize what is going on, but they too may find that it makes more sense to leave the substance in the background if, for instance, they enjoy more support from allies or more autonomy from home on the procedural issue.

When participants lose a debate at the United Nations because of greater support for an alternate substantive proposal, they are likely to be disappointed. However, when participants lose a debate at the United

Nations because the rules were turned against them so that their ideas did not receive adequate attention, the disappointment often deepens into frustration and bitterness (Smith, 1999, p. 182). Consideration of alternate substantive proposals in committees and small groups is seen as being a more fair and inclusive process than any type of procedural manipulation to limit the scope of debate (Kulyk, 1998). Thus participants in UN decisionmaking generally prefer to wield influence through substantive proposals and fall back on procedural manipulation only if it seems they have run out of other options for pursuing and protecting their interests. After all, why risk long-term damage to your reputation through procedural tricks and traps when you could have won a debate based solely on the readily apparent weaknesses of a rival proposal or the merits of your own? Given this, the following discussion will consider substantive strategies first, followed by procedural ones.

Participants who wish to use substantive debate to either advance their own proposal or work to defeat an objectionable proposal "must know what can be sold and what cannot be sold" at the United Nations (Kaufmann, 1980, p. 131). This requires detailed knowledge about the constellation of interests at work in the debate on the issue as well as extensive awareness of how such campaigns have played out in the past. It is also essential to have the strong support of the home ministry (or other appropriate constituency in the case of nonstate actors) and a fine-tuned sense of timing, such that arguments and counterproposals (if used) can be advanced at the precise moment when they are likely to have the greatest impact (ibid., pp. 130, 135). Speeches cannot be used for scoring debating points; instead, they must offer a well-reasoned, logical, passionate, and persuasive argument in favor of one's proposal or pointing out the limitations of the existing alternatives (ibid., pp. 132, 134–137).

Participants using substantive strategies can choose between two possible routes. First, they can seek to substitute their own proposal for one offered by another actor or group of actors that they find problematic. This is easiest to do "if the initiating delegation has given wide advance knowledge to its proposal, thus having forewarned its opponents" (ibid., p. 134). Even in these situations, successfully substituting a later proposal for one introduced earlier is a challenging task, regardless of which one ultimately wins more support in the decisionmaking body. Advancing cogent intellectual arguments for why a newer proposal is better (such as more efficient use of limited resources) is certainly helpful, in that it can force the authors of the original proposal to accept compromises in order to maintain sufficient support for their original goals (Kaufmann, 1988, p. 161, 166). However, it may not be enough to defeat the original proposal if these compromises are not forthcoming, since the general practice is that proposals are voted on in the order in which they were submitted to the Secretariat for circulation to the entire body (Peterson, 1986, p. 69). Thus proposals that refine or improve an earlier submission cannot be voted on until after the earlier submission unless that one is withdrawn by its sponsors. This puts newer proposals at an inherent disadvantage. Participants may be torn between conducting numerous consultations to build more support and increase the chances of approval and conducting the bare minimum of consultations so that their proposal can be first in line. These contradictory pressures are partially offset by the fact that members of the body can motion to change the order in which proposals will come to a vote, especially when informal consultations indicate that a consensus has emerged around a later proposal (ibid., pp. 70–71). As was discussed in Chapter 8, however, these same informal consultations can allow compromises to be reached before proposals are officially introduced, so it is increasingly rare that the order of voting must be changed.

In addition to submitting alternate proposals, participants can attempt to modify existing proposals through "friendly amendments," which are supported by the sponsors of the original proposal, or "unfriendly amendments," which are not supported by the original sponsors (Peterson, 1986, p. 97). Offering amendments can be an effective way to quickly weaken or eliminate objectionable parts of an existing proposal, whether or not they are initially supported by the original sponsors. As was discussed in Chapter 7, there is considerable debate as to how much change an amendment can propose and still be considered an amendment rather than an alternate proposal (for example, see Sabel, 1997, p. 185). Yet even relatively modest changes in language can dramatically alter the intent and expected effectiveness of a proposal, perhaps by softening the language and weakening the obligations imposed on target states (Tolley, 1983, p. 47). Kaufmann provides an illuminating stylized account of the back-and-forth between original sponsors and amendment authors that frequently characterizes this process (1988, p. 16). However, as with offering alternate proposals, the growing use of informal consultations at the UN has had the effect of making formal amendments a strategy of last resort, since many changes can be incorporated before a text is officially introduced into debate (Peterson, 1986, p. 73).

While the use of informal consultations has changed the extent to which competing proposals and amendments make it into formal debate, it has done little to change the tools participants can use to sell their substantive proposals and amendments to other actors. Quite simply, actors can promise rewards to other actors to encourage their support or threaten negative action to try and compel it (Kaufmann, 1988, pp. 162–165). Actors may offer promises through bilateral "logrolling," where increased economic assistance or a contribution toward a peacekeeping mission, for example, is offered in exchange for a favorable vote on a specific proposal (Kaufmann, 1980, pp. 112, 133). Promises may also take the form of "package deals," where a multilateral agreement is constructed on an issue such that gains and concessions are distributed in an acceptable manner among all parties (Feld and Jordan, 1989, p. 130). Threats are similar in that they attempt to change behavior, but they do so in a negative, win-lose fashion rather than through the positive, win-win approach of logrolling and package dealing. Actors might threaten to withhold payment for a particular program, to boycott a specific vote, or even to leave a decisionmaking body if an objectionable proposal is adopted (Kaufmann, 1988, pp. 163–165).

As was discussed above, the line between substantive and procedural issues is often fuzzy and controversial. The same can be true for strategies of influence. For example, Kaufmann has identified a number of common tactics for blocking UN proposals that technically deal with the substance of the issue at hand, but do so in a way that resembles procedural tricks and traps (1988, p. 168). These include giving oral support to a proposal that you have no intention of supporting because you know it is certain to be rejected anyway; using your time on the speakers' list to obfuscate the issues through impenetrable rhetoric; erecting additional hurdles to block support for a proposal after other hurdles have already been cleared; and arguing that a proposal merits consideration but that the time is not ripe for action. In each case, claims about substance are used to hide an agenda of obstruction and delay.

The motives of actors that resort to strategies of procedural manipulation are often, but not always, the same. As was discussed in Chapters 6 and 7, the rules of procedure in international organizations are generally designed to "reflect and promote a spirit of accommodation" (Hovey, 1951, p. 529). They do this by providing clear, consistent mechanisms through which actors can debate and decide on controversial issues without having to recontest the procedures on every issue. However, this predictability can turn into rigidity and harm the chances for building agreement. This can be prevented in many cases if the rules balance consistency with flexibility, so that they can be modified or changed in order to make agreement easier depending on how a debate is unfolding (Smith, 1999, pp. 179, 188). Unfortunately, it is easy to lose sight of the constructive benefits of clear procedures when they are sometimes used to delay and obstruct the UN's political process. While there may be situations when procedural manipulation is perfectly justified (such as to allow time to receive instructions from home), all too often it is used solely as a political weapon (Kaufmann, 1980, p. 130).

Procedural manipulation can be a tempting tool for participants in UN decisionmaking. It offers an opportunity to shape how a debate unfolds without requiring actors to directly target and change the behavior of others (Keohane, 1967, p. 223). This can limit the level of confrontation in parliamentary diplomacy, but there is a tradeoff, for with detailed rules of procedure there are many places in the political process where decisionmaking can be blocked (Hovey, 1951, p. 529). While the rules of procedure used at the UN have historically included mechanisms for overcoming such blocks (such as limiting the time allotted for speeches), the early precedent was that these mechanisms were used in only a fraction of the situations when they could have been (ibid., pp. 520–521). The result was a "slow veto," with "a whole catalogue of parliamentary maneuvers" available "to embroil the Assembly [and other UN bodies] in procedural squabbles" (ibid., p. 517).

At the United Nations it is typically easier to work against a proposal than to work for one (Kaufmann, 1988, p. 160). When supporting a proposal, actors have only one outcome that can be considered a success: getting the proposal approved by the organization. However, when one is trying to block a proposal, two possible outcomes can be considered successful: getting consideration of the proposal deferred or defeating the proposal outright. The first of these goals can be achieved through manipulation of the process of debate; the second is achieved through manipulation of the method of conducting votes.

To delay consideration of a proposal, actors can seek to limit the time allotted to speakers, limit the number of times a delegate can speak, or close the speakers' list altogether. A more substantial delay can be obtained through a motion to suspend the meeting, adjourn the meeting, or adjourn the debate on the item under discussion; these motions take precedence over all others in the rules of procedure for most UN bodies (ibid., p. 167). Finally, consideration of an issue can be deferred when it is sent to another committee or subsidiary body that supposedly has greater expertise for dealing with that particular subject matter (Peterson, 1986, p. 33). This can be an especially effective strategy of delay when a proposal can be bounced in a "ping-pong" fashion among bodies with overlapping mandates within the UN system (Kaufmann, 1980, p. 134).

Procedural manipulation can also be directed toward the process through which voting will be conducted, in hopes of defeating a proposal outright. In some UN bodies like the Security Council, dominance in voting is clear and overwhelming, given the disproportionate power of the veto granted to permanent members (O'Neill, 1997, pp. 76–79). In more egalitarian bodies like the General Assembly, all members can potentially manipulate the voting procedures by changing the required support from a simple majority to two-thirds or by calling for separate votes on individual parts of a proposal (Keohane, 1967, pp. 233–234; Peterson, 1986, pp. 65–69, 75–80). As was discussed in Chapters 6 and 7, before the rise in consensus decisionmaking UN members were more willing to manipulate the voting rules than to limit or defer consideration of an issue. Even with the current preference for consensus-based outcomes at the UN, though, procedural manipulation of the mechanisms of debate and voting is still a common occurrence, as the examples considered below will indicate.

In the final stages of drafting the Comprehensive (Nuclear) Test Ban Treaty (CTBT) in June 1996, procedural manipulation came into play (see Smith, 1999, p. 192; Ramaker, 1998; Hanif, 1998). While France and China had been active in using procedural manipulation to drag out the early stages of the negotiations, they had come to support the "rolling text" by the beginning of 1996. This was an important development, since the Conference on Disarmament (CD), the UN body charged with drafting the CTBT, operated on the basis of consensus. By the spring of 1996 it was clear to most participants that "convergence had reached its peak" on the rolling text; however, India was still not on board, due to its desire to see greater linkages between the CTBT and general nuclear disarmament by the nuclear weapons states. India decided to block the CD from approving the treaty by consensus, as was required. A number of concerned states in the CD and the General Assembly became overtly frustrated with India's efforts to derail what they considered to be an otherwise strong treaty. This created fertile ground for the permanent representative from Australia, Richard Butler, to engage in some procedural manipulation of his own: the draft CTBT was submitted directly to the Assembly in September 1996 with nearly 130 cosponsors, even though it had never been approved by the CD. This procedural trick saved the CTBT, as it was subsequently approved by the Assembly in a vote of 158 to 3 with five abstentions; however, it created considerable lingering resentment on both sides.

The efforts of the General Assembly's Open-Ended Working Group on Security Council Reform to adjust the composition and working methods of the Council also came up against procedural manipulation (Smith, 1999, p. 192). As has been discussed elsewhere in this book, the reform debate came to a head in the spring of 1997, when the dominant proposal at the time, called the Razali Proposal after the president of the Fifty-first Session of the Assembly, seemed—in the eyes of those who were opposed to any quick fix—to be rushing toward a vote. The states most opposed to this approach were Italy, Mexico, Pakistan, and Egypt, but the "Coffee Club," as this group was called, had nearly forty active members. The leaders of this group first tried to counteract the Razali Proposal with alternate substantive proposals regarding the composition of an expanded Council (Fulci, 1998; Tello, 1998). By the fall of 1997 these substantive efforts had failed, so the leaders of the "go slow" approach turned instead to procedural manipulation (Verdier, 1998). They introduced a draft resolution in advance of the Razali Proposal, specifying that any decisions that require Charter amendment (as Council reform would) must be approved by a two-thirds vote of the UN's membership, not just two-thirds of the members "present and voting." Since this would dramatically increase the required threshold of support, the Razali Group immediately introduced a counterproposal reaffirming two-thirds of the members "present and voting." This resulted in a procedural deadlock that caused the discussions on Council composition to fatally stall that year (Kooijmans, 1998; Manley, 1998). Calls for Council reform resumed in 2003; however, no real progress has been made on this issue, due to the suspicion and hostility that the 1997 events generated.

These two examples illustrate both the promise and the peril of procedural manipulation. Procedures can be powerful tools for influencing UN decisionmaking, but they must be used cautiously, only as a last resort, and only on those issues where the short-term need to secure a particular outcome outweighs the sometimes significant long-term costs that can arise due to frustration, suspicion, and bitterness (Keohane, 1967, pp. 236–237). It is one thing to be defeated by an alternate substantive proposal; it is something else entirely to feel that the rules of the game were changed or manipulated such that your concerns were not given due consideration. In the cases of the CTBT and Council reform, procedural manipulation was remarkably effective, but it was also resented by a number of states, which ended up questioning the very legitimacy of the decisionmaking process (Hanif, 1998; Holter, 1998). In the case of the CTBT, India's resentment has kept it from signing the treaty, and this has made it more difficult for the treaty to secure sufficient ratifications to enter into force. In the case of Council reform, the efforts of the Razali Group and the Coffee Club to pursue and protect their interests through any means possible have resulted in a situation where it is not even possible to have a reasoned political debate about an issue that every single UN member feels is a pressing priority. These legacies of procedural manipulation raise important questions about how the processes of reaching a particular outcome at the United Nations affect the way the actors involved ultimately perceive that outcome (Keohane, 1967, p. 237). Put another way, do certain strategies or other elements of the UN's political process either facilitate or inhibit implementation and compliance? Chapter 10 will offer some preliminary answers to these puzzles.

PART 3

Implications of the Dance

10

The United Nations
and State Compliance

OUR DISCUSSION OF THE POLITICS AND PROCESSES THROUGH WHICH THE
United Nations makes its decisions began with the analogy of a global
dance. The various participants in the UN dance—member states,
groups, Secretariat officials, and representatives of nongovernmental
organizations and multinational corporations—often begin to negotiate
on an issue while listening to different music and performing different
routines based on the goals they are pursuing and the mechanisms of
influence they have available. However, as the dance proceeds, various
formal and informal procedures and practices used in UN decisionmaking can make it such that these actors start to move in the same direction in search of effective solutions to pressing problems on the organization's agenda. As Parts 1 and 2 of this book have explored these
actors and procedures, the underlying assumption has been that the
political processes in which they are involved must be better understood
because the decisions, resolutions, and policies that the UN adopts have
an impact on international relations, both within and outside the organization.

Certain academic traditions, like realism and its variants, would
challenge this assumption, arguing that the United Nations and other
international institutions are set up by major powers as an instrument
for pursuing their own self-interests and power (for overviews of realism and institutions, see Mearsheimer, 1994–1995; Schweller and
Priess, 1997). In their eyes, investigating how these organizations make
their decisions involves opening a complicated "black box" of decisionmaking that adds little to our understanding of world politics. After all,
for realists the decisions of international institutions either reinforce the
interests of the dominant powers or remain inoperable because they
have the support only of a large number of small powers that lack the

resources and capacity to implement them. In either case, the processes themselves are irrelevant and epiphenomenal. Other scholars who see greater potential for cooperation in the international system, such as neoliberal institutionalists, are more inclined to accept that international organizations like the UN at a minimum act as a forum through which the interests of states and other actors are aggregated and reconciled (for an overview of this school, see Keohane, 1988; Keohane and Martin, 1995). If international organizations influence interests rather than merely reflect them, then exploring the political processes of these institutions is a critical component of understanding the outcomes that they help shape. Therein lies the primary contribution of this book: providing scholars and students of the United Nations with a conceptual guide to how the organization actually works.

These scholarly debates aside, the questions of *if* and *how* the UN's political processes really matter within and outside the organization merit additional attention. Common mechanisms for evaluating the UN's role in international politics usually focus on one of three things: the level of demand for the organization and its activities, the degree to which the organization successfully performs the tasks with which it is entrusted, and the degree of autonomy the organization enjoys vis-à-vis its member states. After briefly considering these three mechanisms, this chapter focuses on the relationship between processes and outputs as a means of understanding state compliance with the organization's decisions. It also explores how the political processes of the organization matter in world politics even when no discernible outputs emerge from its decisionmaking at all.

▓ Evaluating the United Nations

One common argument used to justify the importance of the United Nations in world politics relates to the issue of demand: do states want to be in the organization, and do they bring their problems to it for resolution? Bennett and Oliver have observed that the "clamor for membership" in the UN and other international organizations is a measure of their utility (2002, p. 443). Nearly every eligible state has sought UN membership. This gave rise to political disputes in the early years of the cold war, but since then membership has pretty much been for the asking. Since Switzerland joined the UN in 2002 (finally putting aside concerns about its neutrality), the only remaining states that are not members are the Vatican (which maintains observer status) and several microstates with extremely small populations. Furthermore, in contrast to the League of Nations, states that have joined the UN have stayed in it. The only state to withdraw was Indonesia for a period of twenty months in the 1960s, to protest the election of Malaysia to the Security Council (ibid., p. 85). While one could argue that UN membership is desirable for states simply so they can be seen as part of "the club," it is also likely that states join and remain in the organization because it provides them with tangible benefits.

Another way to think about demand and the UN's effectiveness relates to its ever-expanding agenda. Especially in the years since the end of the cold war, the UN has been asked to provide management of a growing range of transnational problems (Weiss, Forsythe, and Coate, 2001, p. 14). If the organization were not effective in addressing these issues at least part of the time, why would its members and other actors keep asking it to do more and more? Once might respond that the UN experiences this demand because it has a monopoly on responding to certain types of problems as the world's only general-purpose and universal membership organization. Yet in recent years, states and nongovernmental organizations are more than willing to go outside the UN when they feel it is necessary, as the drafting of the antipersonnel landmines ban and the Statute of the International Criminal Court demonstrate (see the volume by Cooper, English, and Thakur, 2002). Thus the actors covered in Part 1 do have a choice regarding whether or not to use the UN to address their concerns, and many of them, including the major powers, do choose to use it, as was illustrated by the (unsuccessful) US effort to get Security Council backing for its campaign against Iraq in 2003. This must mean that the organization has some value-added function to provide to its members, and it may explain why one of the most common refrains one hears about the UN, especially from US policymakers, is that "if we did not have the UN, something like it would need to be invented."

A second, related mechanism for evaluating the United Nations is to consider the extent to which it performs the tasks with which it has been entrusted. Here the record is clearly mixed, and conclusions certainly vary based on the issue and period under consideration: for every human rights abuse that is addressed by the UN, there are many more that never even make it onto the international agenda; for every country that benefits from UN development assistance, there are others that get either the wrong kind of assistance or none at all; the list of inconsistencies is seemingly endless. Moreover, conclusions regarding the task performance of the UN hinge on the specific measure or yardstick being used by the evaluator. For example, should the work of the UN be judged by the high ideals of the Charter or in light of the political realities in which the organization has operated since its founding? Should the UN focus solely on drafting standards (in which case its work on human rights and the environment is dramatic), or must it also work to implement these standards if it is to be judged successful (in which case these same issues are areas of disappointment and frustration)? Ziring, Riggs, and Plano, like many other UN authors, offer a carefully balanced assessment of the UN in light of these difficulties: "Where UN resolutions have initiated programs to be administered by the Secretariat and members are willing to contribute the necessary resources, the consequences of UN action have been significant. . . . On the other hand, where resolutions have depended on compliance by member states, the record is very checkered" (2000, p. 106).

One of the reasons the UN's record is so checkered is that it is often asked to address only the most intractable problems and disputes, those that no other actor or organization has been able to solve (Narasimhan, 1988, p. 369). Given this, it is common for studies of the UN's activities to conclude, as do Thomas Weiss, David Forsythe, and Roger Coate (1997, p. 330), with words attributed to Secretary-General Dag Hammarskjöld: "The purpose of the UN is not to get us to heaven but to save us from hell."

A third common standard used to evaluate the United Nations and other international organizations relates to an issue introduced at the beginning of Chapter 2: the extent to which the organization can act independently of its member states. That earlier discussion highlighted how Claude (1996, pp. 290–292) and Weiss, Forsythe, and Coate (2001, pp. 12–15) distinguish between "two UNs": one that is merely a framework through which its members pursue their interests and one that is an actor that enjoys significant autonomy to pursue its own interests and programs. A similar, three-category typology has been offered by Clive Archer (1992, pp. 135–153), who differentiates among international organizations as instruments of states to pursue their self-interest, arenas for states to search for common interests, and independent actors that operate outside the strict control of their members. Different international organizations can play different roles within this typology; in fact, a single international organization can play different roles depending on the specific arena and issue under consideration. This variation in autonomy is typically not determined by how much authority the international organization is able to seize from its members (for an exception, see Alter, 1998) but instead by the amount of freedom the member states are willing to allow and whether they have the political will to actually let the United Nations live up to the intentions of its founders as expressed in the Charter (Narasimhan, 1988, p. 370). Furthermore, the relative balance between autonomy and member-state control in an international organization has important implications for evaluating its effectiveness, since it directly affects what the organization can realistically be expected to achieve. Quite simply, an organization with greater autonomy must be judged with a different set of criteria from those applicable to an organization that remains solely a creature of its member states.

So how does this relationship between autonomy and control play out in the United Nations? Scholars and former practitioners have offered a variety of opinions on this issue over time, but many attribute a relatively low degree of autonomy to the UN except under rather narrow conditions. Decades ago, Keohane used four indicators to consider the degree of autonomy found in the UN General Assembly: the distinctiveness of organizational norms and values, personnel controls, the control of material resources, and the impact of organizational norms on political processes (1969, pp. 866–869). While he encountered difficulty in measuring some of these indicators, he found that overall autonomy remained limited if for no other reason than the fact that "governments and other actors might become quite unwilling to cooperate with an organization that had become effectively removed from their control" (ibid., p. 895). Writing in the same period, Jacob, Atherton, and Wallenstein found that while some international organizations had gained a degree of autonomy, the authority of most remained severely limited; they agreed in the end with Hammarskjöld's description of the UN as merely "an institutional system for coexistence" (Jacob, Atherton, and Wallenstein, 1972, p. 17). The UN's lack of autonomy experienced in the 1970s was based on its having only limited resources, all of which were controlled by its member states, and its small staff's having been entrusted with only a narrow range of functions (Jacobson, 1979, pp. 83–87).

More recently scholars have again considered the autonomy of the UN, and their conclusions represent a modest evolution in how the organization is viewed. In a discussion of why states act through formal international organizations, Abbott and Snidal find that states value certain functions performed by these organizations and that a number of these functions require the organizations to have some degree of independence, autonomy, and authority in defined spheres of activity (1998, p. 9). These spheres include direct participation in and contributions to interstate negotiations, as well as managing substantive operations that require a neutral third party to provide information, allocate resources, and monitor compliance (ibid., pp. 16–23). Based on the examples they offer, it is clear that the UN enjoys at least some degree of independence as conceptualized by Abbott and Snidal. However, the extent to which member states have sanctioned (or even really noticed) this independence is unclear. In the conclusion to an edited volume on the foreign policy of eight member states toward the UN, John Trent finds "some movement toward the transformation of the organization into an independent institution in global politics," but he still says that "for most states, most of the time, the United Nations is primarily an instrument of foreign policy to protect interests, enhance influence, or achieve specific goals. Few states (if any) have a coherent United Nations policy in which the United Nations is seen as an object unto itself" (1995, p. 466).

Debates about the degree to which the UN can be an autonomous actor will certainly persist, but a question also remains as to the extent to which autonomy can be equated with effectiveness. It may be tempting for UN supporters to argue that a more autonomous organization is by definition a more effective one, but it is preferable to keep these issues separate, since different degrees of autonomy would lead one to expect different types of behaviors from the organization as examples of effectiveness. Actually both autonomous and tightly controlled bodies within the UN system could be effective, albeit in different ways. This suggests that other mechanisms for evaluating effectiveness would be helpful, so the next section of this chapter focuses on the relationship between processes and outputs as a means of understanding state compliance with the decisions of the United Nations.

▓ Considering State Compliance

While demand, task performance, and autonomy all give windows into the effectiveness of the United Nations, the picture they provide is incomplete, as it neglects to consider whether the outputs of the UN's processes are ultimately implemented. Studying compliance with the resolutions, decisions, and policies of international organizations is fraught with difficulty: the outputs are often complex and ambiguous; there are many member states and other actors that must be monitored; and deciding which behaviors are acceptable or unacceptable often hinges on political judgments. Nevertheless, implementation and compliance are essential components of any consideration of whether the decisionmaking of international organizations actually matters. After all, if decisions do nothing to affect subsequent behavior, then the time and effort spent drafting them has been wasted.

Fortunately, the study of compliance has received considerable attention since the 1990s. Much of this has addressed international law and the implementation of legally binding treaties. While the decisions of most international organizations do not carry the same legal weight as treaties, insights generated from this treaty literature nonetheless have much to offer the study of implementation of and compliance with the decisions of international organizations.

While the terms *implementation* and *compliance* are often used interchangeably, their meanings are related but distinct (Jacobson and Weiss, 1995, p. 123). Implementation involves states' making changes to their domestic laws to make them consistent with the international accords they have joined; compliance involves going a step further to actually adhere to the measures for implementation that a state has instituted. A similar distinction can apply to other actors like nongovernmental organizations and multinational corporations: it is one thing to design a new policy, it is something more to actually follow it. Armed with these definitions, scholars have engaged in serious debate about how to properly conceptualize compliance. One approach begins with the assumption that states enter into only those treaties with which they expect to comply; it is simply not worth the effort to negotiate a treaty that one has no intention of honoring (see Chayes and Chayes, 1993). The expectation is that overall levels of compliance will be high and that noncompliance, in the rare cases it occurs, does not represent an intentional choice to disregard the provisions of the treaty. Instead, noncompliance is an unintended product of ambiguous treaty language, limited state capacity, and unexpected social or economic changes. A different approach to conceptualizing compliance looks specifically at situations in which treaties require a deep commitment on the part of the states seeking to implement them (Downs, Rocke, and Barsoom, 1996). This approach sees compliance in more critical terms, argues that the self-interested calculations of states must be taken into account, and concludes that good compliance is very much a result of good enforcement. As would be expected, the causes of noncompliance are more varied with the second approach.

Scholarship has identified a number of reasons a state may find it in its self-interest not to comply with a treaty it has signed and ratified. George Downs, David Rocke, and Peter Barsoom discuss how domestic political considerations can cause states to avoid the difficult sacrifices required when the time for implementation rolls around (1996, p. 399). Beth Simmons finds that concerns about one's reputation and the level of compliance of other states in the same region determine whether or not states will comply with the par value currency requirements of the IMF (2000). Ronald Mitchell concludes that inherent differences in treaty design explain why one regime for controlling oil pollution in the oceans through limitations on discharges was much less effective than another regime that required tanker owners to install new and costly equipment to prevent discharges in the first place (1994). The list of possible reasons for defection is long, but the key point is that compliance often depends at least in part on the use of strong enforcement mechanisms, including the possibility of punishment through "naming and shaming," economic sanctions, or even military intervention. Unfortunately, these tools are still of only limited availability in the UN system, despite their increased use in the years since the end of the cold war (White, 2002, pp. 301–302).

Jacobson and Weiss build on the case study research discussed in the preceding paragraph to consider numerous possible explanations for the variations in implementation and compliance among eight different actors on five environmental treaties. The factors they cover include the nature of the activity, the characteristics of the accord itself, the characteristics of the states in question, and the impact of the international environment (1995, pp. 124–127). In relation to the characteristics of the accord, Jacobson and Weiss cover one issue especially relevant to this study of UN decisionmaking: how the process by which the accord was negotiated affects implementation and compliance (ibid., p. 125). Does it matter who initiated or participated in the process? What did the negotiations look like? Were decisions made by majority rule or consensus? Unfortunately, Jacobson and Weiss do not return to these questions in their brief conclusion (ibid., pp. 139–140); however, the connection between process and compliance has been suggested by other authors. For example, Young argues that multilateral negotiations are more likely to reach a successful outcome when clear-cut and effective compliance mechanisms are available (1989, pp. 370–371). Of course our concern here is with the opposite relationship: not how expected outcome affects the process but how process affects the likely outcome. A number of considerations related to process can affect how a state responds to an objectionable decision by an international organization: the identity of the body in which the decision is made, the size and composition of the majority supporting the decision, the forcefulness of the language of the decision, and the number of times the same decision has been passed. Larger bodies, larger majorities, broader coalitions, strong language, and repeated action all increase the likelihood of compliance (Claude, 1967, pp. 93–94; Peterson, 1986, pp. 195–206; Feld and Jordan, 1989, p. 132). The relationship between process and outcomes applies to both binding and nonbinding UN decisions; it is especially important in any situation where member states are likely to perceive the UN decision as embodying a double standard (for example, see Franck, 1984).

Binding Decisions

Most decisions made by international organizations take the form of recommendations that their member states are encouraged but not required to honor. While some international organizations are empowered to adopt decisions that are legally binding on their members, "directives authorizing IGOs [international governmental organizations] to issue an enforceable order are not frequent" (Feld and Jordan, 1989, p. 132). In the case of the United Nations, only the Security Council and General Assembly can make binding decisions, and in the case of both bodies, this power can be exercised only under rather narrow parameters. The scope of binding decisions made by both bodies was discussed in Chapter 6, but some of this information bears repeating here, especially in terms of its relationship to compliance.

For the Security Council, the common distinction is that substantive decisions taken under Chapter 6 of the UN Charter (the peaceful settlement provisions) are recommendations but that those taken under Chapter 7 of the Charter (the collective security provisions) can be legally binding on all UN members, including those in the Council that voted against the resolution as well as member states not serving on the Council (see Bailey and Daws, 1998, pp. 266–268; Sands and Klein, 2001, pp. 281–282). However, this common understanding has been the subject of some debate: Can decisions taken under Chapter 6 ever be mandatory? Are all decisions taken under Chapter 7 legally binding? Much of the attention in this debate has focused on Article 25 of the Charter, which specifies that "the Members of the United Nations agree to carry out the decisions of the Security Council in accordance with the present Charter." As a result, when the Council acts under Chapter 7 to exercise its responsibilities for international peace and security, there is little doubt that its decisions are binding. However, an advisory ruling issued by the International Court of Justice has found that Article 25 is not limited to just enforcement action but applies to "'the decisions of the Security Council' adopted in accordance with the Charter" (Bailey and Daws, 1998, p. 268; Sands and Klein, 2001, p. 281). Determining whether a Council resolution should be considered legally binding thus requires a careful analysis of the content and context of the resolution. Reference to the language of Chapter 7 is the most common manner in which the Council conveys its intent that the resolution be mandatory for all UN members.

In their analysis of Security Council practice, Bailey and Daws find that from 1946 to 1989, the Council adopted twenty-two resolutions that either cited or used the wording of Chapter 7 (1998, p. 273). From 1990 to 1996, the Council adopted 107 such resolutions (p. 273), and this pattern of greater use of Chapter 7 has continued into the new millennium (Malone, 2004, pp. 620–622). Legally binding resolutions since the mid-1990s cover both military enforcement and mandatory economic and diplomatic sanctions. While many have seen this as a positive development, since it has allowed the Council to fulfill more of its original mandate than was ever possible during the cold war, it has resulted in some problems. First, as was discussed in Chapter 6 of this book, there is some concern "that Chapter VII was being used to take mandatory decisions on matters outside the traditional jurisdiction of the Council" (Bailey and Daws, 1998, p. 271). Second, despite their legally binding character, the Council found that enforcement of its Chapter 7 decisions was problematic at best in the face of disunity among the five veto powers; nowhere was this more clearly demonstrated than in the Council's handling of Iraq in the twelve years after the end of the Gulf War in 1991. Compliance with the Council's binding decisions can face serious obstacles, then, regarding perceptions of the target state and the political will of UN members.

The General Assembly is also empowered with the ability to make binding decisions; however, these are more limited in scope than the powers of the Security Council. Peterson observes that the Assembly can make binding decisions in eight areas, many of which are matters internal to the UN system, such as oversight of its subsidiary bodies, elections to limited membership bodies, and supervision of the Secretariat (1986, pp. 115, 136, 152). Some of these powers, however, apply directly to its relation with member states: the designation of who can participate in the Assembly, approval of trusteeship arrangements (of which there are currently none), and approval of the regular budget, including the apportionment of assessments among members. It is this last responsibility that receives the most attention in terms of the Assembly's binding powers (Sands and Klein, 2001, p. 280), for its budgetary decisions have frequently been ignored by major financial contributors, such as the United States, that withhold their legally obligated dues as a means of pushing for reform in the organization (for information on the US case, see Smith, 2004). The UN Charter specifies a sanction for the withholding of dues in Article 19: member states whose arrears exceed their assessed contributions for the preceding two full years shall have no vote in the Assembly, unless the Assembly decides to waive this penalty if it determines that the arrears are beyond the control of the member state. This sanction has not been consistently applied, and some members (like the United States) have made sure to keep their arrears barely below this limit even when using withholding as a means of leverage. As of January 2004, twenty-six states were in arrears under the terms of Article 19, but ten of them were allowed to temporarily retain their vote due to economic hardship or other mitigating factors (see UN doc. A/58/688, January 21, 2004).

As a result of these narrow binding powers, Peterson concludes, "Assembly majorities can exert important influence over the UN system," but "they have great trouble exerting much direct influence over member states" (1986, p. 252). One exception is that Assembly resolutions can lead to or approve multilateral treaties, but these treaties are not legally binding until they are signed and ratified by a specified number of states and thus enter into force as statements of international law (Sands and Klein, 2001, pp. 275–276; Baehr and Gordenker, 1994, pp. 53–54). Chapter 6 of this book also briefly considered a debate regarding the extent to which other substantive decisions by the Assembly that technically only carry the weight of recommendations might become part of customary international law. This debate involves some degree of legal hair-splitting. For example, "it is widely accepted that [these recommendations] cannot, as such, be considered as binding on the members of the organization," but that does not mean "that they will produce no legal effects whatsoever outside the organisation's legal order" (Sands and Klein, 2001, pp. 286–287). What these authors have in mind is that Assembly resolutions may have normative value when they "provide evidence important for establishing the existence of a rule" in customary international law (ibid., p. 290). Ultimately, Philippe Sands and Pierre Klein (ibid., p. 291) agree with the opinions of Peterson (1986, p. 145) and Smouts (2000, p. 51), who argue that Assembly resolutions are most likely to have the weight of customary international law when they reflect existing state practice, when they explicitly state that the states involved accept the resolution as binding, and when the resolution is repeatedly adopted by overwhelming majorities. While the debate concerning the relationship between Assembly resolutions and customary international law remains unresolved, it is important to consider these and other factors that can motivate states and other actors to comply with UN recommendations even when they are not legally required to do so.

Recommendations

It is unfortunately easy to provide a list of UN decisions and resolutions that member states and other actors have failed to implement once they were drafted. While there are many such instances for the binding decisions just discussed, nonimplementation is even more common for the vast majority of UN outputs that remain mere recommendations. One can find examples of this persistent problem across almost any issue on the UN's agenda, from disarmament to human rights, from the environment to the status of women. However, these problems are likely to be most apparent when the focus is on a "snapshot" of the UN's work in specific issues at specific times. If one takes a more long-term and holistic view of the UN's decisions, the picture is often quite different. In his study of the roots and reaches of UN decisions, Moses Moskowitz offers the following observation:

> Although opinion is deeply divided on the question of the efficacy of the United Nations, its relevance and its proper role in the larger world, the impact of the international organization for good or evil can be ignored only at our peril. The United Nations remains a world arena in which words and resolutions have moral and political consequences. Like individual tesserae of a mosaic which are but little bits of colored glass or stone until they are put together in a given order, so the individual resolutions or decisions of United Nations bodies often make little sense until they are put together to make a pattern. (1980, p. vii)

Moskowitz goes on to conclude, "There is no nation in the world today, regardless of size, population, wealth or power that is not in one way or another affected by, and in turn does not affect, the United Nations" (ibid., p. 1).

Other observers have used similar analogies to try to capture the long-term impact of UN decisions. In a passage already quoted in Chapter 6, Leon Gordenker says the recommendations of the General Assembly resemble waves: in some rare instances they make great splashes in implementation, but their effects are more likely to be felt as ripples (quoted in Kaufmann, 1980, p. 25). The point of the analogy is that both waves and ripples will ultimately reshape the contours of the shoreline, just on different timetables. Some UN resolutions may have a dramatic and immediate effect, but the impact of most is felt only with the passage of time. Righter offers a similar observation rooted in a more critical analogy: she argues that UN "resolutions bind nobody, but like Chinese water torture, they slowly penetrate the collective skull, promoting (or, all too often, obstructing) a common approach to a particular question and effecting a slow mutation in the terms in which it is discussed. They can nudge governments toward accepting a convention. . . . Such mutations matter" (1995, p. 69).

Some scholars have adopted an even stronger view of the long-term influence of United Nations decisions on the behavior of member states. One classic conceptualization is Claude's notion of "collective legitimization," which he summarized as follows:

A state may hesitate to pursue a policy that has engendered the formal disapproval of the Assembly, not because it is prepared to give the will of that organ priority over its national interest, but because it believes that the adverse judgment of the Assembly makes the pursuit of that policy disadvantageous to the national interest. This is simply to say that statesmen take collective legitimacy seriously as a factor in international politics. (1967, p. 93)

Claude further argues that the degree of collective legitimization conferred by a UN resolution will vary based on the size and composition of the majorities supporting it, the forcefulness of the language it contains, and the number of times its content has been repeated in other resolutions, with unanimous, unambiguous, and recurring decisions having the most influence (ibid., p. 94). Writing in the same period, Catherine Manno echoes some of Claude's findings and adds that the ultimate impact of UN decisions also depends on the intent of the resolution (how much behavioral change it requires) as well as the number of actors whose behavior is targeted (1968, pp. 256–259). This second point is especially important, given the rise in consensus decisionmaking in UN bodies: Manno finds that more selective resolutions are less likely to be implemented than those that adopt a broader focus (ibid., p. 259).

This linkage between collective legitimization and the process of decisionmaking returns us to the discussion of the advantages and disadvantages of consensus found at the end of Chapter 7. UN critics have observed that consensus often results in "least common denominator" outcomes (for example, see Righter, 1995, pp. 69, 138), but this claim has been strongly disputed by others (for example, see Childers and Urquhart, 1991, p. 4). Even if the critics of consensus are correct, the ideas advanced by Claude and Manno decades ago suggest that consensus may still lead to greater compliance than strongly worded but controversial majority-based decisions. Other more recent writings already discussed in this chapter, such as Feld and Jordan (1989, p. 132) and Peterson (1986, pp. 195–206), have found that decisions with broader participation can be more effective in certain circumstances. This suggests that there is a paradox at work in the relationship between consensus and compliance. Majority-rule decisions require less support, so decisions made in this manner usually are written in unambiguous language. On the other hand, consensus requires the support, or at least acquiescence, of all participants, thereby encouraging compromise. The result is that majority-rule decisions appear strong but often remain inoperable due to minority objections (Peterson, 1986, p. 252), whereas consensus decisions seem vague but may nonetheless be more likely to be integrated into the policies of member states and other actors, since states may feel strong pressure not to disrupt these agreements (Finkelstein, 1988c, p. 23). This paradox was highlighted by many of the practitioners who were interviewed for this book; however, no systematic examination of this complex relationship has yet been completed, due at least in part to the difficulty of accurately assessing compliance.

One additional indicator of the power of collective legitimization lies in the fact that most member states appear to have an intense interest in the decisions made by UN bodies. Puchala observes that "most members currently respect the United Nations, accept commitments contained in its policies and programs, adhere to UN-inspired conventions and codes, and accord authority to resolutions that follow from consensus" (1982–1983, p. 587). After all, why would states spend so much time "polishing, promoting, and maneuvering resolutions" if they do not value and fear the political significance of these texts (Baehr and Gordenker, 1994, p. 53)? Claude echoes this realization: "The intensity of the concern exhibited by states about the outcome of votes in the organization indicates that the seal of approval and the stigma of disapproval are taken seriously" (1967, p. 102). More recently, Kaufmann arrives at a similar conclusion: "Although few United Nations decisions are mandatory, the strenuous efforts delegations make in order to amend, defeat or avoid such draft resolutions, even when they contain very vague language, indicates the importance attached to these texts" (1980, p. 119).

These views on the ability of UN recommendations to influence the behavior of its member states and other actors over the long term show that the outputs of the organization's political processes do matter in world politics. Furthermore, the relationship between the drafting process and the level of compliance confirms the importance of the insights offered in the preceding chapters about how the process actually works. But what about the significance of this process when no outputs result? The final section of the book considers how UN decision-making matters even when no decisions are made.

■ Does the Process Itself Matter?

Most studies of the United Nations focus on its outputs: the resolutions, decisions, programs, and policies that emerge from its various decision-making arenas. This is a logical focus, since these outputs are "the final point . . . the official product that is aimed at" when states interact at the UN (Petersen, 1968, p. 128). However, Keith Petersen goes on to observe that "hardly ever [are these outputs] the most important or meaningful point," since they often require "the sacrifice of precision, forthrightness, and even relevance" in order to be adopted (pp. 128, 131). Thus UN resolutions are "debilitated" rather than "defeated" and "the resolution itself is hardly ever the crucial point of the UN process . . . it is the getting there that counts." In other words, Petersen concludes, "the 'parliamentary' battle and its tactics are generally of much greater consequence than the 'legislative' victory and its results," and these dynamics are "the real achievements of the UN" (ibid., p. 131). While some of the authors surveyed in the preceding sections would certainly disagree with Petersen's apparent assessment that UN outputs don't really matter, his observations regarding the importance of the process itself are as relevant today as they were several decades ago. Numerous practices and procedures seem to have an effect inside and outside the organization on their own, regardless of the decisions (if any) that ultimately are made. Several brief examples will be surveyed here to support this important point.

One way the UN's political processes matter regardless of outcomes relates to their participatory nature. Before the advent of universal-membership and general-purpose international organizations, international relations was dominated by a few great powers that fought wars, maintained colonies, and set up the rules that governed the interaction of sovereign states. This study of decisionmaking has found that powerful states still have much influence within and outside the United Nations; however, it has also found that the UN's political processes provide a role and voice to a much wider range of states that are small, poor, or otherwise lacking in international stature (Jacobson, 1979, p. 138). These states are thus able to advance their interests to an extent that would be impossible in the absence of the United Nations or an equivalent institution. Even middle powers that already enjoy a substantial role in international politics, at least at the regional level, can benefit from participation in the UN, since they often end up playing leadership roles in the organization (Peterson, 1986, p. 244). This prominence and visibility can lead to enhanced stature outside the UN as well. Finally, the participatory nature of the UN extends beyond its member states; Part 1 of this book considered how nongovernmental organizations and even multinational corporations can influence the content and direction of UN debates. Members of the Secretariat are able to advance positions not associated with any state and thereby broaden the debate (Jacobson, 1979, pp. 136–137). As was discussed in Chapter 4, they are also able to contribute to effective third-party conflict resolution, even when the political bodies of the UN remain stalemated in regard to a particular situation.

A second way the UN's political processes matter even in the absence of actual decisions concerns their role in the dissemination of information. While this is an important function for almost any international organization (Feld and Jordan, 1989, p. 132), it is especially important for the United Nations, given its broad participatory nature and expansive agenda (Alger, 1961, pp. 134–137; 1965, pp. 277–279). The UN's political process involves the preparation of numerous background reports, the circulation of countless proposals, and frequent formal and informal interaction between participants. Some of this information is available from other sources, but much of it is generated due to the unique environment of the United Nations. The ready availability of this information has direct effects inside and outside the UN, because it requires participants to be concerned with a much wider range of issues and other participants than they would otherwise have on their radar screen. This expanded agenda forces participants to "take public positions on matters that they would sometimes prefer to handle privately" (Baehr and Gordenker, 1994, p. 54), to adapt their own domestic policy agenda accordingly (Karns and Mingst, 1987, pp. 460, 464), and to change the factors they weigh when deciding how to most effectively articulate their national interests at the international level (Peterson, 1986, pp. 241–247). Furthermore, making these changes can necessitate adjustments in other policy positions (for the sake of consistency or due to domestic political considerations, for example), so developments in the UN's political processes may have an impact on issues not even on the organization's agenda.

Finally, the process of UN decisionmaking can matter even when decisions are not made, because international organizations often serve as an important forum for socialization and learning for their participants (Karns and Mingst, 1987, pp. 465–467, Peterson, 1986, p. 243). This can have several positive benefits for the actors involved at the United Nations and their representatives. For example, participation in the UN's political processes results not only in changed attitudes toward the organization but also in changed attitudes toward other participants (see, for example, Alger, 1963; Riggs, 1977). These new attitudes, in turn, can have an impact on subsequent behavior: for example, participants find it harder to identify the "good guys" and "bad guys" on each issue, since the "good guys" sometimes fail to vote with their country, while the "bad guys" on occasion end up being unexpected sources of support (Alger, 1968, p. 123). Furthermore, the sustained interaction between participants that occurs in UN decisionmaking can allow friendships to form between delegates representing different member states, including those from states who have little in common outside of their UN membership (Alger, 1961, pp. 133–134). These friendships provide participants with a network of contacts that they can use to more effectively achieve their objectives at the UN, and over time these networks can extend beyond the organization to other areas of international relations as UN participants rotate into new assignments and positions. Interaction at the UN can thus have a direct impact outside the organization, as these networks provide opportunities for the participants involved to explore areas of potential agreement or cooperation, sometimes despite official government policies to the contrary (Alger, 1965, p. 283; 1968, p. 110).

The observations contained in this chapter are intended to demonstrate that the decisions of the United Nations, whether they are legally binding or not, can influence the behavior of its member states and other actors. They also describe how the organization's political processes can have an impact on the conduct of international relations even in cases where no decisions are made. Developing a deeper understanding of how these processes unfold is therefore an important, even necessary, undertaking. This book represents an important step in this regard, but more research is certainly required. Scholars pursuing this agenda would do well to remember Secretary-General Kofi Annan's characterization of the United Nations is his annual *Report on the Work of the Organization* for 2003:

> The United Nations is not an end in itself. Rather, it is an instrument for achieving common ends. The strength and effectiveness of the Organization depends on the active support of its Member States and their policies. Moreover, achievement of the Organization's purposes requires a shared consensus about its fundamental goals. That does not mean that Member States need to agree on all issues. However, it does mean that they should be ready to use the Organization to achieve mutual objectives and to accommodate different national interests. (Annan, 2003, p. 2)

Looking at the organization in this manner is consistent with the global dance analogy used at various points in this study. The UN brings diverse actors together in a complex routine of procedures and practices where each seeks to shift the music so that the process is moving toward outcomes it prefers. Some strut, others inspire, and a few just remain on the sidelines, but the hope is that the number of participants willing to dance to the same music will increase over time, to the end that effective solutions to pressing global problems can be found.

Acronyms

ACABQ	Advisory Committee on Administrative and Budgetary Questions
ACC	Administrative Committee on Coordination
ASEAN	Association of South East Asian Nations
AU	African Union
CANZ	Canada, Australia, and New Zealand (as a UN group)
CARICOM	Caribbean Community
CD	Conference on Disarmament
CEB	Chief Executives Board for Coordination
CMEA	Council for Mutual Economic Assistance
CONGO	Conference of NGOs in Consultative Status with the United Nations
CSD	Commission on Sustainable Development
CTBT	Comprehensive (Nuclear) Test Ban Treaty
DPI	Department of Public Information
ECOSOC	Economic and Social Council
ECOWAS	Economic Community of West African States
EU	European Union
FAO	Food and Agriculture Organization
G7	Group of 7
G8	Group of 8
G77	Group of 77
IAEA	International Atomic Energy Agency
ICAO	International Civil Aviation Organization
ICJ	International Court of Justice
IFAD	International Fund for Agricultural Development
IGO	international governmental organization
ILO	International Labour Organization

IMF	International Monetary Fund
LDCs	least developed countries
LLDS	Land-Locked Developing States
MNC	multinational corporation
NAM	Non-Aligned Movement
NGLS	Non-Governmental Liaison Service
NGO	nongovernmental organization
NIEO	new international economic order
OAS	Organization of American States
OECD	Organization for Economic Cooperation and Development
OEWG	open-ended working group
OHCHR	Office of High Commissioner for Human Rights
OIC	Organization of the Islamic Conference
OPEC	Organization of Petroleum Exporting Countries
P3	the Western permanent members of the Security Council
P5	the five permanent members of the Security Council
SAARC	South Asian Association for Regional Cooperation
SADC	Southern African Development Community
SIDS	Small Island Developing States
TCN	troop-contributing nation
TNC	transnational corporation
UNCED	UN Conference on Environment and Development
UNCTAD	United Nations Conference on Trade and Development
UNDP	United Nations Development Programme
UNEP	United Nations Environment Programme
UNESCO	United Nations Educational, Scientific, and Cultural Organization
UNHCR	United Nations High Commissioner for Refugees
UNICEF	United Nations Children's Fund
UNIDO	United Nations Industrial Development Organization
UNMOVIC	UN Monitoring, Verification, and Inspection Commission
WHO	World Health Organization
WTO	World Trade Organization

References

Abbott, Kenneth W., and Duncan Snidal. 1998. "Why States Act Through Formal International Organizations." *Journal of Conflict Resolution* 42, no. 1: 3–32.

Adams, Barbara. 1994. "The People's Organisations and the UN: NGOs in International Civil Society." In Erskine Childers, ed., *Challenges to the United Nations: Building a Safer World.* New York: St. Martin's Press, pp. 176–187.

Aggrey-Orleans, Agnes Y. 1998. "The Role, Organization, and Work of a Permanent Mission in Geneva." In M. A. Boisard and E. M. Chossudovsky, eds., *Multilateral Diplomacy: The United Nations System at Geneva—A Working Guide.* The Hague, the Netherlands: Kluwer Law International, pp. 47–52.

Alger, Chadwick F. 1961. "Non-resolution Consequences of the United Nations and Their Effect on International Conflict." *Journal of Conflict Resolution* 5, no. 2: 128–145.

———. 1963. "United Nations Participation as a Learning Experience." *Public Opinion Quarterly* 27, no. 3: 411–426.

———. 1965. "Decision-Making Theory and Human Conflict." In Elton B. McNeil, ed., *The Nature of Human Conflict.* Englewood Cliffs, NJ: Prentice Hall, pp. 274–292.

———. 1966. "Interaction and Negotiation in a Committee of the United Nations General Assembly." Philadelphia Conference. *Peace Research Society: Papers* 5, pp. 141–159.

———. 1967. "Interaction in a Committee of the United Nations General Assembly." In J. David Singer, ed., *Quantitative International Politics: Insights and Evidence.* New York: Free Press, pp. 51–84.

———. 1968. "Personal Contact in Intergovernmental Organizations." In Robert W. Gregg and Michael Barkun, eds., *The United Nations System and Its Functions: Selected Readings.* Princeton, NJ: D. Van Nostrand, pp. 104–127.

———. 1970. "Research on Research: A Decade of Quantitative and Field Research on International Organizations." *International Organization* 24, no. 3: 414–450.

———. 1972. "Negotiation, Regional Groups, Interaction, and Public Debate in the Development of Consensus in the United Nations General Assembly." In James N. Rosenau, Vincent Davis, and Maurice A. East, eds., *The Analysis of International Politics: Essays in Honor of Harold and Margaret Sprout*. New York: Free Press, pp. 278–298.

———. 1973. "Decision-Making in Public Bodies of International Organizations (ILO, WHO, WMO, UN): A Preliminary Research Report." In Dusan Sidjanski, ed., *Political Decision-Making Processes: Studies in National, Comparative, and International Politics*. San Francisco: Jossey-Bass, pp. 205–229.

———. 1976. "The Researcher in the United Nations: Evolution of a Research Strategy." In James N. Rosenau, ed., *In Search of Global Patterns*. New York: Free Press, pp. 58–72.

———. 1989. "Negotiating a Consensus on Peacekeeping Finance: The United Nations Special General Assembly Session of 1963." In Johan Kaufmann, ed., *Effective Negotiation: Case Studies in Conference Diplomacy*. Dordrecht, the Netherlands: Martinus Nijhoff, pp. 1–44.

———. 1994. "Citizens and the UN System in a Changing World." In Yoshikazu Sakamoto, ed., *Global Transformation: Challenges to the State System*. Tokyo: United Nations University Press, pp. 301–329.

———. 1999. "Strengthening Relations Between NGOs and the UN System: Towards a Research Agenda." *Global Society* 13, no. 4: 393–409.

———. 2002. "The Role of the Practitioner-Scholar: Johan Kaufmann's Contributions to Scholarship on Decision Making in the United Nations System." *International Studies Perspectives* 3, no. 2: 209–220.

———. 2003. "Evolving Roles of NGOs in Member State Decision-Making in the UN System." *Journal of Human Rights* 2, no. 3: 407–424.

Alker, Hayward R., Jr. 1967. "Dimensions of Conflict in the General Assembly." In David A. Kay, ed., *The United Nations Political System*. New York: John Wiley and Sons, pp. 161–185.

Allen, Michael J. 1991. "UNESCO and the ILO: A Tale of Two Agencies." In Robert N. Wells Jr., ed., *Peace by Pieces: United Nations Agencies and Their Roles—A Reader and Selective Bibliography*. Metuchen, NJ: Scarecrow Press, pp. 182–215.

Alter, Karen J. 1998. "Who Are the 'Masters of the Treaty'? European Governments and the European Court of Justice." *International Organization* 52, no. 1: 121–147.

Ameri, Houshang. 1996. *Politics of Staffing the United Nations Secretariat*. New York: Peter Lang.

Annan, Kofi A. 1993. "The Secretary-General and the UN Budget." In Benjamin Rivlin and Leon Gordenker, eds., *The Challenging Role of the UN Secretary-General: Making "the Most Impossible Job in the World" Possible*. Westport, CT: Praeger, pp. 98–107.

———. 2003. *Report on the Secretary-General on the Work of the Organization*. UN doc. A/58/1, August 28, 2003. New York: United Nations.

Appathurai, E. R. 1985. "Permanent Missions in New York." In G. R. Berridge and A. Jennings, eds., *Diplomacy at the UN*. London: Macmillan, pp. 94–108.

Archer, Clive. 1992. *International Organizations*. London: Routledge.

Aviel, JoAnn Fagot. 1999a. "The Evolution of Multilateral Diplomacy." In James P. Muldoon Jr., JoAnn Fagot Aviel, Richard Reitano, and Earl Sullivan, eds., *Multilateral Diplomacy and the United Nations Today*. Boulder, CO: Westview Press, pp. 8–14.

———. 1999b. "NGOs and International Affairs: A New Dimension of Diplomacy." In James P. Muldoon Jr., JoAnn Fagot Aviel, Richard Reitano, and Earl Sullivan, eds., *Multilateral Diplomacy and the United Nations Today*. Boulder, CO: Westview Press, pp. 156–166.

Baehr, Peter. 1995. "The Netherlands and the United Nations: The Future Lies in the Past." In Chadwick F. Alger, Gene M. Lyons, and John E. Trent, eds., *The United Nations System: The Policies of Member States*. Tokyo: United Nations University Press, pp. 271–328.

Baehr, Peter R., and Leon Gordenker. 1994. *The United Nations in the 1990s*. New York: St. Martin's Press.

Bailey, Sydney D. 1960. *The General Assembly of the United Nations: A Study of Procedure and Practice*. New York: Frederick A. Praeger.

———. 1962. *The Secretariat of the United Nations*. New York: Carnegie Endowment for International Peace.

———. 1963. *The United Nations: A Short Political Guide*. New York: Frederick A. Praeger.

———. 1969. *Voting in the Security Council*. Bloomington: Indiana University Press.

Bailey, Sydney D., and Sam Daws. 1995. *The United Nations: A Concise Political Guide*. London: Macmillan.

———. 1998. *The Procedure of the UN Security Council*. Oxford: Clarendon Press.

Barringer, Felicity. 2003. "Security Council Adopts U.S. Plan for Iraq in 15–0 Vote." *New York Times*, October 16, Internet edition (www.nytimes.com).

Behnam, Awni. 1998. "The Group System." In M. A. Boisard and E. M. Chossudovsky, eds., *Multilateral Diplomacy: The United Nations System at Geneva—A Working Guide*. The Hague, the Netherlands: Kluwer Law International, pp. 193–204.

Beigbeder, Yves. 1988. *Threats to the International Civil Service*. London: Pinter.

———. 2000. "The United Nations Secretariat: Reform in Progress." In Paul Taylor and A. J. R. Groom, eds., *The United Nations at the Millennium: The Principal Organs*. London: Continuum, pp. 196–223.

Bennett, A. LeRoy, and James K. Oliver. 2002. *International Organizations: Principles and Issues*. Upper Saddle River, NJ: Prentice Hall.

Bisogniero, Claudio. 1998. First counselor, Permanent Mission of Italy to the United Nations. Personal interview, Permanent Mission of Italy to the UN, March 10.

Brühl, Tanja, and Volker Rittberger. 2001. "From International to Global Governance: Actors, Collective Decision-Making, and the United Nations in the World of the Twenty-first Century." In Volker Rittberger, ed., *Global Governance and the United Nations System*. Tokyo: United Nations University Press, pp. 1–47.

Burgess, Stephen F. 2001. *The United Nations Under Boutros Boutros-Ghali, 1992–1997*. Lanham, MD: Scarecrow Press.

Buzan, Barry. 1981. "Negotiating by Consensus: Developments in Technique at the United Nations Conference on the Law of the Sea." *American Journal of International Law* 75, no. 2: 324–348.

Caradon, Lord. 1981. "Reflections and Hopes." In Davidson Nicol, ed., *Paths to Peace: The UN Security Council and Its Presidency*. New York: Pergamon Press, pp. 74–83.

Caron, David D. 1993. "The Legitimacy of the Collective Authority of the Security Council." *American Journal of International Law* 87, no. 4: 552–588.

Chai, Feng-Yang. 1981a. "The Scope of Consensus." In Davidson Nicol, ed., *Paths to Peace: The UN Security Council and Its Presidency*. New York: Pergamon Press, pp. 48–64.

———. 1981b. "A View from the UN Secretariat." In Davidson Nicol, ed., *Paths to Peace: The UN Security Council and Its Presidency*. New York: Pergamon Press, pp. 84–93.

Chandra, A. V. S. Ramesh. 2001. First secretary, Permanent Mission of India to the United Nations. Personal interview, Permanent Mission of India to the UN, January 5.

Chase, Eugene P. 1950. *The United Nations in Action*. New York: McGraw-Hill.

Chayes, Abram, and Antonia Handler Chayes. 1993. "On Compliance." *International Organization* 47, no. 2: 175–205.

Childers, Erskine, and Brian Urquhart. 1991. *Towards a More Effective United Nations*. Uppsala, Sweden: Dag Hammarskjöld Foundation. Reprinted in *Development Dialogue*, nos. 1–2 (1991): 5–85.

Chrispeels, Erik. 1998. "Procedures of Multilateral Conference Diplomacy." In M. A. Boisard and E. M. Chossudovsky, eds., *Multilateral Diplomacy: The United Nations System at Geneva—A Working Guide*. The Hague, the Netherlands: Kluwer Law International, pp. 119–136.

Claude, Inis L., Jr. 1967. *The Changing United Nations*. New York: Random House.

———. 1984. *Swords into Ploughshares: The Problems and Progress of International Organization*. New York: Random House.

———. 1993. "Reflections on the Role of the UN Secretary-General." In Benjamin Rivlin and Leon Gordenker, eds., *The Challenging Role of the UN Secretary-General: Making "the Most Impossible Job in the World" Possible*. Westport, CT: Praeger, pp. 249–260.

———. 1996. "Peace and Security: Prospective Roles for the Two United Nations." *Global Governance* 2, no. 3: 289–298.

Cleary, Seamus. 1996. "The World Bank and NGOs." In Peter Willetts, ed., *"The Conscience of the World": The Influence of Non-governmental Organisations in the UN System*. London: Hurst, pp. 63–97.

Conca, Ken. 1996. "Greening the UN: Environmental Organisations and the UN System." In Thomas G. Weiss and Leon Gordenker, eds., *NGOs, the UN, and Global Governance*. Boulder, CO: Lynne Rienner, pp. 103–119.

Connors, Jane. 1996. "NGOs and the Human Rights of Women at the United Nations." In Peter Willetts, ed., *"The Conscience of the World": The*

Influence of Non-governmental Organisations in the UN System. London: Hurst, pp. 147–180.

Cook, Helena. 1996. "Amnesty International at the United Nations." In Peter Willetts, ed., *"The Conscience of the World": The Influence of Non-governmental Organisations in the UN System.* London: Hurst, pp. 181–213.

Cooper, Andrew F. 2002. "Like-Minded Nations, NGOs, and the Changing Pattern of Diplomacy Within the UN System: An Introductory Perspective." In Andrew F. Cooper, John English, and Ramesh Thakur, eds., *Enhancing Global Governance: Towards a New Diplomacy?* Tokyo: United Nations University Press, pp. 1–18.

Cooper, Andrew F., John English, and Ramesh Thakur, eds. 2002. *Enhancing Global Governance: Towards a New Diplomacy?* Tokyo: United Nations University Press.

Cox, Robert W. 1969. "The Executive Head: An Essay on Leadership in International Organization." *International Organization* 23, no. 2: 205–230.

Cox, Robert W., and Harold K. Jacobson. 1973a. "The Anatomy of Influence." In Robert W. Cox and Harold K. Jacobson, eds., *The Anatomy of Influence: Decision Making in International Organization.* New Haven, CT: Yale University Press, pp. 371–436.

———. 1973b. "The Framework for Inquiry." In Robert W. Cox and Harold K. Jacobson, eds., *The Anatomy of Influence: Decision Making in International Organization.* New Haven, CT: Yale University Press, pp. 1–36.

Crossette, Barbara. 2001. "U.S. Is Voted off Rights Panel of the U.N. for the First Time." *New York Times,* May 4, Internet edition (www.nytimes.com).

Crowe, Sir Colin. 1981. "Some Observations on the Operation of the Security Council Including the Use of the Veto." In Davidson Nicol, ed., *Paths to Peace: The UN Security Council and Its Presidency.* New York: Pergamon Press, pp. 94–97.

Darmanin, Joanna. 1998. First secretary, Permanent Mission of Malta to the United Nations. Personal interview, Permanent Mission of Malta to the UN, February 24.

Dedring, Juergen. 2000. "The Security Council." In Paul Taylor and A. J. R. Groom, eds., *The United Nations at the Millennium: The Principal Organs.* London: Continuum, pp. 61–99.

Dell, Sidney. 1989. "The United Nations Code of Conduct on Transnational Corporations." In Johan Kaufmann, ed., *Effective Negotiation: Case Studies in Conference Diplomacy.* Dordrecht, the Netherlands: Martinus Nijhoff, pp. 53–74.

Dixon, William J. 1989. "The Evaluation of Weighted Voting Schemes for the United Nations General Assembly." In Paul F. Diehl, ed., *The Politics of International Organizations: Patterns and Insights.* Chicago: Dorsey Press, pp. 134–151.

Donini, Antonio. 1996. "The Bureaucracy and the Free Spirits: Stagnation and Innovation in the Relationship Between the UN and NGOs." In Thomas G. Weiss and Leon Gordenker, eds., *NGOs, the UN, and Global Governance.* Boulder, CO: Lynne Rienner, pp. 83–101.

Downs, George W., David M. Rocke, and Peter N. Barsoom. 1996. "Is the

Good News About Compliance Good News About Cooperation?" *International Organization* 50, no. 3: 379–406.

Drayton, Alison. 1998. First secretary, Permanent Mission of Guyana to the United Nations. Personal interview, Viennese Café at UN headquarters, March 10.

Edwards, Michael. 2000. "Civil Society and Global Governance." In Ramesh Thakur and Edward Newman, eds., *New Millennium, New Perspectives: The United Nations, Security, and Governance*. Tokyo: United Nations University Press, pp. 205–219.

Egeland, Jan. 1984. "Focus On: Human Rights—Ineffective Big States, Potent Small States." *Journal of Peace Research* 21, no. 3: 207–213.

Eldon, Stewart. 2001. Deputy permanent representative of the United Kingdom to the United Nations. Personal interview, Permanent Mission of the United Kingdom to the UN, January 18.

Evensen, Jens. 1989. "Three Procedural Cornerstones of the Law of the Sea Conference: The Consensus Principle, the Package Deal, and the Gentleman's Agreement." In Johan Kaufmann, ed., *Effective Negotiation: Case Studies in Conference Diplomacy*. Dordrecht, the Netherlands: Martinus Nijhoff, pp. 75–92.

Fasulo, Linda. 2004. *An Insider's Guide to the UN*. New Haven, CT: Yale University Press.

Feld, Werner, and Robert Jordan. 1989. "Patterns of Decisionmaking in International Organizations." In Paul F. Diehl, ed., *The Politics of International Organizations: Patterns and Insights*. Chicago: Dorsey Press, pp. 117–134.

Finger, Seymour Maxwell. 1990. *American Ambassadors at the UN*. New York: United Nations Institute for Training and Research.

Finkelstein, Lawrence S. 1988a. "Comparative Politics in the UN System." In Lawrence S. Finkelstein, ed., *Politics in the United Nations System*. Durham, NC: Duke University Press, pp. 446–483.

———. 1988b. "The Political Role of the Director-General of UNESCO." In Lawrence S. Finkelstein, ed., *Politics in the United Nations System*. Durham, NC: Duke University Press, pp. 385–423.

———. 1988c. "The Politics of Value Allocation in the UN System." In Lawrence S. Finkelstein, ed., *Politics in the United Nations System*. Durham, NC: Duke University Press, pp. 1–40.

———. 1995. "What Is Global Governance?" *Global Governance* 1, no. 3: 367–372.

Firestone, Bernard J. 2001. *The United Nations Under U Thant, 1961–1971*. Lanham, MD: Scarecrow Press.

Fischer, Dietrich, and Johan Galtung. 1991. "Some Observations About the Significance of CAMDUN-1." In Frank Barnaby, ed., *Building a More Democratic United Nations: Proceedings of CAMDUN-1*. London: Frank Cass, pp. 287–292.

Fomerand, Jacques. 1996. "UN Conferences: Media Events or Genuine Diplomacy?" *Global Governance* 2, no. 3: 361–375.

Forsythe, David P. 1988. "The Politics of Efficacy: The United Nations and Human Rights." In Lawrence S. Finkelstein, ed., *Politics in the United Nations System*. Durham, NC: Duke University Press, pp. 246–273.

Franck, Thomas M. 1984. "Of Gnats and Camels: Is There a Double Standard at the United Nations?" *American Journal of International Law* 78, no. 4: 811–833.

Franck, Thomas M., and Georg Nolte. 1993. "The Good Offices Function of the UN Secretary-General." In Adam Roberts and Benedict Kingsbury, eds., *United Nations, Divided World: The UN's Roles in International Relations.* Oxford: Clarendon Press, pp. 143–182.

Fulci, Francesco. 1998. Permanent representative of Italy to the United Nations. Personal interview, Permanent Mission of Italy to the UN, March 10.

Gaglione, Anthony. 2001. *The United Nations Under Trygve Lie, 1945–1953.* Lanham, MD: Scarecrow Press.

Ghebali, Victor-Yves. 1991. "The Politicisation of UN Specialised Agencies: A Preliminary Analysis." In Robert N. Wells Jr., ed., *Peace by Pieces: United Nations Agencies and Their Roles: A Reader and Selective Bibliography.* Metuchen, NJ: Scarecrow Press, pp. 12–39.

Glennon, Michael J. 2003. "Why the Security Council Failed." *Foreign Affairs* 82, no. 3, available online at www.foreignaffairs.org.

Goodrich, Leland M. 1967. "The Political Role of the Secretary-General." In David A. Kay, ed., *The United Nations Political System.* New York: John Wiley and Sons, pp. 127–141.

Gordenker, Leon. 1993. "The UN Secretary-Generalship: Limits, Potentials, and Leadership." In Benjamin Rivlin and Leon Gordenker, eds., *The Challenging Role of the UN Secretary-General: Making "the Most Impossible Job in the World" Possible.* Westport, CT: Praeger, pp. 261–282.

Gordenker, Leon, and Thomas G. Weiss. 1996a. "NGO Participation in the International Policy Process." In Thomas G. Weiss and Leon Gordenker, eds., *NGOs, the UN, and Global Governance.* Boulder, CO: Lynne Rienner, pp. 209–221.

———. 1996b. "Pluralizing Global Governance: Analytical Approaches and Dimensions." In Thomas G. Weiss and Leon Gordenker, eds., *NGOs, the UN, and Global Governance.* Boulder, CO: Lynne Rienner, pp. 17–47.

Gregg, Robert W. 1977. "The Apportioning of Political Power." In David A. Kay, ed., *The Changing United Nations: Options for the United States.* Proceedings of the Academy of Political Science 32, no. 4: 67–80. New York: Academy of Political Science.

———. 1993. *About Face? The United States and the United Nations.* Boulder, CO: Lynne Rienner.

Grey, Wilfrid. 2000. *U.N. Jigsaw.* New York: Vantage Press.

Groom, A. J. R. 2000. "The Trusteeship Council: A Successful Demise." In Paul Taylor and A. J. R. Groom, eds., *The United Nations at the Millennium: The Principal Organs.* London: Continuum, pp. 142–176.

Gupta, Joyeeta. 2001. "Legitimacy in the Real World: A Case Study of the Developing Countries, Non-governmental Organizations, and Climate Change." In Jean-Marc Coicaud and Veijo Heiskanen, eds., *The Legitimacy of International Organizations.* Tokyo: United Nations University Press, pp. 482–518.

Haas, Ernst. 1958. *The Uniting of Europe: Political, Social, Economic Forces, 1950–1957.* Stanford, CA: Stanford University Press.

———. 1968. "Dynamic Environment and Static System: Revolutionary Regimes in the United Nations." In Robert W. Gregg and Michael Barkun, eds., *The United Nations System and Its Functions: Selected Readings.* Princeton, NJ: D. Van Nostrand, pp. 162–197.

———. 1990. *When Knowledge Is Power: Three Models of Change in International Organizations.* Berkeley: University of California Press.

Haggard, Stephen, and Beth A. Simmons. 1987. "Theories of International Regimes." *International Organization* 47, no. 3: 491–517.

Hamilton, Keith, and Richard Langhorne. 1995. *The Practice of Diplomacy: Its Evolution, Theory, and Administration.* London: Routledge.

Hammarskjöld, Dag. 1967. "Two Differing Concepts of United Nations Assayed." In David A. Kay, ed., *The United Nations Political System.* New York: John Wiley and Sons, pp. 109–126.

———. 1968. "The International Civil Servant in Law and in Fact." In Robert W. Gregg and Michael Barkun, eds., *The United Nations System and Its Functions: Selected Readings.* Princeton, NJ: D. Van Nostrand, pp. 215–228.

Hanif, Navid. 1998. First secretary, Permanent Mission of Pakistan to the United Nations. Personal interview, Delegates' Lounge at UN headquarters, February 26.

Haufler, Virginia. 2000. "Private Sector International Regimes." In Richard A. Higgott, Geoffrey R. D. Underhill, and Andreas Bieler, eds., *Non-state Actors and Authority in the Global System.* London: Routledge, pp. 121–137.

———. 2002. "Industry Regulation and Self-Regulation: The Case of Labour Standards." In Andrew F. Cooper, John English, and Ramesh Thakur, eds., *Enhancing Global Governance: Towards a New Diplomacy?* Tokyo: United Nations University Press, pp. 162–186.

Hayes, Donald. 2000. United States representative for United Nations management and reform. Personal interview, Permanent Mission of the United States to the UN, August 25.

Heller, Peter B. 2001. *The United Nations Under Dag Hammarskjöld, 1953–1961.* Lanham, MD: Scarecrow Press.

Henneberger, Melinda. 2003. "Weight of the World." *Newsweek,* May 26, Internet edition (newsweek.msnbc.com).

Hermann, Charles F. 1993. "Avoiding Pathologies in Foreign Policy Decision Groups." In Dan Caldwell and Timothy J. McKeown, eds., *Diplomacy, Force, and Leadership: Essays in Honor of Alexander L. George.* Boulder, CO: Westview Press, pp. 179–207.

Hocking, Brian, and Dominic Kelly. 2002. "Doing the Business? The International Chamber of Commerce, the United Nations, and the Global Compact." In Andrew F. Cooper, John English, and Ramesh Thakur, eds., *Enhancing Global Governance: Towards a New Diplomacy?* Tokyo: United Nations University Press, pp. 203–228.

Hoggart, Richard. 1996. "UNESCO and NGOs: A Memoir." In Peter Willetts, ed., *"The Conscience of the World": The Influence of Non-governmental Organisations in the UN System.* London: Hurst, pp. 98–115.

Holloway, Steven. 1990. "Forty Years of United Nations General Assembly Voting." *Canadian Journal of Political Science* 23, no. 2: 279–296.

Holter, Dag. 1998. Counselor, Permanent Mission of Norway to the United Nations. Personal interview, Permanent Mission of Norway to the UN, March 12.

Hong, Mark. 1995. "Small States in the United Nations." *International Social Science Journal*, no. 144 (June 1995): 277–287.

Hopmann, P. Terrance. 1996. *The Negotiation Process and the Resolution of International Conflicts.* Columbia: University of South Carolina Press.

Hovet, Thomas, Jr. 1960. *Bloc Politics in the United Nations.* Cambridge, MA: Harvard University Press.

Hovey, Allan, Jr. 1951. "Obstructionism and the Rules of the General Assembly." *International Organization* 5, no. 3: 515–530.

Hurd, Ian. 1997. "Security Council Reform: Informal Membership and Practice." In Bruce M. Russett, ed., *The Once and Future Security Council.* New York: St. Martin's Press, pp. 135–152.

Ignatieff, George. 1981. "Prompt and Regular Access to Political Government at Home is Essential." In Davidson Nicol, ed., *Paths to Peace: The UN Security Council and Its Presidency.* New York: Pergamon Press, pp. 130–139.

Jacob, Philip E., Alexine L. Atherton, and Arthur M. Wallenstein. 1972. *The Dynamics of International Organization.* Homewood, IL: Dorsey Press.

Jacobson, Harold K. 1979. *Networks of Interdependence: International Organizations and the Global Political System.* New York: Alfred A. Knopf.

Jacobson, Harold K., and Edith Brown Weiss. 1995. "Strengthening Compliance with International Environmental Accords: Preliminary Observations from a Collaborative Project." *Global Governance* 1, no. 2: 119–148.

Jakobson, Max. 1981. "The Importance of Periodic Meetings." In Davidson Nicol, ed., *Paths to Peace: The UN Security Council and Its Presidency.* New York: Pergamon Press, pp. 160–163.

———. 1993. *The United Nations in the 1990s: A Second Chance?* New York: Twentieth Century Fund and United Nations Institute for Training and Research (UNITAR).

James, Alan. 1993. "The Secretary-General as an Independent Political Actor." In Benjamin Rivlin and Leon Gordenker, eds., *The Challenging Role of the UN Secretary-General: Making "the Most Impossible Job in the World" Possible.* Westport, CT: Praeger, pp. 22–39.

Jönsson, Christer. 1986. "Interorganizational Theory and International Organization." *International Studies Quarterly* 40, no. 1: 39–57.

Jönsson, Christer, and Peter Söderholm. 1996. "IGO-NGO Relations and HIV/AIDS: Innovation or Stalemate?" In Thomas G. Weiss and Leon Gordenker, eds., *NGOs, the UN, and Global Governance.* Boulder, CO: Lynne Rienner, pp. 121–138.

Jordan, Robert S. 1988. "'Truly' International Bureaucracies: Real or Imagined?" In Lawrence S. Finkelstein, ed., *Politics in the United Nations System.* Durham, NC: Duke University Press, pp. 424–445.

Joyner, Christopher C. 1996. "The United States and the New Law of the Sea." *Ocean Development and International Law* 27, nos. 1–2: 41–58.

Kahler, Miles. 1993. "Multilateralism with Large and Small Numbers." In John Gerald Ruggie, ed., *Multilateralism Matters: The Theory and Praxis of an Institutional Form*. New York: Columbia University Press, pp. 295–326.

Karns, Margaret P., and Karen A. Mingst. 1987. "International Organizations and Foreign Policy: Influence and Instrumentality." In Charles W. Kegley Jr. and James N. Rosenau, eds., *New Directions in the Study of Foreign Policy*. Boston: Allen and Unwin, pp. 454–474.

———. 1995. "The Past as Prologue: The United States and the Future of the UN System." In Chadwick F. Alger, Gene M. Lyons, and John E. Trent, eds., *The United Nations System: The Policies of Member States*. Tokyo: United Nations University Press, pp. 410–460.

———. 2002. "The United States as 'Deadbeat'? U.S. Policy and the UN Financial Crisis." In Stewart Patrick and Shepard Forman, eds., *Multilateralism and U.S. Foreign Policy: Ambivalent Engagement*. Boulder, CO: Lynne Rienner, pp. 267–294.

Kaufmann, Johan. 1980. *United Nations Decision Making*. Rockville, MD: Sijthoff and Noordhoff.

———. 1988. *Conference Diplomacy: An Introductory Analysis*. Dordrecht, the Netherlands: Martinus Nijhoff.

———, ed. 1989. *Effective Negotiation: Case Studies in Conference Diplomacy*. Dordrecht, the Netherlands: Martinus Nijhoff.

———. 1991. "Developments in Decision Making in the United Nations." In Richard A. Falk, Samuel S. Kim, and Saul H. Mendlovitz, eds., *The United Nations and a Just World Order*. Boulder, CO: Westview Press, pp. 125–136.

———. 1994. "The Evolving United Nations: Principles and Realities." John W. Holmes Memorial Lecture. *ACUNS Reports and Papers* 4.

Kay, David A. 1967. "Instruments of Influence in the United Nations Political Process." In David A. Kay, ed., *The United Nations Political System*. New York: John Wiley and Sons, pp. 92–107.

———. 1968. "Secondment in the United Nations Secretariat: An Alternative View." In Robert W. Gregg and Michael Barkun, eds., *The United Nations System and Its Functions: Selected Readings*. Princeton, NJ: D. Van Nostrand, pp. 228–239.

———. 1969. "A Note on Robert O. Keohane's 'Institutionalization in the United Nations General Assembly' and Keohane's Response." *International Organization* 23, no. 4: 951–959.

Keohane, Robert O. 1967. "The Study of Political Influence in the General Assembly." *International Organization* 21, no. 2: 221–237.

———. 1969. "Institutionalization in the United Nations General Assembly." *International Organization* 23, no. 4: 859–896.

———. 1984. *After Hegemony: Cooperation and Discord in the World Political Economy*. Princeton, NJ: Princeton University Press.

———. 1988. "International Institutions: Two Approaches." *International Studies Quarterly* 32, no. 4: 379–396.

Keohane, Robert O., and Joseph S. Nye Jr., eds. 1971. *Transnational Relations and World Politics*. Cambridge, MA: Harvard University Press.

————. 1977. *Power and Interdependence: World Politics in Transition.* Boston: Little, Brown.

Keohane, Robert O., and Lisa L. Martin. 1995. "The Promise of Institutionalist Theory." *International Security* 20, no. 1: 39–51.

Khalikov, Rashid. 1998. Chief of staff, Office of the Under-Secretary-General, United Nations Office for the Coordination of Humanitarian Affairs. Personal interview, UN headquarters, March 10.

Kille, Kent J., and Roger M. Scully. 2003. "Executive Heads and the Role of Intergovernmental Organizations: Expansionist Leadership in the United Nations and the European Union." *Political Psychology* 24, no. 1: 175–198.

Kim, Soo Yeon, and Bruce M. Russett. 1997. "The New Politics of Voting Alignments in the General Assembly." In Bruce M. Russett, ed., *The Once and Future Security Council.* New York: St. Martin's Press, pp. 29–57.

Kirgis, Frederic L., Jr. 1995. "The Security Council's First Fifty Years." *American Journal of International Law* 89, no. 3: 506–539.

Knight, W. Andy. 2002. "The Future of the UN Security Council: Questions of Legitimacy and Representation in Multilateral Governance." In Andrew F. Cooper, John English, and Ramesh Thakur, eds., *Enhancing Global Governance: Towards a New Diplomacy?* Tokyo: United Nations University Press, pp. 19–37.

Knight, W. Andy, and Keith Krause. 1995. "Conclusion: States, Societies, and the United Nations in a Multilateral Context." In Keith Krause and W. Andy Knight, eds., *State Society, and the UN System: Changing Perspectives on Multilateralism.* Tokyo: United Nations University Press, pp. 245–264.

Kondo, Tetsuo. 1998. First secretary, Permanent Mission of Japan to the United Nations. Personal interview, Permanent Mission of Japan to the UN, February 25.

Kooijmans, Adriaan. 1998. Counselor, Permanent Mission of the Kingdom of the Netherlands to the United Nations. Personal interview, Permanent Mission of the Kingdom of the Netherlands to the UN, February 24.

Kosciusko-Morizet, Jacques. 1981. "Conflict and Collaboration Among States." In Davidson Nicol, ed., *Paths to Peace: The UN Security Council and Its Presidency.* New York: Pergamon Press, pp. 164–172.

Kostakos, Georgios. 1995. "UN Reform: The Post–Cold War World Organization." In Dimitris Bourantonis and Jarrod Wiener, eds., *The United Nations in the New World Order: The World Organization at Fifty.* London: Macmillan, pp. 64–80.

Krasner, Stephen D. 1983. "Structural Causes and Regime Consequences: Regimes as Intervening Variables." In Stephen D. Krasner, ed., *International Regimes.* Ithaca, NY: Cornell University Press, pp. 1–21.

Kratochwil, Friedrich, and John Gerald Ruggie. 1986. "International Organization: The State of the Art on the Art of the State." *International Organization* 40, no. 4: 753–776.

Krause, Keith, W. Andy Knight, and David Dewitt. 1995. "Canada, the United Nations, and the Reform of International Institutions." In Chadwick F. Alger, Gene M. Lyons, and John E. Trent, eds., *The United Nations*

System: The Policies of Member States. Tokyo: United Nations University Press, pp. 132–185.

Kulyk, Markiyan. 1998. Legal adviser, Office of the President of the General Assembly. Personal interview, Permanent Mission of the Ukraine to the UN, February 25.

Kunita, Miki. 1998. Attaché, Permanent Mission of Japan to the United Nations. Personal interview, Permanent Mission of Japan to the UN, February 25.

Lankevich, George J. 2001. *The United Nations Under Javier Pérez de Cuéllar, 1982–1991.* Lanham, MD: Scarecrow Press.

Laurenti, Jeffery. 1999. "US Reluctance and UN Revival." *International Spectator* 34, no. 4: 13–20.

Lavrov, Sergey. 1999. "The United Nations Through the Eyes of a Russian Ambassador." In James P. Muldoon Jr., JoAnn Fagot Aviel, Richard Reitano, and Earl Sullivan, eds., *Multilateral Diplomacy and the United Nations Today.* Boulder, CO: Westview Press, pp. 35–42.

Levy, David L., and Daniel Egan. 2000. "Corporate Political Action in the Global Polity: National and Transnational Strategies in the Climate Change Negotiations." In Richard A. Higgott, Geoffrey R. D. Underhill, and Andreas Bieler, eds., *Non-state Actors and Authority in the Global System.* London: Routledge, pp. 138–153.

Luard, Evan, and Derek Heater. 1994. *The United Nations: How It Works and What It Does.* New York: St. Martin's Press.

Luck, Edward C. 1999. *Mixed Messages: American Politics and International Organization, 1919–1999.* Washington, DC: Brookings Institution Press.

Luck, Edward C., Anne-Marie Slaughter, and Ian Hurd. 2003. "Stayin' Alive: The Rumors of the UN's Death Have Been Exaggerated." *Foreign Affairs* 82, no. 4, available online at www.foreignaffairs.org.

Lydon, Anthony F. 1998. "The Making of a United Nations Meeting." In M. A. Boisard and E. M. Chossudovsky, eds., *Multilateral Diplomacy: The United Nations System at Geneva—A Working Guide.* The Hague, the Netherlands: Kluwer Law International, pp. 149–160.

Lynch, Colum. 2000. "U.S. Campaign Against Terrorism Denies Sudan U.N. Security Council Seat." *Washington Post,* October 11, Internet edition (www.washingtonpost.com).

Lyons, Gene M., David A. Baldwin, and Donald W. McNemar. 1977. "The 'Politicization' Issue in the UN Specialized Agencies." In David A. Kay, ed., *The Changing United Nations: Options for the United States.* Proceedings of the Academy of Political Science 32, no. 4: 81–92. New York: Academy of Political Science.

Malik, Yakov A. 1981. "The Veto as a Protective Act of Policy." In Davidson Nicol, ed., *Paths to Peace: The UN Security Council and Its Presidency.* New York: Pergamon Press, pp. 173–177.

Malone, David M. 2000a. "Eyes on the Prize: The Quest for Nonpermanent Seats on the UN Security Council." *Global Governance* 6, no. 1: 3–23.

———. 2000b. "The Security Council in the 1990s: Inconsistent, Improvisational, Indispensable?" In Ramesh Thakur and Edward Newman, eds., *New Millennium, New Perspectives: The United Nations, Security, and Governance.* Tokyo: United Nations University Press, pp. 21–45.

————. 2002. "The New Diplomacy and the United Nations: How Substantive?" In Andrew F. Cooper, John English, and Ramesh Thakur, eds., *Enhancing Global Governance: Towards a New Diplomacy?* Tokyo: United Nations University Press, pp. 38–54.

————. 2004. "Conclusion." In David M. Malone, ed., *The UN Security Council: From the Cold War to the 21st Century*. Boulder, CO: Lynne Rienner, pp. 617–649.

Maniatis, Gregory A. 2001. "On Top of the World." *New York Magazine*, November 19, pp. 42–47.

Manley, Simon. 1998. First secretary, Permanent Mission of the United Kingdom to the United Nations. Personal interview, Permanent Mission of the United Kingdom to the UN, February 25.

Manno, Catherine Senf. 1968a. "Majority Decisions and Minority Responses in the UN General Assembly." In Robert W. Gregg and Michael Barkun, eds., *The United Nations System and Its Functions: Selected Readings*. Princeton, NJ: D. Van Nostrand, pp. 247–265.

————. 1968b. "Problems and Trends in the Composition of Nonplenary UN Organs." In Robert W. Gregg and Michael Barkun, eds., *The United Nations System and its Functions: Selected Readings*. Princeton, NJ: D. Van Nostrand, pp. 368–383.

Marin-Bosch, Miguel. 1987. "How Nations Vote in the General Assembly of the United Nations." *International Organization* 41, no. 4: 705–724.

Martin, Lisa L., and Beth A. Simmons. 2001. "Theories and Empirical Studies of International Institutions." In Lisa L. Martin and Beth A. Simmons, eds., *International Institutions: An International Organization Reader*. Cambridge, MA: MIT Press, pp. 437–465.

McCarthy, Patrick A. 1997. "Positionality, Tension, and Instability in the UN Security Council." *Global Governance* 3, no. 2: 147–169.

Mearsheimer, John J. 1994–1995. "The False Promise of International Institutions." *International Security* 19, no. 3: 5–49.

Meisler, Stanley. 1995. *United Nations: The First Fifty Years*. New York: Atlantic Monthly Press.

————. 2003. "Man in the Middle: Travels with Kofi Annan." *Smithsonian*, January, pp. 32–39.

Mendez, Ruben P. 1997. "Financing the United Nations and the International Public Sector: Problems and Reform." *Global Governance* 3, no. 3: 283–310.

Millar, Caroline. 1998. Counselor (political), Permanent Mission of Australia to the United Nations. Personal interview, Permanent Mission of Australia to the UN, March 11.

Mills, Don. 1999. "The Diplomat at the United Nations: Yesterday and Today." In James P. Muldoon Jr., JoAnn Fagot Aviel, Richard Reitano, and Earl Sullivan, eds., *Multilateral Diplomacy and the United Nations Today*. Boulder, CO: Westview Press, pp. 15–34.

Mitchell, Ronald B. 1994. "Regime Design Matters: International Oil Pollution and Treaty Compliance." *International Organization* 48, no. 3: 425–458.

Mitrany, David. 1943. *A Working Peace System*. Chicago: Quadrangle Books.

Morphet, Sally. 1996. "NGOs and the Environment." In Peter Willetts, ed.,

"The Conscience of the World" : The Influence of Non-governmental Organisations in the UN System. London: Hurst, pp. 116–146.

———. 2000. "States Groups at the United Nations and Growth of Member States at the United Nations." In Paul Taylor and A. J. R. Groom, eds., *The United Nations at the Millennium: The Principal Organs.* London: Continuum, pp. 224–270.

Moskowitz, Moses. 1980. *The Roots and Reaches of United Nations Actions and Decisions.* Alphen aan den Rijn, the Netherlands: Sijthoff and Noordhoff.

Moynihan, Daniel Patrick, with Suzanne Weaver. 1978. *A Dangerous Place.* Boston: Little, Brown.

Muldoon, James P., Jr. 1999. Introduction to James P. Muldoon Jr., JoAnn Fagot Aviel, Richard Reitano, and Earl Sullivan, eds., *Multilateral Diplomacy and the United Nations Today.* Boulder, CO: Westview Press, pp. 1–5.

———. 2004. *The Architecture of Global Governance: An Introduction to the Study of International Organizations.* Boulder, CO: Westview Press.

Mwakawago, Daudi. 2000. Permanent representative of the United Republic of Tanzania to the United Nations. Personal interview, Permanent Mission of the United Republic of Tanzania to the UN, August 30.

Narasimhan, C. V. 1988. *The United Nations: An Inside View.* New Delhi: Vikas.

Natsios, Andrew S. 1996. "NGOs and the UN System in Complex Humanitarian Emergencies: Conflict or Cooperation?" In Thomas G. Weiss and Leon Gordenker, eds., *NGOs, the UN, and Global Governance.* Boulder, CO: Lynne Rienner, pp. 67–81.

Nelson, Jane. 2002. *Building Partnerships: Cooperation Between the United Nations System and the Private Sector.* New York: United Nations Department of Public Information.

Ness, Gayl D., and Steven R. Brechin. 1988. "Bridging the Gap: International Organizations as Organizations." *International Organization* 42, no. 2: 245–274.

Newcombe, Hanna, Michael Ross, and Alan G. Newcombe. 1970. "United Nations Voting Patterns." *International Organization* 24, no. 1: 100–121.

Nicholas, H. G. 1975. *The United Nations as Political Institution.* London: Oxford University Press.

Nicol, Davidson. 1981a. "Andrew Young at the United Nations: A Major Role for the UN in US Foreign Policy." In Davidson Nicol, ed., *Paths to Peace: The UN Security Council and Its Presidency.* New York: Pergamon Press, pp. 310–325.

———. 1981b. "The Security Council." In Davidson Nicol, ed., *Paths to Peace: The UN Security Council and Its Presidency.* New York: Pergamon Press, pp. 3–36.

Nicolson, Harold. 1988. *Diplomacy.* Washington, DC: Institute for the Study of Diplomacy.

Norwegian Nobel Committee. 2001. "The Nobel Peace Prize 2001." Press release, October 12, available online at www.nobel.se/peace/laureates/2001/press.html.

Nyerges, Janos. 1998. "How to Negotiate?" In M. A. Boisard and E. M.

Chossudovsky, eds., *Multilateral Diplomacy: The United Nations System at Geneva—A Working Guide*. The Hague, the Netherlands: Kluwer Law International, pp. 175–180.

Ogata, Sadako. 1995. "Japan's Policy Towards the United Nations." In Chadwick F. Alger, Gene M. Lyons, and John E. Trent, eds., *The United Nations System: The Policies of Member States*. Tokyo: United Nations University Press, pp. 231–270.

O'Neill, Barry. 1997. "Power and Satisfaction in the Security Council." In Bruce M. Russett, ed., *The Once and Future Security Council*. New York: St. Martin's Press, pp. 59–82.

Orr, John. 2000. First secretary, Permanent Mission of Canada to the United Nations. Personal interview, Permanent Mission of Canada to the UN, August 30.

Pathmarajah, Appiah. 1998. "Preparing for a Meeting: Some Practical Advice to Diplomats." In M. A. Boisard and E. M. Chossudovsky, eds., *Multilateral Diplomacy: The United Nations System at Geneva—A Working Guide*. The Hague, the Netherlands: Kluwer Law International, pp. 113–117.

Paul, James. 1999. "NGOs and the United Nations: Comments for the Report of the Secretary-General." New York: Global Policy Forum, available online at www.globalpolicy.org/ngos/docs99/gpfrep.htm.

Penrose, Angela, and John Seaman. 1996. "The Save the Children Fund and Nutrition for Refugees." In Peter Willetts, ed., *"The Conscience of the World": The Influence of Non-governmental Organisations in the UN System*. London: Hurst, pp. 241–269.

Pentland, Charles. 1989. "International Organizations and Their Roles." In Paul F. Diehl, ed., *The Politics of International Organizations: Patterns and Insights*. Chicago: Dorsey Press, pp. 5–14.

Pérez de Cuéllar, Javier. 1993. "The Role of the UN Secretary-General." In Adam Roberts and Benedict Kingsbury, eds., *United Nations, Divided World: The UN's Roles in International Relations*. Oxford: Clarendon Press, pp. 125–142.

Petersen, Keith S. 1968. "The Uses of the United Nations." In Robert W. Gregg and Michael Barkun, eds., *The United Nations System and Its Functions: Selected Readings*. Princeton, NJ: D. Van Nostrand, pp. 127–135.

Peterson, M. J. 1986. *The General Assembly in World Politics*. Boston: Allen & Unwin.

Prantl, Jochen, and Jean Krasno. 2002. "Informal *Ad Hoc* Groupings of States and the Workings of the United Nations." International Relations Studies and the United Nations Occasional Papers 3. New Haven, CT: Academic Council on the United Nations System, Yale University.

Puchala, Donald J. 1982–1983. "American Interests and the United Nations." *Political Science Quarterly* 97, no. 4: 571–588.

———. 1993. "The Secretary-General and His Special Representatives." In Benjamin Rivlin and Leon Gordenker, eds., *The Challenging Role of the UN Secretary-General: Making "the Most Impossible Job in the World" Possible*. Westport, CT: Praeger, pp. 81–97.

Putnam, Robert D. 1988. "Diplomacy and Domestic Politics: The Logic of Two-Level Games." *International Organization* 42, no. 3: 427–460.

Ramaker, Jaap. 1998. Permanent representative of the Netherlands to the United Nations. Personal interview, Permanent Mission of the Netherlands to the UN, March 11.

Ramcharan, B. G. 2000. "The International Court of Justice." In Paul Taylor and A. J. R. Groom, eds., *The United Nations at the Millennium: The Principal Organs*. London: Continuum, pp. 177–195.

Reymond, Henri, and Sidney Mailick. 1985. *International Personnel Policies and Practices*. New York: Praeger.

Richard, Ivor. 1981. "The Council President as Politician." In Davidson Nicol, ed., *Paths to Peace: The UN Security Council and Its Presidency*. New York: Pergamon Press, pp. 242–254.

Riggs, Robert E. 1977. "One Small Step for Functionalism: UN Participation and Congressional Attitude Change." *International Organization* 31, no. 3: 515–539.

Righter, Rosemary. 1995. *Utopia Lost: The United Nations and World Order*. New York: Twentieth Century Fund Press.

Ritchie, Cyril. 1996. "Coordinate? Cooperate? Harmonise? NGO Policy and Operational Coalitions." In Thomas G. Weiss and Leon Gordenker, eds., *NGOs, the UN, and Global Governance*. Boulder, CO: Lynne Rienner, pp. 177–188.

Rittberger, Volker. 1998. "International Conference Diplomacy: A Conspectus." In M. A. Boisard and E. M. Chossudovsky, eds., *Multilateral Diplomacy: The United Nations System at Geneva—A Working Guide*. The Hague, the Netherlands: Kluwer Law International, pp. 15–28.

Rivlin, Benjamin. 1993. "The Changing International Political Climate and the Secretary-General." In Benjamin Rivlin and Leon Gordenker, eds., *The Challenging Role of the UN Secretary-General: Making "the Most Impossible Job in the World" Possible*. Westport, CT: Praeger, pp. 3–21.

———. 1995. "The UN Secretary-Generalship at Fifty." In Dimitris Bourantonis and Jarrod Wiener, eds., *The United Nations in the New World Order: The World Organization at Fifty*. New York: St. Martin's Press.

Rochester, J. Martin. 1986. "The Rise and Fall of International Organization as a Field of Study." *International Organization* 40, no. 4, pp. 777–814.

———. 1995. "The United Nations in a New World Order: Reviving the Theory and Practice of International Organization." In Charles W. Kegley, ed., *Controversies in International Relations Theory: Realism and the Neoliberal Challenge*. New York: St. Martin's Press, pp. 199–221.

Rosenstock, Robert. 1998. Minister counselor, Permanent Mission of the United States to the United Nations. Personal interview, Permanent Mission of the United States to the UN, February 24.

Rowe, Edward T. 1969. "Changing Patterns in the Voting Success of Member States in the United Nations General Assembly: 1945–1966." *International Organization* 23, no. 2: 231–253.

———. 1971. "The United States, the United Nations, and the Cold War." *International Organization* 25, no. 1: 59–78.

Rubin, Seymour J. 1977. "The Transnational Corporations." In David A. Kay, ed., *The Changing United Nations: Options for the United States*. Proceedings of the Academy of Political Science 32, no. 4: 120–127. New York: Academy of Political Science.

Ruggie, John Gerald. 1993. "Multilateralism: The Anatomy of an Institution."
In John Gerald Ruggie, ed., *Multilateralism Matters: The Theory and
Praxis of an Institutional Form.* New York: Colombia University Press, pp.
3–47.
———. 2003. "The United Nations and Globalization: Patterns and Limits of
Institutional Adaptation." *Global Governance* 9, no. 3: 301–321.
Russett, Bruce M. 1968. "Discovering Voting Groups in the United Nations."
In Robert W. Gregg and Michael Barkun, eds., *The United Nations System
and Its Functions: Selected Readings.* Princeton, NJ: D. Van Nostrand, pp.
72–87.
———, ed. 1997. *The Once and Future Security Council.* New York: St.
Martin's Press.
Russett, Bruce M., Barry O'Neill, and James Sutterlin. 1996. "Breaking the
Security Council Restructuring Logjam." *Global Governance* 2, no. 1:
65–80.
Ryan, James Daniel. 2001. *The United Nations Under Kurt Waldheim,
1972–1981.* Lanham, MD: Scarecrow Press.
Sabel, Robbie. 1997. *Procedure at International Conferences: A Study of the
Rules of Procedure of Conferences and Assemblies of International Inter-
governmental Organisations.* Cambridge: Cambridge University Press.
Sands, Philippe, and Pierre Klein. 2001. *Bowett's Law of International
Institutions.* London: Sweet and Maxwell.
Sanger, Clyde. 1987. *Ordering the Oceans: The Making of the Law of the Sea.*
Toronto: University of Toronto Press.
Sankey, John. 1996. "Conclusion." In Peter Willetts, ed., *"The Conscience of
the World": The Influence of Non-governmental Organisations in the UN
System.* London: Hurst, pp. 270–276.
Schechter, Michael G. 1987. "Leadership in International Organizations:
Systemic, Organizational and Personality Factors." *Review of
International Studies* 13:197–220.
———. 1988. "The Political Roles of Recent World Bank Presidents." In
Lawrence S. Finkelstein, ed., *Politics in the United Nations System.*
Durham, NC: Duke University Press, pp. 350–384.
———. 2001a. "Making Meaningful UN-Sponsored World Conferences of the
1990s: NGOs to the Rescue?" In Michael G. Schechter, ed., *United
Nations–Sponsored World Conferences: Focus on Impact and Follow-Up.*
Tokyo: United Nations University, pp. 184–217.
———. 2001b. "UN-Sponsored World Conferences in the 1990s." In Michael
G. Schechter, ed., *United Nations-Sponsored World Conferences: Focus on
Impact and Follow-Up.* Tokyo: United Nations University, pp. 3–9.
Scholte, Jan Aart. 2000. "'In the Foothills': Relations Between the IMF and
Civil Society." In Richard A. Higgott, Geoffrey R. D. Underhill, and
Andreas Bieler, eds., *Non-state Actors and Authority in the Global System.*
London: Routledge, pp. 256–273.
Schweller, Randall L., and David Priess. 1997. "A Tale of Two Realisms:
Expanding the Institutions Debate." *Mershon International Studies Review*
41, suppl. 1: 1–32.
Seary, Bill. 1996. "The Early History: From the Congress of Vienna to the San
Francisco Conference." In Peter Willetts, ed., *"The Conscience of the*

World": The Influence of Non-governmental Organisations in the UN System. London: Hurst, pp. 15–30.

Sell, Susan K. 2000. "Structures, Agents, and Institutions: Private Corporate Power and the Globalization of Intellectual Property Rights." In Richard A. Higgott, Geoffrey R. D. Underhill, and Andreas Bieler, eds., Non-state Actors and Authority in the Global System. London: Routledge, pp. 91–106.

Shestack, Laurie. 1998. Political adviser, Permanent Mission of the United States to the United Nations. Personal interview, Permanent Mission of the United States to the UN, February 25.

Sikkink, Kathryn. 1986. "Codes of Conduct for Transnational Corporations: The Case of the WHO/UNICEF Code." International Organization 40, no. 4: 815–840.

Simmons, Beth A. 2000. "The Legalization of International Monetary Affairs." International Organization 54, no. 3: 573–602.

Smith, Courtney B. 1999. "The Politics of Global Consensus Building: A Comparative Analysis." Global Governance 5, no. 2: 173–201.

———. 2003. "More Secretary or General: Effective Leadership at the United Nations." International Politics 40, no. 1: 137–147.

———. 2004. "The Politics of U.S.-UN Reengagement: Achieving Gains in a Hostile Environment." International Studies Perspectives 5, no. 2: 197–215.

Smouts, Marie-Claude. 2000. "The General Assembly: Grandeur and Decadence." In Paul Taylor and A. J. R. Groom, eds., The United Nations at the Millennium: The Principal Organs. London: Continuum, pp. 21–60.

Stephenson, Carolyn M. 2000. "NGOs and the Principal Organs of the United Nations." In Paul Taylor and A. J. R. Groom, eds., The United Nations at the Millennium: The Principal Organs. London: Continuum, pp. 271–294.

Sutterlin, James S. 1993. "The UN Secretary-General as Chief Administrator." In Benjamin Rivlin and Leon Gordenker, eds., The Challenging Role of the UN Secretary-General: Making "the Most Impossible Job in the World" Possible. Westport, CT: Praeger, pp. 43–59.

———. 1997. "The Past as Prologue." In Bruce M. Russett, ed., The Once and Future Security Council. New York: St. Martin's Press, pp. 1–11.

Talbot, Ross B., and H. Wayne Moyer. 1997. "Who Governs the Rome Food Agencies?" In Paul F. Diehl, ed., The Politics of Global Governance: International Organizations in an Interdependent World. Boulder, CO: Lynne Rienner, pp. 269–286.

Taylor, Paul. 2000a. "The Institutions of the United Nations and the Principle of Consonance: An Overview." In Paul Taylor and A. J. R. Groom, eds., The United Nations at the Millennium: The Principal Organs. London: Continuum, pp. 293–326.

———. 2000b. "Managing the Economic and Social Activities of the United Nations System: Developing the Role of ECOSOC." In Paul Taylor and A. J. R. Groom, eds., The United Nations at the Millennium: The Principal Organs. London: Continuum, pp. 100–141.

Tello, Manuel. 1998. Permanent representative of Mexico to the United Nations. Personal interview, Permanent Mission of Mexico to the UN, March 11.

Terpstra, Rienk W. 1999. "Post–Cold War UN Diplomacy from Up Close: Inside Perspectives from an Outsider." In James P. Muldoon Jr., JoAnn Fagot Aviel, Richard Reitano, and Earl Sullivan, eds., *Multilateral Diplomacy and the United Nations Today*. Boulder, CO: Westview Press, pp. 210–221.

Thakur, Ramesh. 2001. "Human Rights: Amnesty International and the United Nations." In Paul F. Diehl, ed., *The Politics of Global Governance: International Organizations in an Interdependent World*. Boulder, CO: Lynne Rienner, pp. 365–387.

Thalakada, Nigel. 1997. "China's Voting Pattern in the Security Council, 1990–1995." In Bruce M. Russett, ed., *The Once and Future Security Council*. New York: St. Martin's Press, pp. 83–118.

Thoresson, Per. 1998. First secretary, Permanent Mission of Sweden to the United Nations. Personal interview, Permanent Mission of Sweden to the UN, February 26.

Tolley, Howard, Jr. 1983. "Decision-Making at the United Nations Commission on Human Rights, 1979–1982." *Human Rights Quarterly* 5, no. 1: 27–57.

Traub, James. 1998. "Kofi Annan's Next Test." *New York Times Magazine*, March 29, pp. 44–50, 62, 71, 74, 80–81.

Trent, John E. 1995. "Foreign Policy and the United Nations: National Interest in the Era of Global Politics." In Chadwick F. Alger, Gene M. Lyons, and John E. Trent, eds., *The United Nations System: The Policies of Member States*. Tokyo: United Nations University Press, pp. 436–508.

Tsui, Ed. 1998. Director, Policy and Analysis Division, United Nations Office for the Coordination of Humanitarian Affairs. Personal interview, UN headquarters, March 11.

Tsuruoka, Senjin. 1981. "The Council President Should Never Despair." In Davidson Nicol, ed., *Paths to Peace: The UN Security Council and Its Presidency*. New York: Pergamon Press, pp. 304–305.

Tung, William L. 1969. *International Organization Under the United Nations System*. New York: Thomas Y. Crowell.

Tussie, Diana, and Maria Pia Riggirozzi. 2001. "Pressing Ahead with New Procedures for Old Machinery: Global Governance and Civil Society." In Volker Rittberger, ed., *Global Governance and the United Nations System*. Tokyo: United Nations University Press, pp. 158–180.

United Nations. 1998. *Basic Facts about the United Nations*. New York: UN Department of Public Affairs.

———. 2002. "Economic and Social Council Selects Members of Twenty Subsidiary Bodies: United States Among Those Elected to Commission on Human Rights." Press Release ECOSOC/6003. Economic and Social Council, 2002 Organizational Session, 4th Meeting (AM), April 29.

———. 2003. *Permanent Missions to the United Nations*. UN doc. ST/SG/SER.A/289, Executive Office of the Secretary-General Protocol and Liaison Service.

United Nations Handbook. 2002. Wellington: New Zealand Ministry of Foreign Affairs and Trade.

Uvin, Peter. 1996. "Scaling Up the Grassroots and Scaling Down the Summit: The Relations Between Third World NGOs and the UN." In Thomas G.

Weiss and Leon Gordenker, eds., *NGOs, the UN, and Global Governance.* Boulder, CO: Lynne Rienner, pp. 159–176.

Verdier, Alejandro. 1998. First secretary, Permanent Mission of Argentina to the United Nations. Personal interview, Permanent Mission of Argentina to the UN, February 27.

Vincent, Jack E. 1968. "National Attributes as Predictors of Delegate Attitudes at the United Nations." *American Political Science Review* 62, no. 3: 916–931.

Walters, F. P. 1952. *A History of the League of Nations.* London: Oxford University Press.

Weisman, Steven R., and Felicity Barringer. 2003. "U.S. Seeks Nine Votes from U.N. Council to Confront Iraq." *New York Times*, February 21, Internet edition (www.nytimes.com).

Weiss, Thomas G., David P. Forsythe, and Roger A. Coate. 2001. *The United Nations and Changing World Politics.* Boulder, CO: Westview Press.

Wells, Robert N., Jr. 1991. "The UN's Specialized Agencies: Adaptation and Role Changes in an Altered International Environment." In Robert N. Wells Jr., ed., *Peace by Pieces: United Nations Agencies and Their Roles: A Reader and Selective Bibliography.* Metuchen, NJ: Scarecrow Press, pp. 1–11.

White, Nigel D. 2002. *The United Nations System: Toward International Justice.* Boulder, CO: Lynne Rienner.

Willetts, Peter. 1996a. "Appendix A: NGOs and the Structure of the United Nations System." In Peter Willetts, ed., *"The Conscience of the World": The Influence of Non-governmental Organisations in the UN System.* London: Hurst, pp. 277–289.

———. 1996b. "Consultative Status for NGOs at the United Nations." In Peter Willetts, ed., *"The Conscience of the World": The Influence of Non-governmental Organisations in the UN System.* London: Hurst, pp. 31–62.

———. 1996c. "Introduction." In Peter Willetts, ed., *"The Conscience of the World": The Influence of Non-governmental Organisations in the UN System.* London: Hurst, pp. 1–14.

Williams, Marc. 2000. "The World Bank, the World Trade Organisation, and the Environmental Social Movement." In Richard A. Higgott, Geoffrey R. D. Underhill, and Andreas Bieler, eds., *Non-state Actors and Authority in the Global System.* London: Routledge, pp. 241–255.

Williams, Shelton L. 1999. "Citizen Diplomacy and the 1995 NPT Review and Extension Conference." In James P. Muldoon Jr., JoAnn Fagot Aviel, Richard Reitano, and Earl Sullivan, eds., *Multilateral Diplomacy and the United Nations Today.* Boulder, CO: Westview Press, pp. 136–153.

Young, Oran R. 1989. "The Politics of International Regime Formation: Managing Natural Resources and the Environment." *International Organization* 43, no. 3: 349–375.

———. 1991. "Political Leadership and Regime Formation: On the Development of Institutions in International Society." *International Organization* 45, no. 3: 281–308.

Ziring, Lawrence, Robert E. Riggs, and Jack C. Plano. 2000. *The United Nations: International Organization and World Politics.* Forth Worth, TX: Harcourt Brace.

Zyss, Witold. 1998. "The International Civil Servant." In M. A. Boisard and E. M. Chossudovsky, eds., *Multilateral Diplomacy: The United Nations System at Geneva—A Working Guide*. The Hague, the Netherlands: Kluwer Law International, pp. 53–69.

Index

About the Book

HOW DOES THE UNITED NATIONS ACTUALLY WORK? HOW DOES IT RECON-
cile the diverse interests of 191 sovereign member states—plus those of
the numerous NGOs with which it interacts, the diverse international
Secretariat that services it, and the multinational corporations that lobby
it—in the search for effective solutions to the myriad problems it con-
fronts daily? *Politics and Process at the United Nations* answers these
questions, providing a vivid picture of the dynamic interaction between
actors and institutional structures.

Drawing readers into the "global dance" that takes place at UN
headquarters, Courtney Smith introduces the various members of the
troupe and explains the procedures and processes that make up the
movements of the dance. He also addresses an often neglected but
essential issue: do UN decisions really matter? The result is an unusual
book, valuable both for scholars and for students in UN and IO courses.

Courtney Smith is associate professor and associate dean of academic
affairs in the John C. Whitehead School of Diplomacy and International
Relations at Seton Hall University.